THE FACES OF
FORGIVENESS

THE FACES OF FORGIVENESS

Searching for Wholeness and Salvation

F. LeRon Shults
and
Steven J. Sandage

Baker Academic
A Division of Baker Book House Co
Grand Rapids, Michigan 49516

Published by Baker Academic
a division of Baker Book House Company
P.O. Box 6287, Grand Rapids, MI 49516-6287
www.bakeracademic.com

Printed in the United States of America

Library of Congress Cataloging-in-Publication Data
Shults, F. LeRon.
    The faces of forgiveness : searching for wholeness and salvation / F. LeRon Shults
and Steven J. Sandage.
        p. cm.
    Includes bibliographical references and index.
    ISBN 0-8010-2624-5 (pbk.)
    1. Forgiveness—Religious aspects—Christianity. 2. Forgiveness. I. Sandage, Steven J.
II. Title.
BV4647.F55S545 2003
234′.5—dc21   2002043713

To our parents
Fount and Lynda Shults
Duane and Alpha Sandage

CONTENTS

ACKNOWLEDGMENTS

First, both of us wish to acknowledge that the interdisciplinary collaboration and dialogue that went into this book were as challenging as we had expected and as rewarding as we had hoped. We are grateful for the opportunity to work and write together.

I (LeRon) am particularly grateful to Shane Oborn, Ken Reynhout, Elizabeth Shults, and James Wilson for reading early drafts of part 2. Ken deserves special thanks for his excellent work as my research assistant on this project. Much of the material contained in chapter 5 was initially developed in my systematic theology classes. I appreciate the students who patiently faced me as I struggled to articulate these doctrinal issues in response to their questions and comments. The conceptual and existential importance of the "face" was disclosed to me as I interacted with my mentor, James Loder at Princeton Seminary; I am deeply thankful for his contribution to my own search for wholeness and salvation.

For me (Steve), this book is a product of a rich and evolving conversation I have enjoyed with many insightful sojourners. I continue to appreciate the influence of past collaboration with Everett Worthington Jr. and Mike McCullough in shaping my approach to the psychology of forgiveness. Randy Sorenson has not only been a formative influence on my approach to integration but also provided helpful feedback on parts of the manuscript. My research colleagues with the Institute for Research on Psychology and Spirituality at Rosemead School of Psychology have enhanced my awareness of the multidimensionality of forgiveness. I also want to thank several students who have made substantive contributions to my research on forgiveness, including Robert Gordon, Kori Hoffman, Samantha Morgan O'Rourke, Henry C. Vang, and Tina Watson Wiens. My understanding of the cultural and gender implications of discourse on forgiveness has been deepened through dialogue with Carla Dahl, Peter Hill, Richard Lee, Jason Li, Ruben Rivera, Myrla Seibold, Christine Smith, and Leng Xiong. My personal curiosity about the theme of this book involves a debt of gratitude to Ruby Woodin, whose face was for me an early clue for the search.

Finally, we are thankful to our wives and children—and to our parents, to whom this book is dedicated.

1

INTRODUCTION

The word *forgiveness* evokes a variety of powerful emotions. Thinking about forgiveness, some of us smile as we are reminded of a process in our lives that led to the overcoming of pain and bitterness through the healing of an estranged relationship. Others of us grimace as we imagine angry faces trying to coerce us into a passive surrender of our resistance to abuse, betrayal, or injustice. As we reflect on forgiveness, particular human faces can rise to the surface of our consciousness— faces we have forgiven, faces who have forgiven us, or faces we have vowed never to forgive. All of us carry particular moral, political, religious, and therapeutic values into our attempts to understand and practice forgiveness. Our struggle with and for forgiveness is shaped by our deepest hopes and fears as we search for wholeness and salvation in a fragmented and oppressive world. We wonder . . . is forgiveness really good for us?

Forgiveness has become a popular topic in contemporary psychology. Clinicians have been interested in the potential therapeutic benefits of forgiveness for decades,[1] but scientific research on forgiveness

1. M. E. McCullough, K. I. Pargament, and C. E. Thoresen, "The Psychology of Forgiveness: History, Conceptual Issues, and Overview," in *Forgiveness: Theory, Research, and Practice* (ed. M. E. McCullough, K. I. Pargament, and C. E. Thoresen; New York: Guilford, 2000), 1–14.

rapidly accumulated in recent years.[2] There are now substantial bodies of psychological research on forgiveness in the areas of moral development, social and personality psychology, health psychology, psychology of religion, and group interventions. Most of this work focuses on how people forgive others as a way of coping with the hurt and anger generated by interpersonal transgressions. Somewhat less attention is paid to the dynamics of seeking forgiveness from others and of self-forgiveness. Much recent research on forgiveness relates to an emerging interest in positive psychology, that is, the scientific study of the psychological strengths and virtues that shape human flourishing. Forgiveness is proposed as a human strength (or virtue) that may contribute to personal and relational health.

For centuries, particular theological construals of the concept of forgiveness in Christianity dominated the way it was understood and practiced in much of Western society. Since the Enlightenment, however, some of the traditional ways of speaking about forgiveness in Christian theology have been challenged. On the one hand, the Christian idea that we ought to forgive our enemies came under the suspicion of philosophers like Nietzsche and psychoanalysts like Freud. The suggestion that a victim should simply forgive her oppressor was taken as a mask for weakness or as a defensive illusion based on a projected fear of condemnation. On the other hand, the idea that humans receive divine forgiveness only on the basis of a payment made by (or the punishment of) God's innocent Son was intensely criticized. In what sense is this forgiveness if a full payment of the debt was required? Does it make sense to speak of one person's being forgiven on the basis of some other person's taking their place?[3] Research into the history of theology compelled many scholars to conclude that some of the older formulations of divine forgiveness are so enmeshed in ancient or medieval theories of jurisprudence that we must move beyond them and explore new ways to articulate the Christian doctrine of salvation.

Our book engages these developments in psychology and theology and outlines some new models for understanding and practicing forgiveness. At least three factors make our contribution to the dialogue

2. For reviews, see R. D. Enright and R. P. Fitzgibbons, *Helping Clients Forgive: An Empirical Guide for Resolving Anger and Restoring Hope* (Washington, D.C.: American Psychological Association, 2000); F. D. Fincham, "The Kiss of the Porcupines: From Attributing Responsibility to Forgiving," *Personal Relationships* 7 (2000): 1–23; M. E. McCullough, J. J. Exline, and R. F. Baumeister, "An Annotated Bibliography of Research on Forgiveness and Related Concepts," in *Dimensions of Forgiveness: Psychological Research and Theological Perspectives* (ed. E. L. Worthington Jr.; Philadelphia: Templeton Foundation, 1998).

3. Immanuel Kant offers a seminal critique of this idea in his *Religion within the Limits of Reason Alone* (1793; trans. T. M. Greene and H. H. Hudson; New York: Harper, 1960), 66.

unique, and this introductory chapter will spell these out in more detail. First, both authors find an emphasis on "relationality" illuminating not only in our own disciplines, but also in the task of tracing connections between disciplines. As a psychologist and a theologian working together, we hope to enhance understanding on both sides. Second, our approach is integrated by a focus on the theme of the hermeneutics of the face. Interpreting the formative power of facing and being faced in the practice of forgiveness may enable us to discern the therapeutic and redemptive dynamics that promote wholeness and salvation. Third, we delineate three fields of meaning in which the term *forgiveness* is most commonly used. Carefully differentiating these semantic domains and observing their interrelation will help us clarify some of the difficult issues in the dialogue among psychologists and theologians regarding forgiveness. This introductory chapter outlines the unique formal aspects of our treatment of the search for wholeness and salvation and provides an overview of the material contours of our modeling of the dynamics of the faces of forgiveness in psychology and theology.

Relationality and Interdisciplinarity

Our treatment of the topic of forgiveness takes an explicitly interdisciplinary approach, focusing on the essentially relational patterns of human knowing, acting, and being. We believe that careful attention to the philosophical "turn to relationality"[4] opens up new conceptual space for understanding the dynamics of forgiveness. This shift from an emphasis on substances to relational categories and its broader impact on contemporary science and culture will be traced throughout the book. Our primary interest, however, is in the psychological and theological insights that emerge when we consider the idea of forgiveness in the context of the relational interfacings that shape and transform the systems of human existence.

In psychology, the influence of the turn to relationality is illustrated in relational models of psychoanalysis[5] and in empirical research validating the role of relational factors in child development and psychotherapeutic change.[6] Intersubjective psychoanalytic theorists suggest

4. For an extended treatment of the philosophical "turn to relationality," see F. L. Shults, *Reforming Theological Anthropology: After the Philosophical Turn to Relationality* (Grand Rapids: Eerdmans, 2003), chap. 1.

5. For example, S. A. Mitchell, *Relationality: From Attachment to Intersubjectivity* (Hillsdale, N.J.: Analytic Press, 2000); S. A. Mitchell and L. Aron, *Relational Psychoanalysis: The Emergence of a Tradition* (Hillsdale, N.J.: Analytic Press, 1999).

6. J. C. Norcross, *Psychotherapy Relationships That Work* (New York: Oxford University Press, 2002).

that the self is formed and reshaped through a systemic context of re-ciprocally interacting subjectivities.[7] A fascination with the other is one of the primary traits of what is commonly called the "postmod-ern." Many postmodernists in psychology and psychotherapy empha-size and celebrate difference or "alterity" and view the self as consti-tuted and embedded within relationships. This relational view of the self embodied in community is far removed from the classical defini-tion of persons as "individual substances," immaterial souls impris-oned in material bodies. In the individualistic, modernist view, neither social identity (e.g., race, ethnicity, gender) nor communal affiliations (e.g., religious tradition) is considered an important dimension of the true self. In part 1, Steve examines this new view in which the self is mediated to itself through relation to the other and the implications for forgiveness. Chapter 2 describes the role of intersubjectivity in the formation of dispositional capacities for forgivingness. This focus on relationality, intersubjectivity, and otherness serves to broaden models of forgiveness in the social sciences, which tend to focus more exclu-sively on the individual subject attempting to forgive others intrapsy-chically. Interpersonal conflicts always involve a dynamic intersubjec-tive relationship between at least two people in the systemic context of their respective subjectivities. Dilemmas of forgiveness are embed-ded in a social process of saving and losing face. Chapter 3 connects intersubjectivity to the social, spiritual, and psychological dynamics of facing and forgiveness.

In Christian theology it might be more appropriate to refer to a re-turn to relationality. Most of the key doctrines that emerged early in the Christian religion are inherently relational; this applies, for exam-ple, to the uniquely Christian views of God, revelation, and redemp-tion. The doctrine of the Trinity teaches that God is three persons in relation. The incarnation of the word of God in Jesus Christ discloses the relation between human and divine nature. Believers are re-deemed through their intimate relation with the Holy Spirit, who con-stitutes and builds up the relational unity of the Christian community. In part 2, LeRon traces the impact of the turn to relationality in late modernity on the theory and practice of Christian forgiveness. Chap-ter 4 outlines the importance of the concepts of facing and forgiveness for theology and describes the theological loss of relational categories in early modernity and the broader philosophical factors in late mo-dernity that have contributed to a renewed emphasis on the explana-

7. For differing views of intersubjectivity, see J. Benjamin, *Like Subjects, Love Ob-jects: Essays on Recognition and Sexual Difference* (New Haven: Yale University Press, 1995); D. M. Orange, G. E. Atwood, and R. D. Stolorow, *Working Intersubjectively: Con-textualism in Psychoanalytic Practice* (Hillsdale, N.J.: Analytic Press, 2001).

tory power of the category of relation over substance. This renewal took shape in the retrieval of the ideas of Infinity, Trinity, and Futurity in the doctrine of God in the twentieth century. The doctrine of God inevitably shapes the doctrine of salvation, and chapter 5 explores the implications of these developments for understanding and practicing forgiveness. The emphasis on relationality leads to a new appreciation of the systemic and communal dynamics that are often overshadowed in traditional treatments that focus merely on the individual's appropriation of divine forgiveness.

In addition to gaining material insights, a vigorous thematization of relationality also illuminates the formal dimensions of the process of inquiry itself. For example, it raises our awareness of the way in which a person's general social location and particular relations in community both shape her identity and mediate her understanding of and criteria for forgiving. It highlights the danger of the domination of one group over another, drawing out the potential for the abuse of forgiveness as a tool to maintain inequities in social power. Social exclusion and marginalization play a formative role in the dynamics of forgiveness and unforgiveness. Reaching across boundaries, we try to pay special attention to voices from the margins, voices that have previously been excluded from discourse. Both of the authors of this book are white Protestant males and teach in a Christian seminary. This social location influences how we ourselves relate to the process and possibilities of forgiveness. Attending to the relationality that pervades our own psychological and theological inquiry, we are led to acknowledge that we are embedded in our own matrix of concerns; we bring our own particular fears and desires to the text. In these and other ways, starting with communal relationality instead of self-sufficient individuality provides a different perspective on forgiveness.

Attention to relationality also leads to a new awareness of the permeable boundaries between disciplines and invites interdisciplinary dialogue. Not only social locations in general, but also our particular academic contexts shape our approach to forgiveness. Our goal is to reach across these boundaries as well. An emphasis on the intrinsic connections between disciplines leads us to be wary of disciplinary idolatry—allowing one discipline (in this case, psychology or theology) to trump the other discipline when approaching a topic like forgiveness. Dismissing the value of the other discipline can also be a form of hegemony. The science-and-religion multidiscipline can benefit from a dialogue that includes diverse disciplines and methodologies.[8] After the demise of positivism, most scholars recognize that

8. W. Grassie, "Postmodernism: What One Needs to Know," *Zygon: Journal of Religion and Science* 32 (1997): 84.

theories in both the social sciences and in theology are in some sense socially constructed and located within traditions. This does not mean that there are no criteria for evaluating theories. It does mean that theories are thoroughly value laden and related to broader conceptual webs. We can recognize this embeddedness without giving up on the search for more adequate models to explain human experience.

Theological proposals must be connected to real lived experience, not only in our communities of faith, but also in our actual experiences of the general systems in which human life is embedded. Conversely, the social sciences should deal with the religious experiences of persons in faith communities. By acknowledging the overlapping interests and interdependence of these disciplines, social scientists and theologians can become dialogical partners in constructive theory development. Of particular importance for the study of forgiveness is the interrelatedness of construals of ethics and health, which have traditionally been two distinct spheres of inquiry. Ethics was in the domain of philosophical and theological reflection, while health was in the domain of the physical and social sciences. This separation has the advantage of working against the age-old problem of equating health problems with moral failure. It can also occlude the real connection between some moral behaviors or dispositions and physical or psychological health. It is easy to find scholarly treatments of ethical or moral questions of forgiveness from philosophical or theological perspectives, and numerous books and articles in the fields of psychology and psychotherapy relate forgiveness to questions of mental health and wholeness. Only a few books, however, attempt to address both the ethical and health-related questions of forgiveness.[9]

Our emphasis on relationality and interdisciplinarity is connected to the broader debate in academe over postmodernity. Broadly speaking, "the postmodern turn"[10] involves a critique of aspects of the modern worldview that has dominated Western culture since the Enlightenment(s) of the seventeenth and eighteenth centuries. Many postmodern voices focus on the deconstruction of modernist metanarratives, the ideals of objective science, and universal truth claims. But not all postmodern perspectives are the same. Pauline Rosenau distinguishes skeptical postmodernism from affirmative postmodern-

9. Examples include Enright and Fitzgibbons, *Helping Clients Forgive*; R. D. Enright and J. North (eds.), *Exploring Forgiveness* (Madison: University of Wisconsin Press, 1998); S. Lamb and J. G. Murphy, *Before Forgiving: Cautionary Views of Forgiveness in Psychotherapy* (Oxford: Oxford University Press, 2002).

10. For an introduction to these issues, see S. Best and D. Kellner, *The Postmodern Turn* (New York: Guilford, 1997).

ism.[11] Skeptical postmodernism engages in the critical function of un-masking and deconstructing power agendas that lurk behind claims of universal truth and authoritative interpretations of texts. Operating from a strong hermeneutic of suspicion and generally reluctant to articulate ethical or political positions regarding virtue or the good,[12] skeptical post-modernists in the field of psychotherapy deny having a conceptual ideal for healthy human functioning and tend to appeal to pragmatism.

In contrast, affirmative postmodernists are wary of relativism and more open to the value of new ethical and political proposals. There-fore, they are more willing to articulate theories of health, virtue, and justice and are more optimistic about constructing new and less op-pressive models of identity, knowledge, and community using inter-disciplinary methodologies that incorporate empirical science. For ex-ample, Robert Kegan's notion of "reconstructive postmodernism"[13] involves an attempt to move beyond the deconstructive task of cri-tique and to engage in the perennial search for more integrated mod-els for understanding human experience. Our approach in this book is reconstructive in this sense, although the phrase *late modern*[14] might be less misleading since we do not believe that *post*modernism has simply left behind the concerns of the Enlightenment. Contemporary social science and theology continue to operate in a dialectical rela-tion with modern values, critically discerning and refiguring them in the ongoing task of reconstruction. Our goal in the current study is not so much to interpret the phenomena of the postmodern as it is to engage in a transversal performance of interpretation, to make sense *out* of the search for wholeness and salvation in a way that makes sense *in* and *to* contemporary culture.[15]

Hermeneutics and the Face

Our emphasis on relationality and our attempt to interpret forgive-ness across disciplinary boundaries inevitably raise hermeneutical ques-

11. P. M. Rosenau, *Postmodernism and the Social Sciences* (Princeton: Princeton University Press, 1992).

12. I. Prilleltensky, "Values, Assumptions, and Practices: Assessing the Moral Impli-cations of Psychological Discourse and Action," *American Psychologist* 52 (1997): 517–35.

13. R. Kegan, *In over Our Heads: The Mental Demands of Modern Life* (Cambridge: Harvard University Press, 1994).

14. Cf. P. Lakeland, *Postmodernity: Christian Identity in a Fragmented Age* (Minneap-olis: Fortress, 1997), 12–13.

15. For an examination of the relation between hermeneutics and epistemology in recent interdisciplinary dialogue, see F. L. Shults, *The Postfoundationalist Task of Theol-ogy* (Grand Rapids: Eerdmans, 1999), chap. 2.

tions. Facing the challenges of hermeneutics leads us to reflect on the hermeneutics of facing. We suggest that the face represents a powerful interpersonal "text" that evokes an attempt to interpret the feelings and dispositions of the other. We call the ambiguous hermeneutical process that occurs in interpersonal relationships "facial hermeneutics." The multifaceted text of the face is itself shaped intertextually through interaction with a multitude of other faces, accompanied by interpersonal challenges that influence forgiveness and unforgiveness. Psychological research suggests that we are constantly interpreting one another, making attributions about the motives and actions of others. We will review research that suggests that certain kinds of attributions and interpretations significantly impact the process of forgiveness. The early experiences of being faced by caregivers may even serve the formation of internal representations of the face of God, affecting our attribution of emotions to the divine. The following chapters explore the developmental and theological implications of facial intertextuality as it influences the dynamics of forgiveness, both divine and human.

Contemporary psychology and philosophy are fascinated by the dynamics of the human face. On the one hand, by "face" we mean actual physical human faces. Psychological studies show that as early as nine minutes after birth, the child differentiates the face from other patterns. A consistent loving face (usually the mother or primary caregiver) provides the developmental space for the emergence of the child's ego functions, through which she faces the world as a distinct personality. The ability of human beings to recognize their own faces in a mirror at about two years of age is one of the marks of the emergence of self-consciousness.[16] The Latin word *persona* is derived from Greek *prosōpon* and originally referred to the mask of an actor. We commonly hear of social façades, of putting on a happy face, of saving face. A stone face excludes; a warm face welcomes. A face (like Helen of Troy's) can launch a thousand ships—or sink them. Our developmental need to be subjectively recognized, understood, and shown an affirming face and our relational experiences regarding those needs exert a powerful influence on the formation of the self.[17]

On the other hand, these phenomena themselves suggest that we are dealing with something more than just a physical object; the face

16. Adult humans who suffer from neurological problems like prosopagnosia are unable to recognize their own faces, as well as the faces of others. Research with various higher mammals suggests that some chimpanzees and other great apes may also be able to recognize their own faces under certain conditions. See M. D. Hauser, *Wild Minds: What Animals Really Think* (New York: Holt, 2000), 96–103.

17. Cf. J. E. Loder, *The Logic of the Spirit: Human Development in Theological Perspective* (San Francisco: Jossey-Bass, 1998).

confronts us with an overflow of meaning that is beyond objectification. Our being present to each other is mediated through our facing of each other. A lover finds life ecstatically secure when gazing into the face of the beloved as the beloved gazes back. We are granted personal being and called into fellowship through facing and being faced by others. The theme of the face has also become important in the work of several late modern philosophers. Jean-Luc Marion suggests that "the face of the other implies an infinite hermeneutic" and that "to love somebody is always to need more time to know him."[18] Emmanuel Levinas argues that we are primordially bound to the other, whose face speaks to our humanness and invites us to ethical responsibility. By face, Levinas names "the way in which the other presents himself, exceeding *the idea of the other in me* . . . the face of the Other at each moment destroys and overflows the plastic image it leaves me."[19] The human face is an embodied symbolic mediator of intersubjective communication that shapes the relational episodes we call forgiveness and unforgiveness.

Hermeneutics involves the practice of interpreting the meaning of stories and texts, and it plays a significant role in both theology and certain branches of social science. Our interest is in exploring the hermeneutics of the face as it impacts forgiveness. Julia Kristeva articulates the literary notion of intertextuality,[20] which suggests that every text is really a mosaic related to other texts. Whether scientific, religious, or some other genre, a text is comprised of explicit and implicit connections to other texts. Intertextuality is made explicit in scholarly texts through footnotes and reference sections, but there are implicit connections to other texts through the use of language and shared connotations of concepts. Kristeva argues that readers of texts are influenced both by previous texts they have read and by the broader social context of both the reader and the author. Our attention to the "text" of the face follows a general trend that applies that term to a whole range of meaningful activities that involve interpretation. We believe that a moderate[21] use of intertextuality in hermeneutics can be helpful for an interdisciplinary understanding of forgiveness. In urbanized, Western contexts these texts are permeated by

18. J.-L. Marion, "The Face: An Endless Hermeneutics," *Harvard Divinity Bulletin* 28/2 (1999): 9–10 at 10.

19. E. Levinas, *Totality and Infinity* (trans. A. Lingis; Pittsburgh: Duquesne University Press, 1969), 50–51.

20. J. Kristeva, *Desire in Language: A Semiotic Approach to Literature and Art* (ed. L. S. Roudiez; trans. A. Jardine, T. A. Gora, and L. S. Roudiez; New York: Columbia University Press, 1980), 15.

21. Some deconstructive postmodernists employ an extreme form of intertextuality to support the death of authorship and the indeterminacy of meaning and causality.

vestiges of therapeutic and religious language.[22] We suggest that the folk understandings of forgiveness in such contexts are influenced by an intertextual amalgam of cultural and religious texts that include social scripts about repair following interpersonal conflict and the role of forgiveness in the search for wholeness and salvation.

Forgiveness: Three Fields of Meaning

One of the problems in the current literature on forgiveness is the lack of clarity in defining the meaning and use of the term itself. In the chapters that follow we analyze several definitions, but to guide our discussion we propose the following conceptual taxonomy for delineating and linking the semantic domains in which the idea of forgiveness operates as a concept:

> forensic forgiveness
> therapeutic forgiveness
> redemptive forgiveness

Forensic Forgiveness

The first semantic field covers a broad range of popular uses of the word. What they all have in common is the forensic application of forgiveness. Here we mean forensic in the sense of "application to legal issues" not the "art of argumentation." So, for example, we may ask a child to forgive his sister for her infraction of a family rule, such as entering his room without proper authorization. If the child is convinced not to demand the punishment of his sibling, his behavior would be called forgiving. A transaction occurs in which one party agrees not to exact what the law requires. This may be an actual legal decision, or it may be a financial transaction, as when we forgive a debt. A code of conduct that putatively binds the involved parties was transgressed and retribution is required. A transaction that releases one party from retributive justice is forgiveness. This pattern of meaning holds for transactions as small as one sibling mumbling "I forgive

---

22. For example, a client relayed how she had learned to practice forgiveness by watching Oprah on television, who had instructed that unforgiveness damages the soul and that one should start forgiving oneself. In more rural, collectivistic contexts, forgiveness might be related to the cultural texts of proverbs, narratives, and rituals that inform personal accounts (or texts) of interpersonal conflict. In a current study with Hmong informants about forgiveness in the Hmong community, it was common for the informants to move from telling a story about a personal experience of conflict and forgiveness to quote a cultural proverb about the dangers of unforgiveness.

you" before slamming the door and as large as one country forgiving the billion-dollar debt of another.

The legal and financial language of the first semantic field is commonly appropriated metaphorically in the second and third semantic fields. Contextual therapists in the tradition of Boszormenyi-Nagy use the language of "balancing the moral ledger" of relational credits and debits.[23] Forgiveness as a transaction also occurs in couples therapy, for example, when spouses learn the discipline of editing hostile and defensive responses (i.e., biting one's tongue) when they are hurt and frustrated. This can serve the valuable function of preventing the escalation of conflict, but it is a form of forgiveness that is limited to what systems therapists call "first-order" behavioral change and does not effect deeper "second-order" transformation of self and relationship.[24] In theological discourse, one also often hears forgiveness described as the remission of a debt or the removal of a penalty. However, the use of simile requires a simultaneous recognition of the dissimilarity in meaning when terms cross into a new field of discourse. The problems that arise in psychology and theology when forgiveness is limited to this semantic range will be examined throughout the following chapters.

Therapeutic Forgiveness

While legal and financial acts of forgiveness can occur instantaneously, forgiveness in the second semantic field, therapeutic transformation, usually is a process that takes time.[25] This is the range of meaning in which most psychological and psychotherapeutic definitions of forgiveness primarily operate. In this sphere the activity of forgiving may include a forensic transaction, but it always aims for a more transformative effect. For example, forgiveness may be portrayed as "the healing balm for wounds to commitment in rela-

23. See, e.g., T. D. Hargraves, *Families and Forgiveness: Healing Intergenerational Wounds* (New York: Bruner/Mazel, 1994).

24. For a classic work on first-order and second-order change, see P. Watzlawick, J. Weakland, and R. Fisch, *Change: Principles of Problem Formation and Problem Resolution* (New York: Norton, 1974).

25. Enright and Fitzgibbons, *Helping Clients Forgive*; E. L. Worthington Jr., S. J. Sandage, and J. W. Berry, "Group Interventions to Promote Forgiveness: What Researchers and Clinicians Ought to Know," in *Forgiveness: Theory, Research, and Practice* (ed. M. E. McCullough, K. I. Pargament, and C. E. Thoresen; New York: Guilford, 2000), 228–53. For practical psychological approaches to the process of forgiveness, see R. D. Enright, *Forgiveness Is a Choice: A Step-by-Step Process for Resolving Anger and Restoring Hope* (Washington, D.C.: American Psychological Association, 2001); M. E. McCullough, S. J. Sandage, and E. L. Worthington Jr., *To Forgive Is Human* (Downers Grove, Ill.: InterVarsity, 1997); E. L. Worthington Jr., *Five Steps to Forgiving: The Art and Science of Forgiving* (New York: Crown, 2001).

tionships."[26] Kenneth Pargament and Mark Rye describe forgiveness as a transformation in one's goals (e.g., from self-protection to peace) and in the means to those goals (e.g., from resentment to empathy).[27] Michael McCullough conceptualizes forgiveness as a transformation of motivations toward an offender where motivations become less vengeful and avoidant and more benevolent. Whether focused on the individual client or on a dyadic or family relationship or a broader political system, forgiveness in this context involves more personal and interpersonal engagement—aimed at second-order change and the healing and wholeness of the self and/or the other.

Psychologists reach stronger consensus on what forgiveness is *not* than on what it *is*.[28] To forgive someone is different from condoning an offense, which implies that the offender's action was justifiable.[29] Forgiveness is relevant in the case of real interpersonal wrongs. Excusing an offender as having valid reasons for committing an offense is also different from forgiveness. Forgiveness involves a moral judgment that an offender is responsible for harmful actions. Genuine forgiveness is also distinct from forgetting or denying the impact of harmful offenses. Forgiveness involves surveying the damage one incurred through the hurtful actions of another and, eventually, remembering it differently rather than trying to erase it from memory. Finally, forgiveness is not the same as reconciliation, which is the restoration of a trusting relationship.[30] Therapists often assert that it is possible to forgive an offender but not restore the relationship, which may be a wise decision if safe and trustworthy behavior cannot be demonstrated. Everett Worthington and Nathaniel Wade note that forgiveness is one among many ways to reduce feelings of unforgiveness toward an offender. Other ways of reducing these feelings include retaliating, seeking justice, or employing psychological defenses. We presently await scientific comparisons of differing methods for reducing unforgiveness.

26. S. J. Sandage, E. L. Worthington Jr., T. L. Hight, and J. W. Berry, "Seeking Forgiveness: Theoretical Context and an Initial Empirical Study," *Journal of Psychology and Theology* 28 (2000): 21.

27. K. I. Pargament and M. S. Rye, "Forgiveness as a Method of Religious Coping," in *Dimensions of Forgiveness: Psychological Research and Theological Perspectives* (ed. E. L. Worthington Jr.; Philadelphia: Templeton Foundation, 1998), 62–64.

28. See McCullough, Pargament, and Thoresen, "Psychology of Forgiveness," 7–9.

29. Enright and Fitzgibbons, *Helping Clients Forgive*, 40–41.

30. S. R. Freedman, "Forgiveness and Reconciliation: The Importance of Understanding How They Differ," *Counseling and Values* 42 (1998): 200–216; McCullough, Sandage, and Worthington, *To Forgive Is Human*; E. L. Worthington Jr. and D. T. Drinkard, "Promoting Reconciliation through Psychoeducation and Therapeutic Interventions," *Journal of Marriage and Family Therapy* 26 (2000): 93–101.

Drawing primarily upon McCullough's theory and research, we suggest the following broad definition: forgiveness in this semantic field is a process of (a) reducing one's motivation for avoidance and revenge and (b) increasing one's motivation for goodwill toward a specific offender.[31] Forgivingness is the dispositional trait or capacity for practicing forgiveness over time and across situations.[32] Ideas of forgiveness are cultural constructs related to social scripts about the healing and repair of interpersonal conflict. At least in the United States, social scripts about forgiveness are influenced by moral, religious, and psychological discourse. This suggests that interdisciplinary and integrative accounts of forgiveness are needed for developing multidimensional models. Our task in this book is to engage in this interdisciplinary conversation and explore the connections between the various meanings and practices of forgiveness.

Redemptive Forgiveness

This brings us to the third semantic field in which the term *forgiveness* operates: redemption. Theological reflection expands the horizon for understanding forgiveness by including ultimate concerns about the relation of humanity to God. Redemptive forgiveness can and should incorporate the dynamics of forensic and therapeutic forgiveness, but as a theological category it must not be limited to them. As we will see, nowhere have the egregious effects of the domination of legal and financial metaphors of salvation been felt more deeply than in the understanding and practice of forgiveness in Christian life. Primarily forensic models of divine redemption risk placing divine grace under the constraints of a legal system, a system that usually reflects the prevailing jurisprudence of the era in which the model was developed. They also easily lead to a view of forgiving one's neighbor or enemy as a quick fix, an abstract mental accounting that does not actually transform and heal relations.

The New Testament occasionally uses penal and financial metaphors for salvation, especially in the context of parables, but as we shall see, the overarching meaning of forgiveness is manifesting and sharing redemptive grace. In Christian theology, salvation is about grace. In fact, one of the main Greek words translated "forgiveness" in the New Testament literally means "to manifest grace." Theologians who favor primarily forensic models will usually admit that salvation should *also* include healing and redemption. Once the first semantic

31. M. E. McCullough, "Forgiveness: Who Does It and How Do They Do It?" *Current Directions in Psychological Science* 10 (2001): 194–97.

32. Cf. R. C. Roberts, "Forgivingness," *American Philosophical Quarterly* 32 (1995): 289–306.

domain has been privileged in theological construction, however, it is difficult to incorporate the other two fields of meaning into a coherent doctrine of salvation. On the other hand, if we begin by focusing on the redemptive field of meaning we may be able to embrace the concerns of the others within a broader presentation of soteriology.

Many theologians are becoming more critical of what they see as overly therapeutic models of Christian forgiveness. For example, L. Gregory Jones speaks of therapeutic forgiveness (with the model of Lewis Smedes[33] in mind) as a "frighteningly shallow perspective that trivializes and undermines central Christian practices and understandings of forgiveness." Jones goes so far as to say this "therapeutic cancer" impoverishes the church.[34] John Hughes expresses concern about the exclusion of forgiveness from broader political life, which is perpetuated by "the interiorising and therapeutic rhetoric of forgiveness often used by the Church today."[35] On the other hand, psychologists are often guilty of secularizing and stripping the construct of forgiveness from historically religious contexts; and several psychologists are reevaluating this separation. For example, Pargament and Rye note that psychological or transformative forgiveness can be "sanctified" and "invested with sacred meaning."[36] They argue that religious traditions also offer models, methods, and resources for the process of forgiveness that should be empirically investigated.

In this book, we challenge the dichotomy that leads to a forced decision—either psychological or theological. Our delineation of the fields of meaning in which forgiveness operates is intended to open up the dialogue between psychology and theology in a way that recognizes the integrity of each discipline as well as the overlapping of concerns in the domains of therapeutic and redemptive forgiveness. In part 1, Steve describes the dynamics of intersubjectivity and the developmental impact of early caregiving faces in the formation of the capacity for forgivingness. From a psychological perspective, he outlines the practice of saving faces, in both the negative and positive connotations of that phrase. In part 2, LeRon examines these dynamics from a theological perspective, exploring the biblical and doctrinal significance of facing and forgiveness. He presents a model of redemptive forgiveness as sharing in divine grace and integrates forgiveness into

33. Lewis Smedes's popular 1984 book *Forgive and Forget* (Dallas: Word) attracted the interest of many psychologists and therapists and helped catalyze contemporary research on forgiveness. Cf. Smedes, *The Art of Forgiving* (Nashville: Moorings, 1996).

34. L. G. Jones, *Embodying Forgiveness: A Theological Analysis* (Grand Rapids: Eerdmans, 1995), 52, 64.

35. J. Hughes, "The Politics of Forgiveness," *Modern Theology* 17 (2001): 261–87 at 271.

36. Pargament and Rye, "Forgiveness as a Method of Religious Coping," 66–67.

the practical experience of faith, love, and hope in Christian community. In part 3, we interact together with specific case studies about
facing and forgiveness, drawn from contemporary therapeutic practice and from ancient biblical texts. We test our psychological and
theological models by bringing them to bear on particular narratives
that illustrate the struggle for forgiveness. Our overarching goal is to
demonstrate the explanatory power of facial hermeneutics and to illuminate the transforming reality of forgiveness as we search for wholeness and salvation.

PART 1

Faces
of Forgiveness
in Psychology

Steven J. Sandage

2

Forgiveness and Intersubjective Formation

One afternoon I (Steve) was at home working furiously on a writing project to meet a rapidly approaching deadline. I decided to take a quick break, probably at a difficult point in the manuscript, to rush across the street to the grocery store and grab an ingredient I would need for dinner. I snatched what I needed from the shelf and briskly headed for the checkout area. I picked up speed as I heard a clerk announcing that she was opening a new checkout line at register 6. "Great! No line," I thought as I shifted into overdrive. Out of the corner of my eye, I picked up an object moving toward me. Suddenly, I experienced the sharp jab of what felt like knives in the back of my ankles. I gasped out loud in pain and shock and turned to see a woman who had run into me from behind with her shopping cart. We must have converged on the open register from opposing angles and I, unfortunately, beat her to the spot. My shock quickly turned to anger as my reproachful eyes searched for hers, demanding some sign of contrition. Instead, without making any eye contact, she backed up her cart and went around me to claim her victory in our race to the checkout finish line. As she passed me I caught a glimpse of her small, gray-blue eyes staring straight ahead. They looked glassy, as though she would not have been able to see me even if she had looked me in the face. I felt a strange mix of anger and sympathy as I stood there and checked to make sure my feet were still attached to my legs.

This story illustrates three important dynamics that often emerge in the psychological battlefield of life, where the dynamics of forgiveness and unforgiveness occur daily. First, when we are hurt or offended by others, there is often an initial anxious shock with the surprise of physical or emotional pain, which can be followed by anger or other negative emotions. Fear and anxiety are at the core of unforgiveness and relational estrangement.[1]

Second, forgiveness and unforgiveness emerge in a context of intersubjectivity and are influenced by the ways we face one another. By intersubjectivity I mean that interpersonal encounters always involve the interplay and potential recognition between two differing subjectivities. I say *potential* recognition because two subjects frequently fail to overcome the forces of negation to experience recognition or connection with one another. I looked at the face and eyes of my "offender" hoping for some sign of recognition that might mitigate my rising hostility. She and I each had a subjective experience of the event, and we did not connect or recognize one another in a way that bridged our differing subjectivities. The developmental roots and systemic context of intersubjectivity strongly shapes a person's capacities for practicing forgiveness.

Third, forgiveness is prevented by deficits of empathy and humility. I later reflected that it felt easier to access righteous indignation about her competitive rudeness and stone-faced lack of remorse in the moment than to humbly become aware of my own contribution to the situation. The truth is that I probably entered the store feeling anxious and tense about my writing, which served to generate an unconscious demand that the world (namely, other shoppers) cooperate with my time pressures. And once I felt hurt and offended, I found it extremely challenging to consider the possibilities of this other person's subjectivity and life context. Perhaps her husband was at home suffering from terminal cancer. Or maybe she was a widow preparing her house for sale after her kids talked her into moving into a nursing home. Instead, I rushed to form a negating and unforgiving interpretation of this stranger as callous and self-serving. Empathy is more psychologically challenging and involves a compassionate recognition of the humanness of another person who, like me, has a story and life context.

1. S. J. Sandage, "An Ego-Humility Model of Forgiveness: Theoretical Foundations," *Marriage and the Family: A Christian Journal* 2 (1999): 259–76; E. L. Worthington Jr., "The Pyramid Model of Forgiveness: Some Interdisciplinary Speculations about Unforgiveness and Forgiveness," in *Dimensions of Forgiveness: Psychological Research and Theological Perspectives* (ed. E. L. Worthington Jr.; Philadelphia: Templeton Foundation, 1998), 107–38.

Empathy is a way of facing an offender that transcends anxious reactivity and paves the way for forgiveness.

Being hit by that woman's cart would have been painful and frustrating under any circumstances, but it was also a moment of interpersonal estrangement pregnant with the potential for forgiveness or unforgiveness. Most people have probably hundreds or thousands of such interactions over the course of a lifetime, the most important of which involve close relationships. Forgiveness and unforgiveness may serve to influence the fate of many of our relationships, and emerging research suggests that the capacity to forgive might even affect our health.[2] Until recently, psychological science gave very little attention to interpersonal forgiveness. Empirical research on forgiveness is still in the early phases of development, so psychological models of forgiveness must be held tentatively. In this chapter I will synthesize psychological theory and research on human development and personality to outline the characterological formation[3] of capacities for practicing forgiveness or what philosopher Robert Roberts calls "forgivingness."[4] A theme that guides our intersubjective understanding is this: the capacity for forgiveness is formed in response to the face of the other.

Forgiveness and Intersubjectivity

Many psychological models of forgiveness emphasize intrapsychic factors in the development of forgiveness. Forgiveness is often conceptualized as a process that occurs within an individual and is influenced by various developmental and personality factors. Robert Enright and his colleagues at the University of Wisconsin are the pioneers of psychological research on forgiveness and continue to generate an excellent body of work.[5] Enright conceptualizes forgiveness from a structural cognitive developmental framework in the tradition of Piaget and Kohlberg, and his cross-sectional research suggests qualitative differences in the cognitive rationales people use in thinking about for-

2. J. W. Berry and E. L. Worthington Jr., "Forgiveness, Relationship Quality, Stress While Imagining Relationship Events, and Physical and Mental Health," *Journal of Counseling Psychology* 48 (2001): 447–55.

3. Social scientists use the term *development*, while spiritual directors often prefer to speak of *formation*. I use the terms interchangeably, although I appreciate the spiritual connotations of formation.

4. R. C. Roberts, "Forgivingness," *American Philosophical Quarterly* 32 (1995): 289–306.

5. For a review, see R. D. Enright and R. P. Fitzgibbons, *Helping Clients Forgive: An Empirical Guide for Resolving Anger and Restoring Hope* (Washington, D.C.: American Psychological Association, 2000).

giveness.[6] These rationales about forgiving others roughly parallel Kohl-bergian stages of moral development. For example, a person at a pre-operational level of cognitive and moral development understands both morality and relationships primarily in terms of punishments and rewards. Such a person might be willing to forgive an offender if the offender is sufficiently punished or if forgiveness seems to of-fer personal benefits (e.g., reduced guilt for not forgiving). Another person, at a concrete operational level of development may respond to social expectations and norms and forgive out of a social or reli-gious obligation (i.e., "I *must* forgive"). Still a third person could be at a postoperational level of development and forgive out of an in-ternalized sense of the inherent goodness of forgiveness as moral love.[7]

Cognitive developmental and other intrapsychic personality factors certainly influence a person's capacity to forgive. Emerging empirical evidence suggests that there are individual differences in a charactero-logical disposition to practice forgiveness. Some people are more in-ternally predisposed to forgive than others.[8] For example, people who are high in the personality trait of rumination tend to repeatedly expe-rience intrusive thoughts and images about hurtful events.[9] Not sur-prisingly, such people often have trouble forgiving others.

The developmental formation of capacities for interpersonal for-giveness involves both intrapsychic *and* intersubjective dynamics. Models of intersubjective development can complement rather than replace intrapsychic models of development.[10] The intersubjective de-velopment or formation of forgiveness is given less attention in psy-chology than the intrapsychic, no doubt because intersubjectivity is much harder to operationalize and empirically investigate. Yet dilem-mas of interpersonal forgiveness and unforgiveness involve the inter-section of at least two people and their differing subjective experi-ences of conflict within a systemic context.

6. R. D. Enright and the Human Development Study Group, "Piaget on the Moral Development of Forgiveness: Identity or Reciprocity?" *Human Development* 37 (1994): 63–80.

7. Enright and Fitzgibbons, *Helping Clients Forgive*.

8. Berry and Worthington, "Forgiveness, Relationship Quality"; J. W. Berry, E. L. Worthington Jr., L. Parrott III, L. E. O'Connor, and N. G. Wade, "Dispositional Forgiv-ingness: Development and Construct Validity of the Transgression Narrative Test," *Per-sonality and Social Psychology Bulletin* 27 (2001): 1277–90.

9. M. E. McCullough, C. G. Bellah, S. D. Kilpatrick, and J. L. Johnson, "Vengeful-ness: Relationships with Forgiveness, Rumination, Well-Being, and the Big Five," *Per-sonality and Social Psychology Bulletin* 27 (2001): 601–10.

10. J. Benjamin, *Like Subjects, Love Objects: Essays on Recognition and Sexual Dif-ference* (New Haven: Yale University Press, 1995); idem, *Shadow of the Other: Intersub-jectivity and Gender in Psychoanalysis* (New York: Routledge, 1998).

Intersubjectivity is a relational construct that generates interest and differing understandings across a number of disciplines. In the social sciences, intersubjectivity is a vibrant topic of study in contemporary psychoanalysis, developmental psychology, and critical theory.[11] Philosophers such as Gadamer, Buber, and Levinas also emphasize intersubjectivity as the primordial "always already thereness" of relationality. These differing accounts of intersubjectivity share a move beyond the monadic Cartesian view of selfhood in modern philosophy and science to explore a dialogical and relational construal of mind and self, although theorists differ on the definition of intersubjectivity. Psychoanalyst Jessica Benjamin frames the questions of intersubjectivity in this way: "But how is the meeting of two subjects different from the meeting of a subject and an object? Once we have acknowledged that the object makes an important contribution to the life of the subject, what is added by deciding to call this object another subject? And what are the impediments to the meeting of two minds?"[12] For Benjamin, intersubjectivity is not simply the general subjective interplay of two persons but the qualitative capacity to *recognize* the other as a subject and an equivalent center of being. In contrast, Robert Stolorow and his colleagues argue the more phenomenological position that intersubjectivity is not a specific developmental capacity but rather the systemic context that is the precondition for all interpersonal experience.[13] These differing uses of the language of intersubjectivity are not easily reconciled, yet each contributes something important to contemporary discourse on relationality. The estrangement of unforgiveness can be the expression of one developmental impediment to intersubjectivity or "the meeting of two minds," and it can represent the ruptured primordial context some theologians call

11. In psychoanalysis, see Benjamin, *Like Subjects, Love Objects*; S. A. Mitchell, *Relationality: From Attachment to Intersubjectivity* (Hillsdale, N.J.: Analytic Press, 2000); D. M. Orange, G. E. Atwood, and R. D. Stolorow, *Working Intersubjectively: Contextualism in Psychoanalytic Practice* (Hillsdale, N.J.: Analytic Press, 2001). In developmental psychology, see J. V. Jordan, "The Meaning of Mutuality," in *Women's Growth in Connection: Writings from the Stone Center* (ed. J. V. Jordan, A. G. Kaplan, J. B. Miller, I. P. Stiver, and J. L. Surrey; New York: Guilford, 1991), 81–96; D. N. Stern, *The Interpersonal World of the Infant: A Viewpoint from Psychoanalysis and Developmental Psychology* (London: Karnac, 1985). In critical theory, see J. Habermas, *Moral Consciousness and Communicative Action* (Cambridge: MIT Press, 1990); idem, *Justification and Application* (Cambridge: MIT Press, 1993).

12. Benjamin, *Like Subjects, Love Objects*, 29.

13. For greater depth on the contours of this psychoanalytic debate over the definition of intersubjectivity, see Jessica Benjamin, afterword to *Relational Psychoanalysis: The Emergence of a Tradition* (ed. S. A. Mitchell and L. Aron; Hillsdale, N.J.: Analytic Press, 1999), 201–10; and the contrasting position of R. D. Stolorow, D. M. Orange, and G. E. Atwood, "Cartesian and Post-Cartesian Trends in Relational Psychoanalysis," *Psychoanalytic Psychology* 18 (2000): 468–84.

"original sin." Intersubjective theorists describe intersubjectivity in the following ways: as (a) a developmental capacity, (b) a systemic context, or (c) both context and capacity.

Intersubjectivity as Developmental Capacity

Daniel Stern's model of the psychological development of intersubjectivity and selfhood is novel, while building on the earlier work of relational developmentalists such as Lev Vygotsky and Harry Stack Sullivan.[14] Stern challenges the Piagetian view that the social development of learning to interact with other persons can be likened to learning to engage physical objects. Unlike physical objects, human caregivers respond to infants and children out of their own subjective states with varying qualities of responsiveness and empathic attunement. This represents a shift from a "one-person psychology" viewing individuals as closed systems to a "two-person psychology" studying the individual in intersubjective, relational context.[15]

Stern also challenges Margaret Mahler's influential theory that development moves in a largely unidirectional manner from unrelatedness to symbiosis with caregivers to separation and individuation. He suggests that infants are born as active organisms with an innate sense of separateness from others in the context of interpersonal relatedness. According to Stern, around the age of seven to nine months, infants can develop the expanded capacity for intersubjective awareness of sharing mental states with a caregiver. This preverbal awareness involves a mutual process between infant and caregiver of inferring that the subjective mental states of the other, including intentions and emotions, are distinct but can be shared. Intersubjectivity is this growing awareness that minds and subjective states are separate but "interfaceable."[16] Stern explains intersubjectivity:

> It is rather a working notion that says something like, what is going on in my mind may be similar enough to what is going on in your mind that we can somehow communicate this (without words) and thereby experience intersubjectivity. For such an experience to occur, there must be some shared framework of meaning and means of communication such as gesture, posture, or facial expression.[17]

14. Cf. Stern, *Interpersonal World of the Infant*.
15. R. A. Watson, "Toward Union in Love: The Contemplative Spiritual Tradition and Contemporary Psychoanalytic Theory in the Formation of Persons," *Journal of Psychology and Theology* 28 (2000): 282–92.
16. Stern, *Interpersonal World of the Infant*, 124.
17. Ibid., 124–25.

The development of intersubjectivity transforms the experience of caregiver empathy from simply a source of soothing to a dyadic process of mutual disclosure, impenetrability, and intimacy. This involves the sharing of attention between infant and caregiver where, for example, infants visually follow the direction a caregiver points, using the caregiver's face to confirm they have found the intended target. By nine months, infants show the ability to notice the congruence between their own emotional states and the emotional expression on the face of someone else. Lab studies of one-year-old infants being coaxed across a visual cliff (i.e., a glass-covered apparent drop-off) with a toy show infants looking at their mothers' facial expressions to interpret the uncertainty and potential danger. This is essentially an intersubjective process of sharing inner states through facial expressions, among other mediums of communication.

Stern argues that intersubjective affective attunement is not synonymous with empathy but that the two share in common a tacit process of emotional resonance with another person. This connection between attunement and empathy is significant for forgiveness. Psychological research, described later in this chapter, indicates that a personal capacity for empathy is strongly related to forgiving a specific offender and becoming a forgiving person.

Benjamin describes intersubjectivity as the development of mutual recognition of self-reflective, agentic persons where "the other must be recognized as another subject in order for the self to fully experience his or her subjectivity in the other's presence."[18] This suggests that affective attunement by caregivers, a particular form of responsive intersubjectivity, enables infants to develop both independent agency and intersubjective connection to others.[19] In a paradoxical sense, we develop awareness of our own subjectivity and agency only if faced and recognized by another. As D. W. Winnicott says in countering Descartes, "When I look I am seen, so I exist."[20]

Winnicott relates the intersubjective unfolding of face-to-face recognition between infant and caregiver to the need for mirroring. He asks, "What does the baby see when he or she looks at the mother's face? . . . what the baby sees is himself or herself. In other words, the mother is looking at the baby, and what she looks like is related to what she sees there."[21] Winnicott is suggesting that infant-caregiver mirroring is foundational to the formation of intersubjectivity and selfhood and that children literally look at their parents' faces to as-

18. Benjamin, *Like Subjects, Love Objects*, 30.
19. J. S. Auerbach and S. J. Blatt, "Self-Reflexivity, Intersubjectivity, and Therapeutic Change," *Psychoanalytic Psychology* 18 (2001): 427–50; cf. Stern, *Interpersonal World of the Infant*.
20. D. W. Winnicott, *Playing and Reality* (1971; New York: Tavistock, 1982), 114.
21. Ibid., 112.

sess their present relationship with that parent. If a caregiver's face chronically mirrors hostility, anxiety, or simply nonresponsiveness, the formation of a healthy sense of selfhood and relationality will be hindered. The infant, in turn, influences this reciprocal process to the degree that the face of the infant seems to recognize the caregiver.

The growing self-reflexivity in the second year of life that contributes to the development of intersubjectivity, such as facial self-recognition in a mirror or photograph, coincides with both an increased potential for shame and the emergence of transitional object usage.[22] Both shame and the use of transitional objects, as I will argue later, have important implications for the formation of capacities for forgiveness. Shame represents a self-conscious moral emotion rooted in relational experiences of estranging conflict that can communicate personal worthlessness. Shame typically interferes with healthy forgiveness and relational repair. Transitional objects are creatively employed by children to deal with the dilemma of becoming separate and autonomous while remaining attached. Internalized images of God represent one form of sacred transitional object that mediates the space between self and other, thereby potentially shaping internal models related to forgiveness and repair.

The capacity for intersubjectivity is also applied to models of adult development. One example includes Judith Jordan's model of the relational selfhood of women. Jordan describes intersubjectivity as "understanding the other from her or his subjective frame of reference,"[23] and she goes on to describe an intersubjectivity in relationship that is mutual or goes both ways. In a manner reminiscent of Stern, Jordan defines mutual intersubjectivity as "an interest in, attunement to, and responsiveness to the subjective, inner experience of the other at both a cognitive and affective level. The primary channel for this kind of mutuality is empathic attunement, the capacity to share in and comprehend the momentary psychological state of another person."[24] Such mutual intersubjectivity involves an openness to both affecting and being affected by the other person. Through empathic attunement, the other's subjective frame of reference is "held" and taken into account. This does not imply boundaryless merger with the other or a loss of one's own sense of self, since mutuality implies safety to reveal one's own self as well. This kind of mutual intersubjectivity and empathic attunement among adults could be expected to facilitate forgiveness and perhaps prevent the compounding of severe relational injuries.

22. Cf. Auerbach and Blatt, "Self-Reflexivity, Intersubjectivity, and Therapeutic Change."

23. Jordan, "Meaning of Mutuality," 83.

24. Ibid., 82.

Another application of intersubjectivity to adult relationships comes from the marriage and family love ethic articulated by Don Browning and his colleagues.[25] Browning et al. build on the communication theory of Jürgen Habermas and the psychoanalytic theory of Benjamin to suggest that contemporary couples and families in the highly democratic United States need to develop communicative competence in intersubjective dialogue. The erosion of traditional role definitions and communal supports makes intersubjective communication vital to developing healthy and forgiving relationships. Browning and colleagues offer an ethic of love as equal regard, mutuality, and intersubjective dialogue as an alternative to the more limited and more common views of love as self-sacrifice or self-fulfillment. In marriage, virtues like love and justice (and I would add forgiveness) must be experienced intersubjectively if the relationship is to be grounded in the politics of equal regard and mutuality rather than dominance and submission.

Intersubjectivity as Systemic Context

Some psychoanalysts articulate a theory of intersubjectivity not as a developmental achievement or capacity but as the psychological field or systemic context "constituted by the intersection of two subjectivities."[26] In this systemic view intersubjectivity can occur between any two people as subjects. A person's mental experience and sense of self is shaped throughout development in the context of intersubjective systems.[27] This second view of intersubjectivity as systemic context is closer to the meaning of intersubjectivity posited by philosophers in the phenomenological tradition, such as Gadamer, Buber, and Levinas. From this philosophical perspective, intersubjectivity itself is not actually developed but is the primordial relational sphere of facing which is "always already there."[28]

Intersubjectivity as Capacity and Context

While I am partial to the definition of intersubjectivity as developmental capacity advanced by theorists such as Benjamin, Stern, Jordan, and Browning, it is possible to also utilize the view of intersub-

25. D. S. Browning, B. J. Miller-McLemore, P. D. Couture, K. B. Lyon, and R. M. Franklin, *From Culture Wars to Common Ground: Religion and the American Family Debate* (2d ed.; Louisville: Westminster John Knox, 2000).

26. G. E. Atwood and R. D. Stolorow, *Structures of Subjectivity: Explorations in Psychoanalytic Phenomenology* (Hillsdale, N.J.: Analytic Press, 1984), 64.

27. R. O. Piehl, "Marbles, Clocks, and the Postmodern Self," *Journal of Psychology and Theology* 26 (1998): 83–100.

28. E. Farley, *Good and Evil: Interpreting a Human Condition* (Minneapolis: Fortress, 1990), 36.

jectivity as systemic context. J. S. Auerbach and S. J. Blatt advocate this position:

> It is this mutual recognition by the caregiver and child, of each other's mental states, that ultimately constitutes the intersubjective situation. Thus, intersubjectivity as an interpersonal interaction—in Aron's (1996) phrase, a meeting of minds—and intersubjectivity as a psychological capacity are deeply intertwined concepts, with the former constituting the transactional matrix from which the latter emerges.[29]

Obviously, healthy mutual intersubjectivity is rare in human relationships. From a contextual perspective, the intersubjective nature of interpersonal conflict is so complex because it always involves a dance, often a chaotic one, between the subjective experiences of two people. From the developmental perspectives, affective attunement and mutual empathy are obstructed by various anxieties, distortions, and projections. What is called unforgiveness is often a failure of mutual intersubjectivity and empathic attunement, and forgiveness typically develops in response to intersubjective attunement and empathy. While it is possible to forgive an offender whom we feel does not recognize us intersubjectively, it is interesting to note that forgiveness of a specific offender is highly correlated with (a) offender apology, (b) empathy toward the offender, and (c) closeness in the relationship both before and after the conflict. This implies an intersubjective process whereby we are more likely to forgive when someone close to us apologizes for an offense (probably at least attempting to recognize and enter our subjectivity), which prompts our empathy and forgiveness in return. But this dyadic process unfolds in a broader sociocultural context. Broader intersubjective dynamics of the systemic context or matrix can promote estrangement (e.g., scapegoating) rather than forgiveness.

The Sociocultural Context of Forgiveness

Forgiveness and related social processes of repairing hurt in relationships are also formed and embedded in sociocultural contexts. Forgiveness and unforgiveness are not only intrapsychic and intersubjective, for there is always a cultural and historical context that shapes the ways in which individuals and relational partners approach conflict. Lev Vygotsky (1896–1934) was a Russian psychologist whose theories of human development are finally attracting attention in the West, especially in the past thirty years. Whereas Piaget emphasizes the biological maturation and cognitive discovery of the developing individual, Vygotsky suggests that the sociocultural and historical context of development is pivotal. Vygotsky believes that children are

---

29. Auerbach and Blatt, "Self-Reflexivity, Intersubjectivity, and Therapeutic Change," 429.

guided or acculturated into development through intersubjective or "intermental" relationships of mutual understanding and attention with parents, teachers, and mentors.[30] Through these relationships we come to internalize the customs, practices, and values of our communities, primarily through the mediating tool of language. Language is such a powerful tool, according to Vygotsky, because it is a vital part of social interaction and eventually leads to the ability to influence oneself (e.g., through self-talk).

A Vygotskian understanding of the formation of forgiveness can provide a helpful complement to the Piagetian cognitive developmental model of Enright. Intraorganismic factors certainly influence the dynamics of forgiveness, but so do social and cultural factors. Two main implications for models of forgiveness can be drawn from Vygotsky's understanding of development. First, models and construals of forgiveness will be likely to differ across cultural and historical contexts. To date, this is a neglected issue in Western psychological research on forgiveness. While all cultural groups need ways to resolve interpersonal conflict, and something like forgiveness might be a common method, there appear to be cultural differences in the motivations and mechanisms of forgiveness.[31] For example, some initial fieldwork research with highly collectivistic Hmong (a Southeast Asian refugee group) in the St. Paul, Minnesota, area suggests that cultural norms can influence the practice of forgiveness. For traditional Hmong, interpersonal offenses do not occur between individuals but between families and clans. The group orientation of the Hmong means that forgiveness could require a ceremony between two clans that involves the offender offering a formal apology and a gift, which culminates in a feast. In such collectivistic cultures, forgiveness and relational reconciliation are closely connected and preserve social harmony.

This is quite a contrast from the more individualistic-therapeutic approach to forgiveness of one my former therapy clients, a suburban Euro-American woman who was trying to continue a process of forgiving her drug-abusing son. When I asked how she was approaching forgiveness she reached into her purse and pulled out a very tattered piece of paper that was a self-help newsletter she had found in the office of a previous therapist. The newsletter contained a brief article on forgiving others by "letting go of resentment," and this woman explained that she reread some key lines from the article on a daily basis. Her cultural and therapeutic context had taught her that forgiveness was an individual decision that did not de-

---

30. L. S. Vygotsky, *Thought and Language* (ed. and trans. E. Haufmann and G. Vakar; Cambridge: MIT Press, 1962).

31. D. Augsburger, *Conflict Mediation across Cultures: Pathways and Patterns* (Louisville: Westminster John Knox, 1992); S. J. Sandage and T. W. Wiens, "Contextualizing Models of Humility and Forgiveness: A Reply to Gassin," *Journal of Psychology and Theology* 29 (2001): 201–11.

pend on the actions of her son, which she experienced as freeing her from responsibility for her son's behavior. One of the reasons this woman came to a professional therapist's office was to try to sustain and elaborate her experience of forgiveness since she could not locate specific tools or resources on forgiveness in her personal religious community.

Community and Forgiveness

Cultural and religious communities, however, often provide the models, tools, and resources for socially facilitating forgiveness,[32] which is a second implication of a Vygotskian perspective. Philosophers and theologians suggest that virtues like forgiveness are formed in and through community. Sociologist Robert Wuthnow finds evidence that religious groups in the United States might facilitate forgiveness for many people. In a nationally representative sample of over 1,300 adults involved in prayer groups, Bible studies, or other religiously oriented small groups, the majority of respondents reported that their religious groups had helped them to forgive someone.[33] It appears that the focus of such groups, however, makes a difference in facilitating forgiveness. Spiritual and emotional group activities such as prayer and the sharing of personal problems were more strongly associated with forgiveness than more general group activities like eating together or discussing books. Groups that paid particular attention to forgiveness were also more likely to be associated with forgiving behavior. Wuthnow concludes that religious and spiritual content in small groups might help shape a language of forgiveness, and a group climate that encourages sharing personal problems might promote the emotional safety to explore the need for forgiveness in relationships. It makes sense that the faces of those in our relational worlds, our communities, would shape how we approach such a social and intersubjective practice as forgiveness.

The Facial Mediation of Forgiveness

Perhaps faces—both our own faces and the faces of others in our community—actually mediate the process of forgiveness.[34] Faces ap-

32. K. I. Pargament and M. S. Rye, "Forgiveness as a Method of Religious Coping," in *Dimensions of Forgiveness: Psychological Research and Theological Perspectives* (ed. E. L. Worthington Jr.; Philadelphia: Templeton Foundation, 1998), 62–64.

33. R. Wuthnow, "How Religious Groups Promote Forgiving: A National Study," *Journal for the Scientific Study of Religion* 39 (2000): 125–39.

34. In this case, my use of the term *mediate* does not refer to statistical mediation. Rather, I mean *mediate* in the Vygotskian sense of human action mediated through tools and signs. Facial expressions represent one set of tools or signs that serve to mediate forgiveness-related actions. Obviously, faces play a different role interpersonally for individuals with visual and other impairments. These issues are explored helpfully by Jonathan Cole, *About Face* (Cambridge, Mass.: MIT Press, 1998).

pear to influence our experiences of forgiveness and unforgiveness at three levels of analysis. First, as just argued, forgiveness is influenced by our sociocultural and relational context or the faces of those around us. Second, scientific evidence is emerging that the actual anatomy of our own faces may reflect our psychological levels of forgiveness. Our physical faces can provide clues to the depth of our forgiveness. And third, dilemmas of forgiveness typically involve the intersubjective interaction of our own faces and the faces of others, including our offenders. This can involve ongoing face-to-face interaction between a victim and offender, or it can simply involve the subjective influence of the face of the other within oneself. The ways we face one another strongly influence the process of forgiveness.

But how do our faces reflect our levels of forgiveness? One study suggests that our faces might change depending upon whether we imagine forgiving or unforgiving responses to an offender. Charlotte vanOyen Witvliet and her colleagues conducted a psychophysiological laboratory study of forgiveness and unforgiveness.[35] They asked participants to remember a relationship in which they were offended by someone and to imagine making unforgiving responses and then forgiving responses. Various physiological measures were recorded during the imagery exercises, including facial electromyogram (EMG) at the corrugator (i.e., brow) muscle region. Previous studies on facial expressions of emotion showed that negative imagery stimulated greater muscle tension in the brow region than did positive imagery. Participants rated their emotional responses throughout the imagery exercises using a video display and computer joystick. Facial expressions of muscle tension were significantly greater during the unforgiving condition than the forgiving condition during both the imagery and recovery periods. Participants also indicated feeling significantly more negative, aroused, angry, sad, and in control during the unforgiving condition than during the forgiving condition. Heart rate, blood pressure, and sympathetic nervous system arousal were also all higher for participants during the unforgiving condition. This study involved relatively brief periods of forgiveness and unforgiveness, but the findings suggest the possibility that chronic patterns of making forgiving or unforgiving responses to interpersonal offenses might result in differential health consequences.

A second study on facial expressions of forgiveness suggests that, at least in certain cultural contexts, our faces might not only reflect the presence of forgiveness but also the depth and maturity of our forgive-

35. C. V. Witvliet, T. E. Ludwig, and K. L. Vander Laan, "Granting Forgiveness or Harboring Grudges: Implications for Emotion, Physiology, and Health," *Psychological Science* 12 (2001): 117–23.

ness. Shih-Tseng Tina Huang and Robert Enright conducted a study in Taiwan investigating the relationship between developmental levels of forgiveness and physiological and facial indices of anger.[36] The investigators used an initial screening to select thirty pairs of adults who were at level 4 or level 6 on Enright's cognitive developmental model of forgiveness. In Enright's model, level 4 forgivers understand forgiveness as a social obligation that rests on the authority of social and religious leaders; level 6 forgivers understand forgiveness at a more mature level and view forgiveness as internalized commitment to moral love. The pairs of participants—matched in age, religion, education, gender, type of conflict, severity of conflict, and length of conflict—all reported forgiving someone following an interpersonal conflict within the previous three years. They were asked to recount the story of conflict and how it was resolved, while their blood pressure was monitored and their facial expressions were videotaped. Huang and Enright used the videotapes to code the number of times participants showed masked smiles and casting down of their eyes, both expressions of residual negative emotions. Masked smiles, in particular, are associated with anger. While there was no difference between the level 4 and level 6 forgivers on their conscious self-reports of anger, level 4 forgivers exhibited more frequent masked smiles and casting down of the eyes than level 6 forgivers while telling the story of the conflict. Level 4 forgivers also showed higher blood pressure levels than level 6 forgivers during the first part of telling their conflict stories. These results suggest that, contrary to their self-reports, level 4 forgivers did have more residual anger and emotional discomfort related to their interpersonal conflicts than the more mature forgivers at level 6. Forgiveness that is internalized and transcends social duty looks different on the face of the forgiver.

These two studies provide some limited but interesting preliminary data to suggest that our ability to forgive can be reflected in our faces. There is also a considerable body of theoretical and empirical research on facial expressions and emotions.

The Face of Emotion

The human face is the primary site for displaying and communicating emotion. Our faces can reveal our inner worlds or what Dan Allender calls "the disposition of the soul."[37] At given moments, our psychological feelings and spiritual longings converge in our facial

36. S. T. Huang and R. D. Enright, "Forgiveness and Anger-Related Emotions in Taiwan: Implications for Therapy," *Psychotherapy* 37 (2000): 71–79.

37. D. Allender, "Emotions and the Pathway to God," *Christian Counseling Today* 4 (Winter 1996): 35.

displays. At other times, our faces may conceal what is happening inside of us.

Charles Darwin developed one of the earliest scientific theories of facial expressions of emotion, although his work was not particularly helpful to modern researchers.[38] Silvan Tomkins is the leading modern theorist on the facial expression of emotion.[39] Tomkins suggests that emotions are our primary motivational mechanism and are expressed through the skin, especially the skin of the face. Throughout the 1970s, Carroll Izard and Paul Ekman were leading researchers on facial expressions of emotion, which has been called "the single most important idea in the psychology of emotion."[40] Ekman developed the most widely used methodologies for research in this area, and his work also advanced the controversial thesis that facial expressions of some basic emotions might be universal.[41]

This body of work suggests that we not only express emotions through our faces but also that we react emotionally and facially to the facial expressions of others.[42] In other words, face-to-face interactions often generate something like a biologically driven emotional dance of reciprocal influence. For example, an angry face in one person often prompts neural activity, autonomic responses, and a face of fear in the other person. This can in turn generate a face of superiority or regret on the first person, depending upon his or her characterological dispositions and affective regulation. And much of this interpersonal process unfolds below conscious awareness. Recent studies find that facial expressions spontaneously evoke emotions and facial muscle reactions at an automatic, unconscious level.[43] One theory suggests that angry faces could produce a mimicry or contagion effect in the recipient, who essentially mimics back facial expressions of anger. It is easy to imagine how this could be

38. C. Darwin, *The Expression of Emotions in Man and Animals* (Chicago: University of Chicago Press, 1872); see also J. A. Russell and J. M. Fernandez-Dols, "What Does a Facial Expression Mean?" in *The Psychology of Facial Expressions* (ed. J. A. Russell and J. M. Fernandez-Dols; Cambridge: Cambridge University Press, 1997), 3–30.

39. S. S. Tomkins, *Affect, Imagery, and Consciousness*, vol. 1: *The Positive Affects* (New York: Springer, 1962); see also D. L. Nathanson, *Shame and Pride: Affect, Sex, and the Birth of the Self* (New York: Norton, 1992).

40. Russell and Fernandez-Dols, "What Does a Facial Expression Mean?" 4.

41. P. Ekman and E. Rosenberg (eds.), *What the Face Reveals: Basic and Applied Studies of Spontaneous Expression Using the Facial Action Coding System* (New York: Oxford University Press, 1998).

42. U. Dimburg, M. Thunberg, and K. Elmehed, "Unconscious Facial Reactions to Emotional Facial Expressions," *Psychological Science* 11 (2000): 86–89; V. Surakka, M. Sams, and J. K. Hietanen, "Modulation of Neutral Face Evaluation by Laterally Presented Emotional Expressions," *Perceptual and Motor Skills* 88 (1991): 595–606.

43. Ibid.

part of escalating cycles of face-to-face interpersonal conflict with each person largely unaware of what their face is symbolically communicating to the other person.

The abilities to both make and read faces are vital social skills that can impact our health and our interpersonal relationships, a set of skills not all people possess.[44] Autism, schizophrenia, depression, and Parkinson's disease all seem to inhibit facial expressions of emotion, which can be a challenging part of the interpersonal difficulties associated with those disorders. A lack of facial animation might even impede the formation of close relationships.

This ability to read or interpret the faces of others, what we could call facial hermeneutics, is a complex skill that is crucial to healthy relationships. Empirical evidence shows that we use others' facial expressions of emotion not only to interpret their emotional states but also their interpersonal intentions.[45] People who have been abused or neglected as children often struggle with accurately interpreting the faces and intentions of others.[46] Those who have been abused, for example, often tend to overinterpret anger when trying to interpret the emotions of others through their facial expressions. Such inaccurate and hostile interpretations of faces could obviously create or exacerbate relational estrangement and unforgiveness. From a psychodynamic perspective, this can include a defensive process of projection and projective identification where one person projects his or her own anger or insecurity onto the other person, who then starts to identify with those projections. This projection may even occur via the facial expressions of the other person, where faces (and intentions) are misread as excessively hostile or malevolent. For some people, this defensive projection may have served an important survival function early in life when family relationships were hostile and dangerous and it was necessary to "assume the worst" of others' intentions. Unfortunately, this defense of overinterpreting hostile faces and intentions can be carried into adult relationships that could actually be safer and healthier than earlier abusive relationships.

44. D. Keltner, A. M. Kring, and G. A. Bonanno, "Fleeting Signs of the Course of Life: Facial Expression and Personal Adjustment," *Current Directions in Psychological Science* 8 (1999): 18–22.

45. U. Hess, S. Blairy, and R. E. Kleck, "The Influence of Facial Emotional Displays, Gender, and Ethnicity on Judgements of Dominance and Affiliation," *Journal of Nonverbal Behavior* 24 (2000): 265–83.

46. S. D. Pollack, D. Cichetti, K. Hornung, and A. Reed, "Recognizing Emotion in Faces: Developmental Effects of Child Abuse and Neglect," *Developmental Psychology* 36 (2000): 679–88.

The Face of the Other

The human face of the other becomes a significant influence on both our sense of self and others early in development. We seem to enter the world programmed to read faces. At the age of about three months, infants begin responding to the faces of caregivers, even smiling back at a smiling mother or father. James Loder suggests that this early face-to-face smiling between infant and caregiver is foundational to psychosocial and spiritual development and "is like imprinting on what it means to be human."[47] Loder explains: "This smiling response to the face or the consistent nurturing presence of another is a cosmic ordering, self-confirming presence of a loving other."[48] The face of the caregiver becomes a central part of the intersubjective relational matrix for the infant, which includes some sense of safety, nurturance, and affirmation related to human presence. The early developmental achievements of focusing eye contact, directing attention, and smiling allow formation of social engagement and attunement with others.[49] This intersubjective facial copresence even precedes language development.

The philosophy of Levinas is consonant with our postmodern intersubjective understanding of the formation of forgiveness. Levinas suggests that ethics and morality begin in experience of obligation through being faced by the other. Our responsibilities to others are grounded in face-to-face encounters that beckon us to care for those outside of ourselves. Levinas explains: "The irreducible and ultimate experience of relationship appears to me in fact to be . . . in the face to face of humans, in sociality, in its moral signification."[50] It is easier to avoid our moral obligations to others or even go through the motions of inauthentic moral acts, if we do not actually encounter the face of the other person. This is why television commercials soliciting funds for relief efforts often include the faces of needy children.

Developmental research complements Levinas's moral philosophy of the face by demonstrating the psychological significance of the human face. The distressed face and vocalizations of an infant typically elicit concerned responses from caregivers.[51] And while infants cannot appreciate the moral implications of face-to-face encounters, there is evidence that at as early as two months of age infants display facial

47. J. E. Loder, *The Logic of the Spirit: Human Development in Theological Perspective* (San Francisco: Jossey-Bass, 1998), 90.

48. Ibid.

49. B. Vandenberg, "Levinas and the Ethical Context of Human Development," *Human Development* 42 (1999): 31–44.

50. E. Levinas, *Ethics and Infinity* (trans. R. Cohen; Pittsburgh: Duquesne University Press, 1985), 77.

51. Cf. Vandenberg, "Levinas and the Ethical Context."

smiles and other self-regulatory behaviors in response to the expressionless faces of their mothers, seemingly trying to reconnect and then resolve feeling a sense of relational failure.[52] Our early experiences of the face of the other begin to intersubjectively shape our internal models about forgiveness and relational repair.

Faces in Therapy

Psychoanalyst Harold Searles proposes an intriguing theory of the role of facial expressions in psychotherapy.[53] Searles makes the observation through his own clinical work that a vital step in the healing process was when patients began to realize that they actually affected his facial expressions as a therapist. He believes that therapists needed to be aware of their own facial expressions to maximize the therapeutic impact of their relationship with clients. He suggests that many patients project their own emotions (e.g., anger) onto the face of the therapist, while others make use of the therapist's facial expressions as a symbolic bridge to gain access to their own dissociated emotions. In this sense, Searles advances the notion that facial expressions "belong" as much to the other person as to oneself. Connecting back to Winnicott's insights about intersubjective facing between mothers and infants, he posits that facial expressions can serve as transitional phenomena that mediate the space between two people and impact the self of both. This understanding of human facial expressions as transitional phenomena has a fascinating parallel in the qualitative research of Ana-Maria Rizzuto and others, suggesting that internalized representations of God's face also form developmentally and serve as transitional objects to mediate anxieties throughout life.[54]

A clear example of interpersonal facing in therapy occurred in my own clinical practice with a client who was struggling with depression and deep resentment at his former wife. He was self-medicating his pain with alcohol, and in one highly charged session I told him he would need to get a chemical dependency evaluation in order for us to continue with therapy. He became verbally aggressive with me for the first time, even questioning my motives and whether I had any addictions myself. I thought we had ended the session with a more agreeable tone, but I happened to pass him in the lobby after the session on my way to the rest room. At the start of the next session, he told me that I "scowled" at him with an angry expression when we passed in

52. Cf. Blum, "Face It!"

53. H. F. Searles, "The Role of the Analyst's Facial Expressions in Psychoanalysis and Psychoanalytic Therapy," *International Journal of Psychoanalytic Psychotherapy* 10 (1984–85): 47–73.

54. A.-M. Rizzuto, *The Birth of the Living God: A Psychoanalytic Study* (Chicago: University of Chicago Press, 1979).

the lobby. Now I do not believe I scowled at him nor was I aware of being particularly angry at him at that moment; I did, however, remember perceiving what I would call an angry scowl on *his* face. Curiously, we both perceived an angry lack of forgiveness in the face of the other. And this raises one of Searles's fascinating questions: To whom do facial expressions belong? Did he project angry unforgiveness onto my face because he was angry at me for confronting him? Was I simply unaware of the anger on my own face? Did I project my own repressed anger onto his face? Whatever the truth of the encounter, it highlights the intersubjective role of the face in relationships and the power of perceived negation. That client and I went on to initiate a meaningful and constructive conversation about our mutual frustration in therapy, which allowed a form of delayed recognition, and shared what we really wanted to communicate in the context of our therapeutic relationship. This provided an episode of relational repair where facial misinterpretations did not perpetuate estrangement.[55] It is interesting to consider how our impressions of the other would have been different if that meeting in the lobby had been our last or if we had not had the space of therapy to talk openly about our perceptions of each other and work through the estrangement that had occurred.

Faces of Anxiety

The core barrier to forgiveness is the anxiety of relational estrangement. When we are hurt or betrayed by another person, especially someone we trusted, we can experience it as an attack on our dignity and security in life. The interpersonal offense can offer us a taste of the existential estrangement that is a central part of the human predicament. The mistreatment or betrayal can symbolize deeper threats to our safety and existence and provoke unconscious anxiety about death and loss.

Interpersonal offenses activate defense mechanisms to cope with anxiety over this sense of threat.[56] Worthington developed a fear-conditioning model of unforgiveness and suggested that fear becomes associated with a particular offender (perhaps even the face of an offender), resulting in fight or flight responses of revenge or avoidance.[57] In this model, fear or anxiety is more basic to unforgiveness than even

55. On the development of relational repair and forgiveness, see R. Karen, *The Forgiving Self: The Road from Resentment to Connection* (New York: Doubleday, 2001).

56. P. C. Vitz and P. Mango, "Kleinian Psychodynamics and Religious Aspects of Hatred as a Defense Mechanism," *Journal of Psychology and Theology* 25 (1997): 64–71; idem, "Kernbergian Psychodynamics and Religious Aspects of the Forgiveness Process," *Journal of Psychology and Theology* 25 (1997): 72–80.

57. Worthington, "Pyramid Model of Forgiveness."

anger or hostility. Anxiety can give rise to aggressive feelings of anger or can mobilize other emotional responses associated with avoidance.

The development of defense mechanisms to cope with anxiety is an ego function that begins early, as anxiety becomes a central influence on personality.[58] Maladaptive defenses have been linked theoretically with characterological problems in forgiving. Some defenses more seriously distort the realities of self and other, which is like pouring gasoline onto the fires of relational anxiety. For example, projection of one's own anger and aggression onto the intentions of another operates on paranoia that could create a subjective need for unforgiveness.[59] Paranoia generates enemies that must be hated, excluded, and punished. Splitting, which is common in borderline personality disorder and involves viewing self or others as either all-good or all-bad, is another defense mechanism that reduces human complexity and interferes with forgiving others and feeling forgiven.[60] Authentically forgiving another person is impossible if that person is viewed as all-bad or all-good because such a construal represents a gross distortion of the other person and the self. This too results in an intrapsychic desire to punish the self or the other person for being so totally despicable.

Forgiveness can also be precluded by our human propensity for stranger anxiety. Researchers in the area of child-caregiver attachment show that it is normal for the presence of strangers to create anxiety in children around the age of six months, which peaks around ten to fourteen months. Stranger anxiety is actually a healthy sign that a child has a secure attachment to parents or caregivers and usually dissipates as children become more confident in exploring their environments. But it is also true that much of the human race appears to struggle against a more pernicious xenophobia or fear of the *other* who seems strange and alien.

Theologian Miroslav Volf suggests that a deeper "stranger anxiety" motivates a core psychological and spiritual dynamic of sin—the propensity to exclude the other who seems threatening and different.[61] This exclusion can be practiced by construing the other as an enemy who must be ejected and avoided or by viewing the other as an "inferior being" who must be assimilated and dominated. Setting boundaries with another person is not exclusion, and boundaries are a nec-

58. Loder, *Logic of the Spirit*.

59. D. W. Augsburger, *Helping People Forgive* (Louisville: Westminster John Knox, 1996); Karen, *Forgiving Self*.

60. J. Gartner, "The Capacity to Forgive: An Object Relations Perspective," *Journal of Religion and Health* 27 (1988): 313–20; Vitz and Mango, "Kernbergian Psychodynamics."

61. M. Volf, *Exclusion and Embrace: A Theological Exploration of Identity, Otherness, and Reconciliation* (Nashville: Abingdon, 1996).

essary part of healthy relationships. Exclusion sets up "impenetrable barriers that prevent creative encounter with the other."[62] One woman told me that she would be willing to forgive her former husband but she refused to ever even think of him or acknowledge his existence again. I could understand the pain that motivated her exclusion, but I was not optimistic that she would experience much authentic forgiveness out of that internal stance if that was her goal. If forgiveness is to unfold in a person's heart, what is eventually required is at least a creative internal encounter with the other that moves beyond exclusion, even if actual interpersonal boundaries remain firm with that offender.

Those, like this woman, hurt or offended by someone, especially someone they trusted, often wrestle with anxiety over the mystery of a relational trauma. For example, research with victims of romantic betrayal often reveals an anxious felt need to ruminate on the mystery of the other person and his or her actions.[63] After a betrayal, the former friend or lover can feel like a mysterious stranger. Why did he do it? Who is she really? How did I miss the signs that something was wrong? What does this say about me? It seems that there is an anxious pull to try to figure out the mystery in order to recover from the injury to self and to protect against future injuries. Unfortunately, factual information rarely alleviates the anxiety of such mysteries or generates much forgiveness. When forgiveness happens, the differentness and dangerousness of the offender are viewed from a new frame that mitigates this stranger anxiety and results in some sense of renewed meaning and security.

Linguist and psychoanalyst Julia Kristeva argues that our xenophobia or fear of the foreign other is rooted in our difficulty in acknowledging and accepting our own strangeness: "Strangely, the foreigner lives within us: he is the hidden face of our identity. . . . By recognizing him within ourselves we are spared detesting him in himself."[64] When we are mistreated or hurt by others it can provoke our psychological fear of not belonging, of not being home, of being a stranger. This is probably why for many of us our first impulse after being hurt by someone is to find friends or family members, if we have them, who will listen sympathetically and symbolically reaffirm our sense of belonging to the human community. In some relational systems this can also serve the function of building a coalition against the enemy.

62. Ibid., 67.
63. R. F. Baumeister, S. R. Wotman, and A. M. Stillwell, "Unrequited Love: On Heartbreak, Anger, Guilt, Scriptlessness, and Humiliation," *Journal of Personality and Social Psychology* 64 (1993): 377–94.
64. J. Kristeva, *Strangers to Ourselves* (trans. L. Roudiez; New York: Columbia University Press, 1991), 1.

Others might respond to interpersonal hurt by denying the impact it has on them. A middle-aged man at a forgiveness seminar told me that throughout his years growing up he was teased mercilessly by other kids at school for being "a hick," among an assortment of other insults. But he said "it was really no big deal" and he didn't even need to forgive them because he just "considered the source." He somehow found a way to conclude, at least on the surface, that he was not a stranger because the other kids were not really competent to practice such exclusion.

But if we all really are strangers here on earth perhaps we will not overcome the estrangement of unforgiveness by clinging to relational coalitions or minimizing the impact of others. Perhaps Kristeva is correct that we must face our own strangeness and our deep fears of exclusion. The author of the Book of Hebrews commended those heroes of the faith who "admitted that they were aliens and strangers on earth" (11:13 New International Version) and found a way to hold their own longings for a spiritual home beyond this life. Those who develop a forgiving character do not rigidly defend against their own strangeness or lack of belonging, but they are also not overly reactive to the strangeness of others. They are characterized by what family therapist Murray Bowen calls "differentiation of self," which includes the ability to experience both intimacy with and independence from others.[65] People who are higher in differentiation of self can handle the anxiety of both interpersonal connection and solitude and show higher levels of forgiving others.[66] The differentness of others does not typically provoke the reactive anxiety of unforgiveness because such people are not fundamentally estranged from themselves.

The Existential Void

The psychological and spiritual challenges of forgiveness call for the differentiation of self that transforms stranger anxiety. But the crucible of forgiveness has additional developmental roots in separation anxiety. Around six months of age most infants develop an anxiety of being separated from their parents or caregivers. Caregivers go away at times. This separation represents the loss of the face and presence of those attachment figures who provide the most basic security necessary in life for survival.[67] In Loder's existential model of development, this separation leaves an infant anxiously facing the void of

65. M. Bowen, *Family Therapy in Clinical Practice* (New York: Aronson, 1978).

66. Augsburger, *Helping People Forgive*.

67. Loder, *Logic of the Spirit*. For an introduction to attachment theory and the psychological importance of caregiver presence and loss, see R. Karen, *Becoming Attached: First Relationships and How They Shape Our Capacity to Love* (New York: Oxford University Press, 1994).

loss, aloneness, and nonbeing. Infants usually protest this separation and then search for means of soothing the accompanying anxiety if the caregiver does not quickly return. Throughout development we build ego capacities and defenses to contend with the underlying negation and loneliness of the void, but we long for the presence of "a face that will not go away."[68]

Attachment researchers have identified three main styles of infant-caregiver attachment, attachment styles that are also assessed and studied in adult relationships. Attachment theorists suggest that out of early experiences with separation and the void infants form an internal working model of self and others that is a blueprint for future relationships.[69] An infant who develops a secure attachment perceives his or her caregiver to be a reliable source of warmth and protection and a secure base for exploring the environment. The securely attached infant experiences the caregiver as sensitively attuned and responsive to needs, fostering a sense of intersubjectivity.[70] The separations of the void do not overwhelm the coping resources of such infants or their developing sense of relational security. Securely attached adults tend to have a healthy approach to emotional closeness, distance, loss, and conflict in relationships. Preliminary evidence shows that securely attached adults are likely to report a propensity to forgive others and themselves.[71] Agreeableness and emotional stability, two personality traits associated with a secure attachment style, are also positively correlated with dispositional forgiveness and negatively correlated with vengefulness.[72]

In contrast, two primary types of anxious or insecure attachment are identified—ambivalent and avoidant—both of which manifest in response to the void of separation from caregivers. Infants with an ambivalent caregiver-attachment are often clingy and demanding, which limits exploration. They are often angry and difficult to soothe after separations from the caregiver. Caregivers may be anxious themselves and overly fo-

68. Loder, *Logic of the Spirit*, 94.

69. By drawing on attachment theory and other perspectives that emphasize early relational influences on personality, I am not suggesting that genetics plays no role in the formation of dispositional forgiveness. Researchers have started exploring the potential contribution of genetics to forgiveness, so there is likely to be data to address that question in the coming years.

70. P. Fonagy and M. Target, "Mentalization and the Changing Aims of Child Psychoanalysis," *Psychoanalytic Dialogues* 8 (1998): 87–114; cf. Stern, *Interpersonal World of the Infant*.

71. J. Tangney, R. Fee, C. Reinsmith, A. L. Boone, and N. Lee, "Assessing Individual Differences in the Propensity to Forgive" (paper presented at the annual meeting of the American Psychological Association, Boston, 1999).

72. M. E. McCullough, "Forgiveness: Who Does It and How Do They Do It?" *Current Directions in Psychological Science* 10 (2001): 194–97.

cused on the baby's anxiety. Ambivalently attached adults tend to fear abandonment in close relationships, become preoccupied with relational conflicts, and pull for large doses of reassurance from others.

Avoidantly attached infants are also anxious upon separation from caregivers but tend to avoid contact when the caregiver returns. Caregivers of the avoidantly attached are often emotionally unavailable or even rejecting, and they reinforce independence. Avoidantly attached adults tend to dismiss the importance of relational connection and often struggle with trust and commitment in relationships. As adults, the ambivalently attached have trouble resolving relational losses or disappointments, while the avoidantly attached deny the impact of others and their impact on others.

Both the ambivalent and avoidant attachment styles can work against authentic forgiveness. In the Tangney et al. study, the avoidant style was negatively correlated with a self-reported propensity to forgive others.[73] Avoidantly attached adults often hold others to extreme standards and struggle with trust, both of which impede forgiveness. The ambivalent style was not correlated with a propensity to forgive others. In my clinical experience with couples, however, an ambivalently attached person often reports a willingness to forgive a partner who has hurt them but then actually vacillates between anger and fear of losing the relationship. They often feel like they are forgiving because they want the relationship to continue, but their insecurity may feel suffocating to their partner.

At their worst, the ambivalent and avoidant styles offer different faces of the void to their relational partners. An avoidant wife described her ambivalent husband as "a black hole" and "an emotional whirlpool." Given her avoidant set of anxieties, she had repeatedly pulled back from him and retreated into her personal cocoon to avoid the feeling of being sucked into the void. Her husband, who was seeking forgiveness for an affair, described her as "a robot." Her lack of emotional availability provoked his fear of emptiness and death and had sent him searching for someone who felt responsive and alive. This is another common example of the intersubjective context of unforgiveness and estrangement: two people with contrasting narratives about their relationship each reflect a lack of the subjective attunement necessary for mutual forgiveness.

Evil and Trauma

One of the most difficult topics related to forgiveness involves the traumatizing impact of encounters with evil. The evils of abuse, violent crime, political genocide, and other unspeakable acts of human

73. Tangney et al., "Assessing Individual Differences."

cruelty render sentimental notions about forgiveness absurd. Victims of such offenses are often traumatized, which can result in emotional numbing, intrusive memories of the victimization, perpetual anxious mistrust and hostility, and other symptoms that impair psychological functioning. In some cases, victims tragically internalize the abuse and violence, resulting in self-injurious and self-defeating patterns of behavior. Forgiveness seems like a very strange or even dangerous idea for a traumatized person who, for example, has blocked out most of their childhood from conscious awareness or who feels they are re-experiencing sexual abuse every time their spouse tries to get close to them. One study of post-traumatic stress disorder found that patients with higher levels of PTSD symptoms tended to be lower in both forgiving others and forgiving themselves.[74]

Understandings of forgiveness that imply one can forgive any offender through a simple conscious decision are insulting, particularly in cases of traumatic victimization and post-traumatic stress disorder. This leads some therapists to argue that forgiveness is inappropriate and potentially damaging to survivors of abuse and other traumas.[75] In place of these simplistic construals of forgiveness, such therapists often prioritize goals such as recovering emotionally, empowering a healthy sense of self, utilizing anger constructively, and pursuing justice. Conversely, some therapists suggest that forgiveness can be relevant to the traumatized but should be handled very sensitively and noncoercively within the context of a broad, long-term approach to treatment.[76] I concur that it is unjust and controlling to demand or expect immediate forgiveness from traumatized victims, which may serve to protect those with more power in relational systems. As suggested in chapter 1, at least theoretically there are other methods of reducing unforgiveness besides forgiveness.[77] A more just approach

74. Cf. L. S. Heinze and C. R. Snyder, "Forgiveness Components: Mediators of PTSD and Hostility in Child Abuse" (paper presented at the annual meeting of the American Psychological Association, San Francisco, 2001).

75. For examples, see E. Bass and L. Davis, *Courage to Heal: A Guide for Women Survivors of Sexual Abuse* (3d ed.; San Francisco: Harper, 1994); S. Lamb and J. G. Murphy, *Before Forgiving: Cautionary Views of Forgiveness in Psychotherapy* (Oxford: Oxford University Press, 2002); A. Miller, *Banished Knowledge* (New York: Doubleday, 1990); J. Safer, *Forgiving and Not Forgiving: A New Approach to Resolving Intimate Betrayal* (New York: Avon, 1999).

76. M. Seibold, "When the Wounds Run Deep: Encouragement for Those on the Road to Forgiveness," in *Care for the Soul: Exploring the Intersection of Psychology and Theology* (ed. M. R. McMinn and T. R. Phillips; Downers Grove, Ill.: InterVarsity, 2001), 294–308; S. Tracy, "Sexual Abuse and Forgiveness," *Journal of Psychology and Theology* 27 (1999): 219–29.

77. Lamb and Murphy, *Before Forgiving*; E. L. Worthington Jr. and N. G. Wade, "The Psychology of Unforgiveness and Forgiveness and Implications for Clinical Practice," *Journal of Social and Clinical Psychology* 18 (1999): 385–418.

than demanding or coercing forgiveness is to create safe relational contexts with space for the healing of trauma. Quick decisions to forgive following trauma are more likely to be a defense against the pain and loss than genuine forgiveness. A safe, noncoercive context will lead some people to want to explore the meaning of forgiveness as part of a healing journey.

Only a few studies have investigated relationships between trauma and forgiveness. Suzanne Freedman and Robert Enright found that incest survivors in a forgiveness-oriented psychotherapy intervention that lasted an average of eighteen months were higher in hope and self-esteem and lower in depression than the control group at the end of treatment.[78] N. A. Peddle interviewed ninety adolescent and adult war refugees living in the Chicago area and administered measures of both trauma recovery/resilience and forgiveness. Forgiveness was positively correlated with trauma recovery/resilience, and all participants who were rated as forgiving also rated as recovered from the trauma.[79] E. Staub and L. A. Pearlman conducted a comparison of treatments to promote psychological healing from the traumatic impact of genocide and group conflict in Rwanda.[80] Participants in the study, which included trauma recovery interventions, not only decreased in symptoms of trauma at posttest but also increased positive other group orientation and openness to forgiveness. These three studies offer only preliminary data and are in need of replication. But, if replicated, evidence could emerge that for some victims of trauma forgiveness might be part of a healing process. Forgiveness may be a way that some people renarrate traumatic events so their lives are not defined by the horror.

Shame and Pride

Interpersonal offenses present a shaming attack on our dignity as persons and activate our ways of facing ourselves. Shame and pride are two interrelated dynamics of the self system that strongly impact

78. S. R. Freedman and R. D. Enright, "Forgiveness as an Intervention Goal with Incest Survivors," *Journal of Consulting and Clinical Psychology* 64 (1996): 983–92.

79. N. A. Peddle, "Forgiveness in Recovery/Resiliency from the Trauma of War among a Selected Group of Adolescents and Adult Refugees" (doctoral diss., Fielding Institute, 2001).

80. E. Staub and L. A. Pearlman, "Healing, Forgiveness, and Reconciliation in Rwanda: Project Summary and Outcome" (unpublished paper, 2000); E. Staub and A. Gubin, "Healing through Connection and Understanding Project Research Findings: Results from Community Members" (unpublished paper, 2001); see also E. Staub and L. A. Pearlman, "Healing, Reconciliation, and Forgiving after Genocide and Other Collective Violence," in *Forgiveness and Reconciliation: Religion, Public Policy, and Conflict Transformation* (ed. R. G. Helmick and R. L. Petersen; Philadelphia: Templeton Foundation, 2001), 195–218.

the process of forgiveness. Pride is a positive feeling about the self, and shame is a negative feeling about the self.[81] When someone treats us poorly it can feel like a loss of face and a shameful assault on our pride and self-esteem. This can mobilize defensive efforts to save face, recover pride and esteem, and guard against feelings of vulnerability. Those high in personality traits of shame-proneness and narcissistic pride can be expected to struggle with forgiving others and seeking forgiveness.

Several forgiveness theorists describe ways in which shame interferes with forgiving others.[82] The etymology of the word *shame* has roots in the Old High German word *sceme*, which means "to cover or mask."[83] The experience of shame often involves a feeling of exposure and the desire to hide or disappear. The well-attuned caregivers of securely attached children usually notice expressions of shame on the faces of their children (e.g., averted gaze) and are responsive to repairing a rupture of the social bond.[84]

Tangney differentiates the personality traits of shame-proneness and guilt-proneness and conducts a program of research on these differing moral emotions.[85] The highly shame-prone often experience a sense of worthlessness, particularly in the context of interpersonal conflict where they quickly become defensive. These defensive maneuvers frequently involve anger, aggressiveness, hiding, shifting blame, and self-contempt. Shame-proneness tends to be positively correlated with psychopathology and negatively correlated with forgiving others and forgiving oneself.[86]

In contrast, guilt-proneness involves a tendency to be able to focus on specific wrong actions one has committed (i.e., "I did a bad thing") rather than the global negative self-evaluation of shame (i.e., "I am a bad person"). Tangney's research shows that guilt-proneness is positively correlated with empathy, apology, forgiving others, seeking for-

81. Nathanson, *Shame and Pride*.

82. M. G. Alter, *Resurrection Psychology: An Understanding of Human Personality Based on the Life and Teachings of Jesus* (Chicago: Loyola University Press, 1994); S. Halling, "Shame and Forgiveness," *Humanistic Psychologist* 22 (1994): 74–87; J. Patton, *Is Human Forgiveness Possible? A Pastoral Care Perspective* (Nashville: Abingdon, 1985); Sandage, "Ego-Humility Model of Forgiveness: Theoretical Foundations."

83. H. Wharton, "The Hidden Face of Shame: The Shadow, Shame, and Separation," *Journal of Analytical Psychology* 35 (1990): 279–99.

84. A. N. Schore, "Early Shame Experiences and Infant Brain Development," in *Shame: Interpersonal Behavior, Psychopathology, and Culture* (ed. P. Gilbert and B. Andrews; New York: Oxford University Press, 1998), 57–77.

85. J. P. Tangney, "Shame and Guilt in Interpersonal Relationships," in *Self-Conscious Emotions: Shame, Guilt, Embarrassment, and Pride* (ed. J. P. Tangney and K. W. Fischer; New York: Guilford, 1995), 114–39.

86. Tangney et al., "Assessing Individual Differences."

giveness, and other reparative actions in relationships. It appears that guilt-proneness represents certain qualities of humility, while shame-proneness represents a proclivity toward humiliation.

Narcissistic pride is another personality trait closely related to the dynamics of selfhood and forgiveness. In fact, Robert Emmons suggests that narcissism might be one of the central personality traits related to forgiveness, even calling the narcissistic personality "the antithesis of the forgiving personality."[87] Narcissism is usually defined as extreme self-admiration and grandiose self-involvement that goes beyond healthy personal pride and prevents empathy, intersubjectivity, and a willingness to lose face. Highly narcissistic individuals have trouble getting along with others due to these failures of empathy and intersubjectivity. Other people tend to serve as extensions of the self, not as separate individuals. As Auerbach and Blatt observe, "there is always a wish to retreat from the tensions of intersubjectivity to the safety of narcissism."[88] When narcissistic individuals do become aware of hurt and vulnerability in others, it can provoke contempt at perceived weakness rather than intersubjectivity and empathy.

While highly narcissistic individuals exhibit grandiosity and elevated self-esteem, their self-images are low in complexity and highly vulnerable to ego-threats.[89] This vulnerability creates a demand for positive evaluations from others and an angry reactivity toward those who fail to support the grandiose self. Psychoanalyst Heinz Kohut suggests that pathological narcissism develops in childhood through empathic failures and poor emotional attunement on the part of caregivers, which children can experience as shameful rejection.[90] This sense of rejection generates shame about personal needs and defensive self-involvement. Narcissism is then an "ill-fitting mask" or defense to avoid the painful vulnerability of shame.[91]

Kohut describes "narcissistic rage" as a defensive reaction of a shame-prone and narcissistically vulnerable individual to criticism or other perceived ego-threats. Narcissistic rage is an "unforgiving fury" against the source of the ego-threat.[92] This rage and accompanying

87. R. A. Emmons, "Personality and Forgiveness," in *Forgiveness: Theory, Research, and Practice* (ed. M. E. McCullough, K. I. Pargament, and C. E. Thoresen; New York: Guilford, 2000), 156–75 at 164.

88. Auerbach and Blatt, "Self-Reflexivity, Intersubjectivity, and Therapeutic Change," 430.

89. F. Rhodewalt and C. C. Morf, "Self and Interpersonal Correlates of the Narcissistic Personality Inventory: A Review and New Findings," *Journal of Research in Personality* 29 (1995): 1–23; cf. Emmons, "Personality and Forgiveness."

90. H. Kohut, "Narcissism and Narcissistic Rage," *Psychoanalytic Study of the Child* 27 (1972): 379–92.

91. Nathanson, *Shame and Pride*, 349.

92. Kohut, "Narcissism and Narcissistic Rage," 386–87.

vengeful fantasies can feel empowering and serve to bolster the injured self.

Psychological research shows that those higher in narcissism are also higher in hostility and more prone to aggression and violence.[93] Narcissism has been negatively correlated with forgiving others and seeking forgiveness from others.[94] Narcissistic individuals are unlikely to acknowledge guilt to others or apologize because such loss of face feels overwhelming and intolerable. The underlying narcissistic splitting involves the projection of bad self-representation ("I am hateful") onto others, resulting in anxious mistrust and feelings of being persecuted. This perpetuates a vicious cycle of anxiety-shame-rage and chronic relational conflict and estrangement.

The narcissistic tendencies toward exploitiveness and entitlement might be among the strongest barriers to forgiveness. Highly narcissistic individuals can be interpersonally exploitive, and they often feel entitled to use other people as means to their own ends. They also operate from a profound sense of entitlement and believe they deserve special treatment and constant affirmation. Tangney and her colleagues found the exploitive dimension of narcissism to be the primary dimension negatively correlated with a propensity to forgive.[95] Julie Exline also found narcissistic entitlement to be negatively correlated with forgiving others.[96] The narcissistic tendencies toward exploitiveness and entitlement reflect a desire to use power against others and a sense of deserving excessive admiration and respect, both of which can greatly inhibit genuine forgiveness in the context of interpersonal conflict.

For both narcissistic and shame-prone individuals, the faces of those with whom they are in conflict represent faces of the void and the underlying anxiety of nonbeing. Healthy individuals with rela-

93. On narcissism and hostility, see M. H. Kernis and C. R. Sun, "Narcissism and Reactions to Interpersonal Feedback," *Journal of Research in Personality* 28 (1994): 4–13; Rhodewalt and Morf, "Self and Interpersonal Correlates." On narcissism and violence, see R. F. Baumeister, L. Smart, and J. M. Boden, "Relation of Threatened Egotism to Violence and Aggression: The Dark Side of High Self-Esteem," *Psychological Review* 103 (1996): 5–33.

94. On narcissism and forgiving others, see D. L. Davidson and G. J. Jurkovic, "Forgiveness and Narcissism: Consistency in Experience across Real and Hypothetical Hurt Situation" (paper presented at the First National Convention on Forgiveness, Kansas City, 1993). On narcissism and seeking forgiveness, see S. J. Sandage, E. L. Worthington Jr., T. L. Hight, and J. W. Berry, "Seeking Forgiveness: Theoretical Context and an Initial Empirical Study," *Journal of Psychology and Theology* 28 (2000): 21–35.

95. Tangney et al., "Assessing Individual Differences."

96. J. J. Exline, B. Bushman, J. Faber, and C. Phillips, "Pride Gets in the Way: Self-Protection Works against Forgiveness" (paper presented at the annual meeting of the Society for Personality and Social Psychology, Nashville, 2000).

tively mature ego development have sufficient defenses and coping resources to work through interpersonal encounters that symbolize the
negation of the void. But excessive narcissism and shame are symptoms of serious cracks in the structures of ego development that allow
the negating forces of the void to frequently overwhelm coping capacities in the midst of relational conflict.

Forgivingness

If anxiety, shame, and narcissism sabotage forgiveness, what fos-
ters a capacity to be a forgiving person? Mature forgivers or those
with a disposition toward forgivingness are characterized by two primary virtues: empathy and humility. Empathy involves the ability to
transcend narcissistic self-interest in facing the humanness of others
with compassion. Humility involves the capacity to overcome shame
by facing oneself nondefensively and facing others redemptively. Empirical evidence shows that empathy is positively related to forgiveness and facilitates forgiveness. Humility has been difficult to study
empirically but figures prominently in numerous theoretical models
of forgiveness.[97]

Empathy

Empathy includes cognitive and affective dimensions. Cognitive
empathy is the ability to temporarily detach from our own concerns
and take the perspective of another person. The affective dimension of
empathy involves feelings of compassion and tenderness toward another person. In the case of forgiveness, empathy finds rapprochement with the virtue of compassion, which promotes concern for the
suffering of another person.[98] When one is hurt or offended by someone, the natural response for most people is to view their offender as
fundamentally different from themselves. We tend to demonize people
who have hurt us by making global internal attributions about their
negative characteristics (e.g., "He's such a jerk!" or "She always stabs
people in the back"). This helps us feel psychological distance from

97. On empathy and forgiveness, see M. E. McCullough, E. L. Worthington Jr., and
K. C. Rachal, "Interpersonal Forgiving in Close Relationships," *Journal of Personality and
Social Psychology* 73 (1997): 321–36; M. E. McCullough, K. C. Rachal, S. J. Sandage, E. L.
Worthington Jr., S. W. Brown, and T. L. Hight, "Interpersonal Forgiving in Close Relationships, II: Theoretical Elaboration and Measurement," *Journal of Personality and Social Psychology* 75 (1998): 1586–1603. On humility and forgiveness, see J. M. Brandsma,
"Forgiveness: A Dynamic, Theological, and Therapeutic Analysis," *Pastoral Psychology* 31
(1982): 40–50; Emmons, "Personality and Forgiveness"; Roberts, "Forgivingness"; Sandage, "Ego-Humility Model of Forgiveness: Theoretical Foundations."
    98. Cf. Roberts, "Forgivingness."

them, since most people tend to attribute their own failures to external causes (e.g. "I'm having a stressful week"), and justifies excluding our offenders from our internal sense of community.

Empathy and compassion enable us to become aware of the humanness of our offenders as people (subjects rather than objects) who, like us, also suffer from stories of painful victimization. This does not mean that empathy forces us into condoning or exonerating our offenders, as though they cannot be held responsible for their actions. In fact, empathy is at times part of understanding more deeply the pathological motives of an offender. But empathy does reduce the psychological distance we place between ourselves and our offenders that serves a self-protective function when we have been hurt or traumatized. Empathy helps us face people within the context of a broader horizon of humanness.

Empathy also helps explain the ease with which we can almost always forgive someone who apologizes. Empathy and compassion appear to mediate the connection between apologies and forgiveness.[99] Offenders are more likely to offer apologies in close, satisfying relationships, and mutual empathy is also more common in relationships where there is a secure and healthy attachment. This is what makes forgiveness so difficult in unhealthy relationships and for victims of traumatic abuse who have never received a meaningful apology. The anxiety and shame of human estrangement and trauma can motivate a self-protective resistance to empathy and forgiveness. Relationally traumatized persons have deeply internalized fears about the dangers of other people. One abuse survivor who fervently resisted forgiving others, even people he cared about, explained to me, "Hate is all I've got!" What he meant was that he had learned early in life that hate was his only defense against the massive psychological pain of being physically abused by those he trusted most in life—his parents. Hate helped him form a self-protective armor and fueled his determination to survive his family battleground. In relying on such hate he could not afford to empathize or take the perspective of others, which is quite understandable given his early life context. A challenge for him in adulthood was to eventually make room in his personality for the empathy and forgiveness that would help him overcome his family legacy of pathological relationships.

Humility

Humility is another characterological virtue closely related to empathy and forgiveness. Empathy helps us appreciate the humanness (subjectivity) of our offenders, and humility helps us face our own hu-

---

99. McCullough et al., "Interpersonal Forgiving in Close Relationships, II."

manness. I define ego-humility as "a realistic orientation toward self and other that includes a willingness to acknowledge one's strengths and face one's limitations."[100] Humility is different from low self-esteem and shame-proneness.[101] In fact, humility involves a nondefensive, differentiated stance toward self and other. Humble people do not feel a need to distort feedback from others in self-protective or self-enhancing ways. While open to feedback from others, humble people are likely to have a deeper sense of self-acceptance that is not dependent upon the appraisals of others.[102] They have an ability to transcend their own self-focus and show low levels of entitlement because they tend to view others as equals. Humility is a trait of mature ego development that represents healthy flexibility and openness in contending with ego-threats and the accompanying forces of existential negation. As Exline and her colleagues point out, humble people probably tend to see themselves as small in comparison to God or the broader universe, "but also as valuable and safe."[103]

Humility is very difficult to study empirically, primarily because it is so hard to measure. Humility is something of a paradoxical virtue—humble people probably do not identify themselves as such. But, like empathy, humility offers rich promise as a pathway toward forgiveness. Forgiving others requires that we abandon the pretense of our own moral superiority or at least gross differences in moral achievement. Recent studies by Exline and her colleagues find that students induced to feel morally similar (as opposed to morally superior) to a perpetrator and those who wrote essays about personal experiences of feeling humble (as opposed to feeling important) were more likely to forgive.[104] Humility helps us face our own failures and need for forgiveness.

Humility may also facilitate forgiveness by helping us to abandon egocentrism and move toward empathy.[105] The early relational experiences of humble and forgiving people were probably characterized by intersubjectivity, empathy, and relational repair following conflict. It is particularly valuable for children to have experiences of repair with

100. Sandage, "Ego-Humility Model of Forgiveness: Theoretical Foundations," 262.
101. J. J. Exline, W. K. Campbell, R. F. Baumeister, T. E. Joiner, and J. Krueger, "Bringing Ourselves Down to Size: Toward a Positive Psychology of Humility" (unpublished paper); J. P. Tangney, "Humility: Theoretical Perspectives, Empirical Findings, and Directions for Future Research," *Journal of Social and Clinical Psychology* 19 (2000): 70–82.
102. Cf. Emmons, "Personality and Forgiveness."
103. Cf. J. J. Exline, W. K. Campbell, R. F. Baumeister, T. Joiner, and J. Krueger, "Humility and Modesty," in *The Values in Action (VIA) Classification of Strengths* (ed. C. Peterson and M. Seligman; Cincinnati: Values in Action Institute, forthcoming).
104. Cf. Exline, Bushman, et al., "Pride Gets in the Way."
105. Cf. Brandsma, "Forgiveness."

their parents where, for example, parents admit they were wrong and apologize.[106] Children, too, need to have experiences of feeling angry at their parents and having those feelings recognized without reactive retribution or abandonment. These experiences form inner beliefs that anger, shame, and conflict do not have to prove deadly to authentic connections. Humble people likely have developmental reservoirs of gratitude for forgiveness received as well as hope that conflicts can be repaired. Their "internal museums" include the faces of people who reflected responsive forgiveness, not just faces of the void.[107]

The main personality factors that are empirically related to forgiveness in psychological science are theoretically organized in the table below.[108] I argue that intersubjectivity is profoundly formative in the positive development of an array of healthy forgiveness-related traits such as emotional stability, secure attachment style, agreeableness, differentiation of self, empathy, and humility. In contrast, developmental failures in intersubjective attunement and recognition contribute to a trajectory that is more likely to involve some combination of forgiveness-impeding personality traits such as vengefulness, rumination, narcissism, or shame:

Intersubjective Deficits Promote Negative Forgiveness Traits	Intersubjective Formation Promotes Positive Forgiveness Traits
Anxiety/Insecure Attachment Style	Emotional Stability/Secure Attachment Style
Vengefulness	Agreeableness
Rumination	Differentiation of Self
Narcissism	Empathy
Shame-proneness	Humility (or Guilt-proneness)

Conclusion

Our characterological dispositions toward forgiveness and unforgiveness—the ways we face ourselves and others—are formed through a complex social fabric of relational and cultural influences. Early attachment relationships provide human faces of otherness that shape the formation of selfhood and internal working models of relationships. Christian theology suggests that we all long for the presence of God—"the face that does not go away." But the degree of warmth and

---

106. This is a point made by Karen in *The Forgiving Self*.

107. Augsburger, *Helping People Forgive*.

108. For research on forgivingness and personality traits, see Berry et al., *Dispositional Forgivingness*; McCullough, "Forgiveness: Who Does It?" 194–97; Tangney et al., "Assessing Individual Differences."

responsiveness in the faces of our caregivers and the quality of inter-subjectivity we experience early on sets the stage for how we later approach interpersonal conflict and forgiveness. Some children suffer from relational environments characterized by overwhelming anxiety or a severe lack of empathic attunement, which can mobilize the development of various combinations of anxiety, shame, narcissism, and forgivencss-impeding defenses. Authentic forgiveness can be learned later but is likely to require significant personal transformation within a new relational context. Other children reap the benefits of secure early attachments that form foundational experiences of trust, mutual intersubjectivity, and empathy. This provides a relational pathway toward later development of traits of self-differentiation and humility, which foster forgivingness.

3

Saving Faces

It was a warm but breezy summer afternoon as I (Steve) walked toward the entrance to one of our prisons here in Minnesota. I had been invited by a prison psychologist to speak on forgiveness to inmates who were part of a "lifers group." These inmates were serving a life sentence, and the group included a component on forgiveness, a topic in which many of the men were quite interested. I had previously worked in a number of juvenile detention centers and adult prisons as a chaplain and a psychologist, but it had been a couple of years since I had set foot in a prison. And, I had never been asked to speak on the psychology of forgiveness in a correctional setting. I had no idea what to expect from the men in the group, but I could still see the face of an inmate at a federal prison who had roared with laughter when I had simply raised the possibility of forgiveness as a way of dealing with interpersonal conflict. So, I felt a mix of anxiety and curiosity as I approached the guard stand at the prison entrance.

The familiar electronic hum of the grill sounded, and the wall of bars retracted for me to enter into the next security station. The clang of metal behind me indicated that the grill had shut and I was "inside." A guard arrived and led me through a couple more security checks to a pale green classroom in the educational wing of the prison where the group met. The room was empty, and I was left to nervously scan my notes one last time, hoping to come up with a clever line that would buy me some rapport with this unpredictable audience. Soon the men started to saunter into the room, about fifteen in all. They were a diverse-looking group, though they were united in wearing khaki pants and either a matching shirt or a white T-shirt. Most looked like they were in their forties or fifties, but a few were younger and a few were older than that. My host psychologist followed them in and greeted me by saying, "Thanks for coming, Steve. They like to talk, so I'll have them introduce themselves and we'll get rolling." I wanted a little more orientation, but liked the idea of at least hearing their voices before I launched into my talk.

The first inmate started with something like, "My name is Joe"—not his real name—"and I have a life sentence for first-degree murder. My crime was that I came home drunk from a party and found my wife in bed with another man. I was enraged and grabbed the guy by the hair, drug him into the living room, and threw him through the front window. The glass severed an artery in his neck and he died." Most of the rest of the introductions were like that—candid confessions of tragedies for which the inmates accepted blame. Only one man denied committing the crime with which he was charged.

Now I have spoken to classes or groups at universities, seminaries, counseling centers, academic and professional conferences, and various organizations. But thirty minutes into my dialogue with these inmates I realized that this was one of the most authentic groups of people I had ever encountered. Many of these men had been a part of this group for eight to ten years, some even longer. They had spent hundreds or even thousands of hours facing themselves, their crimes, and each other in an effort to find healing and hope. Some of us approach a topic like forgiveness with a kind of mild curiosity, but it was obvious that for many of these men forgiveness was a matter of psychological life and death. On the one hand, several spoke of the reality that to act like a forgiving person in the world of the prison would be to lose face and appear vulnerable, a dangerous position in that environment. On the other hand, many voiced the significance of seeking forgiveness from family members and victims, learning to not retaliate against people who angered them, and struggling to forgive themselves. Their insights about the challenges and the gravity of forgiveness were among the most penetrating I have ever heard.

One man who looked like he could have been an offensive tackle for a pro football team gave a poignant testimony to some of the core dilemmas of forgiveness. His voice throbbing with sadness, he explained, "You know, all this talk about forgiving and seeking forgiveness sounds good. But what do you do when you are not forgiven? Society sure won't forgive us. And I have apologized in writing to the family of my victim a couple of times with no response. And you know what, I have to admit that if I was in their place, I wouldn't forgive me either. Every year at the anniversary of his death that family grieves it all over again. So I've tried to do the right thing, but how do you stay motivated to seek forgiveness when it never comes?"

Those men taught me several things about forgiveness that day, and questions like this one linger with me. Why would any of us keep seeking forgiveness when we feel there is no hope of seeing a face of recognition that will relieve our shame and invite us back into the human community? When I explained to a colleague what I found so attractive about the authenticity of the men in this group in contrast to other groups where we all pretend we have it all together, she commented, "Isn't it true that there is a spiritual advantage in knowing you are a sinner? Those guys have committed public crimes so they can be free from the need to save face." She was right. And this illustration and her comment speak to the heart of the relationship between forgiveness and saving face.

Saving and Losing Face

We have probably all felt a pull to try to save face when we hurt or offend someone. Saving face refers to strategies we use to protect our self-image and social identity from shame and embarrassment when we fail or commit a moral offense. Sociologist Erving Goffman describes the ways people manage their impression with others in order to save face and avoid shame.[1] Goffman suggests that people are in an ongoing social process of honoring or legitimating the social worth of one another. According to Goffman painful emotions such as embarrassment or shame come from a loss of face or dishonor in front of others. Interpersonal offenses can be thought of as not only a moral affront to interpersonal fairness, but also as an attack on the victim's self-esteem.[2] Offenses communicate dishonor and disrespect to the victim, and they can generate defensive shame in the offender. Whether primarily the victim or offender in a conflict, a humiliating loss of face often "kindles the flames of anxiety"[3] because we unconsciously sense a diminishment of our worth and very being. This diminishment offers us an anxious taste of the estrangement that is at the core of the human predicament.

1. E. Goffman, *The Presentation of Self in Everyday Life* (New York: Doubleday, 1959); idem, *Interaction Ritual: Essays on Face-to-Face Behavior* (New York: Aldine, 1967).

2. F. D. Fincham, "The Kiss of the Porcupines: From Attributing Responsibility to Forgiving," *Personal Relationships* 7 (2000): 1–23.

3. T. Peters, *Sin: Radical Evil in Soul and Society* (Grand Rapids: Eerdmans, 1994), 11.

In some cultures saving face is a valuable social process of conflict resolution that restores harmony and community with norms of prioritizing the face needs of others.[4] But the ways we attempt to save our own social face can negatively impact the legitimate face needs of others. As I write this chapter, Catholic leaders in America are holding national meetings on sexual abuse by priests to face the pain and injustice caused by decades of institutional decisions to try to save face. And the Catholic Church is not alone. There is no shortage of examples of leaders in religion, education, business, government, and healthcare who have abusively tried to avoid losing face and thereby avoided acknowledging the needs of their victims. Jesus said, "Whoever wants to save their life will lose it, but whoever loses their life for me . . . will find it" (Mark 8:35 New International Version). It seems there is often a similar paradox to saving face: whoever tries to save face will eventually lose it, but whoever loses face redemptively can find it.

The forgiveness-seeking inmate described above reminds us that, even when we are willing to humbly and courageously lose face, we have no guarantee that we will encounter human forgiveness. In this chapter, I will consider the intersubjective dynamics of interpersonal estrangement and forgiveness and pay particular attention to the ways in which our own efforts to save face can obstruct the process of both seeking and extending forgiveness.

The title of this chapter ("Saving Faces") also represents an ironic double meaning. Saving face refers to a largely defensive process of impression management, but we hunger to be faced by a face that saves. As suggested in chapter 2, early in life we start looking for human faces that confirm our security and affirm our worth. But those human faces are not always present, and so we long for a sacred saving face that will always be warmly available, that will not go away.[5] Ultimately, we believe this leads to theological and spiritual questions about the possibility of a transcendent face that saves us from the estranging void of sin and shame. Our human ways of facing each other are not salvific in this ultimate sense of transcending the spiritual void. Social-science theories and research suggest that our internal images of the face of God might be shaped by how we have been faced by others. Psychological research shows forgiveness to be one way, albeit a challenging one, of saving ourselves and others from passing on further pain and estrangement. Research shows that the intersubjec-

---

4. On the role of social face, see H. C. Triandis, *Individualism and Collectivism* (Boulder, Colo.: Westview, 1995).

5. J. E. Loder, *The Logic of the Spirit: Human Development in Theological Perspective* (San Francisco: Jossey-Bass, 1998).

tive impact of face-to-face encounters serves to move relationships toward estrangement or intimacy, agony or ecstasy.

Face to Face

In chapter 2 I described psychological research demonstrating that the human face is the primary site for displaying and communicating emotions. This means that face-to-face interpersonal encounters can be expected to be emotionally provocative, perhaps especially because we are not always aware of what our faces are communicating to or concealing from others. Three main areas of social-science theory and research on face-to-face encounters between couples are relevant to our understanding of forgiveness and saving face: (a) faces of conflict, (b) faces of violence, and (c) faces of intimacy.

Faces of Conflict

Psychological research on faces primarily involves studying individuals in response to mental stimuli. A valuable exception is a laboratory study conducted by John Gottman and his colleagues of the facial expressions of marital couples engaging in conflicted discussion.[6] The faces of the couples were videotaped and coded using the Emotion Facial Action Coding System of P. Ekman and E. Rosenberg.[7] Four years later, the researchers followed up with the same couples. Facial expressions of anger, disgust, contempt, sadness, fear, and unfelt happiness proved to be significantly related to a variety of marital and health outcomes. Remarkably, facial expressions of emotions by one or both partners during the initial taping were predictive four years later of (a) the couple's feelings about their marriage, (b) the number of months the couple had been separated over the four years, and (c) the amount of illness experienced by both husband and wife over the four years. Less surprising was the finding that facial expressions correlated with physiological variables such as heart rate and blood pressure and ratings of back-and-forth dialogue (as opposed to monologue) during the conflict session.

This study by Gottman and his colleagues is only initial and not directly related to measures of forgiveness. Nevertheless, the methodology and results of this study of couples builds upon two studies show-

6. J. M. Gottman, R. Levenson, and E. Woodin, "Facial Expressions during Marital Conflict," *Journal of Family Communication* 1 (2001): 37–57.

7. P. Ekman and E. Rosenberg (eds.), *What the Face Reveals: Basic and Applied Studies of Spontaneous Expression Using the Facial Action Coding System* (New York: Oxford University Press, 1998).

ing that the physiology and facial expressions of individuals are both related to the level and maturity of forgiveness.[8] Perhaps our faces symbolically mediate internal physiological and external interpersonal processes. When we experience defensive feelings of unforgiveness, such as contempt, during conflict with another person, our faces often display those feelings. This in turn elicits feelings and physiological reactions in the other person and impacts the back-and-forth process of the relationship. If our primary motivation is to save face, this may elicit expressions on our own faces that aggravate the face needs of the other person. Our physiology is the "hardware" and our faces the "software" of this symbolic social process of saving and losing face.

Gottman establishes in other studies that couples become estranged, in part because they develop hostile and defensive patterns that lead to becoming too physiologically aroused ("flooded") during conflict.[9] A key part of this pattern is the development of contempt where one or both partners begin to add an insult to a complaint (e.g., "You lazy slob! You never remember to take out the trash!"). Contempt on the face of a spouse, parent, or some other person is likely to instigate feelings of shame in the recipient. Eventually, chronic defensiveness sets in to avoid further shame, which blocks the possibility of experiencing mutual intersubjectivity. Partners start responding to anticipated challenges and insults before they even happen. The negative cycles of shame and arousal become so aversive, if only at the physiological level, that many partners begin stonewalling or emotionally withdrawing from interactions. This can lead to entertaining alternatives to staying in the relationship. Some divorce, and others stay married but build impenetrable walls of self-protection. Gottman suggests that developing capacities for repairing conflict and extending forgiveness can mitigate a cascade of marital estrangement.[10]

Faces of Violence

A number of theorists and researchers note the tendency for shame to initiate, rather than curb, angry and violent reactions toward oth-

8. See S. T. Huang and R. D. Enright, "Forgiveness and Anger-Related Emotions in Taiwan: Implications for Therapy," *Psychotherapy* 37 (2000): 71–79; C. V. Witvliet, T. E. Ludwig, and K. L. Vander Laan, "Granting Forgiveness or Harboring Grudges: Implications for Emotion, Physiology, and Health," *Psychological Science* 12 (2001): 117–23.

9. J. M. Gottman, "A Theory of Marital Dissolution and Stability," *Journal of Family Psychology* 7 (1993): 57–75.

10. J. M. Gottman and N. Silver, *The Seven Principles for Making Marriage Work* (New York: Three Rivers Press, 1999).

ers.[11] Helen Lewis postulates a link between shame and anger, or what she calls "humiliated fury."[12] She views shame as the emotional aspect of disconnection between persons. Building on Bowlby's theory of attachment, Lewis considers shame an "attachment emotion" that signals a threat to the social bond. Shame initially involves hostility toward the self due to the sense of a disapproving other. Turned inward, this hostility can be so threatening and aversive that the shame-prone individual defensively turns the hostility outward. Lewis further suggests that shamed individuals may become motivated toward anger at others to mobilize the impaired self beyond self-condemnation. This shame-anger-shame process can escalate into interpersonal violence, a process described by Thomas Scheff and Suzanne Retzinger as the triple spiral of shame.[13]

Scheff and Retzinger integrate the sociological perspectives of Goffman with the intrapsychic perspective of Lewis on the connection between shame and anger. Retzinger carried out several studies using qualitative methods to analyze videotaped marital quarrels. Scheff and Retzinger offer support of Lewis's theory by observing that the intensity and escalation of conflict increases for couples through rapid alternation of shame and anger states. One partner feels shame and responds with anger both verbally and nonverbally, including facial responses. These angry facial expressions and responses shame the other person and provoke angry counters that can escalate into violence.

Scheff and Retzinger conclude that anger alone is usually relatively benign and diffuses quickly, a view supported by Gottman's research. Anger admixed with defensive shame is particularly emotionally damaging and potentially volatile. Scheff and Retzinger build on Lewis to implicate unacknowledged or bypassed shame as the primary mechanism that leads to interpersonal hostility potential violence. Lewis suggests that shame can be acknowledged or unacknowledged between persons. She believes that shame can either strengthen the social bond between individuals or estrange them, depending on whether the shame is acknowledged. Acknowledged shame

11. T. J. Scheff and S. M. Retzinger, *Emotions and Violence: Shame and Rage in Destructive Conflicts* (Lexington, Mass.: Lexington, 2001). See also S. M. Retzinger, "The Role of Shame in Marital Conflict," *Perspectives on Social Problems* 3 (1992): 135–54; T. J. Scheff, "Emotion and Illness: Anger, Bypassed Shame, and Heart Disease," *Perspectives on Social Problems* 3 (1992): 117–34; idem, "Shame and Related Emotions: An Overview," *American Behavioral Scientist* 38 (1995): 1053–59.

12. H. B. Lewis, *Shame and Guilt in Neurosis* (New York: International Universities Press, 1971); see also G. Kaufman, *Shame: The Power of Caring* (Rochester, Vt.: Schenkman, 1985).

13. Scheff and Retzinger, *Emotions and Violence*.

usually subsides rather quickly. In Western cultures, shame is often unacknowledged and takes two forms. Lewis calls the first form "overt" shame because the person is aware of feeling emotional pain and slows down the rate of thought and speech. In her discourse analyses of therapy sessions, Lewis finds that clients experiencing overt shame often relabeled the feelings "awkward" or "insecure." The other form of unacknowledged shame described by Lewis is "bypassed" shame. Bypassed shame involves more primitive denial as the individual defensively speeds up his or her rate of thinking, talking, or other behavior to keep the emotional pain of shame outside his or her conscious awareness. She believes that this bypassed shame can even result in obsessive behavior as a defense against the painful affect. Unacknowledged shame can inhibit intersubjective recognition and promote internalized negation. The interpersonal process that leads to violence seems to involve one person feeling a shameful loss of face and then defending against shame with an angry counterattack of narcissistic blows against the face needs of the other with an escalating reciprocal spiral of shame and anger. This is also a common spiral of face-to-face estrangement between couples who do not escalate all the way to violence. When conflicted couples indicate they cannot forgive one another, this could be the face-to-face process they have experienced.

Faces of Intimacy

Face-to-face encounters involving intense negative emotions such as shame and contempt often exacerbate the estrangement of unforgiveness. Stonewalling and violence are two opposing ways of defending against the painful tension of facing a person who provokes anxiety and shame. But it is not just faces of agony that summon our defenses. Many of us also fear face-to-face encounters of intimacy and ecstasy.

David Schnarch develops a model of sexual therapy and sexual potential that involves likening both sexuality and marriage to a crucible or severe test where unresolved relational dynamics like anxious shame and resentment come to the surface.[14] Schnarch raises the question of why so few people seem to engage in eyes-open sex with their partners when sustained eye contact during face-to-face encounters creates such potential for deepened intimacy. He goes on to suggest that eye contact during sex can be part of a move toward greater intimacy but that many people uncon-

14. D. M. Schnarch, *Constructing the Sexual Crucible: An Integration of Sexual and Marital Therapy* (New York: Norton, 1991); idem, *Passionate Marriage: Keeping Love and Intimacy Alive in Committed Relationships* (New York: Norton, 1997).

sciously resist this because authentic intimacy is so anxiety provoking. The risk of being seen and being known on the inside activates our personal insecurities about being accepted and creates ambivalence about intimacy. Schnarch suggests that the risk of face-to-face intimacy where another is allowed to see inside requires mature differentiation of self and the ability to self-validate and self-soothe in the face of anxiety. Mike Mason poetically describes the other side of this maturity, the healthy humility that leads to relational intimacy: "Even the simple act of kissing is powerfully symbolic of the crush of personalities, as each partner pushes his features against those of the other as if to make one new face out of two. Kissing implies losing face; it is inherently a free and wholehearted gesture of self-effacement."[15]

Given the vulnerability and risk of face-to-face intimacy, it is no wonder that hurts and betrayals involving sexuality (e.g., abuse, assault, affairs) are among the most complex and painful cases of shame and unforgiveness. Schnarch's theory also helps explain why couples in therapy will sometimes make progress toward forensic or behavioral forgiveness, have their first intense sexual encounter in months or years, and then immediately regress back into estrangement. The experience of intimacy can feel surprising and threatening, as though one has perhaps revealed too much. Again, Mason is illuminating: "To be naked with another person is a sort of picture or symbolic demonstration of perfect honesty, perfect trust, perfect giving and commitment, and if the heart is not naked along with the body, then the whole action becomes a lie and a mockery."[16]

Intimacy, like conflict, tests the bonds of trust between two people, and the trust that can undergird forgiveness is refracted through a broader systemic context. Too often, however, that systemic context engenders estrangement rather than forgiveness.

Systemic Estrangement

A systemic perspective suggests that the tension between forgiveness and unforgiving estrangement unfolds within a social and relational context of social power. Social systems such as families and communities shape the contours of power and identity that influence the forgiveness process. Individual self-identity is, in part, an internalization of the power dynamics of the social system.

15. M. Mason, *The Mystery of Marriage* (Portland: Multnomah, 1985), 133.
16. Ibid., 117.

Yet literature on forgiveness largely fails to address the relationship between forgiveness and social power.[17] Forgiveness is often confused with submissive capitulation to inequities in social power. As mentioned before, this rightly generated the concern among some therapists as to whether forgiveness is consistent with psychological well-being and recovery from relational conflicts.[18] When forgiveness is construed as simply canceling a debt and moving on, there is a risk of denying inequities in social power that will continue to cause systemic problems. Forgiveness is actually better understood as a stance of promoting personal differentiation and inviting relational change toward just relations rather than a slave mentality of conflict-avoiding submission. Mature forgiveness can include nonviolent protest that invites change.

Before forgiveness can be applied systemically, it is necessary to diagnose dynamics of systemic estrangement that impede the process of forgiveness. I will describe five dynamics of systemic estrangement: (a) totalizing the other, (b) scapegoating, (c) exclusion, (d) self-surveillance, and (e) narcissistic families.

Totalizing the Other

Emmanuel Levinas describes the tension between totality and infinity.[19] "Totality" refers to our tendency to categorize and the perception that something or someone is *nothing-more-than* whatever our categories make of it. This is an ego-adaptive function of our attempt to comprehend and control our worlds. "Infinity" refers to the reality that others are *always-more-than* we can know or categorize or judge. As G. Kunz puts it, "Other persons facing me are infinitely more than a member of my convenient categories."[20] There is an irreducible mystery to the other who is always beyond our grasp or comprehension.

The danger of totalizing the other is that it can become a destructive process of reducing the other based on social stereotypes and controllable categories. This is not to suggest that using categories, such

17. This point is raised by Fincham, "Kiss of the Porcupines"; C. Madanes, *Sex, Love, and Violence: Strategies for Transformation* (New York: Norton, 1991); S. J. Sandage, "An Ego-Humility Model of Forgiveness: Theoretical Foundations," *Marriage and the Family: A Christian Journal* 2 (1999): 259–76; M. Seibold, "When the Wounds Run Deep: Encouragement for Those on the Road to Forgiveness," in *Care for the Soul: Exploring the Intersection of Psychology and Theology* (ed. M. R. McMinn and T. R. Phillips; Downers Grove, Ill.: InterVarsity, 2001), 294–308.

18. Cf. S. Lamb and J. G. Murphy, *Before Forgiving: Cautionary Views of Forgiveness in Psychotherapy* (Oxford: Oxford University Press, 2002).

19. E. Levinas, *Totality and Infinity* (trans. A. Lingis; Pittsburgh: Duquesne University Press, 1969).

20. G. Kunz, *The Paradox of Power and Weakness: Levinas and an Alternative Paradigm for Psychology* (Albany: State University of New York Press, 1998), 36.

as personality descriptors, is inherently bad. The problem arises when we attempt to control relational estrangement by totalizing the other. For example, when we are hurt by a coworker or relative we might find ourselves groping for a condemning label that will provide us with some sense of control (e.g., "No one could ever work with him" or "He's nothing but a jerk"). At times we explicitly use totalizing language in face-to-face combat (e.g., "You are a total ———!").

Two systemic problems with totalizing perpetuate estrangement and unforgiveness. First, social stereotypes often supply convenient but oppressive categories for totalizing. These could be stereotypes about gender, race, ethnicity, class, sexual orientation, intelligence, beauty, religion, or any number of other categories. Stereotypes reduce the complexity of human diversity and often mask deeper resentments. For example, in leading groups with men I have found that totalizing stereotypes about women are a frequent temptation for men discussing problems in their lives. If the stereotypical discourse is not challenged, the group members will simply enable one another in unforgiveness and find it hard to make progress in facing the anxieties and resentments that create the desire for stereotypes.

The second systemic problem with totalizing is that it often serves as a method of gatekeeping and recruiting others into one's exclusion or punishment of a perceived enemy. I once worked in an organization where a staff person became offended by a peer in another department. Rather than dealing with his resentment or directly addressing the other person, he started referring to her with the clinical label "borderline." He meant it in a demeaning fashion and would say to other staff, "Has Borderline been bugging you for that report yet?" Soon, others who hardly knew the person picked up the label and it became uncommon to hear the actual name of the staff person. She was simply known as "Borderline," a clinical category that has been overdiagnosed in women. Unforgiveness became contagious through totalizing discourse about the other.

Scapegoating

Scapegoating is related to totalizing and occurs in families or social systems where one person is assigned total blame for all the problems in the system. The scapegoated person then bears the brunt of all the anger and pain in the system.[21] The assigning of the scapegoat role is not a conscious process but simply emerges in the anxious dynamics of conflict in the system. It represents a detouring of conflict away from others in the system and allows narcissistic individuals or dyads

21. V. Pillari, *Scapegoating in Families: Intergenerational Patterns of Physical and Emotional Abuse* (Philadelphia: Brunner-Routledge, 1991).

to focus blame on another person and thereby save face and exonerate themselves. For example, parents sometimes become focused on an adolescent child that is acting out and avoid facing problems in their marriage or other family relationships. Soon, the adolescent is labeled rebellious, and the rest of the family system builds a false cohesion by trying to "straighten out" the kid. This is not to suggest that the adolescent in a case like this does not have any problems. But the pathology and unforgiveness of the system can be missed, and an unfair burden placed on a single person. The scapegoated person can then be banished from the system or held at arm's length without other members of the system acknowledging this as a form of unforgiveness.

I have seen cases where good kids have been sent away or submitted to "tough love" approaches aimed at breaking rebelliousness. In one case a parent suggested an exorcism for a teenage daughter who was doing well in school and all other areas of life but had "a bad attitude" at home. When the parents began actually spending some time with the girl and attending to their own serious marital problems, her "bad attitude" remitted.

Scapegoating perpetuates systemic estrangement and unforgiveness. In some cases the scapegoated person may internalize the scapegoat role and struggle with chronic self-hatred. In such cases, the person will need to shed the role of scapegoat and move toward a healthier, more differentiated sense of self before meaningful forgiveness of others will be possible.

Exclusion

Scapegoating often leads to exclusion, which is another dynamic of systemic estrangement. Miroslav Volf's theology of exclusion and embrace suggests that exclusion of those we find different, strange, or "outgroup" is an ubiquitous dynamic of sin and the identity formation processes that can war against forgiveness and reconciliation. The formation of a healthy, differentiated sense of self does not necessitate exclusion. Volf's theological perspective is consistent with the differentiated, relational view of selfhood we have been developing. He explains: "Identity is a result of the distinction from the other *and* the internalization of the relationship to the other; it arises out of the complex history of 'differentiation' in which both the self and the other take part by negotiating their identities in interaction with one another."[22]

Unfortunately, this healthy process of creative differentiation is often maligned by the sinful dynamics of exclusion. The formation of

22. M. Volf, *Exclusion and Embrace: A Theological Exploration of Identity, Otherness, and Reconciliation* (Nashville: Abingdon, 1996), 66.

identity can result in a motivation to exclude that which is perceived as other. This can take the form of cutting off connection to specific individuals or groups of people and denying interdependence. For example, an elder at a very conservative church raised some questions to the elder board about the possibility of allowing a group of women to meet for a Bible study without a male teacher present. Amazingly, the board rejected the proposal and became so defensively entrenched that they labeled the elder a divisive person and excluded him from the elder board. The elder had called into question an exclusionary practice that was a central part of the patriarchal identity of both the church and the elders themselves. For this he became unforgiven and excluded.

According to Volf, exclusion can also take the form of denying differences and forcing assimilation. In this case the otherness of the other is excluded. A cultural example is the refusal to acknowledge ethnic differences in social practices. In some families, children are not allowed to differ from their parents in terms of political views or likes and dislikes. I heard a father explain that he never got to golf growing up and his sixteen-year-old son would golf in tournaments "whether he likes it or not!" By contrast, embrace involves an openness to the other that is not present in the posture of exclusion.

Systems that practice exclusion perpetuate estrangement and unforgiveness by making it unsafe to acknowledge conflict or even simple differences. This can maintain what Scott Peck calls "pseudo-community."[23] Conflicts are denied, and those in power may feel a certain fragile security, while those with less power often feel forced to wear masks that hide their real faces. Meaningful forgiveness and reconciliation are never achieved in such systems because real conflicts are not allowed or they are cut off before the anxiety gets too intense. By not facing the anxiety of conflict and difference, there is no chance for the creative encounter that Volf associates with forgiveness and embrace. Volf describes forgiveness as "the boundary between exclusion and embrace"[24] that removes walls of hostility and leaves space for noncoerced decisions about the future of the relationship.

Criminologist John Braithwaite developed a theory of the role of shame and forgiveness that is related to exclusion and social space.[25] Braithwaite proposes that some societies, usually collectivistic or communal ones, practice "reintegrative" shaming and forgiveness to

23. M. S. Peck, *The Different Drum: Community Making and Peace* (New York: Simon & Schuster, 1987).

24. Volf, *Exclusion and Embrace*, 125.

25. J. Braithwaite, *Crime, Shame, and Reintegration* (Cambridge: Cambridge University Press, 1989); idem, *Restorative Justice and Responsive Regulation* (Oxford: Oxford University Press, 2001).

socially control crime. Reintegrative shaming can lead to effective crime control by simultaneously shaming criminals for their offense while also offering them some form of social forgiveness and reintegration back into the space of community based on repentance. In contrast to reintegrative shaming, Braithwaite suggests that stigmatizing shame results when individuals who commit crimes are separated or excluded from the community with no means of reintegration or forgiveness. This was the dilemma of the inmate I described at the start of this chapter, spatially removed from a society he experiences as unwilling to ever face and forgive him.

According to Braithwaite, individualistic societies like the United States are more likely to rely upon impersonal bureaucratic forms of social control that make it harder to facilitate community reintegration and forgiveness. He argues that stigmatizing shame damages the social bond between the offender and the punisher by not offering any means of forgiveness and reintegration into the community. Stigmatizing shame can promote the formation of criminal subgroups whereby excluded and alienated criminals can find some sense of belongingness.

Self-Surveillance

Systemic estrangement can also foster what French cultural historian Michel Foucault describes as "self-surveillance." Foucault is interested in the systemic connections between knowledge and power in institutions such as hospitals and prisons where people became both objects of knowledge and objects of domination. Foucault believes that power and expert knowledge are so interrelated that he prefers to speak of power/knowledge. He suggests that modern institutions are shaped by power but disguise the power dynamics behind a humanitarian façade and claims to objective knowledge.

In his book *Discipline and Punish: The Birth of the Modern Prison*, Foucault traces the transition from medieval approaches to criminology that involved physical punishment of the body and public shaming to the modern correctional methods of more privatized punishment of the soul through social control.[26] Foucault is particularly intrigued by the Panopticon, a French prison invented by nineteenth-century reformer Jeremy Bentham, which Foucault held to be the quintessential example of modern social control. The Panopticon was a circular, light-filled building with a guard tower in the middle that allowed the guard to potentially see into any of the rows of individual cells. Yet the tower was designed in a way that the prisoners could not

---

26. M. Foucault, *Discipline and Punish: The Birth of the Modern Prison* (New York: Pantheon, 1977).

see where the guard was looking, and so they had to assume they were under constant surveillance. Inmates became subjects of "the ever present gaze." The intended effect of the Panopticon and of all modern institutions, argues Foucault, is to promote self-surveillance of the individual to facilitate efficient social control. He goes on to suggest that modern institutions such as prisons, hospitals, or government agencies employ the surveillance tools of files, databanks, and documents as mechanisms of control and manipulation. Foucault charges these systems of surveillance with using categorizing and labeling to subjugate people.

Angela Davis traces the historical influence of Bentham's Panopticon prison design on the construction of prisons in the United States.[27] She draws chilling parallels between the surveillance philosophy of the Panopticon and the increased use of impersonal, technological surveillance in the rising number of supermaximum-security ("supermax") prisons where normal cells often lack any bars or glass to see out of and inmates are monitored by video. Davis argues that two important differences are that supermax prisons in the United States have confined a vastly higher percentage of African American men than in the general correctional population and have also dropped Bentham's correctional goal of rehabilitation. She concludes, "The supermax draws upon—even as it also serves to feed—the perpetuation of racism at every level of our society."[28] Systemic factors such as racism, sexism, and classism infiltrate public perceptions about who is potentially forgivable and worth facing as a society.

Foucault and his theory of self-surveillance also have a significant influence on postmodern narrative therapies.[29] Narrative therapists suggest that systemic forces of oppression encourage people to internalize mechanisms of self-surveillance. Eating disorders like anorexia nervosa are a prime clinical target for narrative therapists applying the concept of self-surveillance. Women in the United States are surrounded by images of the ideal female body as thin.[30] Parents and family members may reinforce this oppressive standard for success, which can serve to create family power struggles for the control of food and the body. And as was the case with the Panopticon, once the ideal image and the ever present gaze of the social standards are inter-

27. A. Y. Davis, "Race, Gender, and Prison History: From the Convict Lease System to the Supermax Prison," in *Prison Masculinities* (ed. D. Sabo, T. A. Kupers, and W. London; Philadelphia: Temple University Press, 2001), 35–45.

28. Ibid., 44.

29. For example, M. White and D. Epston, *Narrative Means to Therapeutic Ends* (New York: Norton, 1990).

30. W. Polinska, "Bodies under Siege: Eating Disorders and Self-Mutilation among Women," *Journal of the American Academy of Religion* 68 (2000): 569–89.

nalized, the individual will place herself under the control of self-surveillance and feel shame if she deviates from that standard. Narrative therapists suggest that healing, and what could be considered forgiveness, will come in such cases when the standard for surveillance is deconstructed and a new, less oppressive narrative identity is formed.

Foucault is also interested in what he calls "the hermeneutics of the self," which involves examining the historically and culturally prescribed methods for defining and transforming the self.[31] He calls these methods "technologies of the self." He is concerned that certain institutions like the Catholic Church and the psychiatric establishment practice a dangerous form of social control by defining the categories of sin or mental illness while at the same time also controlling the technologies or mechanisms of expiation and healing. In other words, these institutions have a stake in defining the self as comprised of certain problems so they can profit from providing the technologies of transformation. Foucault focuses particular attention on the way in which the Catholic practice of confession serves as a technology of selfhood by requiring people to search within themselves for sins, which are also defined by the church. He sees this as a technology of the self that creates subjugation within the power structure of the church.

Foucault's insights about power structures in systems and technologies of selfhood serve a valuable deconstructive and prophetic function, although there are important limitations to his work and his critique of Christian technologies of the self.[32] His work is a reminder that the social construction of forgiveness will always be related to the moral discourse a particular system or community uses to define sin and pathology. It is neither possible nor desirable for communities, particularly the religious or therapeutic, to stop engaging in moral discourse. It is wise, however, for such communities to attend to the power dynamics that could potentially generate an oppressive theology of sin or definition of pathology.

Foucault's notion of self-surveillance also contributes to our consideration of forgiveness by providing a useful depiction of a powerful barrier to self-forgiveness and feeling forgiven by God. Some people seem to have internalized voices or images of God that generate self-surveillance by providing a constant source of incrimination and internal estrangement. These internalized voices and God images are in-

31. M. Foucault, "About the Beginnings of the Hermeneutics of the Self: Two Lectures at Dartmouth," *Political Theory* 21 (1993): 198–227.

32. For examples of critiques, see S. J. Sandage, "Power, Knowledge, and the Hermeneutics of Selfhood: Postmodern Wisdom for Christian Therapists," *Mars Hill Review* 12 (1999): 65–73; A. Thiselton, *Interpreting God and the Postmodern Self* (Grand Rapids: Eerdmans, 1995); Volf, *Exclusion and Embrace*.

trojected within the self from a person's community and social system, constituting a theology of self-denigration.[33] Self-surveillance differs from healthy self-control in that the latter is not anxiety driven and shame inducing. The ever present gaze of self-surveillance means the person never feels a sense of internal grace and forgiveness and never discovers the freedom of an authentic voice. This perpetuates relational estrangement from self and others.

Narcissistic Families

A fifth dynamic of systemic estrangement that influences the process of forgiveness is that of the "narcissistic family" described by therapists S. Donaldson-Pressman and R. M. Pressman.[34] They work with many clients who seem to have a similar constellation of symptoms, including denial of feelings, a chronic sense of emptiness, recurrent interpersonal problems, periodic anxiety and depression, and unacknowledged anger. These clients had not grown up in alcoholic or otherwise abusive families. These clients did share growing up in family systems where the primary responsibility for meeting needs had been inversed from the parents meeting the needs of the child to the children meeting the needs of the parents. In healthy family systems, parents are not perfectly altruistic or always attuned to their children, but they do make a consistent attempt to respond to the emotional needs of their children. In narcissistic families, parents do not provide a healthy, supportive, or reality-based mirror for their children. Instead, these parents provide a mirror that reflects their own needs, with the implicit demand that their children meet those needs.

Since children in narcissistic families can never adequately meet parental needs, the shame of failure is internalized in the child. Such children have difficulty developing a sense of voice or the ability to identify their own wants and needs and to develop strategies for meeting them. This can create an underlying frustration, and narcissistic families lack healthy ways of acknowledging such frustrations and repairing the relational damage. Parents in these families likely experienced the same family dynamics themselves while growing up, and they probably find it hard to admit that they are wrong and to apologize to their children, because this was never modeled for them. This invalidates morally legitimate feelings of hurt and frustration in other family members. Children from such families may learn to split from their feelings and may have a confused sense of conscience. Narcissis-

---

33. Cf. C. Crysdale, *Embracing Travail: Retrieving the Cross Today* (New York: Continuum, 2001).

34. S. Donaldson-Pressman and R. M. Pressman, *The Narcissistic Family: Diagnosis and Treatment* (New York: Lexington, 1994).

tic systems could be expected to create defensively shame-prone people who take responsibility for what they cannot control and deny responsibility for what they can control resulting in internalizing disorders. Since narcissistic individuals are also more prone to aggression following ego-threats, narcissistic parents may be likely to punish children in harsh or explosive ways that do not include sensitivity or restoration. Conversely, narcissistic parents may use denial to maintain a façade of having a "perfect family," thereby ignoring or minimizing the problems their children are experiencing.

Narcissistic family systems also tend to be characterized by several forgiveness-impeding patterns, such as passive-aggressive communication, triangulation, lack of parental accessibility, and unclear boundaries. Triangulation is particularly toxic for the development of forgiveness in families since it involves building coalitions or alliances to manage anxiety rather than using more direct conflict resolution. For example, a parent "confides" in a child in a manner that carries the goal of gaining support against the other parent or some other family member. The coalition then exerts power (usually unspoken) against the other family member.

Summary of Systemic Estrangement

All five of these dynamics of systemic estrangement—totalizing, scapegoating, exclusion, self-surveillance, and narcissistic families— involve the misuse of power to control the space between self and other. They represent insidious systemic responses to the inevitable anxiety of human estrangement, and yet they generate further estrangement by constructing relational architecture that obstructs the process of forgiveness. Boundaries are too rigid, too diffuse, or nonexistent. The forgiveness that does happen in such systems is probably often no deeper than that of behavioral transaction, because systemic feedback loops prevent more meaningful transformation. For individuals inhabiting such systems, experiencing transforming forgiveness requires significant differentiation of self and, at least eventually, connection to a healthier community. These psychological realities find a parallel in the gospel stories that expose a narcissistic pharisaic religious system and corrupt political system that totalizes, scapegoats, and excludes. Jesus is the Messiah whose differentiation from the prevailing system is empowered by sharing in divine grace, which grounds the deepest level of forgiveness. Throughout the gospels, this enables Jesus to be the forgiving face of transformation to people who were hungry for the wholeness of salvation.

Systems shape the way we interpret what unfolds in our relationships with others. Depending upon the kinds of interpretations we make and the ways in which we hold our interpretations, this can move us toward further estrangement or the possibility of forgiveness. This is the process of relational hermeneutics.

Relational Hermeneutics

We engage in a constant process of interpreting or making cognitive attributions about the causes of others' behavior. Making attributions about the causes of another's behavior is essentially an interpretive or hermeneutical process that both involves and influences human subjectivity. Attribution theories suggest that our emotional responses are driven by the cognitive attributions or interpretations we make. When hurt or offended by someone we almost automatically make attributions about their motivations and culpability. If we attribute their behavior to an intentional desire to harm us, we will likely feel unforgiving and consider either retaliation or avoidance or both. If we attribute their behavior to a situational mistake, we will likely feel less outraged and less need to defend against future attacks. We make such attributions, in part, to try to make sense out of our relational world and to be able to predict those people that pose a future threat. These attributions of blame have a powerful effect on the process of forgiveness.

Attributions of Blame

An impressive body of research on attributions demonstrates the importance of our cognitive judgments about the responsibility for another's behavior.[35] Psychologists describe the relevance to forgiveness of the basic human tendency toward self-serving biases by attributing our own negative behavior to external causes while attributing the negative behavior of others to exclusively internal causes.[36] When the negative behavior of others is attributed strictly to internal causes (e.g., "He's just a rude person"), emotional empathy or compassion for that person is unlikely to follow. Rather, anger is likely to gain momentum from such global internal attributions of blame toward others.

Attributions or interpretations of intentionality and responsibility are particularly central to relational estrangement and the process of forgiveness.[37] It is well established in marital research that the degree

35. B. Weiner, "On Sin Versus Sickness: A Theory of Perceived Responsibility and Social Motivation," *American Psychologist* 48 (1993): 957–65.

36. M. E. McCullough, "Marital Forgiveness: Theoretical Foundations and an Approach to Prevention," *Marriage and Family: A Christian Journal* 1 (1997): 81–96.

37. Fincham, "Kiss of the Porcupines"; K. C. Gordon and D. H. Baucom, "Understanding Betrayals in Marriage: A Synthesized Model of Forgiveness," *Family Process* 37 (1998): 425–49.

of intentionality attributed to the negative behavior of one's spouse significantly impacts the desire to retaliate with negative behaviors. Frank Fincham finds that forgiveness mediated or accounted for the relationship between responsibility attributions and positive relationship behaviors among a sample of British couples. This suggests that forgiveness is not only related to cognitive attributions of responsibility but that forgiveness impacts marital behavior over and above those attributions.

Attributions of the stability of the negative behavior of one's partner also greatly influence the probabilities of forgiveness. A woman in therapy recently asked me to determine whether her husband would have another affair in the future. She intended to use my assessment in her decision about forgiving him and working on the relationship. It is hard to accept our human limitations in predicting the future behavior of another person because, in cases like this one, so much is at stake.

Apologies and the sincerity of an offender's remorse can influence the nature of attributions and forgiveness. A strong positive correlation is found between the apology of an offender (as perceived by the victim) and the levels of empathy, forgiveness, and relational closeness described by the victim.[38] In other words, we tend to empathize, forgive, and restore closeness with an offender to the degree that that person apologizes. This again speaks to the intersubjective nature of forgiveness. When an offender apologizes, at least two things can happen psychologically. First, that person affirms the face needs of the victim. Second, the offender offers a story or account of the incident that mitigates against making global attributions about the offender's character. The offender's apology serves as a contrast to limit the scope of their negative behavior (i.e., the person doesn't seem all bad).

Stories of Facework

We not only make interpretations about the blameworthiness of others, but we offer our own stories or accounts when we find ourselves in what psychologists call a social predicament. Numerous studies in social psychology explore the impact of differing styles of accounts offered by offenders when faced with the need to explain ourselves to others, as in the case of being late to a meeting or forgetting an important date. This research builds upon the impression management tradition of Goffman and seeks to understand the ways

38. Cf. M. E. McCullough, K. C. Rachal, S. J. Sandage, E. L. Worthington Jr., S. W. Brown, and T. L. Hight, "Interpersonal Forgiving in Close Relationships, II: Theoretical Elaboration and Measurement," *Journal of Personality and Social Psychology* 75 (1998): 1586–1603.

we socially negotiate saving and losing face ("facework"). Most people work to maintain social interactions that allow them to save face and feel social worth from others. One way people negotiate face needs is to offer "accounts" to other people. Accounts are explanations people offer to others for their own behavior, the stories we tell about ourselves. These accounts are frequently designed to defend against threats to social identity and to maintain a positive impression management.

Social psychologists who study the ways people manage their face needs describe four account strategies:[39]

1. Confession involves acknowledging one's offense, accepting full responsibility, expressing regret and apology, possibly offering restitution, and surrendering the effort to protect one's own face.
2. An excuse involves acknowledging the offense, but only partial blame is accepted due to extenuating circumstances. An excuse minimizes the link between the person giving the account (the "actor") and the undesirable event.
3. Justification involves accepting responsibility for the offense, but then redefining the offense so it is less objectionable. Justification can also take the form of scapegoating by blaming the victim or diffusing personal responsibility.
4. Refusal involves blatant denial of responsibility for the offense or denying the victim the legitimacy of offering a reproach about the offense. Refusal is the most defensive strategy and represents the greatest threat to the face needs of the victim. An absence of empathy for the victim's hurt and perception of reality may be the most damaging feature of extreme refusals. Refusal represents the most extreme strategy of externalizing blame with excuses and justifications as milder forms.

Gender socialization might be a factor that influences our relational hermeneutics and the process of forgiveness. Some consistent gender differences emerge in research on accounts of facework. Women generally attend more to the face needs of others and offer more complex and mitigating (as opposed to aggravating) accounts than do men.[40] For example, in two studies of hypothetical predicaments Marti Hope Gonzales and her colleagues find that women offer

---

39. P. Schonbach, *Account Episodes: The Management and Escalation of Conflict* (Cambridge: Cambridge University Press, 1990).

40. For a review, see H. S. Hodgins, E. Liebeskind, and W. Schwartz, "Getting out of Hot Water: Facework in Social Predicaments," *Journal of Personality and Social Psychology* 71 (1996): 300–314.

more complex accounts than men and that (in one of the studies) men offer fewer confessions and more lies than women.[41] In general, the accounts of men in this study appear less intersubjectively responsive than those of women to the face needs of others.

In a subsequent study, Gonzales finds that women report more severe interpersonal costs (anger and damage to the relationship) than do men in response to hypothetical offenses by an offender.[42] Gonzales and her colleagues suggest that this effect may be due to gender differences in social orientation with women socialized toward greater socioemotional concern. Not surprisingly, both men and women generally prefer mitigating accounts over aggravating accounts, and both men and women respond negatively to intentional transgressions, regardless of account strategy. However, in the case of nonintentional offenses (accidents and negligence), men and women respond differently to proffered accounts. Following accidents, men respond more positively to mitigating accounts than to aggravating accounts, whereas women do not discriminate. Gonzales suggests that following an accident women may tend to be satisfied with a simple apology while men, more frequently oriented to issues of power and status, may expect more facework from offenders. Following negligent offenses, women respond significantly more positively to confessions than to refusals, whereas men do not discriminate. Negligent offenses are particularly ambiguous in terms of face implications, and Gonzales et al. suggest that women might pay more attention to the nature of an explanation in ambiguous predicaments. This seems consistent with Carol Gilligan's suggestion that women often approach moral situations with an ethic of care and by empathically attending to the context.[43]

Holley Hodgins and her colleagues approach the question of gender differences and accounts from a different direction.[44] The participants imagine themselves as perpetrators of hypothetical offenses and write accounts to the victims. The experimenters manipulate the status and relational closeness of the victims in the scenarios and ask participants about the expectations for the future of the relationship and how their self-esteem would be affected if the victim does not forgive.

41. M. H. Gonzales, D. J. Manning, and J. A. Haugen, "Explaining Our Sins: Factors Influencing Offender Accounts and Anticipated Victim Responses," *Journal of Personality and Social Psychology* 62 (1992): 958–71.

42. M. H. Gonzales, J. A. Haugen, and D. J. Manning, "Victims as 'Narrative Critics': Factors Influencing Rejoinders and Evaluative Responses to Offenders' Accounts," *Personality and Social Psychology Bulletin* 20 (1994): 691–704.

43. C. Gilligan, *In a Different Voice: Psychological Theory and Women's Development* (Cambridge: Harvard University Press, 1982).

44. Cf. Hodgins, Liebeskind, and Schwartz, "Getting out of Hot Water."

As in prior research, women attend more to the face concerns of others, offer more mitigating accounts (as opposed to aggravating), and use more complexity in their accounts than do men. These effects were particularly strong when victims were friends as opposed to mere acquaintances, which offers some support to the relationship-maintenance hypothesis. Men use more aggravating accounts than women, which reflects higher defensiveness. Interestingly, men who use aggravating strategies tend to expect bright future horizons to the relationship. To a greater extent than do men, women predict that their self-esteem would be harmed if the victim does not forgive, and this effect was even stronger when the victim was a friend. The authors relate this finding to literature in the psychology of women that suggests that women's identities and epistemologies are more strongly based on empathy, intersubjectivity, and relational connection than are men's.[45] Perhaps empathy and intersubjectivity are psychological strengths or virtues that are so strongly related to forgiveness because they shape how a person accounts for their own story and how they interpret the stories of others when the perils of saving and losing face are on the line.

Virtue Epistemology

As suggested above, the relational process of making attributions about the behavior of others can be likened to the hermeneutical process of interpreting a text. This involves epistemology or our ways of knowing. Postmodern theorists argue that it is neither impossible nor even desirable to fully remove the personal and subjective dimensions of knowing.[46] The subjectivity of our social contexts, our personalities and character, and our emotional moods affect what we see and the interpretations we make. Our gender socialization might even influence the stories we tell and the ways we respond to the stories of others.

Subjectivity could be viewed as a liability to knowing and interpretation, but characterological virtues might actually enhance the quality of knowing. While virtue epistemology gained interest among some philosophers,[47] psychologists studying relational attributions largely

45. See M. F. Belenky, B. M. Clinchy, N. R. Goldberger, and J. M. Tarule, *Women's Ways of Knowing: The Development of Self, Voice, and Mind* (rev. ed.; New York: Basic Books, 1997); cf. J. V. Jordan, "The Meaning of Mutuality," in *Women's Growth in Connection: Writings from the Stone Center* (ed. J. V. Jordan, A. G. Kaplan, J. B. Miller, I. P. Stiver, and J. L. Surrey; New York: Guilford, 1991), 81–96.

46. Cf. W. Grassie, "Postmodernism: What One Needs to Know," *Zygon: Journal of Religion and Science* 32 (1997): 84.

47. Cf. A. Fairweather and L. Zagzebski (eds.), *Virtue Epistemology: Essays on Epistemic Virtue and Responsibility* (New York: Oxford University Press, 2001).

ignore the role of virtue in knowing. Yet several virtues appear to influence what we know and how we interpret the behavior of others. For example, virtue capacities for compassion and forgiveness affect the interpretive process of making attributions. Jeanne Zechmeister and Catherine Romero studied empathy in relation to narratives written by research participants about incidents of being either a victim or an offender in an interpersonal conflict. Interestingly victims tended to tell their stories as if the offense was continuing into the future horizon, while offenders tended to describe their offenses as over and located in the past horizon. Also noteworthy was the finding that dispositional empathy on the part of victims was associated with more benign interpretations of offenses, and empathy for the offender was associated with higher levels of forgiveness. However, offender empathy for the victim was associated with lower levels of self-forgiveness.[48] There is also evidence that relational commitment influences cognition and forgiveness in close relationships.[49] People who are more committed to a partner seem motivated to make more forgiving interpretations. The virtue of humility appears particularly relevant to forgiving interpretations. This "hermeneutical humility" involves the ability to lessen one's certainty of completely understanding the causes of an offender's behavior and a willingness to consider external factors that help view an offender's behavior in context.[50] This humility requires the ability to tolerate ambiguity and facilitates openness and complexity in interpreting another's behavior. For example, an individual client deeply hurt by his father's verbal abusiveness might begin to include in his account of his family mention of his father's financial stress and even his father's painful childhood. As I suggested in chapter 2, the virtue of humility is consistent with a high degree of self-differentiation, which includes the ability to self-soothe when anxious and physiologically stressed. Humble self-differentiation allows the flexible cognitive processing that increases capacities for forgiving others.[51]

48. J. Zechmeister and C. Romero, "Victim and Offender Accounts of Interpersonal Conflict: Autobiographical Narratives of Forgiveness and Unforgiveness," *Journal of Personality and Social Psychology* 82 (2002): 675–86.

49. E. J. Finkel, C. E. Rusbult, M. Kumashiro, and P. A. Hannon, "Dealing with Betrayal in Close Relationships: Does Commitment Promote Forgiveness?" *Journal of Personality and Social Psychology* 82 (2002): 956–74.

50. S. J. Sandage, "An Ego-Humility Model of Forgiveness: Implications for Couple and Family Dynamics and Therapy," *Marriage and the Family: A Christian Journal* 2 (1999): 277–92.

51. V. Holeman, "Mutual Forgiveness: A Catalyst for Relationship Transformation in the Moral Crucible of Marriage," *Marriage & Family: A Christian Journal* 2 (1999): 147–58.

We "bring something to the text" of interpersonal conflict, and this includes our personal subjectivity and characterological propensities that are formed by the ways we are interpreted and faced by others. We might expect that for Christians, ways of relating to the sacred face of God and internalized images of being faced by God are profoundly determinative of interpersonal capacities for forgiveness.

Sacred Faces

The historical connections between forgiveness and various world religions lead a number of psychologists to explore the relationship between forgiveness and the sacred. Two main areas of theory and research are (a) the influence of religious identity on the practice of forgiveness and (b) the role of sacred faces in forming our ways of approaching the challenges of forgiveness.

Religious Identity

Are highly religious people more forgiving? It appears to depend upon what we mean by "religious" and what we mean by "forgiving." Religious identity is a diverse phenomenon that may be related to a general disposition toward forgiving others. Michael McCullough and Everett Worthington review the empirical literature on religion and forgiveness and find discrepant results.[52] Highly religious people tend to be more forgiving in some studies but not in others. A key factor in these studies is whether the measure of forgiveness is one of a general disposition toward forgiving or forgiveness of a specific offender. Several studies find that people with an intrinsic commitment to their religious faith tend to report higher levels of valuing and practicing forgiveness than individuals with less intrinsic religious commitment. There is even evidence that intrinsic religiosity is associated with positive changes in forgiveness over time.[53] This suggests that people for whom religion is an intrinsic part of their self-identity describe themselves as more forgiving than those who view religion as more peripheral to their values and self-identity.

A creative study supporting this thesis utilized an autophotographic methodology for studying religious identity.[54] College students were asked to arrange photos in response to the question "who

---

52. Cf. M. E. McCullough and E. L. Worthington Jr., "Religion and the Forgiving Personality," *Journal of Personality* 67 (1999): 1141–64.

53. J. Tsang, M. E. McCullough, and W. T. Hoyt, "Psychometric and Rationalization Accounts for the Religion-Forgiveness Discrepancy" (forthcoming).

54. S. J. Dollinger, "Religious Identity: An Autophotographic Study," *International Journal for the Psychology of Religion* 11 (2001): 71–92.

are you?" Stephen Dollinger coded the photos for religiosity and depictions of the sacred. For example, one student chose a picture of himself with a cross over his head, and others chose pictures of Bibles, churches, nature, stained-glass windows, and other expressions of religious identity. Descriptions were provided by the students to support coding interpretations. Based on these photos, those who depicted religious photos tended to rate forgiveness as a personal value more strongly than those who did not include religious photos. The ways in which we represent ourselves and our own faces may be related to values like forgiveness, at least self-reported forgiveness.

Religious identity, however, seems to have little relationship to self-reports of forgiving a specific offender.[55] A variety of psychometric issues might explain these findings, but the most obvious explanation is that forgiveness in any given relationship can be hard for anyone. Even intrinsically religious people who value forgiveness find it hard to forgive in certain relationships. As suggested throughout these first three chapters, there is more to forgiveness than simply our conscious values and level of religious commitment. Forgiveness is multidimensional and involves our intrapsychic and intersubjective formation in a broader relational context.

Faces of God

Imagine being asked to draw a picture of God. What would you draw? How would you depict God? To some it might seem like a silly idea and to others an invitation to idolatry. Psychoanalyst Ana-Marie Rizzuto conducted a classic qualitative study by doing just that, asking twenty adult psychiatric patients to "draw a picture of God."[56] Some patients drew a face of God, and some who drew a face depicted God's eyes as open while others had them shut. Some drew pictures of God smiling, seemingly friendly, while others depicted God serious, stern, or even hostile. Psychiatrist Robert Coles conducted a similar study with children and found that Christian children usually drew God with a face. One girl in Coles's study explained her drawing in this way: "When God came here, He looked like a man; He was Jesus. But then He went back to being God, and I don't know what he looks like now, but you have to have a face!"[57]

In her study of adult pictures of God, Rizzuto conducted in-depth interviews of the patients' psychological and religious histories. Based on her interviews and the patients' drawings, Rizzuto developed the

---

55. Cf. McCullough and Worthington, "Religion and the Forgiving Personality."

56. Cf. A.-M. Rizzuto, *The Birth of the Living God: A Psychoanalytic Study* (Chicago: University of Chicago Press, 1979).

57. R. Coles, *The Spiritual Life of Children* (Boston: Houghton Mifflin, 1990), 41.

theory that our internal images or representations of God or the sacred are formed through the various relational experiences and influences in our developmental histories. Freud thought images of God are based on one's father, but Rizzuto concludes that relationships with many people, including mothers and fathers, shape internalized, unconscious images of God. Following object relations theorist Donald Winnicott, Rizzuto suggests that representations of God serve as transitional objects, like a teddy bear or a blanket. Transitional objects help us creatively manage the transitional space between our internal experience and external reality. Unlike the teddy bear or blanket, however, sacred and relational connotations of God images make them powerful symbolic resources that can be unconsciously carried forward to be employed throughout the lifespan. This is not to suggest that God and theological beliefs are nothing more than subjective projections of the psyche.[58] Rather, the "unconscious theology" of our images of God are formed through internalizing relational experiences, and these images interact with our more conscious theological beliefs in a bidirectional, intertextual manner.

Provocatively, Rizzuto again builds upon Winnicott and other developmentalists by suggesting that the earliest manifestations of a child's ability to internally form representations of relations with God and others emerge through "eye contact, smiling, and the child's fascination with the configuration of the human face."[59] Through mutual facing and eye contact during nursing, infants and mothers "respond to each other beyond the boundaries of need satisfaction."[60] As suggested in the last chapter, the eyes and faces of mothers and other caregivers provide the first mirror for the child's emerging sense of self. This unfolds during the development of basic trust, which surely exerts a pivotal unconscious influence on later representations of God.

Smiling on both human and sacred faces provides a powerful symbol of an affirming presence. There are many references to the smiling face of God in the spiritual writings of mystics. One example comes from the journals of Simone Weil (1909–43), a French philosopher and political activist who experienced spiritual surrender in a twelfth-century chapel in Assisi where "something stronger than I was compelled me for the first time in my life to go down on my knees."[61] Her spiritual transformation seemed to culminate in 1938:

58. See A. B. Ulanov, *Finding Space: Winnicott, God, and Psychic Reality* (Louisville: Westminster John Knox, 2001).

59. Rizzuto, *Birth of the Living God*, 184.

60. Ibid.

61. S. Weil, *Waiting for God* (1951; trans. E. Craufurd; New York: Harper & Row, 1973), 67–68.

I spent ten days at Solesmes, from Palm Sunday to Easter Tuesday, following all the liturgical services. I was suffering from splitting headaches; each sound hurt me like a blow; by an extreme effort of concentration I was able to rise above this wretched flesh, to leave it to suffer by itself, heaped up in a corner, and find a pure and perfect joy in the unimaginable beauty of the chanting and the words. This experience enabled me by analogy to get a better understanding of the possibility of a loving divine love in the midst of affliction. It goes without saying that in the course of these services the thought of the Passion of Christ entered into my being once and for all. . . .

I only felt in the midst of my suffering the presence of a love, like that which one can read in the smile on a beloved face.[62]

In Coles's study of children, a twelve-year-old boy named Mark also described the power of the smiling face of God in helping him excel at track: "I've been lucky that God has picked me. It's His smile. . . . When I'm running and I see His smile, I feel my body change—it's like shifting into high gear, daddy says."[63] Another significant relational connection emerges later in the interview with Mark: "God's face is the face of love, our teacher said, and I think of him saying that, I hear him saying it, and then there's God, coming to me with a smile, and I thank Him."[64] Mark's descriptions of God's face and his spiritual experiences of relating to God are interspersed with references to relational figures. It is as though the face of God and the face of significant attachment figures cannot be neatly partitioned.

The thesis that the faces of relational figures significantly influence our representations of the face of God has important implications for the process of forgiveness. First, those who were chronically faced by caregivers in anxious, hostile, or unresponsive ways will likely find it harder to form an internal representation of God as warmly accepting, available, and forgiving. God may feel intrusively controlling, like the ever present gaze described by Foucault. Or God may feel disinterested and withholding of love, affection, or forgiveness. Perhaps worst of all, God may feel dangerously violent, like an alcoholic father or mother who might erupt at any time. Not surprisingly, Tsang and her colleagues find that students who held primarily vengeful images of God show lower levels of forgiving others than those who held primarily loving and benevolent images of God.[65]

When children are traumatized through abuse or other experiences and there is an absence of caring responsiveness from those

62. Ibid., 68–69.
63. Coles, *Spiritual Life of Children*, 49.
64. Ibid., 50.
65. Tsang, McCullough, and Hoyt, "Psychometric and Rationalization Accounts."

around them, internal images of the absence of God may form and desecrate previous images of the sacred.[66] This problem of spiritual and existential absence is actually at the heart of the Christian story of the crucifixion, where Jesus cries out in the agony of abandonment before the "dark face of God."[67] The resurrection narratives provide the return of God's presence in the face of Christ. The internal return of the sacred face of God is often challenging for those who have been traumatized by evil and is even hindered by coercive or premature efforts to get victims to forgive offenders.[68] A more psychologically healing and saving representation of the Christian gospel for victims of abuse and oppression is of a loving and just God who sees and identifies with innocent victimization yet ultimately overcomes evil with good.

A Model of the Forgiveness Process

But how does forgiveness happen when it does unfold? Dozens of psychological models outline phases of a process of forgiving others. Many of these models are theoretically consistent and have been developed through clinical or psychoeducational group work with people who are trying to forgive a specific offender. Numerous studies test interventions to promote forgiveness with groups and individuals.[69] Most of these studies are with nonclinical samples of people trying to forgive a specific offender, and these studies usually screen out individuals who have experienced abuse or severe psychological distress. These studies typically find that forgiveness interventions are effective in helping people forgive a specific offender. The empirical research on forgiveness to date, however, has not advanced to the point of validating a specific sequence of phases of a forgiveness process.

Donald Walker and Richard Gorsuch attempt to discover the underlying dimensions of seventeen published models of the forgiveness process.[70] They developed a questionnaire with items representing the various phases or dimensions of these seventeen models. For example,

66. C. Doehring, *Internal Desecration* (Lanham, Md.: University Press of America, 1993); idem, "The Absent God: When Neglect Follows Sexual Violence," *Journal of Pastoral Care* 47 (1993): 3–12.

67. Volf, *Exclusion and Embrace*, 26.

68. Seibold, "When the Wounds Run Deep"; S. Tracy, "Sexual Abuse and Forgiveness," *Journal of Psychology and Theology* 27 (1999): 219–29.

69. For a review, see E. L. Worthington Jr., S. J. Sandage, and J. W. Berry, "Group Interventions to Promote Forgiveness: What Researchers and Clinicians Ought to Know," in *Forgiveness: Theory, Research, and Practice* (ed. M. E. McCullough, K. I. Pargament, and C. E. Thoresen; New York: Guilford, 2000), 228–53.

70. D. Walker and R. Gorsuch, "Dimensions Underlying Seventeen Models of Forgiveness and Reconciliation" (forthcoming).

many of the models have a dimension that involves empathizing with one's offender, so they constructed items to represent empathy. They recruited research participants (predominantly Protestant Caucasian females) from area universities and asked them to think about a person who had hurt and offended them and then respond to the questionnaire. They conducted a factor analysis of responses to the questionnaire and grouped the responses into five separate factors: (a) reconciliation, (b) emotional forgiveness, (c) receiving God's forgiveness, (d) empathy, and (e) hurt and anger.

Walker and Gorsuch followed this by conducting a path analysis to identify pathways toward reconciliation using the other four factors. As suggested earlier, most psychological models differentiate forgiveness and reconciliation. In other words, it is possible to forgive an offender without reconciling. Some empirical evidence, however, shows a strong positive correlation between forgiveness and reconciliation,[71] suggesting that the two may often occur in tandem or not at all. Path analysis allows for modeling a potential sequence of steps in a process. Walker and Gorsuch find two separate models of the pathway to reconciliation. One model describes a three-step process to reconciliation and the other model a five-step process. The three-step process model consists of (a) hurt and anger, (b) empathy, and (c) reconciliation. The five-step process model consists of (a) hurt and anger, (b) empathy, (c) receiving God's forgiveness, (d) emotional forgiveness, and (e) reconciliation.

An important limitation of this study is that participants were not actually followed during the process of therapy or a forgiveness-intervention program to see how forgiveness and reconciliation unfolded. Rather, they were tested once and asked for a retrospective self-report about their experience of a hurtful relationship. Future experimental research may better clarify causal connections between steps in various forgiveness models. Since forgiveness and reconciliation are value-laden and culturally embedded constructs, it is unlikely that a single model will emerge that describes the process for people of all cultures and religions. Nevertheless, this study provides a useful heuristic for considering some of the primary phases that people may go through when they forgive and reconcile.

My own version of the forgiveness process is a three-phase model based on review and synthesis of numerous models, including the two path models from the Walker et al. study. My three phases are (a) engaging in lament, (b) encouraging empathy and humility, and (c) ex-

71. Cf. M. E. McCullough, E. L. Worthington Jr., and K. C. Rachal, "Interpersonal Forgiving in Close Relationships," *Journal of Personality and Social Psychology* 73 (1997): 321–36.

tending narrative horizons. We should think of general phases of the forgiveness process rather than a tight system of sequential steps. In an earlier version of this model, I referred to the second phase as "encouraging ego-humility."[72] The current label broadens the second phase to explicitly acknowledge the pivotal role of empathy, although ego-humility remains a central dimension of our model. Ego-humility refers to a flexible, mature ego orientation toward self and other that includes a willingness to acknowledge one's strengths and face one's limitations. Ego-humility facilitates open, nondefensive engagement in relational hermeneutics and dialogue that do not involve anxiety-driven face-saving strategies. Several interpersonal characteristics associated with ego-humility enhance the process of forgiveness, including (a) little need to defensively control interpersonal encounters, (b) the intersubjective capacity to empathize and take the perspective of others, (c) a willingness to acknowledge and take responsibility for one's own actions and wrongdoing and seek repair when appropriate, (d) a stronger sense of gratitude than entitlement, and (e) a proclivity to view others as one's equal.

This model suggests that interpersonal conflict and states of unforgiveness arise from the human predicament of anxious relational estrangement. Estrangement represents the nexus of sin and shame that both arises from and causes further alienation between persons and between persons and God. The anxiety of this estrangement is rooted in the negation of the void, which haunts our ego structures when we face various levels of death and loss.[73] This root anxiety over the underlying void and potential nonbeing mobilizes us to action whenever our dignity is diminished or we are shamed into losing social face in some way. The person with well-developed ego-humility does not simply fortify existing ego structures whenever confronted with conflicts and loss but, rather, faces the anxiety of the void and cultivates an open posture inviting deeper transformation and forgiveness. Over time, ego-humility also enhances the formation of a resilient, differentiated self that is typically less personally reactive and defensive in the face of interpersonal conflict.

Engaging in Lament

Lament is a psychological and even spiritual practice of facing and experiencing the emotional pain caused by an interpersonal conflict. This involves relaxing anxious defenses like denial in a safe environment that provides a secure base for surveying the damage. This cor-

72. Sandage, "Ego-Humility Model of Forgiveness: Theoretical Foundations"; idem, "Ego-Humility Model of Forgiveness: Implications."
73. Loder, *Logic of the Spirit*.

responds to the first phase in both path models from the Gorsuch et al. study. Enright and his colleagues refer to this first phase as "uncovering" and "acknowledging your anger," and Worthington calls it "recalling the hurt."[74]

Lament means complaint and refers to the spiritual practice of authentically engaging God with the honest expression of questions, doubts, or cries of agony and despair. Psalms of lament in the Hebrew Bible give poetic voice to raw emotions of anger, shame, and sadness. These psalms were used by the Hebrews in corporate prayer and even singing.

Since I view anxious shame as a core barrier to forgiveness, the initial phase of working toward forgiveness involves a psychological and spiritual grief process that can be likened to lament, or what David Augsburger calls "forgrieving."[75] This involves empathically helping the client acknowledge shame, anger, sadness, and confusion and sensitively moving past defenses to uncover unacknowledged or bypassed shame.[76] Shame is often mixed with anxiety and anger, and such feelings need to be encountered in a safe relational context. Interpersonal offenses such as infidelity and criminal victimization can come as a traumatic shock to many people, so some clients will initially feel numb and need to emotionally process the events. Empathic involvement by a therapist or counselor can move past the isolating effect of estrangement and begin to restore the dignity of face. Clients may begin to internalize "good self-objects" through a face-to-face relationship with a caring therapist who helps legitimate their pain.[77] Clients can be encouraged to give voice to their feelings in session, including grief and disappointment over relational needs that were unmet. Writing about feelings also shows promise in recent studies of forgiveness.[78] As suggested in the last chapter, cognitively ruminating about

74. R. D. Enright and R. P. Fitzgibbons, *Helping Clients Forgive: An Empirical Guide for Resolving Anger and Restoring Hope* (Washington, D.C.: American Psychological Association, 2000); E. L. Worthington Jr., *Five Steps to Forgiving: The Art and Science of Forgiving* (New York: Crown, 2001).

75. D. W. Augsburger, *Helping People Forgive* (Louisville: Westminster John Knox, 1996).

76. Cf. M. G. Alter, *Resurrection Psychology: An Understanding of Human Personality Based on the Life and Teachings of Jesus* (Chicago: Loyola University Press, 1994); R. D. Enright, *Forgiveness Is a Choice: A Step-by-Step Process for Resolving Anger and Restoring Hope* (Washington, D.C.: American Psychological Association, 2001); S. Halling, "Shame and Forgiveness," *Humanistic Psychologist* 22 (1994): 74–87; J. Patton, *Is Human Forgiveness Possible? A Pastoral Care Perspective* (Nashville: Abingdon, 1985).

77. M. R. McMinn, *Psychology, Theology, and Spirituality in Christian Counseling* (Wheaton, Ill.: Tyndale, 1996).

78. J. J. Exline and N. Molnar, "Letters, Logic, and a Lack of Self-Righteousness: Facilitators of Forgiveness?" (paper presented in "Forgiveness as Positive Science: Theory, Research, and Clinical Applications," a symposium cochaired by P. C. Hill and S. J. Sandage and conducted at the annual meeting of the American Psychological Association, San Francisco, 2001).

feelings of hurt and resentment impede forgiveness, but verbalizing in a safe context or writing can move people toward healing.

It is not simply the expression or catharsis of painful emotions that facilitates movement toward forgiveness. I once worked with a client who had been threatening to kill his former wife and was daily praying the imprecatory psalms that call for God to wipe out his enemies. This was not the kind of lament that results in forgiveness. Emotional disclosure that leads to reframing the meaning of a conflict and that provides a sense of coherence is associated with psychological health and healing.[79] This translation of the emotional chaos of relational estrangement into language is the poetry of lament.

In this initial phase of lament people may or may not have forgiveness as a goal. Unless a person indicates that they want to work toward forgiveness, becoming too directive or even raising forgiveness as a goal might foreclose the entire process of healing. A primary goal at this phase in the process is helping a person find the space to discover a restored sense of face, that is, a sense of healthy self-acceptance in a trusting relational context. A second vital goal is to help the person form the relational architecture of wise boundaries that maintain safe internal space for healing but do not isolate the person from positive sources of community.

Encouraging Empathy and Humility

The second major phase in the forgiveness process involves encouraging intersubjective empathy and humility. Empathy proves to be a common dimension of the forgiveness and reconciliation models in the Walker et al. study.[80] To date, empathy is the most empirically validated mediator or causal mechanism of forgiveness in psychological research.[81]

Empathy is embodied in the virtue of compassion. Forgiving empathy or compassion is the capacity to become aware of the suffering and weakness of our offenders while still holding them responsible for moral wrongdoing.[82] Cognitively, empathy requires the intersubjective capacity to temporarily detach from our own face concerns and take the perspective of another person. Empathy enables us to see our offenders in context, not to excuse their offenses, but to reduce the to-

79. J. W. Pennebaker, *Emotion, Disclosure, and Health* (Washington, D.C.: American Psychological Association, 1995).

80. Cf. Enright, *Forgiveness Is a Choice*; Worthington, *Five Steps to Forgiving*.

81. Cf. McCullough, Worthington, and Rachal, "Interpersonal Forgiving in Close Relationships"; McCullough, Rachal, et al., "Interpersonal Forgiving in Close Relationships, II."

82. Cf. R. C. Roberts, "Forgivingness," *American Philosophical Quarterly* 32 (1995): 289–306.

talizing effect of the global attributions (e.g., "He's just a jerk") we described earlier.[83] This cognitively reduces the psychological and moral distance between offenders and ourselves. This form of empathy is closely related to the humility that can allow us to realize we might be capable of similar failures and offenses.

Emotionally, empathy involves feelings of care and concern for another person as a fellow human being. It is this connection with the shared humanness of the other that is at the core of empathy. As Kristeva suggests, the face of the other should "reveal the nonexistence of banality in human beings."[84] Estranging feelings of a desire for revenge or avoidance can preclude empathic concern and goodwill toward an offender. It is challenging to integrate feelings of empathy for an offender with feelings of anger about an offense. But as empathy for an offender develops, anger often turns to sadness for the conflict or the problems in the offender's life. Empathic care and feelings of goodwill for an offender do not necessarily equate to a desire for reconciliation or continuing a relationship. Divorced spouses, for example, sometimes forgive one another and experience empathic concern and a desire for good things in the future life of the other person. If children and coparenting are involved, this form of forgiveness may be crucial to the future well-being of everyone in the family.

Empathy can sometimes be generated by reflecting on one's own need for forgiveness. This is usually true if a person is characterized by humility more than by shame. Humility is consistent with self-acceptance and gratitude for forgiveness received. Experiencing God's forgiveness provides the deepest restoration of face possible and should contribute to the spiritual and psychological formation of healthy humility as opposed to defensive shame. Remembering and reencountering God's forgiveness appears to be an explicit dimension of the forgiveness process for many, though not all, forgivers.[85]

Humility also facilitates forgiveness by encouraging a willingness to face any contributions one has made to an interpersonal conflict. This is not always relevant, as there are cases of conflict where a given person is innocent. And those who have been abused or harmed as children often assume too much responsibility for adult sins. But in some cases a humble openness to facing one's own part in a conflict leads to discoveries and reduces the moral distance from an offender.

83. Cf. Gordon and Baucom, "Understanding Betrayals in Marriage."
84. J. Kristeva, *Strangers to Ourselves* (trans. L. Roudiez; New York: Columbia University Press, 1999), 3.
85. Cf. Walker and Gorsuch, "Dimensions Underlying Seventeen Models"; J. P. Pingleton, "Why We Don't Forgive: A Biblical and Object Relations Theoretical Model for Understanding Failures in the Forgiveness Process," *Journal of Psychology and Theology* 25 (1997): 403–13.

Extending Narrative Horizons

The third phase of the forgiveness process involves extending narrative horizons. Narrative psychologists suggest that the development of self-identity and relationship histories are a process of story construction.[86] We construct stories to gain a sense of meaning and control in life. Some cases of unforgiveness can be understood as confusion over how to make sense of the chaos of hurt and injustice in an interpersonal relationship. Painful interpersonal conflicts can make it difficult to envision a positive future story or narrative horizon. The process of forgiveness should ultimately move beyond experiencing forgiveness of a specific offense or offender toward wrestling with the potential meaningfulness of forgiveness as an overall life practice and a theme in one's future story.[87]

Early in the process forgiveness is unlikely to seem meaningful and the pain of the conflict unnecessary. Later, after movement toward healing, forgiveness might be described as a way of finding meaning in the midst of suffering.[88] People should not be rushed into such notions of the meaningfulness of forgiveness prematurely. But as individuals move past shame and anger and begin to experience forgiveness, the natural human tendency is to want to construe the pain suffered as meaningful. Hurtful events that seemed random or tragic can begin to be redeemed as part of a narrative plot that offers opportunities to grow in the character of forgiveness or even reverse the effects of painful family legacies. Examining the impact of a partner's hurtful behavior might lead to the realization that it served as a symbolic reminder of deeper hurts experienced in other relationships.[89] Some individuals begin to see how little forgiveness and relational repair existed in their family relationships and desire to help end the intergenerational transmission of hostility.

This third phase of the forgiveness process involves moving from viewing forgiveness a strategy for coping with a particular conflict or crisis to exploring forgiveness as a life practice. Forgiveness as a life practice requires cultivating a community that nurtures the craft of forgiveness.[90] For Christians, the church and religious small groups can be a source of community that encourages forgiveness. As sug-

---

86. D. P. McAdams, *The Stories We Live By: Personal Myths and the Making of the Self* (New York: Guilford, 1993).

87. Cf. L. G. Jones, *Embodying Forgiveness: A Theological Analysis* (Grand Rapids: Eerdmans, 1995).

88. Augsburger, *Helping People Forgive*; cf. E. A. Gassin and R. D. Enright, "The Will to Meaning in the Process of Forgiveness," *Journal of Psychology and Christianity* 14 (1995): 38–49.

89. Cf. Fincham, "Kiss of the Porcupines."

90. Cf. Jones, *Embodying Forgiveness*.

gested in chapter 2, this depends on what happens in a specific church or small group.[91] Groups like Alcoholics Anonymous and other therapeutic, educational, or support groups can also foster the ongoing practice of forgiveness for individuals and couples. Forgiveness will be sustained if people gain wisdom from their suffering and develop strategies for avoiding the same conflicts or problems in the future.

Forgiveness is also associated with the capacity for hope, and hope is the crucial virtue that enables people to envision a positive future horizon. C. R. Snyder develops personality measures of both forgiveness and hope and finds that people higher in forgiveness of self and others tend to also be more hopeful.[92] Research on forgiveness and hope is limited, but the theoretical connections are promising. For example, couples in therapy who learn to practice forgiveness toward each other often feel more hopeful about the future of their relationship. Individuals who struggle with chronic anger to the point of losing jobs and relationships can gain the hope of greater self-control and better health through forgiveness.[93] Becoming a forgiving person does not remove all problems or relational pain, but it can open the horizon of possibilities in ways that unforgiveness cannot.

Forgiveness and reconciliation are also guiding themes in the plot of the Christian narrative. God's larger story of forgiveness and reconciliation is the Christian narrative horizon that provides the context of our personal life stories. If self-identity is shaped through the internalization of an overall life narrative, then Christian psychology suggests that the theme of forgiveness can be a point of intersection for two narrative horizons—the personal horizon of our relational stories of conflict and the transcendent horizon of God's larger story of forgiveness and reconciliation. Our personal stories or autobiographies become theological by offering episodes of estrangement and forgiveness that invite theological reflection. This can be like the Samaritan woman at the well trying to figure out why this male Jewish prophet was facing her and then risking deeper spiritual questions about access to God's presence (John 4). Our experiences of human faces of forgiveness can offer us just enough hope to keep searching for the divine face of forgiveness.

91. Cf. R. Wuthnow, "How Religious Groups Promote Forgiving: A National Study," *Journal for the Scientific Study of Religion* 39 (2000): 125–39.

92. C. R. Snyder, L. Y. Thompson, S. T. Michael, L. Hoffman, H. N. Rasmussen, L. S. Billings, L. Heinze, J. E. Neufeld, C. M. Robinson, J. R. Roberts, and D. E. Roberts, "The Heartland Forgiveness Scale: Development and Validation of a New Measure of Dispositional Forgiveness" (unpublished paper, 2001).

93. F. Luskin, *Forgive for Good: A Proven Prescription for Health and Happiness* (San Francisco: Harper San Francisco, 2001).

Conclusion

The systemic and intersubjective nature of saving and losing face makes the realization of interpersonal forgiveness an incredibly complex endeavor. The forgiveness-seeking inmate described at the beginning of this chapter had the humility and courage to risk losing face in the hope that he would be faced with a forgiveness that could save him from social exile. His questioning lament reflected both empathy and estrangement, as well as a longing for wholeness and community. In the absence of a human face that saves, either the search intensifies or despair encroaches. And from a Christian narrative worldview, it is because human faces cannot ultimately save that the search becomes spiritual and the questions theological. In part 2, LeRon engages the theological dimensions of the faces of forgiveness, extending the horizon in our search for salvation.

PART 2

Faces of Forgiveness in Theology

F. LeRon Shults

4

FACING, FORGIVENESS, AND THE CHRISTIAN DOCTRINE OF SALVATION

As we suggested in the introduction, the deleterious effects of the dominance of legal metaphors in the Christian doctrine of salvation have nowhere been felt more deeply than in the understanding and practice of forgiveness. In part 1, Steve demonstrated the importance of extending the horizons of our understanding of forgiveness to include the reality of *therapeutic* transformation. Here the social sciences provide insight into the formation of human facing and the dynamics that characterize the move toward integrity and wholeness in community. My purpose in part 2 is to examine these issues from a theological perspective, attending to the dynamics of the search for salvation within the horizon of *redemptive* forgiveness. The first step is to clarify the biblical and theological significance of "facing" and "forgiveness" for the Christian doctrine of salvation. This chapter explores the possibility of an intrinsic relation between the substantial problems that now face some traditional formulations of the doctrine of salvation and the anemic practices of forgiveness that hinder the gracious and peaceful facing of one another that ought to distinguish the Christian community.

The critical analysis of chapter 4 provides the background for the constructive proposal of chapter 5. As will become clear, I believe that the best way to conserve the intuitions of the living biblical tradition is to liberate them *from* the constraints of obsolete philosophical and scientific assumptions and to liberate them *for* transforming dialogue in contemporary culture.

The Christian doctrine of salvation has to do with the good (*salus*)—with wholesome and healthy life together. Salvation brings persons into embodied relations of justice and peace in community. Psychological insights into the structures of this salubrious transformation cannot be ignored by theologians without detriment. However, the work of healing is threatened on every side by the faces of the void—loneliness, despair, anxiety, depression—and finally by death itself. For this reason, all merely human (psychological) efforts to save face ultimately fail to secure the self vis-à-vis this final vulnerability. The search for ultimate wholeness is the search for salvation, and for this humans are wholly dependent on divine grace. Saving faces is indeed a divine prerogative. Too often, however, when forgiveness is discussed in North American churches, it is abstracted from the real concrete practices of shared life together in community. We need an understanding of divine grace and forgiveness that invades, permeates, and empowers the life of the church. Today people still long for wholeness and salvation, but some traditional formulations of forgiveness appear irrelevant and even incoherent. The ongoing reconstructive task of theology requires careful attention to the biblical texts, the historical tradition, and contemporary culture in order to articulate a compelling presentation of the lived Christian intuitions about redemption.

The first two sections of this chapter explore the theological significance of the ideas of facing and forgiveness respectively. What could be more significant than the issues of God's being present to humanity and the specific nature of the relation that this presence creates? The ideas of "face" and "forgiveness" are used to organize and clarify these theologically significant issues. The first section reviews the idea of the face of God by examining the mysterious divine countenance in the Hebrew Bible, which is the subject of both fascination and longing as well as fear and anxiety. It also outlines the testimony of the New Testament that the glorious mystery of God is made known in the face of Jesus Christ, and describes the scriptural understanding of the presence of the Holy Spirit who creates, blesses, and keeps the community of God. The second section explores the theological significance of forgiveness, which has been a central organizing concept for the Christian religion from the beginning. The ways in which it has been interpreted and taught, however, differed widely, and so it is important to trace the development of its various expressions throughout Scripture and in the history of the Christian tradition. This will illustrate the extent to which interpretations of forgiveness are embedded in broader philosophical and theological conceptualizations of salvation.

The third and final section examines the challenges that face some of the early modern formulations of the doctrine of salvation and explores new opportunities for articulating the meaning of forgiveness after the philosophical "turn to relationality." Especially relevant here is the so-called *ordo salutis* (order of salvation), which hardened in the seventeenth century as a way of delineating the series of efficient causes that move an individual soul from one status to another. Reflection on the communal aspects of redemption may lead us to understand the goal of the human longing for salvation as a real *salutary ordering*, in which peace and justice reign in embodied social life. Drawing on several resources throughout the tradition and in recent theological thought, the final subsection explores the renewed interest among Western theologians in the biblical concept of becoming "sharers in the divine nature" (2 Peter 1:4). These developments in the doctrine of God can help open up conceptual space for understanding forgiveness as sharing in divine grace (chap. 5). The following exegetical, historical, and philosophical analyses, then, serve as the background for the development of a theological presentation of the dynamics of Christian faith, love, and hope in the redemptive patterns of the faces of forgiveness.

The Theological Significance of Facing

Both the Greek term *prosōpon* and the Hebrew term *panim* may be translated as "face" or "presence." This intriguing parallel suggests that there may be a significant theological link between the face of God and the saving divine presence. James Loder argues that the human face is a "personal center that is innately sought by a child and the focus of the earliest sense of one's humanity. . . . What is established in the original face-to-face interaction is the child's sense of personhood and a universal prototype of the Divine Presence."[1] Ideally, the face of the primary caregiver provides an affirming presence that orders the cosmos of the infant. This singular face brings peace to the child's world in a way that no other face can. Human caregiving is never ideal, however, and soon the baby learns that this face often

1. J. Loder, *The Transforming Moment* (2d ed.; Colorado Springs: Helmers & Howard, 1989), 163.

goes away, causing anxiety of cosmic proportions. As the child grows to adulthood and agonizes over issues of ultimate concern, she continues to long for a faithful and loving face that will never go away. Only the Face (Presence) of God can satiate this existential desire; as we will see below, Scripture is full of testimony to the faithful presence of the divine countenance of the loving Creator whose promise of the redemption of the cosmos is already ordering human life anew as we search together for wholeness and salvation.

From the beginning of recorded history, humans have expressed this longing for transcendence, for a relation to that which is ultimately "Other." The struggle with and against the mysterious forces that are beyond human control was expressed in early religions in various ways in diverse narratives and rituals. Like their ancient neighbors, the Israelites found their personal and communal existence overshadowed by anxiety, by a longing for a peaceful life they could not themselves secure. Their understanding of the dynamics of this longing was shaped by their narrative experience of YHWH (the LORD). They expressed their desire for wholeness and salvation in terms of seeking the face (*panim*) of God. The early Christians, who were for the most part Jews who had been looking for the salvation of Israel, believed that the ultimate answer to this longing was manifested in the revelation of the mystery of God in the face (*prosōpon*) of Jesus Christ and made available to all people through the presence of the Holy Spirit. While this Christian witness to the loving countenance of God is good news, it is important to remember that this Face is like no other—the experience of the infinite divine Face is ambiguous and evokes not only delight but also terror.

The Mysterious Divine Countenance

A trembling fascination with the face of God may be found in every genre of the Hebrew Bible. One of the most important allusions to the divine countenance is in Numbers 6:24–26, where Aaron is instructed to bless the people of Israel by saying to them:

> The LORD bless you and keep you;
> the LORD make his face to shine upon you, and be gracious to you;
> the LORD lift up his countenance upon you, and give you peace.[2]

The blessing and keeping of the LORD takes concrete form in the manifestation of grace and the provision of peace. The experience of

---

2. In this way, the LORD promises, Aaron and his sons "shall put my name on the Israelites, and I will bless them" (Numbers 6:27). The correlation between face and name will be observed below.

wholeness and salvation depends wholly on the bright and smiling face of God.[3] The community is called into existence and held together by the LORD, whose presence (face) brings the promise of gracious and peaceful life. The Hebrew word for grace (*hen*) means good favor or affection expressed by one person to another, usually on the part of someone in a high place.[4] Being gracious means intending well-being for the other. The Hebrew word for peace (*shalom*) means more than simply the absence of war. It refers to the reign of God's justice and mercy, which bring flourishing to persons in community.

In the Wisdom literature, the wise and upright are those who long for the face of God. The image of the shining divine countenance expresses the intended beauty of the relation of humanity to the LORD. We hear echoes of the blessing and keeping of Numbers 6, and God's facing presence is linked not only to grace and peace, but also explicitly to salvation:

> Let your face shine upon your servant;
> save me in your steadfast love.
> —Psalm 31:16

> May God be gracious to us and bless us
> and make his face to shine upon us,
> that your way may be known upon earth,
> your saving power among all nations.
> —Psalm 67:1–2

> Restore us, O God;
> let your face shine, that we may be saved.[5]
> —Psalm 80:3

Being faced by the shining countenance of God brings grace and peace—this is almost a précis of the Jewish understanding of salvation. Sometimes the English translation obscures the reference to the face or countenance of God. For example, we might take "and set me in your presence forever" (Psalm 41:12b) to mean "and place me be-

3. The idiomatic expression *to lift one's face* means to show favor or to smile. Cf. Proverbs 16:15a: "In the light of a king's face there is life." For an analysis of the use of this phrase, see M. I. Gruber, "The Many Faces of Hebrew נשא פנים 'Lift up the Face,'" *Zeitschrift für die alttestamentliche Wissenschaft* 95 (1983): 252–60.

4. The term can be extended to refer to the object of favor, with a derivative meaning of graciousness or beauty. Cf. P. C. Phan, *Grace and the Human Condition* (Wilmington: Glazier, 1988), 12.

5. This last phrase is used as a refrain in Psalm 80:7, 19. Cf. 119:135, where the psalmist prays for God's face to shine upon the people.

fore your face forever." Similarly, "in your presence there is fullness of joy" (16:11) could be rendered "your face fills me with joy." One might even take the liberty of paraphrasing the final vocative appellation of 43:5 as "my saving face and my God."

The face of God is to be desired above all things. The deepest existential longing of the righteous Israelite would be satisfied with nothing less than the joy of being in the very presence of God: "My soul thirsts for God, / for the living God. / When shall I come and behold / the face of God?" (Psalm 42:2). Conversely no ruination is more to be feared than being hidden from the shining glory of the divine countenance. The Israelites expressed this sense of divine absence, or we might say this presence of the divine absence, with the idiomatic phrase *hiding the face of God*:[6] "You hid your face; / I was dismayed" (30:7b). "'Come,' my heart says, 'seek his face!' / Your face, LORD, do I seek. / Do not hide your face from me" (27:8–9a). Psalm 44:3 claims that the deeds performed in days of old were not by the Israelites' own strength, but were accomplished by "your right hand, and your arm, / and the light of your countenance, / for you delighted in them." The same psalm, however, agonizes over a feeling that God has turned away from Israel: "Why do you hide your face? / Why do you forget our affliction and oppression?" (44:24). If the divine face is hidden, sickness or death are at hand: "Do not hide your face from me, / or I shall be like those who go down to the Pit" (143:7b; cf. 132:10). "When you hide your face, they [living creatures] are dismayed; / when you take away their breath, they die / and return to their dust" (104:29).

The divine countenance is not a presence like any other. On the one hand, it cannot be escaped—it searches out and gazes upon the psalmist, addressing and obliging him to respond: "Where can I flee from your presence [face]?" (Psalm 139:7). On the other hand, the face of God cannot be manipulated, not even by the religious cultic sacrifice. The divine blessing is not mechanistic; it cannot be reduced to simple cause and effect. This is a major theme in the Book of Job. His friends believe that suffering is a result of sin and that God hides his face from those who have earned it. Job's experience challenges this facile commodification. As they all learn from the whirlwind, the ways of the divine countenance are mysterious; suffering does not

6. The most detailed exegetical study of this idiom is S. E. Balentine, *The Hidden God: The Hiding of the Face of God in the Old Testament* (Oxford: Oxford University Press, 1993). For a more accessible study, which examines the issues in the broader context of contemporary culture and science, see R. E. Friedman, *The Hidden Face of God* (San Francisco: HarperCollins, 1995). The one case in which hiding the face is used in a positive sense is when the psalmist prays "hide your face from my sins" (51:9), but this is soon followed by the plea: "Do not cast me away from your presence (*panim*)" (51:11).

necessarily mean judgment for sin. Just because a person does not sense the face of God does not mean that God is not attending to the person. For example, Job is aware that even though "he hides, and I cannot behold him," still God "knows the way that I take" (23:8–10; cf. 30:20). In the climactic last chapter, the LORD announces (42:8) that he will "accept [Job's] prayer" (i.e., lift up Job's face), and the LORD shows favor (42:9) to Job (i.e., lifts up Job's face).[7] The Hellenistic categories of transcendence and immanence are not equivalent to the Hebrew categories of the hiding and shining of the face of God. The divine face (like the divine name and glory) are "present" differently than the way finite objects are present to (or absent from) other finite objects. The Israelites cannot make God's face appear through ritual magic or incantations. This experience led to the idea of divine sovereignty; this mysterious countenance elicits both fascination and terror because it is wholly beyond human control, and yet humans cannot escape its confrontation.

The agony and ecstasy evoked by the divine countenance could be illustrated in the stories of several biblical characters,[8] but the enigmatic experiences of Jacob (who is renamed "Israel") and Moses (who mediates the law) are particularly salient. Even in these intimate encounters with the face of God, however, the divine countenance remains essentially mysterious. The presence of the LORD is not simply given to them in a way that can be manipulated or objectified. The most relevant episode in Jacob's life is the nocturnal struggle that he experiences near Jabbok on his way to meet his brother Esau (Genesis 32:3–33:17). Jacob is so anxious about his imminent confrontation with Esau, whom he had cheated out of the firstborn birthright, that he sends waves of gifts ahead of him to Esau, hoping that these might "appease him" (32:20a; i.e., pacify his face). Then, thinks Jacob, "afterwards I shall see his face; perhaps he will accept me" (32:20b; i.e., lift up my face). That very night Jacob wrestles with a "man" (32:24); when the man does not prevail against Jacob by daybreak, he knocks Jacob's hip out of joint and asks to be released (32:25–26). Jacob refuses to let the man go unless he blesses him. Jacob asks: "Please tell me your name." The man responds, "Why is it that you ask my name?" and then blesses him (32:29).

7. See Gruber, "Many Faces of Hebrew נשא פנים," 254–55.

8. For example, Adam and Eve "hid themselves from the presence (*panim*)" of God after taking of the forbidden tree (Genesis 3:8). When the LORD does not have regard for his offering, Cain's face "fell" (4:5). The LORD notices his fallen countenance (4:6), and his punishment is being driven away from the soil; this is more than he can bear, and he cries out, "I shall be hidden from your face" (4:14). After receiving a mark of protection, Cain goes away "from the presence (*panim*) of the LORD" (4:16).

Jacob interprets this experience explicitly in terms of being faced by God,[9] and here again the presence of a blessing is significant. Jacob calls the place Peniel (face of God), saying, "For I have seen God face to face, and yet my life is preserved" (Genesis 32:30). This self-interpretation is ambiguous; the divine presence, which cannot be seen, is so powerfully present to Jacob that he is compelled to speak of seeing God. The experience is existentially transforming, but it is important to note that even here God's facing of Jacob is still intrinsically mysterious. This is expressed in the refusal of the man to give his name, since the power of naming was a symbol of control in the ancient Near East.[10] That very morning Jacob "looked up and saw" Esau coming (33:1). The blessing had not completely absolved Jacob's guilt and fear, because he continues to behave anxiously as he anticipates facing his brother. After putting his wives and children behind him, he approached Esau, bowing his face to the ground seven times (33:3). In shocking contrast, Esau engages in several intense facial interactions: he "ran to meet him, and embraced him, and fell on his neck and kissed him, and they wept" (33:4). Jacob realizes that Esau is not going to destroy him. He will not have to wrestle again. Jacob insists that Esau accepts his gifts, "for truly to see your face is like seeing the face of God—since you have received me with such favor" (33:10). Jacob's experience of the grace and peace of the divine countenance is somehow mediated through the face of his brother. Conversely, the resolution of his anxiety about facing his brother is mediated by an agonizing night of struggle with the divine presence. Esau manifests grace, and Jacob enters into a time of peace.

The terror and delight of being faced by God is also evident in the story of Moses and the redemption of Israel from slavery. When he first confronts the angel of the LORD who "appeared to him in a flame of fire out of a bush" (Exodus 3:2), Moses "hid his face, for he was afraid to look at God" (3:6). After trying to talk God out of choosing him, Moses receives an answer to the question he shared with Jacob: What is God's name? Perhaps the most compelling translation of the divine response (3:14) is "I will be there as who I am shall I be there."[11] The name is linked to the future and cannot be controlled by human beings. The name is also in the first person, which means that

9. The text simply says a "man," but later the prophet Hosea will refer to the stranger as an "angel" and say that Jacob "strove with God" (Hosea 12:3–4).

10. Cf. T. N. D. Mettinger, *In Search of God: The Meaning and Message of the Everlasting Names* (trans. F. H. Cryer; Philadelphia: Fortress, 1988). Even today, women in some contexts are named by their husbands (or fathers) and required to wear veils over their faces.

11. For argumentation in favor of this translation, in light of other options, see J. C. Murray, *The Problem of God* (New Haven: Yale University Press, 1964).

only God may properly speak it. The divine name implies the divine presence. Only God can name God and so manifest the grace and peace of divine glory. The people of Israel are successfully liberated from Egypt and eventually led to Mount Sinai, where Moses delivers the law. When Moses stayed on the mountain too long for their comfort, however, they begged Aaron to make gods for them. In the context of the divine response to the famous golden calf incident, we read that "the LORD used to speak to Moses face to face, as one speaks to a friend" (33:11).

Here we find the story of Moses' request to see God's glory. Moses does not want to lead the people away from Sinai unless the face of God goes with them; YHWH promises: "My presence (*panim*) will go with you, and I will give you rest" (Exodus 33:14). Moses asks to see God's glory, but is told that he cannot see God's face, and he ends up hearing the LORD pronounce the name: "I will make all my goodness pass before you, and will proclaim before you the name, 'The LORD.' . . . But . . . you cannot see my face; for no one shall see me and live" (33:18–20). Desire, enigma, and revelation—all folded into each other in a transforming experience of the divine presence. Later, after the Israelites fearfully resist entering the promised land, Moses convinces the LORD not to destroy them, by recalling the events of Exodus 33–34. He points out to the LORD that in the midst of this people "you . . . are seen face to face" (Numbers 14:14), and striking the Israelites now would lead the other nations to think that the LORD "slaughtered them in the wilderness" (14:16). While Moses knew God so closely that his own face had to be veiled, the violence and terror at Mount Sinai led many of the Israelites to respond ambiguously to the presence of the divine countenance.

Toward the end of the Pentateuch, we read that "never since has there arisen a prophet in Israel like Moses, whom the LORD knew face to face" (Deuteronomy 34:10). In the same context, we also read that the LORD will hide his face from the Israelites because of the evil they will do and their idolatry (31:17–18). In Moses' final song these words are attributed to the LORD: "I will hide my face from them, / I will see what their end will be" (32:20a). By the end of the narrative in 2 Kings, this judgment had been realized: of both Israel (17:23) and Judah (23:27), it is said that the LORD removed them "out of his sight." The classical prophets[12] also speak of the terrible judgment of God's hidden face: "Truly, you are a God who hides himself, / O God of Is-

---

12. In *Theology of the Old Testament: Testimony, Dispute, Advocacy* (Minneapolis: Fortress, 1997), W. Brueggemann argues that Torah, kingship, the prophets, the cult, and the sages were all mediators of the divine presence. They were signs in the sense that "they decisively enact the thing (Yahweh's presence and purpose) to which they point" (576). He suggests that these modes of mediation have a "sacramental force."

rael, the Savior" (Isaiah 45:15). God is portrayed as actively hiding his face, but it is precisely this hidden face that lures the righteous person in Israel. From the human side, it can be said that "your sins have hidden his face from you" (59:2). The warning is clear: "Then they will cry to the LORD, / but he will not answer them; / he will hide his face from them at that time, / because they have acted wickedly" (Micah 3:4). In reference to the siege of Jerusalem by Babylon, the LORD tells Jeremiah (32:31) that he will "remove it from my sight [i.e., from before my face]" and that "I have hidden my face from this city because of all their wickedness" (33:5).

Yet, the hope and promise of restoration remains, both in the historical books and in the prophets: "For the LORD your God is gracious and merciful, and will not turn away his face from you, if you return to him" (2 Chronicles 30:9b). Isaiah says, "I will wait for the LORD, who is hiding his face from the house of Jacob, and I will hope in him" (8:17). The anticipated Messiah would be the prince of peace (9:6) and would bring an age of peace (2:2). Grace and peace represent the ultimate manifestation of God; the hiding of the divine face is not permanent: "In overflowing wrath for a moment / I hid my face from you, / but with everlasting love I will have compassion on you, / says the LORD, your Redeemer" (54:8). In Ezekiel, this eschatological future is depicted through the LORD's promise to restore Israel: "And I will never again hide my face from them, when I pour out my spirit upon the house of Israel" (39:29).

Invoking poetic license, I suggest that we might even paraphrase the first commandment (Exodus 20:3) with this simple imperative: "Just look at my face!"[13] If the face of God was as important to Israel as this brief survey suggests, it is not unreasonable to think that they would have been able to understand this passage in a way that was a more intimate calling into fellowship: "You shall not have other gods before my face" or "let no other gods get in the way of my facing you." Attending only to the divine countenance frees a person fully to attend to his or her neighbors. Resting under the gaze of the smiling face of God is an experience of absolute loving attentiveness in which one's being is secured in relation to the living God; this is what the Israelites longed for in their relation to YHWH. In Jesus Christ they were confronted by a person who fulfilled this commandment, manifesting through his entire life a focus on his heavenly Father, relying on the life-giving presence of the Spirit, even to death on a cross.

13. The original Hebrew may be translated literally as: "Other gods shall not be to-you before the face-of-me."

The Face of Jesus Christ

The language of the Hebrew Bible about the ambiguous divine countenance is appropriated throughout the New Testament.[14] Early Christians believed that the "mystery" of God had been made known in and through Jesus Christ (Ephesians 1:9; Colossians 1:26–27). Yet, the mysterious presence (or face) is not simply unveiled and objectified. This is not the kind of mystery that is solved; it is *the* mystery of the world that always and everywhere calls creatures toward sharing in its infinitely mysterious glory. Believers continue to anticipate a future coming of Jesus, which is linked to "times of refreshing" in the "presence (*prosōpon*) of the Lord" (Acts 3:20). The worshiping servants of God still expect an eschatological consummation in which "they will see his face, and his name will be on their foreheads" (Revelation 22:4).[15] Paul tells the Corinthians that "now we see in a mirror, dimly [enigmatically], but then we will see face to face" (1 Corinthians 13:12).

That the presence of God is inherently mysterious, even in the manifestation of Jesus Christ, did not diminish the apostolic witness to the ultimacy of this revelation. After Jesus' resurrection, the biblical authors were compelled to say that "in him all the fullness of God was pleased to dwell" (Colossians 1:19) and described him as "the reflection of God's glory and the exact imprint of God's very being" (Hebrews 1:3). Insofar as God was in Christ "reconciling the world to himself" (2 Corinthians 5:19), Jesus faced his contemporaries as the very presence of divine grace and peace. The Johannine Jesus tells his disciples that "whoever has seen me has seen the Father" (John 14:9). The Synoptic writers depict Jesus' personal ministry as confronting the people of Israel with the arrival of the kingdom of God (e.g., Matthew 12:28). Having faced this man from Nazareth, the church begins the journey of interpreting the mysterious divine countenance in trinitarian terms.

The most explicit biblical language about the face of Jesus Christ is in Paul's Second Letter to the Corinthians: "And all of us, with unveiled faces, seeing the glory of the Lord as though reflected in a mir-

---

14. For example, eternal destruction is linked to being "separated from the presence (*prosōpou*) of the Lord" (2 Thessalonians 1:9). First Peter 3:12 quotes Psalm 34, which notes that "the face of the Lord is against those who do evil."

15. In the Book of Revelation, facing is a recurrent theme. Leaving aside the various comments on the faces of the beasts, serpents, and elders, two examples stand out. First, the fear of those experiencing divine judgment leads them to call on the rocks to fall on them "and hide us from the face of the one seated on the throne" (6:16). Second, the whole cosmos dreads the coming purification: "The earth and the heaven fled from" the face (20:11) of the one on the throne. This same one brings about a new heaven and a new earth, "making all things new" (21:5).

ror, are being transformed into the same image from one degree of glory to another; for this comes from the Lord, the Spirit. . . . [God] has shone in our hearts to give the light of the knowledge of the glory of God in the face (*prosōpon*) of Jesus Christ" (3:18; 4:6).

In this context, Paul is comparing the glory of Jesus' face with the glory of Moses' face, which had to be veiled before the early Israelites. Because they rely on the law of Moses, some are still veiled and unable to see "the light of the gospel of the glory of Christ, who is the image of God" (2 Corinthians 4:4).[16] Paul's letter contains more allusions to facing and being faced than most English translations indicate. In 1:11 he is hopeful that many (lit., "many faces") will give thanks for the blessing (*charisma*) of God. Paul tells them that he forgives (*charizomai*) anyone whom they forgive. Why? "For your sake in the presence (*prosōpon* = face) of Christ" (2:10). It is in this face that Paul finds the abundant glory of God (4:6); this presence allows him to face "slight momentary affliction" in his own ministry as he anticipates "an eternal weight of glory beyond all measure" (4:17).

Not all who encounter Jesus (then or now) perceive the glory of God. The face of Jesus is not simply a given, an object for human subjectivity to grasp. As with all human faces, encountering the face of Jesus is enigmatic. The face-to-face relations of human personhood are inherently mysterious; we cannot control the face of the other in the way we manipulate nonpersonal objects (without destroying what makes them personal). What is it about the face of *this* man from Nazareth that led his followers to proclaim that his presence was the unique manifestation of the mysterious divine countenance? They were brought to this conclusion in light of the way that Jesus faced God and others in his *ministry*, the way he entrusted himself to God on the *cross*, and the way he appeared to them after his *resurrection* from the dead. I will examine in turn each of these three ways of facing.

The evangelists explicitly connected their experience of Jesus' ministry with the Jewish anticipation of the Messiah. The Spirit of the LORD would be upon the Messiah, and the reign of God would be displayed in a radically new way. Jesus' facing of others in his ministry reminded the disciples of Isaiah's Suffering Servant, who had neither external majesty nor a desirable appearance, but was "as one from whom others hide their faces" (53:3). The inherent ambiguity of facing is illustrated by the possible translation of this idiomatic expres-

16. A similar comparison is made in the story of the transfiguration, where Moses and Elijah appear, but Jesus' "face shone like the sun" (Matthew 17:2). In Romans 5:12–21 Paul compared Jesus not only to Moses, but also to Adam; neither the law nor the flesh, but only sharing in the righteousness and life of Jesus Christ can bring us into the intimate relation to God for which humans are created.

sion "as one who hides his face from us."[17] Isaiah 50:6 more clearly indicates that it is the servant who does not hide his face from others. As with the servant, Jesus' interfacing (although agonizing) leads to the people's redemption.[18] The servant will be humiliated but vindicated: "The LORD God helps me; / therefore I have not been disgraced; / therefore I have set my face like flint, / and I know that I shall not be put to shame; / he who vindicates me is near" (50:7–8a). Luke says of Jesus that "he set his face to go to Jerusalem" (9:51). Jesus was determined to face the suffering that comes from manifesting love. This setting of his face was the explicit reason one village of Samaritans would not receive him (9:53), although he sent messengers "ahead of him" (lit., "before his face") to prepare for his arrival.[19]

The Synoptic Gospels all use ambiguous facial idioms to express Jesus' way of relating to others. When the disciples of the Pharisees question Jesus about paying taxes, they begin by observing: "Teacher, we know that you are sincere, and teach the way of God in accordance with truth, and show deference to no one; for you do not regard people with partiality [lit., do not look to (*eis*) the face of men]" (Matthew 22:16). This same phrase had already appeared in Mark's account (12:14). In Luke's telling of the story (20:21) we find a slightly different expression; the spies acknowledge that Jesus shows "deference to no one [lit., does not receive a face]." Paul applies a similar phrase to God in Galatians 2:6—although typically translated "God shows no partiality," a more literal rendering would be "God does not receive the face of a person." In contrast to the grumblers of Jude 16, who are "flattering people to their own advantage [lit., admiring faces for the sake of advantage]," Jesus (like God) looks behind people's façades and is not fooled by the duplicity of false faces.

Jesus' facing of others and his facing of the Father as he depended on the life-giving presence of the Spirit were not empty formal structures—the material reality of the dynamics of his life demonstrated what God is like. Jesus' confronting of others reveals the faithful, promising love that is the trinitarian life. In his sermons and parables, in his practice of table fellowship with sinners, in his healing of the sick, and ultimately in laying down his life, Jesus shows us what love

17. For a more detailed analysis of this and similar passages, see Balentine, *Hidden God*, 65–79.

18. The words of the servant—"I gave my back to those who struck me, / and my cheeks to those who pulled out the beard; / I did not hide my face / from insult and spitting" (Isaiah 50:6)—had obvious implications for the crucifixion of Jesus as well.

19. The idea of messengers being sent "before the face" of another was applied not only to John (Matthew 11:10; Mark 1:2; Luke 7:27—echoing Malachi 3:1 and Isaiah 40:3; cf. Acts 13:24), but also to the seventy who were sent out by Jesus in pairs (Luke 10:1).

is (1 John 3:16). He teaches and manifests the fulfillment of the greatest commandments: face God in love with all of your being and face your neighbor in love as you face yourself (cf. Matthew 22:37–39). Jesus looked only to his Father for sustenance, and his ministry was immersed in the Spirit. The history of this man who called others to share in his relation to God manifested the trinitarian structure of the eternal divine life. With his appearance, the reign of divine grace and peace (i.e., the kingdom of God) arrives. This is the same grace and peace that is promised with the arrival of the smiling divine countenance. It is not accidental that almost all of Paul's letters, as well as the Epistle of Titus and the Book of Revelation, contain in the prologue a blessing of "grace and peace." These two concepts, while not exhausting what may be said about our experience of salvation, were clearly central in the New Testament presentation of the gospel. As we will see in chapter 5, the contemporary church may understand its own experience of sharing in Jesus' ministry in terms of life in sacramental, baptized, and eucharistic community—that is, facing God and neighbors in faith, love, and hope.

The early disciples also perceived the revelation of divine grace and peace in the face of the crucified Jesus. His passion leading up to and on the cross manifested the same way of facing that characterized his ministry: to the very end he faced the Father with faith, love, and hope. This becomes even clearer when we observe Christ's last words on the cross, some of which were quotations from well-known psalms. Most of those who heard Jesus (and who read the gospels) would have been familiar with the whole text from which these quotations were derived. If we think of Jesus' words as calling to memory the totality of the psalm, we may see how his experience on the cross was linked to the Israelite longing for the face of God. For example, Jesus' cry "My God, my God, why have you forsaken me?" (Matthew 27:46) comes from Psalm 22:1. The psalm continues: "Why are you so far from helping me, from the words of my groaning? . . . / On you I was cast from my birth, / and since my mother bore me you have been my God. . . . / They stare and gloat over me; / they divide my clothes among themselves, / and for my clothing they cast lots" (22:1, 10, 17–18). In the face of suffering, however, the psalmist also expresses hope in the one who "did not hide his face from me, / but heard when I cried to him" (22:24b). This does not downplay the real agony of Jesus' experience on the cross; even in the garden of Gethsemane, he "fell on his face" (Matthew 26:39 King James Version) in anticipation of his suffering and death. Yet Jesus' invocation of this psalm also points to his trust in the attentive face of his Father.

In Luke 23:46 Jesus quotes the first part of Psalm 31:5: "Into your hands I commend my spirit." The psalm continues—"you have redeemed me, O Lord, faithful God"—and goes on to express gratitude for God's attentiveness even in affliction (31:7). The poet then calls out: "Let your face shine upon your servant; / save me in your stead-fast love" (31:16). God's abundant goodness leads the psalmist to trust that "in the shelter of your presence (*panim* = face)" those who fear the Lord will be protected (31:20). Given Jesus' life of trusting in the presence of God, it makes sense to understand his statements on the cross as another expression of his attitude toward the sheltering di-vine countenance, even at the moment of death. Jesus models the ap-propriate way to face death.

This theme is taken up explicitly in the story of the murder of Stephen, the model martyr. Stephen's trial begins with the observation that all were looking intently at him for "his face was like the face of an angel" (Acts 6:15). After his summary of the gospel, which begins with the God of glory appearing to Abraham (7:2) and ends with Stephen himself gazing into heaven and seeing the glory of God (7:55), Stephen echoes Christ on the cross with an important modifi-cation: "Lord Jesus, receive my spirit" (7:59). Stephen's dying words—"Lord, do not hold this sin against them" (7:60)—again parallel Jesus' own prayer for his torturers: "Father, forgive them; for they do not know what they are doing" (Luke 23:34). Christians are called to par-ticipate in Jesus' suffering as they manifest divine love in and to the world. Death has no terror when one trusts the Spirit of God to up-hold one's own spirit. This expansion of horizons opens up a new way of understanding and practicing forgiveness.

Reflection on the face of the crucified Jesus has long been an im-portant part of the contemplative piety of many saints and mystics throughout the Christian tradition. David Ford describes this transfor-mation as the experience of "the worshipping self, before the face of Christ and other people, in an 'economy of superabundance.'"[20] Among his various examples, Ford's depiction of Thérèse of Lisieux is of particular interest; this nineteenth-century saint called herself Thérèse "of the Holy Face." Although tragically cut short, her entire life was wholly devoted to the face of Jesus Christ. This devotion took shape in several ways, including her contemplation of Jesus' face while on the cross and while sleeping on the boat while the disciples struggled during a storm. She took seriously Jesus' call not to "disfig-ure" one's face when fasting (Matthew 6:16), and despite terrible phys-ical and psychological suffering, Thérèse was famous for her smiling countenance. Ford argues that the face of Jesus became "for Thérèse a way into the basic truths of faith, from God to eschatology." Her "little

20. D. Ford, *Self and Salvation: Being Transformed* (Cambridge: Cambridge Univer-sity Press, 1999), 9.

way" of following Christ was "living before this face . . . as a life of joyful responsibility."[21]

The early Christians' testimony of their experience of fellowship with God was also based on the face of the resurrected Jesus. Both the agony of the cross and the ecstasy of resurrection disclose the ultimate dynamics of the saving face of God. Jesus' glory was not fully known or declared prior to his resurrection (Romans 1:4). Left merely with the image of the dead Jesus, the disciples were left without hope; they were cowering behind locked doors or heading away from Jerusalem. After the resurrection appearances and the outpouring of the promised Holy Spirit, the facing presence of Jesus comes to be interpreted in terms of *parousia*. This Greek word means both "presence" and "coming." Now the resurrected Christ faces the community as the coming one through the redemptive presence of the Spirit (cf. 1 Corinthians 15:23; 1 Thessalonians 2:19; James 5:8; 1 John 2:28). The face of the risen Jesus is the Parousia of the divine countenance, the coming presence of the kingdom of peace, the arriving reality of eternal life. John writes in his vision of "one like the Son of Man" (Revelation 1:13) that "his face was like the sun shining with full force" (1:16).[22] As the *eschatos adam* (1 Corinthians 15:45), Jesus Christ faces the community as "a life-giving spirit." He confronts believers as the coming one, yet they already taste the eternal life of knowing God (John 17:3) because the same Spirit that raised him from the dead dwells in them (Romans 8:11).

Facing Christ today continues to be ambiguous. Believers interpret the revelation of Jesus in terms of the second person (*prosōpon*) of the Trinity, who invites them to participate in the trinitarian life of love, peace, and joy. For them, the face of Jesus makes present the beauty of the divine countenance.[23] Nonbelievers are suspicious that this is merely a desperate search for a face that will offer protection for the weak or confirmation of the authority of the strong. There will always be the danger of projection, of looking for Jesus at the bottom of a well and seeing our own faces.[24] Mirrors deceive us because we like them to. James observes that a person who is merely a hearer but

21. Ibid., 228–29.

22. The author of Hebrews depicts Jesus as appearing for us before the face of God (9:24). Jesus describes heaven as seeing "the face of my Father" (Matthew 18:10).

23. Because the name and face of God are so closely related, as we have seen, we could spell out these dynamics in terms of the naming of Jesus and our being named into the Trinity in baptism. Jesus is called *kyrios* (Lord), which in the first century was the Greek translation of YHWH. Jesus is given "the name that is above every name" (Philippians 2:9).

24. Cf. J. D. Crossan, "Our Own Faces in Deep Wells: A Future for Historical Jesus Research," in *God the Gift and Postmodernism* (ed. J. D. Caputo and M. J. Scanlon; Bloomington: Indiana University Press, 1999), 282–310.

not a doer of the word is deceived, like one who looks at her own face in a mirror (1:22–25). To help avoid the dangers of a well or mirror phenomenon, we might learn from the Eastern Orthodox use of icons. After all, Colossians 1:15 says that Jesus Christ is the *eikōn* (image) of God. An icon is not intended to draw attention to itself or to reflect back the image of the observer. It is meant to lead one's gaze toward the infinite glory of God.[25] Jesus is the image of God precisely by not drawing attention to himself or allowing us to attend only to our own reflections, but by calling us to share in the glory of the Father through life in the Spirit.

The Presence of the Holy Spirit

The face of God and the presence of the Spirit are explicitly linked in the Hebrew Bible. Ezekiel's prophecy illustrates this connection: "I will never again hide my face from them, when I pour out my spirit upon the house of Israel" (39:29). Following the common practice of pairing inherently related concepts, the psalmists also express a parallelism between the divine presence (*panim*) and the divine spirit (*ruach*):

> Do not cast me away from your presence,
> and do not take your holy spirit from me.
> —Psalm 51:11

> When you hide your face, they are dismayed;
> when you take away their breath, they die
> and return to their dust.
> —Psalm 104:29

> Where can I go from your spirit?
> Or where can I flee from your presence?
> —Psalm 139:7

As with the mysterious face of God, so with the Spirit we find a dialectic between a general awareness of and a particularly redemptive experience of the divine presence. The Hebrew Bible testifies both to the general creative presence of the Spirit of God, which is necessary for the contingent existence of all creatures, and to intensified confrontations by or in the Spirit, which bring renewed life and joy. As the Psalms illustrate, the Spirit of God is the basis of life (104:29) and present in all places (139:7). At the same time, the Spirit is not simply

---

25. Cf. L. Ouspensky and V. Lossky, *The Meaning of Icons* (2d ed.; Crestwood, N.Y.: St. Vladimir's, 1999).

there: the poets still seek God's presence and long for a redemptive relation to the *Holy* Spirit (51:11). The Book of Job acknowledges a general dependence on the divine Spirit for life: "The spirit of God has made me, / and the breath of the Almighty gives me life" (33:4; cf. Genesis 1:2; Isaiah 44:3–4). Yet, in the same context, we see that the *ruach* of the Almighty also makes possible the gaining of specific wisdom and understanding (Job 32:8; cf. Exodus 31:3). The prophets of Israel were aware that the hope for new redeemed life depends on the specific active presence of the Spirit of the LORD. Ezekiel's vision of the dry bones that are granted breath (*ruach*) depicts the divine promise of new life: "I will put my spirit within you, and you shall live" (37:14).

It is important to note the difference in meaning between the Hebrew term *ruach* and the Greek term *pneuma* and to see how Paul and the other canonical authors refigure the meaning of both in light of the ministry, death, and resurrection of Jesus Christ. John Breck points out that "whereas *pneuma* denotes a natural physical or psychological force of divine origin, *ruach* signifies *the presence of divinity itself*. The Spirit of the Old Testament and of most Hellenistic Jewish writings is the personal manifestation of God within human life and history."[26] Two important developments between the Testaments affected the way in which the New Testament authors reshaped these terms.[27] First, the Dead Sea Scrolls indicate that in the Palestinian Judaism of this period, the term *ruach* was carried over into Israelite appropriation of the Zoroastrian dualism between the "spirit of truth" and the "spirit of falsehood." While the New Testament speaks of the Spirit of truth (e.g., John 15:26), this is not simply one of the cosmic powers in an eternal battle, but the Spirit of the living God who gives life to all things. A second important development was in Hellenistic Judaism, where the Greek concept of *pneuma* was altered as it came in contact with the Wisdom (*sophia*) literature of Israel. As it was linked to the *sophia* of the Book of Proverbs and other texts, *pneuma* came to be understood not as an abstract divine force (stoicism), but as the creative and redemptive presence of God (Proverbs 8:22–23; cf. Wisdom of Solomon 7:24–8:1).

Can we speak of the Holy Spirit as a person or as a face? Although the New Testament does not explicitly speak of the face of the Spirit, clearly the presence of the Spirit is essential to life itself as well as to redemption. Paul makes this clear in Romans: God's redemptive "love has been poured into our hearts through the Holy Spirit" (5:5). The "Spirit of life

26. "*Pneuma*, on the other hand, is never personified in Greek usage, nor does it ever acquire personal attributes or qualities"; J. Breck, *Spirit of Truth* (Crestwood, N.Y.: St. Vladimir's, 1991), 99.

27. For a detailed treatment of these developments, see A. I. C. Heron, *The Holy Spirit* (Philadelphia: Westminster, 1983), 23–38.

in Christ Jesus" (8:2) has set his readers "free from the law of sin and of death." He explains: "You are not in the flesh; you are in the Spirit, since the Spirit of God dwells in you" (8:9). This mutual indwelling is explicitly trinitarian and redemptive: "The Spirit of him who raised Jesus from the dead dwells in you. . . . [He] will give life to your mortal bodies also through his Spirit that dwells in you" (8:11). The Second Letter to the Corinthians also illuminates the constitutive role of the presence of the Spirit in the lives of believers: the letter of the law kills but "the Spirit gives life" (3:6). The "ministry of death" (3:7) that came through Moses had such a glory that the people could not look at Moses' face unveiled; "how much more will the ministry of the Spirit come in glory?" (3:8). The veil is removed for those who are linked to Christ, and they are being transformed "from one degree of glory to another; for this comes from the Lord" (3:18). The importance of the presence of the Spirit for the liberation of redemption is explicit: "Now the Lord is the Spirit, and where the Spirit of the Lord is, there is freedom" (3:17).

In 1 Corinthians 2:10–11 Paul makes an analogy between the Holy Spirit and the human spirit: "These things God has revealed to us through the Spirit; for the Spirit searches everything, even the depths of God. For what human being knows what is truly human except the human spirit that is within? So also no one comprehends what is truly God's except the Spirit of God." This searching dynamic makes us think of the inherent movement contained in the very idea of spirit (which is sometimes translated as breath or wind). John points out that the Spirit of God is not under our control, for no one knows where the Spirit blows (3:8). Nevertheless, the mysterious presence of the infinite divine Spirit is the source, condition, and goal of the searching of the human spirit. The Spirit is at work in Paul's facing of himself in Romans 9:1: "I am speaking the truth in Christ—I am not lying; my conscience confirms it by the Holy Spirit [lit., my conscience witnesses to me in the Holy Spirit]." Loder identifies five general steps in what he calls the "transformational logic" of the spirit: conflict, interlude for scanning, constructive act of imagination, release and openness, and interpretation. This logic characterizes all of the various arenas in which the human spirit searches, from scientific inquiry to psychotherapy to religious conversion.[28] The Spirit of God

---

28. Loder, *Transforming Moment*, 40. Loder's anthropology relies heavily on the work of nineteenth-century philosophical theologian Søren Kierkegaard, who wrote of the human self as spirit: "A human being is spirit. But what is spirit? Spirit is the self. But what is the self? The self is a relation that relates itself to itself or is the relation's relating itself to itself in the relation; the self is not the relation but is the relation's relating itself to itself"; *The Sickness unto Death* (trans. H. V. Hong and E. H. Hong; Princeton: Princeton University Press, 1980), 13. For Kierkegaard, the power that establishes this relation is the infinite presence of the eternal Spirit of God.

not only provides the conditions for self-facing in consciousness or self-consciousness, but also creates and upholds the conditions for the facing of other persons in community. The Christian church recognizes that its existence depends on the *koinōnia*-creating reality of the Spirit as Christ's presence in the world.[29] Being built together as "a dwelling place for God" (Ephesians 2:22) occurs "in the Spirit." The manifestations of the Spirit (1 Corinthians 12:7–11) make the church a *koinōnia* as believers become "one body" (12:12), baptized in "one Spirit" (12:13) for the common good.

As an Eastern Orthodox theologian, John Breck argues that it is appropriate to speak explicitly of "the face of the Spirit." He notes that "especially in Johannine tradition the image—the 'face' or person—of the Paraclete or Spirit of Truth is made visible, perceptible, as a direct reflection of Jesus' own personal traits and his revelatory, saving work."[30] The purpose of the presence of the Spirit is to lead persons to the face of Jesus, who draws them into relation with the Father: "The 'face' of the Spirit, like that of the Father, is revealed to us in the face of Jesus himself."[31] In another work, Breck acknowledges that "the name of the Spirit, like His image or 'face,' remains shrouded in darkness impenetrable to the intellect."[32] This is because, as the early church fathers insisted, "the Spirit is the only *hypostasis* or 'person' of the Trinity whose image or 'face' (*prosōpon*) is not revealed in another."[33] The Spirit is not personal in the same way that the Father and Son are personal; further, the Father and the Son have their own distinct ways of being person in relation. In Eastern Orthodox Pneumatology, the person of the Holy Spirit is the giver of uncreated grace, which is sometimes called the "energy" of the divine essence.[34]

The Christian tradition in the (Latin) West has typically had a weaker Pneumatology than the (Greek) Eastern church; the former is more hesitant to speak of the Holy Spirit as a third person of the Trinity. This is due in part because in the West the concept of person was defined (in the famous phrase of Boethius) as "an individual substance of a rational nature." If God is three persons in this sense, then tritheism seems unavoidable, because then we have three individual

---

29. Cf. P. Lehmann, *Ethics in a Christian Context* (New York: Harper & Row, 1963), 59.

30. J. Breck, "The Face of the Spirit," *Pro Ecclesia* 3 (1994): 167.

31. Ibid., 173.

32. Breck, *Spirit of Truth*, 1.

33. Ibid.

34. See, e.g., V. Lossky, *The Mystical Theology of the Eastern Church* (Crestwood, N.Y.: St. Vladimir's, 1998), 172–73. For a summary and analysis of these ideas and comparison with the Western tradition, see D. Reid, *Energies of the Spirit: Trinitarian Models in Eastern Orthodox and Western Theology* (Atlanta: Scholars Press, 1997).

substances. This is precisely, however, what the early church intended to avoid when it insisted that God is "one substance in three persons" (e.g., Tertullian). For many early Greek-speaking Christian theologians and especially for the fourth-century Cappadocian fathers, the concept of person had primacy over the concept of nature. For them, the source of the being and renewal of human persons is not an abstract divine nature, but the communion of the divine persons (Father, Son, and Spirit).[35]

The need to take Pneumatology more seriously in the West arose not only as a result of the renewal of Pentecostal and charismatic experience worldwide,[36] but also in response to the collapse of the Enlightenment dualism that canalized many early modern theological treatments of the role of the Holy Spirit in salvation. The harsh bifurcation between object and subject led to a separation between the objective work of Christ on the cross (using primarily legal metaphors) and the subjective work of the Spirit *after* a person is forgiven. The presence of the Spirit had little or no role in the decisive judicial act. Further, the general life-sustaining activity of the Spirit was often not connected to the new life actualized by the atoning death of Christ. The demise of this modernist subject/object dualism and the rise of more holistic concepts of human experience in late modernity provide an opportunity for Western theology to develop a more robust understanding of the objectivity of the person of the Spirit.

Brief reference to two Reformed theologians will suffice. Jürgen Moltmann touches on our theme of the face of God, arguing that it is "a symbol of God's commitment, the attention with which he looks at us, and his special presence. . . . God's 'shining countenance' is the source of the outpouring of the *Spirit* and of God's life, love and *blessing*."[37] This is not merely a subjective experience: "Christ's Spirit is our immanent power to live—God's Spirit is our transcendent space for living."[38] Michael Welker suggests that we speak of the "public person" of the Spirit that corresponds to the individual person Jesus Christ. The Spirit of God generates a "force field" of love, faith, and hope, cre-

35. Cf. K. P. Wesche, "'Mind' and 'Self' in the Christology of Saint Gregory the Theologian: Saint Gregory's Contribution to Christology and Christian Anthropology," *Greek Orthodox Theological Review* 39 (1994): 48. See also Breck, "Face of the Spirit," 174–75.

36. R. Shaull and W. Cesar, *Pentecostalism and the Future of the Christian Churches* (Grand Rapids: Eerdmans, 2000).

37. J. Moltmann, *The Source of Life* (trans. M. Kohl; Minneapolis: Fortress, 1997), 13 (emphasis added).

38. J. Moltmann, *The Spirit of Life* (trans. M. Kohl; Minneapolis: Fortress, 2001), 179. Moltmann explicitly critiques Boethius's substance-oriented definition of "person" and suggests that "the personhood of God the Holy Spirit is the loving, self-communicating, out-fanning and out-pouring presence of the eternal divine life of the triune God" (289).

ating the communion of the body of Christ through which God's grace is manifested publicly in the world. As the mediator of the fellowship of the church, the Spirit is not so much an "individual" as a "domain of resonance"—specifically the resonating domain of the same reality that took place in the individual Jesus Christ: "Real fleshly life is enabled by the Spirit and in the Spirit to be the place where God's glory is made present."[39]

The promised Holy Spirit is the manifestation of the divine countenance, bringing grace and peace to the community of God. The face of the Spirit unifies the community and opens up the future, granting space and time for loving fellowship. Based on the New Testament witness, then, we may articulate the Christian experience of the face of God as an evocative presence that calls persons to participate in the peaceful communion of the Son's facing of the Father in the Spirit. The Book of Acts makes clear the intrinsic link between the presence of the Holy Spirit and forgiveness. This is most explicit in Peter's Pentecost sermon in 2:38: "Repent . . . so that your sins may be forgiven; and you will receive the gift of the Holy Spirit." Peter calls his hearers to "repent . . . so that your sins may be wiped out, so that times of refreshing may come from the presence of the Lord" (3:19–20). Jesus had promised the Holy Spirit (1:5, 8), and on the day of Pentecost they are "filled" with the Holy Spirit (2:4), which fulfilled the divine promise to pour out the Spirit on all flesh (2:18; cf. Joel 2:28–32). Having "received from the Father the promise of the Holy Spirit" (Acts 2:33), they are opened up to new dimensions of fellowship (koinōnia; 2:42) and even "had all things in common (koina)" (2:44). A link is also implied when the Holy Spirit falls on Cornelius and the rest of Peter's listeners, as Peter says, "All the prophets testify about him that everyone who believes in him receives forgiveness of sins through his name" (10:43). Throughout the remainder of Acts, the Spirit of Christ is depicted as the presence of God's grace that transforms the structures of human facing through the in-breaking reality of divine forgiveness.

The Theological Significance of Forgiveness

Persons in contemporary Western culture still long for wholeness and salvation, but most can no longer accept ancient Greek or early

39. M. Welker, *God the Spirit* (trans. J. F. Hoffmeyer; Minneapolis: Fortress, 1994), 330. Although discussion continues on precisely how to speak of the person of the Spirit, we find a growing retrieval of the more robustly trinitarian understanding of the early church among leading theologians in the West. Cf. the proposal of Lutheran theologian R. Jenson, *Systematic Theology* (Oxford: Oxford University Press, 1997), 1.156–61.

modern conceptions of reality, which are presupposed in some theological formulations of the doctrine of forgiveness. Healing this theoretical and existential fracture requires fresh articulation of the gospel of forgiveness that connects to the real practice of facing each other every day. This is all the more important if forgiveness is at the center of the Christian religion.[40] Many discussions of forgiveness in early modernity were limited to an objective legal transaction that took place on the cross. That one does not subjectively feel forgiven is a different problem entirely. When forgiveness is confined to a formal juridical declaration, it does not immediately touch the material agony of shame and anger that crush real human life in community. When theology no longer connects to practice, we are compelled to examine Scripture more closely and to engage traditional proposals more critically. We may discover ways to liberate the Christian concept and experience of forgiveness from the domination of abstract judicial metaphors and thereby conserve the intuition of the living biblical tradition that forgiveness really changes lives, making persons whole and good.

In both the Hebrew Bible and the New Testament we can trace a trajectory in the development of the understanding of God: in light of the revelation of Jesus Christ in the power of the Holy Spirit, the ultimate statement is that God *is* love. Divine justice is not opposed to divine mercy, but is encompassed within and fulfilled by it. I suggest that the overarching meaning of forgiveness in Scripture is manifesting and sharing grace. To demonstrate this, I must display the broader understanding of forgiveness that emerges in the biblical witness.

Forgiveness in the Hebrew Bible

The most common Hebrew word translated as forgiveness in the Bible is *salah*, and it is used only with respect to God's activity. This term is usually rendered by the Greek phrase *hileōs einai* (to be merciful, gracious) in the Septuagint. The other popular term for forgiveness is *nasa*, which denotes "carrying" or "taking away." Occasionally humans are said to forgive another person in this sense,[41] but for the most part the Israelites are concerned about *divine* forgiveness. God is usually the agent of forgiveness, and the object of this agency is either

40. M. Marty suggests that Christianity = forgiveness in his essay "The Ethos of Christian Forgiveness," in *Dimensions of Forgiveness: Psychological Research and Theological Perspectives* (ed. E. L. Worthington Jr.; Philadelphia: Templeton Foundation, 1998), 11. C. Gestrich claims that "the whole of Christianity comes down to God granting the forgiveness of sins"; *The Return of Splendor* (trans. D. W. Bloesch; Grand Rapids: Eerdmans, 1997), 265.

41. For example, Joseph forgives his brothers (Genesis 50:17), and David forgives Nabal because of Abigail's petition (1 Samuel 25:28).

the people (when the meaning is "showing mercy") or sin (when the meaning is "taking away").

Many people imagine the God of the Hebrew Bible as a God of wrath, while the God of the New Testament is seen as a God of forgiveness. Although a cursory reading of the texts may appear to support this distinction, a closer look reveals a clear development in Israel's understanding of God's justice and mercy—a trajectory that continues in the New Testament. We must view the various stories about divine judgment and forgiveness in their appropriate context within the history of Israel's testimony about its ongoing experience of the LORD from the call of Abraham to the return from exile. In the early chapters of Genesis, the possibility of divine forgiveness is hardly considered. When Adam and Eve eat from the tree of the knowledge of good and evil, God is concerned that these beings might live forever, so they are cast out of Eden (3:22–24). Regret is identified as the primary emotion that provokes God to send the great flood to "blot out" (6:7) human beings who had turned to evil and wickedness. Noah alone is righteous before the LORD (7:1) but in contrast to later spiritual leaders, he apparently does not even think to ask God to forgive the people. The story of the tower of Babel (11:1–9) does not indicate that God had any hesitation once the attempt of the people to "make a name for [them]selves" was perceived. The LORD "came down to see" and expresses concern that "nothing that they propose to do will now be impossible for them." To keep this from happening, the people are immediately confused and scattered without any warning or opportunity to repent. These early anthropomorphic pictures of God are similar to the view of the gods among Israel's ancient neighbors: anxious, regretful, destructive, but not at all forgiving. It is important to recognize that these stories were written in the context of an ancient worldview in which divine forces were part of nature and geographically limited. Israel's experience of YHWH over time challenged these presuppositions.

With the call of Abram (later called Abraham) in Genesis 12, we have a radical new development. The covenant with Abraham is couched in the legal language of that era, but the material promise of faithfulness to the covenant introduces a new understanding of God. In several different genres of the Hebrew Bible, the LORD's grace and compassion toward the people of Israel (despite their sins) are explicitly connected to God's promise of covenant faithfulness (e.g., Micah 7:18, 20; 2 Kings 13:23; Deuteronomy 9:27). Later in the story of Abraham, we read that the sins of Sodom and Gomorrah led the LORD to move toward them with punishment and destruction. But Abraham comes near and intercedes for the city, urging forgiveness. He appeals to a sense of justice to which God ought to be obliged; "what is just" should outweigh the divine anger. "Suppose there are fifty righteous within the city; will you then sweep away the place and not forgive it for the fifty righteous who are in it? Far be it from you to do such a thing, to slay the righteous with the wicked. . . . Far be that from you! Shall not the Judge of all the earth do what is just?" (Genesis 18:24–25). Abraham holds God morally accountable, and eventually the LORD agrees not to destroy the city if ten righteous persons are found in it.

Later Moses appeals to God's covenant faithfulness when the people's experience leads them to perceive God as angry and ready to wipe them off the face of the earth. After they make the golden calf at Sinai, God is ready to destroy them but Moses pleads for divine forgiveness. The LORD plans to let his wrath burn hot and consume the people and make of Moses a great nation (Exodus 32:10). But Moses implores, "But now, if you will only forgive their sin—but if not, blot me out of the book you have written" (32:32; cf. Deuteronomy 9:27). Immediately after Moses secures God's forgiveness for the people, he expresses his longing to see the divine glory. Moses is told that no one can see the divine face and live; yet, God's goodness and glory will pass by him. After Moses ascends Mount Sinai, God proclaims "the name," passes before Moses, and proclaims:

> The LORD, the LORD,
> a God merciful and gracious,
> slow to anger,
> and abounding in steadfast love and faithfulness,
> keeping steadfast love for the thousandth generation,
> forgiving iniquity and transgression and sin,
> yet by no means clearing the guilty,
> but visiting the iniquity of the parents
> upon the children
> and the children's children,
> to the third and the fourth generation.
>
> —Exodus 34:6–7

Many biblical scholars consider this to be the most important statement of forgiveness in the Hebrew Bible.[42] One of the reasons for this judgment is that the influence of the formula may be traced throughout the rest of Israel's testimony, which suggests that it expresses something fundamental about their view of God.

42. Cf. T. M. Raitt, "Why Does God Forgive?" *Horizons in Biblical Theology* 13 (1991): 38–58 at 45.

Moses explicitly appeals to this divine proclamation when the people recoil and cower at the spies' report of giants in the land after forty years of wandering in the desert. The Lord had decided to "strike them with pestilence and disinherit them" and to make of Moses a new and greater nation (Numbers 14:12). Once again, Moses reminds God of his covenant promise at Sinai and quotes the Exodus 34 formula with minor variations:

> The LORD is slow to anger,
> and abounding in steadfast love,
> forgiving iniquity and transgression,
> but by no means clearing the guilty,
> visiting the iniquity of the parents
> upon the children
> to the third and the fourth generation.
> —Numbers 14:17–18

Moses then urges God: "Forgive the iniquity of this people according to the greatness of your steadfast love, just as you have pardoned this people, from Egypt even until now" (14:19). To this the Lord responds: "I do forgive, just as you have asked" (14:20).[43]

Even after the return from exile centuries later, Ezra appeals to the formula in the context of recounting God's faithfulness despite the people's disobedience: "But you are a God ready to forgive, gracious and merciful, slow to anger and abounding in steadfast love, and you did not forsake them" (Nehemiah 9:17). The new emphasis as well as the omissions in the restatement of the formula are unmistakable.

When the psalmists appropriate the Exodus 34 proclamation, they too feel free to emphasize mercy and grace, expressing divine forgiveness in new poetic ways:

> But you, O LORD, are a God merciful and gracious,
>   slow to anger and abounding in steadfast love and faithfulness.
> —Psalm 86:15

> The LORD is merciful and gracious,
>   slow to anger and abounding in steadfast love.
> He will not always accuse,
>   nor will he keep his anger forever.

43. Later Amos too (like Abraham and Moses) begs God to forgive (7:1–6); in this case, God's answer involves a relenting of the destruction of the land. Cf. D. F. O'Kennedy, "'It Shall Not Be': Divine Forgiveness in the Intercessory Prayers of Amos," *Old Testament Essays* 10 (1997): 92–108.

> He does not deal with us according to our sins,
>   nor repay us according to our iniquities.
>
> —Psalm 103:8–10

> The LORD is gracious and merciful,
>   slow to anger and abounding in steadfast love.
> The LORD is good to all,
>   and his compassion is over all that he has made.
>
> —Psalm 145:8–9

Other psalms are imprecatory, imploring God *not* to forgive the wicked, while still others express the writer's anxiety about *not* being forgiven (e.g., Psalm 79:9). Nevertheless, we see an increasing tendency to emphasize God's mercy and grace:

> For you, O LORD, are good and forgiving,
>   abounding in steadfast love to all who call on you.
>
> —Psalm 86:5

> If you, O LORD, should mark iniquities,
>   LORD, who could stand?
> But there is forgiveness with you,
>   so that you may be revered.
>
> —Psalm 130:3–4

Already in Deuteronomy 24:16 the second part of the Exodus 34 formula was being challenged. The penalty for the iniquities of parents should not be passed on to their children. Later in the prophecy of Ezekiel, the LORD explicitly contradicts those who think that the son should suffer for the iniquity of the father (18:14–20). This false belief is corrected by the LORD's insistence that one person should not be punished for another's sins (cf. Jeremiah 31:30a). By the time of the writing of the Book of Jonah, the Israelites had come to understand that the LORD is not just the God of one mountain, region, or even one country, but is the God of all the heavens and the earth.[44] Jonah's inability to hide from God outside of the land portrays this expansion of the concept of the divine. The author of Jonah also illustrates a new understanding of the nature of God when he appeals to the Exodus 34 formula, but gives it a significant interpretive twist: "For I knew that

---

44. This is the move from henotheism to monotheism. Jonah may have been written as late as the third century B.C.E.

you are a gracious God and merciful, slow to anger, and abounding in steadfast love, and ready to relent from punishing" (Jonah 4:2).

This statement and a parallel passage in Joel 2:13 ("return to the LORD, your God, / for he is gracious and merciful, / slow to anger, and abounding in steadfast love, / and relents from punishing"), observes Harold C. Washington, "intensify the earlier formula's emphasis on mercy by replacing the terms of retribution in Exod 34:7 ('yet by no means clearing the guilty . . .'), with the statement that God 'relents from punishing.'" Here, notes Washington, "forgiveness does not simply moderate judgment but overcomes it completely."[45] This may be a slight overstatement since the consequences of one's actions must often still be faced even when grace and mercy are extended. Forgiveness excludes judgment only when one understands forgiveness *merely* as a legal or financial transaction. The point, however, is clear: the Israelites increasingly came to view God as essentially gracious.

How is forgiveness related to the presence (or hiding) of the face of God as the Israelites turn away from God to idolatry and wickedness? Are there conditions for divine forgiveness? Throughout the Hebrew Bible, forgiveness is experienced by the people as they turned toward God. Turning to the LORD seems to be the summation of the prophetic message.[46] Those who turn are given or promised forgiveness (e.g., 2 Kings 17:13–14; cf. Jeremiah 3:11–14; 35:15; Malachi 3:7; Zechariah 1:4; Ezekiel 18:30–32), while those who do not turn from their evil will not experience forgiveness (cf. Isaiah 22:14; Jeremiah 5:1–9; Lamentations 3:42; Hosea 1:6). Earlier in the sacrificial cultus, forgiveness was linked to the fulfillment of the conditions of the law (cf. Leviticus 4–5). Although during some periods of Israel's history, they understood divine forgiveness as primarily related to the sacrificial system, at the same time they were also aware that forgiveness is not limited to or controlled by the cultic ritual.[47] Sometimes God forgives without a sacrifice (e.g., when Moses pleads for the people), and not every sin could be dealt with by a sacrificial atonement (Numbers 15:22–36).

It becomes clear by the time of the classical prophets that these conditions are not mechanical. If the attitude of repentance is not present, sacrifices do not mediate forgiveness (e.g., Amos 5:21–24; Isaiah 1:11–12, 14–17; Hosea 6:6). Increasingly, the Israelites realized

45. H. C. Washington, "The Lord's Mercy Endures Forever: Toward a Post-Shoah Reading of Grace in the Hebrew Scriptures," *Interpretation* 54 (2000): 135–45 at 141.

46. Cf. W. Eichrodt, *Theology of the Old Testament* (trans. J. A. Baker; Philadelphia, Westminster, 1967), 2.466–67.

47. Even in the context of the tabernacle and temple sacrifices, mercy was central: the "place" of atonement was called the "mercy" seat.

that God is interested in the heart, in the embodied practices of love in community, not in the abstract accounting of legal codes. All of this suggests that salvation is about more than a forensic application of forgiveness. Yes, human turning to God is part of the experience of forgiveness, but this is not the reason for forgiveness—it is not the cause of a legal effect. Israel discovers the broader explanation for divine forgiveness as it recognizes mercy (*rahum*), grace (*hannun*), and steadfast loving-kindness (*hesed*) as essential attributes of God. All three of these characteristics of the LORD appear in the Exodus 34:6–7 pronouncement and are taken up in various ways throughout the Hebrew Bible.[48]

It is clear, however, that Israel's conception of forgiveness included a transactional element even if it was not their primary focus. It is particularly important to account for the idea of a "substitute" for sin, which became so important for many later Christian theologies of the atonement. In Leviticus, a scapegoat (16:22) "takes on" or "carries away" (*nasa*) the sins of the people. As high priest, Aaron shall "take on himself" the guilt of the Israelites (Exodus 28:38; cf. Leviticus 10:17; Numbers 18:1). Neither the priest nor the scapegoat, however, are being punished for or making a payment *instead of* the sinner(s). Rather, their "bearing" represents the removal of the sin and its damaging effects so that communal health may be restored. These rituals signify the forgiveness of sins by God, who takes the load off of sinners so that they may be freed into righteous relations. The Book of Isaiah challenges the idea that God delighted in sacrifices (1:11–12) and speaks of a Suffering Servant who bears (*nasa*) the iniquities of us all:

> Surely he has borne our infirmities
>   and carried our diseases.
> . . . .
> And the LORD has laid on him
>   the iniquity of us all.
> . . . .
>   The righteous one, my servant, shall make many righteous,
>   and he shall bear their iniquities.
> . . . .
> Yet he bore the sin of many,
>   and made intercession for the transgressors.
>   —Isaiah 53:4, 6, 11–12

48. For exegetical analyses of these key terms, see Raitt, "Why Does God Forgive?"; and G. Müller-Fahrenholz, "Turn to the God of Mercy: New Perspectives on Reconciliation and Forgiveness," *Ecumenical Review* 50 (1998): 196–204.

While some Christian theologians interpret this bearing in the sense of a sacrificial substitute who is punished in the place of another, others question whether the text can bear this interpretation. At the very least, we must recognize that the English word *substitute* carries connotations that are foreign to the Hebrew concept of *nasa*. In the Hebrew Bible, the idea of taking the place of another (*Stellvertretung*),[49] whether applied to the scapegoat, to the normal sacrificial process, or to the place-taking of the Suffering Servant, signifies the enabling of particular persons at the "place" of their pain and alienation.[50] I will return to this issue in the next chapter.

The classical prophets anticipate a future in which the divine mercy, grace, and steadfast love will call the people back into a new and redemptive relation to God; this anticipated forgiveness will transform the real dynamics of their mutual facing of one another in community. This forgiveness will overcome shame and open up the community to a more intimate knowledge of God:

> I will establish with you an everlasting covenant. . . . I will establish my covenant with you, and you shall know that I am the LORD, in order that you may remember and be confounded, and never open your mouth again because of your shame, when I forgive you all that you have done, says the Lord GOD.
>
> —Ezekiel 16:60–63

> I will make a new covenant with the house of Israel and the house of Judah. . . . I will put my law within them, and I will write it on their hearts. . . . No longer shall they teach one another, or say to each other, "Know the LORD," for they shall all know me, from the least of them to the greatest, says the LORD; for I will forgive their iniquity, and remember their sin no more.
>
> —Jeremiah 31:31, 33–34

In both of these quotations, we get a clear sense that divine forgiveness takes the initiative and enables human repentance. Humans are depen-

---

49. For an introduction to the discussion of German *Stellvertretung* (place-taking), which is broader than the English *substitution* or *representation*, see D. P. Bailey, "Concepts of *Stellvertretung* in the Interpretation of Isaiah 53" and "The Suffering Servant: Recent Tübingen Scholarship on Isaiah 53," in *Jesus and the Suffering Servant: Isaiah 53 and Christian Origins* (ed. W. H. Bellinger Jr. and W. R. Farmer; Harrisburg, Pa.: Trinity, 1998), 223–59.

50. N. Hoffmann, *Sühne: Zur Theologie der Stellvertretung* (Einsiedeln: Johannes Verlag, 1981), argues that the atoning work of Jesus Christ in the New Testament should be understood as the Son (through the Spirit) making a "place" for humanity to be in relation to the Father. See especially pp. 51–53, 68–81, and 94–97.

dent on the initiative of divine grace, and this dependence takes shape as an orientation toward a promised future in which forgiveness heals the community.[51]

We have seen a trajectory in the Hebrew Bible that moves from an early interpretation of God as not at all forgiving, to a picture of God as easily angered but open to forgiving, to a vision of an essentially merciful, gracious, and loving God who promises the blessing of full forgiveness. This trajectory is taken up and transformed in the New Testament texts as they witness to the manifestation of divine forgiveness in Jesus Christ through the power of the Spirit.

Forgiveness in the New Testament

Let us briefly overview the basic teaching of the New Testament on forgiveness.[52] Jesus of Nazareth, argues Hannah Arendt, was "the discoverer of the role of forgiveness in the realm of human affairs."[53] It may be too much to claim that Jesus discovered the role of social forgiveness, since prophets and sages before him were also aware of this phenomenon, but clearly he transformed its meaning and significance in a way that has had a profound effect on human history.

If we examine the books of the New Testament in roughly chronological order, once again we find a trajectory that moves toward imagining forgiveness in ways that transcend purely legal or financial metaphors. Mark, the earliest of the gospels, clearly links the arrival of Jesus with the Hebrew prophets' anticipation of the promise of forgiveness and the coming of the Messiah.[54] Unlike the longer introductions of the other gospels, Mark quotes from the prophets and then

51. Cf. Jeremiah 33:7–9; 50:20; Isaiah 33:24; 55:3–7; and especially Micah 7:18–19:
> Who is a God like you, pardoning iniquity
> and passing over the transgression
> of the remnant of your possession?
> He does not retain his anger forever,
> because he delights in showing clemency.
> He will again have compassion upon us;
> he will tread our iniquities under foot.
> You will cast all our sins
> into the depths of the sea.

52. The idea of forgiveness is often present even if the term is not used, as in the parable of the prodigal son. For the sake of space, our focus will be primarily on the use of the Greek terms *aphiēmi* and *charizomai*, although we will attend to their connection to other key terms, such as grace, release, and reconciliation. For a more detailed treatment of the term *forgiveness* in the New Testament, see the classic work by V. Taylor, *Forgiveness and Reconciliation* (London: Macmillan, 1952), and the more recent references in the footnotes below.

53. H. Arendt, *The Human Condition* (Garden City: Doubleday, 1959), 214.

54. Cf. P. G. Bolt, "Jesus and Forgiveness in Mark's Gospel," *Reformed Theological Review* 57 (1998): 53–69.

simply states that John the Baptist "appeared" and proclaimed a baptism of repentance for (or into or toward) the forgiveness of sins (1:4). Jesus heals a paralytic and tells him that his sins are forgiven (2:5). In response to the scribes' antagonism toward him, Jesus announces that "people will be forgiven for their sins and whatever blasphemies they utter," except against the Holy Spirit (3:28–29). Of the two Greek terms translated "forgive" in the New Testament, Mark prefers *aphiēmi*, which literally means "to send (or set) away."

In the Septuagint, *aphiēmi* was used to render not only the Hebrew term *nasa* (as we would expect), but also *salah* and *kipper* (to cover, make atonement for). In the New Testament the semantic range of *aphiēmi*, especially when it occurs in the phrase *aphesis (tōn) hamartiōn* (forgiveness of sins), generally covers what we call "forensic" forgiveness.[55] As in the Hebrew Bible, however, this meaning does not have a totalitarian role, but freely interacts with other expressions of redemption. For example, it is in connection with healing that Jesus announces the forgiveness of the paralytic; this reminds us of Psalm 103:2–3: "Bless the LORD, O my soul, / and do not forget all his benefits— / who forgives all your iniquity, / who heals all your diseases." The Book of James will later also make this connection: "The prayer of faith will save the sick, and the Lord will raise them up; and anyone who has committed sins will be forgiven. Therefore confess your sins to one another, and pray for one another, so that you may be healed" (5:15–16).

The other Synoptic Gospels emphasize even more strongly the role of forgiveness in the experience of fellowship with God and with one another. In Matthew, we find a close relation between divine and human forgiveness, which are linked together with the coming of the kingdom of heaven as it impacts life on earth. The petition "and forgive us our debts, / as we also have forgiven our debtors" is preceded in Matthew's version of the Lord's Prayer by the request for God's kingdom to be present on earth "as it is in heaven" (6:9–13). Luke's shorter version of the prayer[56] makes essentially the same point, and

55. According to F. W. Keene, the forgiveness of sins "takes on an implication of a release from sin (or from the penalty of sinning) or a release from debt; it does not have an implication of a religious or a cultic cleansing"; "Structures of Forgiveness in the New Testament," in *Violence against Women and Children* (ed. C. J. Adams and M. M. Fortune; New York: Continuum, 1995), 124.

56. Luke's shorter version (11:2–4) reads as follows:
> He said to them, "When you pray, say:
> Father, hallowed be your name.
>> Your kingdom come.
>> Give us each day our daily bread.
>> And forgive us our sins,
>>> for we ourselves forgive everyone indebted to us.
>> And do not bring us to the time of trial."

he also reports Jesus' forthright saying: "Forgive, and you will be forgiven" (6:37). Although Mark does not contain the prayer itself, he does include the following instructions: "Whenever you stand praying, forgive, if you have anything against anyone; so that your Father in heaven may also forgive you your trespasses" (11:25). The Matthean parable of the unforgiving slave begins with the phrase "the kingdom of heaven may be compared to . . ." (18:23). Even more vividly than the Lord's Prayer, this story demonstrates the essential connection between receiving divine forgiveness and manifesting forgiveness to one's neighbors. In part 3 Steve and I will examine these passages and several others in conjunction with some contemporary therapeutic case studies.

Are there conditions to divine forgiveness in the New Testament? In the preaching of John the Baptist, repentance is linked to forgiveness (Mark 1:4), and Jesus takes up the call to repentance (1:15), although his primary concern is for people to enter the kingdom of God (which implies forgiveness in some sense). The risen Christ tells the disciples: "Thus it is written, that the Messiah is to suffer and to rise from the dead on the third day, and that repentance and forgiveness of sins is to be proclaimed in his name to all nations, beginning from Jerusalem" (Luke 24:46–47). In the early apostolic proclamation, the link between repenting and forgiveness is even more explicit. On the day of Pentecost, in response to his listeners' question "what should we do?" Peter tells them to "repent, and be baptized every one of you in the name of Jesus Christ so that your sins may be forgiven; and you will receive the gift of the Holy Spirit" (Acts 2:38). Later, in his defense to the high priest after a night in prison, Peter says of Jesus that "God exalted him at his right hand as Leader and Savior that he might give repentance to Israel and forgiveness of sins" (5:31). Rebuking Simon, who had offered money for control of God's gift of the Spirit, Peter exclaims: "Repent therefore of this wickedness of yours, and pray to the Lord that, if possible, the intent of your heart may be forgiven you" (8:22). A similar connection is implied by the voice out of the light that knocked Saul of Tarsus off of his horse and called him to the Gentiles: "To open their eyes so that they may turn from darkness to light and from the power of Satan to God, so that they may receive forgiveness of sins and a place among those who are sanctified by faith in me" (Acts 26:18). In these cases, the term *aphiēmi* or *aphesis* is consistently used.

The idea that repentance is a condition for forgiveness sounded like "salvation by works" to many Protestant theologians, and these passages are troubling for those who want to insist on salvation by grace alone. It is interesting that Augustine, famous for his polemic against the Pelagian call for good works, insisted (e.g., *City of God* 21.27) that

the forgiveness of others is a condition for experiencing divine forgiveness. As we will see below, so did Martin Luther and John Calvin!
Perhaps the trouble is not the passages themselves, but a hermeneutic
that conflates salvation with a forensically applied concept of forgiveness. This in turn leads to a view of grace that is also imprisoned in
the categories of legislative clemency. Rather than giving up on the
doctrine of salvation by grace alone, we need to explore the possibility
that both salvation and grace in the New Testament are broader than
the legal, mechanical, and individualistic soteriological concepts that
have so deeply shaped large streams of Protestant thought. Although
aphiēmi and *aphesis* continue to register an effect,[57] in later books of
the New Testament more general terms for salvation are increasingly
emphasized,[58] and another Greek word for forgiveness (*charizomai*)
comes to the fore.

Paul in particular prefers *charizomai*, which literally means "to
manifest grace." This is not surprising for the apostle of grace! In the
Pauline literature, both divine and human forgiveness are about sharing grace (*charis*) with the other in a way that evokes joy (*chara*) and
thanksgiving (*eucharistia*). The community of God is created and upheld by the presence of divine grace, which is manifested as believers
forgive one another and serve one another with the gifts (*charisma*) of
the Spirit. The term *charizomai* is not always translated forgiveness
because it has a broader semantic range. For example, it can refer to
the bestowal of a gift (1 Corinthians 2:12; Romans 8:32), and it often
implies release (Acts 3:14). In ancient Greece, *charis* was commonly

57. The Book of Hebrews, which describes forgiveness in Christ by comparing it to
the Jewish sacrificial system, naturally uses the term *aphesis*. The difficulties, however,
in interpreting the author's intention in linking Jesus' death and the "taking away" of
sin are notorious. On the one hand "it is impossible for the blood of bulls and goats to
take away sins" (10:4), but on the other hand "without the shedding of blood there is no
forgiveness of sins" (9:22). This latter phrase is probably a popular proverb that should
not be taken as a universal condition for forgiveness, since this was not universally true
even in the Hebrew Bible (e.g., offerings of grain or the petitions of Moses). The main
point is that Jesus "remove[d] sin" (9:26). Besides the passages in Hebrews, the Greek
terms *thyō* (to sacrifice, offer) and *thysia* (sacrifice, offering) are used twice to picture
what happened in the life and death of Jesus (1 Corinthians 5:6–8; Ephesians 5:1–2).
Other uses of these terms are obviously metaphorical, referring to Paul or his readers
(Philippians 2:17; Romans 12:1).

58. Other terms for salvation that move beyond legal and financial metaphors are
much more common than *aphiēmi*. Derivatives of *sōzō* (to rescue, liberate, save) and
sōtēr (savior, deliverer), e.g., occur almost two hundred times. The semantic range of
these terms incorporates the ideas of safely preserving, healing, and delivering (e.g.,
John 4:42; Acts 4:11–12; Romans 1:16; 1 Corinthians 1:18; Philippians 3:20–21;
1 Timothy 1:15; 2:3–4; 2 Peter 1:11). See also the common use of liberation-oriented
terms like those derived from *lyō* (to loose, untie, set free, release; e.g., Matthew 20:27–
28; Luke 1:68; 2:38; 24:21; 1 Timothy 2:3–6; Hebrews 9:11–15).

attributed to a person or work of art that evoked a response of joy and gratitude. A person elevated by true joy is full, complete, wrapped up in the response to the source of grace, whether God (Romans 15:13) or others (Philemon 7). Here forgiveness has a surplus of meaning that overflows the boundaries of transactional metaphors. Paul is focused on the dynamic gracious divine presence that heals the anger and shame that block peaceful life in community through redemptive forgiveness. That the Greek term *charizomai* is broader and can incorporate the meaning of *aphiēmi* is indicated in the story of the woman who anoints Jesus' feet with her tears; in the parable told to Simon the Pharisee, *charizomai* is used to speak of the creditor's cancellation of the debt (Luke 7:42–43).

Paul occasionally uses the term *aphiēmi*,[59] but his main concern is to testify to the reality of divine grace, which actually transforms personal life in community so that righteousness and justice are manifested in practical ways. Paul's tendency to eclipse the pharisaic emphasis on judicial or transactional forgiveness may have arisen out of his own experience of the deleterious effects of religious life under the law.[60] In the Pauline writings, juridical concepts of forgiveness are subsumed into a larger picture of life "in Christ." The main point of the gospel is that salvation comes through the real presence of divine grace in community:

Anyone whom you forgive, I also forgive. What I have forgiven, if I have forgiven anything, has been for your sake in the presence of Christ.

—2 Corinthians 2:10

And be kind to one another, tenderhearted, forgiving one another, as God in Christ has forgiven you.

—Ephesians 4:32

59. Paul uses *aphiēmi* in a quotation of Psalm 32:1–2 found in Romans 4:7–8. Luke reports the following statement of Paul at the synagogue at Perga: "Let it be known to you therefore, my brothers, that through this man forgiveness (*aphesis*) of sins is proclaimed to you; by this Jesus everyone who believes is set free (*dikaioutai*) from all those sins from which you could not be freed by the law of Moses" (Acts 13:38–39). Even here forgiveness has to do with freedom from those things that bind human life, not merely an acquittal from punishment. Paul's interest is in the actual release of persons into a life of righteousness (*dikaiosunē*). The only other occurrences of the *aphiēmi* word group used to connote forgiveness in the Pauline literature are found in the formula "forgiveness (*aphesis*) of sins" in the context of listing various metaphors for salvation (Ephesians 1:7–8; Colossians 1:13–14).

60. This is the rationale for the paucity of Paul's uses of *aphiēmi* given by J. D. G. Dunn, *The Theology of Paul the Apostle* (Grand Rapids: Eerdmans, 1998), 327.

And when you were dead in trespasses and the uncircumcision of your flesh, God made you alive together with him, when he forgave us all our trespasses.

—Colossians 2:13

Bear with one another and, if anyone has a complaint against another, forgive each other; just as the Lord has forgiven you, so you also must forgive.

—Colossians 3:13

Charizomai is consistently used in all of these texts. Forgiveness in the Pauline literature has primarily to do with relationships, and this qualitative concern seems to be the goal of any dealings with the "quantum" of sin.[61] Yes, God "reckons" faith as righteousness (Romans 4:5), but this is not the reckoning of blind justice—it is based on the real righteousness manifested in Christ and those bound to him in faith (3:21–26), as an "accounting" of those who are being made righteous through Christ (5:19; 8:29–30) and are alive in the Spirit "because of righteousness" (8:10). The creative and healing address of the justifying divine Word both reckons and makes righteous. Paul's understanding of forgiveness is not primarily a decision marked on a legal or financial balance sheet; it is the real presence of divine grace that heals human relations. In both divine and human forgiveness, we are dealing with the reconciling intentionality of grace. This is why Paul so commonly describes salvation more broadly in terms of reconciliation.[62]

It is interesting that the word *forgiveness* appears only three times in the writings of John, which are generally considered among the latest in the New Testament canon. Only one passage in the Gospel of John deals with forgiveness: "Jesus said to them again, 'Peace be with you. As the Father has sent me, so I send you.' When he had said this, he breathed on them and said to them, 'Receive the Holy Spirit. If you forgive the sins of any, they are forgiven them; if you retain the sins of any, they are retained'" (20:21–23). Although *aphiēmi* is used here, John's concern is with the operation of grace among believers in the community. In contrast to Matthew's version of Jesus' giving of the "keys to the kingdom," which focuses on the power of a single leader

61. Cf. C. F. D. Moule, "The Theology of Forgiveness," in Moule's *Essays in New Testament Interpretation* (Cambridge: Cambridge University Press, 1982), 250–60.

62. *Katallassō* (to reconcile) and *katallagē* (reconciliation) are among Paul's favorite terms for the goal of divine grace (e.g., Romans 5:10–11; 2 Corinthians 5:17–21; cf. Ephesians 2:15–18; Colossians 1:19–22). Reconciliation means the restoration of good relations between two or more parties. The factors that produce enmity or block relationship must be removed in order for the unity of atonement to be actualized.

(Peter) to bind or loose sins,[63] John's version emphasizes that all the disciples ("you" plural) have the responsibility for forgiving sins.[64] Forgiveness is a manifestation of the peace that comes from life together in the Holy Spirit.

In his first epistle, John uses *aphiēmi* in two places: once to emphasize its connection to being cleansed from unrighteousness (1:9) and again to underline the importance of the name of Jesus Christ, through whom believers are able to walk in the light (2:12). These statements are embedded in John's larger exhortation to the "beloved" to rejoice in their fellowship with God and one another and to live out their faith through self-giving love. These statements are also important because they occur in the context of John's use of the term *hilasmos* (1 John 2:2; 4:10), which has evoked significant exegetical controversy. These texts are sometimes used to buttress views of salvation in which Jesus (as a human) pays a debt or provides legal satisfaction to God. The other important use is Romans 3:25, where Paul speaks of Christ Jesus as a *hilastērion* "put forward" by God. These terms are related to the Hebrew ideas of the place of atonement or mercy seat (cf. *hileōs*, gracious or merciful). If one thinks of the *hilastērion* as something primarily directed toward the offended party (i.e., God), it will be translated "propitiation." If one thinks of it as directed by God toward that which blocks reconciliation (i.e., sin), the translation "expiation" makes more sense. The Romans passage clearly states that the gift of grace in Christ was put forward by God, and 1 John 4:9–10 speaks of God's sending the Son "so that we might live." The immediate context of 2:2 expresses concern that believers fully experience abiding in God and loving each other as God has loved them.

It is also in this epistle that we find the ultimate theological definition of the divine nature: "God is love" (1 John 4:8). Forensic applications of forgiveness are illuminative, but they are slowly subsumed by (not destroyed but taken up into) a more robust and dynamic understanding of salvation. Overall, then, the whole of Scripture leads us toward an understanding of divine forgiveness as manifesting grace and of human forgiveness as sharing in that grace. This trajectory provides a new opportunity for presenting and living out forgiveness in ways that can transcend the limits of legal and financial metaphors.

63. Cf. Matthew 16:17–19, where the power is given to Peter ("you" singular). Matthew does not use the term *forgiveness*, and he may have been making a connection to rabbinic literature, which commonly used the ideas of binding and loosing to describe the authority of the rabbi.

64. Cf. P. N. Anderson, *The Christology of the Fourth Gospel* (Valley Forge, Pa.: Trinity, 1996), 239.

Forgiveness in the Christian Tradition

The church has not always taken advantage of this opportunity; in fact, some streams of the Christian tradition moved back toward primarily forensic applications of the term *forgiveness*. A full examination of the development of the theological concept of forgiveness is beyond the scope of this chapter; my more modest goal is to outline the major factors contributing to those formulations of the doctrine that have come under heaviest scrutiny in modern times. It is important to realize that in the first few centuries after the death of the apostles, the texts that comprise what we now call the New Testament had not yet been officially canonized. Some of the early church fathers did not have access to all of the texts (or perhaps only translations), and their concepts of forgiveness were deeply shaped by the Hebrew Bible as well. The importance of forgiveness as a central tenet of Christian faith was solidified early in the history of the church. This is evident from the last article of the Apostles' Creed: "I believe in the Holy Ghost, the holy catholic church, the communion of saints, the forgiveness of sins, the resurrection of the body, and the life everlasting. Amen."

Although the majority of patristic writers held "Christ as Victor" or "Christ as Healer" models of the atonement, by the second century C.E. we find a movement among some Latin-speaking theologians (e.g., Tertullian) to integrate Roman concepts of justice into Christian soteriology. A key concept in Roman law was the demand for satisfaction to be made to the offended party before "forgiveness" could be granted. Alongside the incorporation of this dominant cultural and philosophical view of jurisprudence into the Christian doctrine of forgiveness, the practice of penance developed. By the early third century, we can trace the emergence of an increasingly common distinction among theologians (e.g., Clement of Alexandria) between the forgiveness that comes with Baptism and the forgiveness that believers may obtain for postbaptismal sins by engaging in specific acts of mercy. Over time, specific rules were developed and institutionalized; particular penitential activities were satisfactory for (balanced out) particular sinful activities. For the most egregious sins, reparation was extremely difficult. In most cases, the penitent had to confess the sin in public before the bishop and then follow the prescribed order of penance.[65]

65. For an accessible overview of the history of the sacrament of confession, see J. Forest, *Confession: Doorway to Forgiveness* (Maryknoll, N.Y.: Orbis, 2002). Cf. the more detailed treatment of P. E. Fink, "History of the Sacrament of Reconciliation," in *Alternative Futures for Worship*, vol. 4: *Reconciliation* (ed. P. E. Fink; Collegeville, Minn.: Liturgical Press, 1987), 73–89.

Only after satisfactory penance had been carried out or adequate reparation had been made could a person receive forgiveness and be welcomed back to the Eucharist—a serious matter since grace (and so salvation) is mediated through this sacrament. Penance could last for weeks, months, or years and typically involved fasting, weeping, and serving the poor. As the power of bishops grew in ecclesiastical governance, eventually only they could absolve sins. This was accomplished by the laying on of hands, but only after full penance had been completed. After the church became the official religion of the Roman Empire in the fourth century, some bishops argued that those who had failed to remain firm during times of persecution should not be forgiven; no penance could provide a counterweight for apostasy. Donatus was the leading voice against forgiveness in such cases. Augustine played a crucial role in this debate, and eventually he prevailed: given the appropriate satisfaction of the formal procedures demonstrating true repentance, such persons could be absolved and receive the Eucharist. The political issues involved here led to the strengthening of the bishop's role in forgiveness.

Augustine distinguished between the forgiveness (or remission) of original sin, which occurred at Baptism, and the forgiveness of actual sins committed after Baptism, which was mediated through other sacraments. This strong distinction emerged out of his reflection on infant Baptism. He did not think that a baby could have committed any actual sins. Since, however, Baptism in fact remits sins, the infant must be washed of something. Augustine argued that the baptismal waters cleanse children of the original sin which they had inherited from Adam (*On the Merits and Forgiveness of Sins* 1.39). Although the law of sin (concupiscence) has not yet resulted in actual sins, unbaptized infants are implicated as guilty and as "children of wrath" and condemned, even if they die in infancy (2.4). Augustine believed that in order to receive divine forgiveness for actual sins repentance was necessary. This was not merely an abstract theological belief; it emerged out of his experience of weeping over his own iniquity, as he tells us in his *Confessions* (1.5). Augustine describes his bitter contrition after reading the psalmist's cries for forgiveness; in the midst of repentance, he hears a voice: "Take up and read" (8.12). After reading Scripture, he turned to Christianity.

By the fifth century, Christianity was well entrenched as the dominant religion in the empire, and the process of penance had been formalized into an "Order of Penitents." These persons often wore plain clothing ("assumed the habit"), and their confession and weeping had a regular place during the public liturgy. Not until 459 was the demand that penitents confess in public laid aside by Pope Leo I. Meanwhile, monasteries had begun to emerge, and some of the same penitential practices were carried over into the lives of these communities. It was in these monastic settings that the practice of private confession was developed: younger monks would confess their sins to the elders responsible for communal life. Over time this practice was adopted more broadly in the church as a whole and slowly became institutionalized. By the end of the first millennium, private confession was a central part of church life, but one thing had not changed: the penitent was not forgiven until penance had been completed. These formal rules worked both ways, however, as the eleventh-century story about Pope Gregory VII and Holy Roman Emperor Henry IV illustrates so well. Henry stood barefoot outside the pope's lodgings for three days, and although the pope did not want to forgive him he was eventually compelled to do so because Henry had completed the appropriate penance. Ironically, this incident shows Henry's power to manipulate the system more than it does the pope's power to determine who receives forgiveness.

The concept of satisfaction plays an enormous role in Saint Anselm's theory of atonement. This eleventh-century theologian set out to prove rationally that it is unfitting for God simply to forgive without the full and proper payment for all human sin (*Why God Became Man*, Book I). Here legal metaphors again come to the fore, but the forensic application in this case is not expressed in terms of classical Roman jurisprudence (as with Tertullian) but in terms of the legal customs of Anselm's medieval world of knights and castles. Lawbreakers had to pay back the lord of the land, financially or through slave labor, or be punished: *aut satisfactio aut poena*. It was necessary that either satisfaction or punishment occur because a legal infraction was a threat to the honor of the lord, who was responsible for maintaining the balance of the social structures. It would be unfitting for a lord simply to forgive, even if he wanted to, because his honor would be challenged and the stability of society threatened. Satisfactory payment merited reinstatement into one's previous place in the social order. This transactional emphasis in atonement theory fit well with the penitential system of the church. As the Middle Ages progressed, the requirement of an extended period of penance between confession and absolution was dissolved, and they occurred in succession. The appropriate penance was, however, still required after leaving the confessional. It is only after Anselm applied the Teutonic concept of satisfaction (which sometimes involved financial reparation) to soteriology that the purchase of indulgences was initiated for the payment of nonmortal sins.

In the thirteenth century, Thomas Aquinas strengthened the distinction between the sacrament of Baptism, which is for the forgiveness of original sin, and the other sacraments, especially penance, which are remedies for washing away postbaptismal sins (*Summa Contra Gentiles* 4.72.1). In this context, Thomas also explicitly affirms the need for satisfaction—the fulfillment of an obligation or the payment of the penalty—before the person receives absolution (4.72.14). Thomas also outlined the rationale for having seven sacraments (*Summa Theologica* 3.65), which are necessary for salvation (3.61) insofar as they are "causes of grace" (3.62). By the fourteenth century, private confession had become perhaps the most important sacrament after Baptism; it was the dominant expression of continued life in the church and the reception of divine forgiveness. After the Protestant Reformation, many of the abuses of the system were acknowledged and the Council of Trent (1545 63) not only developed new guidelines, but also emphasized that confession is not just about isolated individuals, but about life in community.

Much like Augustine, Martin Luther experienced deep misery over his sin, and it took a long time for him to feel assurance of his forgiveness. Assurance came only with the sixteenth-century Reformer's rediscovery of the Pauline doctrine of justification by faith. God's free gift of justification is by Christ alone, by grace alone, by the word alone, and by faith alone. It is important to note that Luther was not against the sacrament of confession (nor against penance per se), but protested against the abuses of the system and particularly the selling of indulgences by the Roman church during his time. For Luther, the forgiveness of sins is mediated through the sacraments as well as through the gospel word of promise. In the context of discussing the "sacrament of the altar" in his Small Catechism (1529), Luther asks, "What is the benefit of such eating and drinking?" to which he expects the answer: "We are told in the words *for you* [1 Corinthians 11:24] and *for the forgiveness of sins* [Matthew 26:28]. By these words the forgiveness of sins, life, and salvation are given to us in the sacrament, for where there is forgiveness of sins, there are also life and salvation."[66]

Luther's main concern was to insist that God's gracious justification cannot be merited or bought—otherwise these categories of the "law" control "grace." He did use the idea of penal satisfaction as well as other images and themes to depict the atonement. Luther emphasized anew the patristic model of Christ as victor over the devil. Sometimes "satisfaction" and "Christus Victor" expressions are held together in the same passage.[67] However, Luther disliked the term *satisfaction*: he preferred not to allow it "in our schools or on the lips of our preachers, but would rather send it back to the judges, advocates, and hang-

---

66. Book of Concord, p. 352.
67. E.g. Book of Concord, p. 414 (Large Catechism).

men, from whom the pope stole it."[68] Clearly he believed that the gospel could not be limited to a legal concept of satisfaction. Elsewhere in his Large Catechism (1529), Luther accepted that the fifth petition of the Lord's Prayer meant that God's assurance of pardon was "on the condition that we also forgive our neighbor." If forgiveness and justification are simplistically identified and both refer to a single event, then this sounds like salvation by works. It makes more sense to think that Luther had a broader understanding of forgiveness that was not limited to legal images. Perhaps the main point of salvation for Luther was indeed "union with Christ," as several scholars argue.[69] For Luther, the event of this union is a dynamic process in which forgiveness plays an important role in our sharing in God's gracious gift of life and righteousness.

For Calvin, too, union with Christ appears to be the overarching concern in the doctrine of salvation.[70] Although he uses judicial metaphors, which were taken up with great earnestness by many of his seventeenth-century followers, Calvin is clear in his *Institutes* about what is of highest importance:

> That indwelling of Christ in our hearts—in short, that *mystical union*— are accorded by us the *highest degree of importance*, so that Christ, having been made ours, makes us sharers with him in the gifts with which he has been endowed. We do *not*, therefore, contemplate him outside ourselves *from afar* in order that his righteousness may be *imputed* to us but because we put on Christ and are engrafted into his body—in short, because he deigns to *make us one with him*.[71]

This does not mean that forgiveness is left out or diminished in Calvin's soteriology. On the contrary, he saw both justification and imputation of righteousness as included by Paul "within forgiveness of sins" (*Institutes* III.11.4). He even says that the righteousness of faith *is* reconciliation with God and that this "consists solely in the forgiveness of sins" (III.11.21).

Calvin does not want to mix forgiveness of sins and rebirth (regeneration), which was Osiander's mistake, but he does see the need to link them together somehow. Calvin did this by depicting both justification and sanctification within the broader context of reconciliation

---

68. Luther's Works 34/1.301–2, summarized and paraphrased in G. Aulén, *Christus Victor* (New York: Macmillan, 1954), 118.

69. Cf. the essays in C. E. Braaten and R. W. Jenson (eds.), *Union with Christ: The New Finnish Interpretation of Luther* (Grand Rapids: Eerdmans, 1998).

70. See, e.g., D. E. Tamburello, *Union with Christ: John Calvin and the Mysticism of St. Bernard* (Louisville: Westminster John Knox, 1994).

71. J. Calvin, *Institutes of the Christian Religion* (2 vols.; ed. J. T. McNeill; trans. F. L. Battles; Library of Christian Classics 20–21; Philadelphia: Westminster, 1960), 1.737 (emphasis added).

with God through union with Christ. For example, he argues that "in our sharing in Christ, which justifies us, sanctification is just as much included as righteousness" (III.16.1). Calvin begins part III of the *Institutes* with ten chapters on the Christian life before turning explicitly to justification by faith. Justification is integrated into sanctification, rather than vice versa, and both are incorporated within the broader rubric of gracious union with Christ. This union takes shape not abstractly, but in concrete community: "Forgiveness of sins, then, is for us the first entry into the church and Kingdom of God" (IV.1.20).[72] Like Luther, Calvin connects the forgiveness of sins not only to the preaching of the gospel, but also to the administration of the sacraments to believers through the ministers of the church (IV.1.22).

The year before Calvin died, the Heidelberg Catechism (1563) posed the question "What do you believe concerning the forgiveness of sins?" and expected the answer: "That, for the sake of Christ's reconciling work, God will no more remember my sins or the sinfulness with which I have to struggle all my life long; but that he graciously *imparts* to me the righteousness of Christ so that I may never come into condemnation" (Q. 56, emphasis added). The connotation of gracious imparting must have sounded (to some) too much like the Catholic view of salvation (real substantial change in the inner being of the person); by the middle of the seventeenth century Reformed language about salvation had significantly shifted back toward legal metaphors. The Westminster Confession of Faith (1647) insists that God freely justifies those who are effectually called, "not by infusing righteousness into them, but by pardoning their sins . . . by *imputing* the obedience and satisfaction of Christ unto them" (11.1, emphasis added).

The soteriological debate between Luther's and Calvin's seventeenth-century followers (often called the Protestant Scholastics) was focused on the *ordo salutis*: what are the causal forces of salvation and in what predetermined order do they move an individual from one status to another? In particular, at what point does the legal decision (or imputation) occur in this order? The Lutheran Scholastics did not all agree, but in general they preferred the following order: vocation, illumination, conversion and regeneration, justification, mystical union, renovation, conservation, sanctification, and glorification. Many Lutheran theologians today find this development troubling, not least because justification loses its overarching importance and easily be-

---

72. Calvinists later abolished the practice of penance and put confession back into the liturgical life of the community. Like Luther, Calvin himself acknowledged (in light of Matthew 6:12) that our forgiving others is a "condition" of divine forgiveness, although not in the sense that the former merits the latter (*Institutes* III.20.45).

comes one step in a psychological process rather than witnessing to the divine eschatological act.[73] For Luther, justifying faith is a rapturous ecstasy of union with Christ, a dynamic existence in the life-giving presence of the Creator Spirit. Already with Philip Melanchthon, however, one can observe a movement away from relational, holistic images and toward an individualistic, mechanical ordering of the causes of grace. After Melanchthon, much Lutheran theology drifted toward a "secularization and psychologizing of the concept of faith in the absence of an adequate doctrine of the Holy Spirit. One begins to think of faith as the first human step in a process of conversion, leading to justification, after which comes sanctification."[74]

Like their Lutheran counterparts, most of the Reformed Scholastics treated forgiveness within the broader context of justification. For the Reformed, however, almost always the first step in the *ordo salutis* was predestination, which was then typically followed by calling, justification, sanctification, and finally glorification. Theodore Beza (Calvin's successor in Geneva) explicitly attempted to ground the *ordo salutis* in the divine will and particularly in the divine decree of predestination.[75] On the one hand, he insisted that this decree was the cause of all things, but, on the other hand, he wanted to maintain real human causality. In his attempt to hold on to both, he relied heavily on the medieval distinction between primary and secondary causality. Among Reformed thinkers in England, William Perkin's *Golden Chaine* (1591) stands out as one of the most schematized articulations of the *ordo salutis*. His concern was to outline the precise order of the causes of salvation and damnation. To this end, he constructed a chart that showed the links in the causal chain of salvation. Around the middle of his "chaine," we observe that remission of sins is caused by justification, which in turn may be traced up the causal links in the chain to God's foreknowledge of the decree of election.[76] This obsession with causality was not unrelated to the growing interest in early modern science in the mechanical laws of causality among bodies in motion.

Later in the mid-seventeenth century Johannes Cocceius attempted to link the *ordo temporum* (scheme of salvation history) with the *ordo*

73. See, e.g., G. O. Forde, "Christian Life," in *Christian Dogmatics* (ed. C. E. Braaten and R. W. Jenson; Philadelphia: Fortress, 1984), 2.395–469 at 429.

74. P. R. Hinlicky, "Theological Anthropology: Toward Integrating Theosis and Justification by Faith," *Journal of Ecumenical Studies* 34 (1997): 38–73 at 61.

75. For analysis, see R. Muller, *Christ and the Decree: Christology and Predestination in Reformed Theology from Calvin to Perkins* (Durham, N.C.: Labyrinth, 1986), 79–91.

76. For a reproduction of Perkin's "chaine," see R. Muller, "Perkin's *A Golden Chaine*," *Sixteenth Century Journal* 9 (1978): 69–81.

salutis (steps in the salvation of the individual).[77] The struggle between the covenant of works (which is being abrogated) and the covenant of grace (which is progressing) characterizes both the whole plan of salvation history and the particular outworking of salvation in the elect individual. Reformed soteriology in North America was deeply shaped by the work of Jonathan Edwards in the eighteenth century and the Old Princeton theologians in the nineteenth century. The influence of Charles Hodge, who defended the satisfaction theory of atonement with vigor and spent several chapters in his *Systematic Theology* delineating his view of the *ordo salutis* (3.15–18), is evident in the work of several contemporary conservative American theologians. The thread of the Christian tradition that focuses on the salvation of individuals through the payment of a penalty may be traced through Anselm to the introduction of Roman jurisprudence into Christian theology at least as early as Tertullian and is now woven into the theological fabric of those who continue to view forgiveness primarily as a step in the order of salvation.

Luther and Calvin had understood forgiveness within the context of a broader conception of salvation as union with Christ by the Spirit, which occurs through life in community.[78] This emphasis has much in common with the Eastern Orthodox understanding of forgiveness, which is embedded within its general soteriological emphasis on *theosis* or participation in God. As Kallistos Ware points out, the sacrament of repentance in the East often contains the statement by the priest that the penitent has "come to the house of the Physician." In reference to confession and forgiveness, Ware argues: "Here, as always, we should think primarily in therapeutic rather than juridical terms."[79] Of course, the Western church too has other resources besides the early Reformers for reconstructing a more transformative understanding of forgiveness, even *within* the work of Tertullian, Augustine, Anselm, and the others; the point of my brief survey is that their privileging of its forensic application overshadowed its broader role in redemption. One objective remains before setting out on the reconstructive task: coming to terms with the cultural, philosophical,

77. For analysis, see W. J. van Asselt, "*Amicitia Dei* as Ultimate Reality: An Outline of the Covenant Theology of Johannes Cocceius," *Ultimate Reality and Meaning* 21 (1998): 35–47.

78. Something similar might be argued for John Wesley. R. Rakestraw shows Wesley's emphasis on union with or "participation in" Christ and its connection to *theosis* in "Becoming Like God: An Evangelical Doctrine of Theosis," *Journal of the Evangelical Theological Society* 40 (1997): 257–69; cf. K. Collins, "A Hermeneutical Model for the Wesleyan *Ordo Salutis*," *Wesleyan Theological Journal* 19/2 (1984): 23–37.

79. K. Ware, *The Inner Kingdom* (Crestwood, N.Y.: St. Vladimir's, 2000), 52.

and theological factors that have shaped the context within which Christian forgiveness must be proclaimed and practiced today.

Soteriology after the Turn to Relationality

As this brief survey of forgiveness in church history illustrates, one's understanding and practice of forgiveness will be shaped by one's general interpretation of salvation. This reciprocity suggests that any new articulation of the gospel of forgiveness should be aware of contemporary trends in the formal study of the Christian doctrine of salvation. In the first subsection below, I outline the philosophical shift toward privileging relationality over substance as an explanatory category. Space limitations preclude a detailed treatment of this expansive sweep of history; yet, an overview of the philosophical assumptions that underlie divergent theories of salvation may help us not only to broaden and deepen our understanding of the Christian past but also to overcome barriers to ongoing dialogue. The second subsection traces the impact of this turn to relationality on contemporary soteriological doctrine; we find a movement away from a focus on an individual's experience of an *ordo salutis* and toward what I call *salutary ordering* in community. Finally, I attempt to outline a general understanding of "sharing in the divine nature" (2 Peter 1:4) that both captures the intuition that salvation has to do with communion with God and responds to the common worry in the West that this biblical phrase may too easily be taken to mean that humans "become God" as they are absorbed into the divine substance.

Substantial Problems in the Doctrine of Salvation

New challenges face every generation of the church, and the hard work of discernment is required as we mediate the tradition to the next generation. Believers and nonbelievers alike find many expressions of the Christian understanding of forgiveness implausible and irrelevant or even destructive. I cannot respond to these objections without dealing more broadly with the general doctrine of salvation, which also faces substantial objections today. Before turning to the deepest problem, which is the dependence of many soteriological concepts on a particular understanding of substance, it is important to observe a few of the more popular objections to some of the traditional models.

Simply put, even on their own terms, theories that rely primarily on legal or financial metaphors raise logical and theological questions that still beg for answers. If God arranged for the debt of humans to be fully paid (satisfied), then in what sense should we call this forgiveness? If a legal penalty or financial debt is forgiven, then it does *not* have to be satisfied.[80] If God (or God the Son) has in fact already paid the debt (made full satisfaction), then there is no need anymore for God to forgive.[81] If a payment is made, should we not speak of "settlement" rather than forgiveness? As we saw in our review of the New Testament above, believers are called to forgive one another as God forgives them (e.g., Ephesians 4:32). Does this mean believers should forgive only after they demand satisfaction? If humans are to forgive seventy-seven times (Matthew 18:22) and are not to repay evil for evil (1 Thessalonians 5:15), then it appears that they are held to a higher standard of forgiveness than God, who *ex hypothesi* will forgive an individual only if they or another person (Jesus) are satisfactorily punished (or pay the full debt). Further, this view faces exegetical objections. The Bible does not say that Jesus had to die in order for God to forgive sins.[82] After all, God already forgave sins in the Hebrew Bible (often without a sacrifice or payment), and Jesus was proclaiming the forgiveness of sins well before his death (e.g., Mark 2:5; Luke 7:48). Finally, the idea that Jesus was punished or paid a penalty in a way that excludes those who are actually wounded by sin from the transaction seems to conflict both with Israel's practice of the sacrificial cultus and with the insights of Israel's classical prophets (e.g., Jeremiah 31:30; Ezekiel 18:14–20). All of this compels us to explore the possibility that Christian discourse on forgiveness should not be limited to legal categories.

Another important philosophical problem with placing forgiveness within an *ordo salutis* is the causal determinism that seems to be implied by many modern formulations of this view of salvation. The philosophical and scientific context in which post-Reformation soteriology operated was fixated on the mechanistic physical laws that determine the causes and effects of bodies in motion. In fact, it was the logical implications of this kind of causality applied to salvation that led Arminius and his followers to object to the views of the Bezaists in the early seventeenth century. Among his objections in *Declaration of Sentiments* (1608) to the deterministic models of his contemporaries was Arminius's point that, from their premise that the divine decree is the efficient cause of all things, one must deduce that God really sins and that God is the only sinner. Followers of Beza over the centuries often attempted to avoid these conclusions either by retreating to Ar-

80. See, e.g., E. Stump, "Atonement according to Aquinas," in *Philosophy and the Christian Faith* (ed. T. V. Morris; Notre Dame: University of Notre Dame Press, 1988).

81. See, e.g., P. L. Quinn, "Christian Atonement and Kantian Justification," *Faith and Philosophy* 4 (1986): 440–62.

82. See the classic exegetical treatment of Taylor, *Forgiveness and Reconciliation*, chap. 1.

istotelian and medieval categories of causation or by appealing to mystery. In the wake of twentieth-century developments in physics such as quantum indeterminacy, chaos theory, and complexity science, it no longer makes sense to structure theological debate about salvation around early modern categories of causation. Today the dynamism of physical structures is interpreted not in terms of predetermined causes but in terms of the emergence of ever more complex relational systems.

This brings us to the main point of this subsection. The most substantial philosophical problem in these formulations of the doctrine of salvation is their reliance on ancient or early modern concepts of "substance." Underneath and alongside the violent collapse of Enlightenment models of nature (space filled with substances) and humanity (the substantive soul of the individual "man of reason"), we may trace a turn away from substance and toward relationality as a key explanatory category.[83] A brief outline of this shift will elucidate one of the major factors contributing to the developments in soteriology. To understand this shift, we must go back at least to Aristotle (384–322 B.C.E.), who was the primary source of Western philosophical privileging of the concept of substance over relation. In his *Categories*, Aristotle argued that "things that are said" (simply, not in combination with other things) fall into ten categories: "Each signifies either substance or quantity or qualification or a relative or where or when or being in a position or having or doing or being affected" (1ᵇ25).[84]

The term *substance* is not only first on Aristotle's list, but it also takes ontological priority because a substance must be included in any predication. That is, to make an affirmation (or negation) requires combining a substance, such as "the man," with a predicate that fits into one of the other categories, such as "running" (doing).[85] As exam-

83. I trace this history in more detail in F. L. Shults, *Reforming Theological Anthropology: After the Philosophical Turn to Relationality* (Grand Rapids: Eerdmans, 2003), chap. 1, and parts of that analysis are incorporated in what follows.

84. Quotations and references are from *The Complete Works of Aristotle* (ed. J. Barnes; 2 vols.; Princeton: Princeton University Press, 1984).

85. This is where Aristotle introduces his influential distinction between primary and secondary substances. Primary substances are particular things like an individual person. Secondary substances are the species and genera to which particular things belong, which in the case of an individual person would be "rational" and "animal." The more concrete the more substantial, argues Aristotle, for "of the secondary substances the species is more a substance than the genus, since it is nearer to the primary substance" (*Categories* 2ᵇ7). All of the other categories are said of primary or secondary substances. Aristotle clearly gives the category of substance (*ousia*) priority over the fourth category, which is the category of relation, that is, the "toward something" (*pros ti*) of a thing. What we might call a thing's "towardness" does not really get at its "whatness" for Aristotle.

ples of the category of relation, Aristotle offers the terms *half, double,* and *greater.* He suggests "we call *relatives* all such things as are said to be just what they are, *of* or *than* other things, or in some other way *in relation to* something else" (6ª37). In *Metaphysics,* he explains that "the great and the small, and the like, must be relative to something; but the relative is *least of all things a real thing or substance* and is posterior to quality and quantity; and the relatives are accidents of quantity" (1088ª21–25, emphasis added; cf. *Posterior Analytics* 83ª15–24). While debate continues among Aristotle's interpreters over his precise intentions here, the important point for our purposes is not controversial: his model led to a hard distinction between substances and accidents (including relations), in which the latter are not essential to what a thing is.[86]

In the third century after Christ, the Neoplatonist philosopher Plotinus rejected Aristotle's list itself, taking instead the five "kinds" in Plato's *Sophist* as the ultimate categories (Being, Motion, Stability, Difference, and Identity). Immediately following his exposition of these five primary genera, Plotinus goes out of his way to stress that the term *Relation* is "remote from Being" (*Enneads* 6.1–2). He asks: "As for Relation, manifestly an offshoot, how can it be included among primaries? Relation is of thing ranged against thing; it is not self-pivoted, but looks outward" (6.2.16).[87] In the patristic period and the early middle ages we find a mixture of Neoplatonic and Aristotelian influences in the theological appropriation of the categories of substance and accidents—and this shaped the medieval debate over the existence of universals. Plotinus insisted that one cannot apply the same categories in the same way to both the intelligible and sensible worlds, and he explored the way in which these "kinds" existed. Porphyry, a pupil of Plotinus, accepted the ten Aristotelian categories in his *Isagoge,* but asked very Plotinian questions about them: Do genera and species exist only in the understanding or also outside of it? If the latter, are these categories corporeal or incorporeal? Are they separable from or do they only reside in sensible things?

When Boethius translated the *Isagoge* into Latin in the sixth century, he also offered his own answers to these questions. This set the stage for the debate over universals that dominated the high middle ages. Whether the answer is moderate realism (Thomas Aquinas) or nominalism (William of Ockham), Christian theologians for the most

---

86. In his *Nichomachean Ethics,* Aristotle clearly makes use of relational categories in his treatment of morality and virtue. Perhaps the separation of metaphysics and ethics in later Western philosophy contributed both to the diminishing of relationality in ontology and to the slow divorce between morality and the substantiality of the good.

87. Cited from Plotinus, *The Enneads* (trans. S. MacKenna; new edition; Burdett, N.Y.: Larson, 1992), 553.

part accepted the validity of Porphyry's way of formulating the question, which presupposed the basic distinction between substance and (accidental) relations. Thomas Aquinas's massive appropriation of Aristotle, including the separation between the substance of a thing and its accidental (relational) properties, set the tone for Roman Catholic theology for centuries. His solutions to soteriological problems relied on these categories. For example, tran*substant*iation involves the change of the substance of the bread and wine, but not their accidental properties (such as being crusty or fermented).

As modern science arose in the fifteenth through seventeenth centuries, we see a slow but revolutionary shift in the understanding and use of categories. For Aristotle, the generic qualities of a thing (like its being "green" or "fragrant") are very real. In fact, they are more real than the quantitative predicates that we apply to things like their being "larger" than other things (since largeness implies a "relation"). As the mathematical models of Copernicus, Galileo, and others explained more of the world, philosophers began to think that quantitative analysis may get us closer to the "whatness" of a thing than does a description of its qualities. During this period, it was still assumed for the most part that what is most real is substance (not relations). The major metaphysical debate was over what types of (and how many) substances compose the world. By the seventeenth century the most popular options were Descartes's dualism (two substances: "thinking thing" and "extended thing") and Spinoza's monism (one absolute substance). It was in this early modern philosophical environment that the *ordo salutis* of Protestant Scholastic soteriology emerged, which we traced above. Unlike Luther and Calvin,[88] for whom relationality was a key concept for articulating salvation, some of their followers were surprisingly quick to revert to Aristotelian categories, which they borrowed from the medieval Scholastic discussion.

In Lutheranism, this philosophical issue even gets mentioned in the Formula of Concord: the terms *substance* and *accident* should be avoided in sermons, but because Luther did not explicitly correct them, they may be used by scholars among themselves (2.1.54). As we saw above, most of the Scholastics linked the forgiveness of sins

---

88. Neither Reformer was enthusiastic about most of the medieval categories they had inherited and often railed against them or at least suggested they were not helpful. For example, M. Luther, *Lectures on Genesis* (ed. and trans. Jaroslav Pelikan; Luther's Works 1; St. Louis: Concordia, 1958), 60; Calvin, *Institutes* I.15.7: "Let not those minutiae of Aristotle delay us here." This may have been one of the major reasons why the Romists misunderstood Luther, even in the specific debate over the order of salvation. They were simply using different categories. See, e.g., S. Ickert, "Defending and Defining the *Ordo Salutis*: Jacob van Hoogstraten vs. Martin Luther," *Archive for Reformation History* 78 (1987): 81–97, esp. 92–94.

closely to justification. Lutherans emphasized that justification is not a real and internal change in or of the justified person, but an external judicial act. As David Hollaz puts it: "Since this action takes place apart from man, in God, it cannot intrinsically change man." When discussing regeneration, Hollaz emphasizes that the spiritual change is not substantial, but only accidental, that is, it introduces new qualities into the person but does not essentially change the substance. Regeneration is metaphorical: "Literally speaking, neither Christ is born in us, nor is there a new man in us."[89] These categories are also prevalent in J. A. Quenstedt's treatment of the same topic: "As in the resurrection of the body the flesh, numerically the same which we have borne, shall be reproduced, furnished, however, with different properties; so, in regeneration, the same natural *substance* of our body remains, the *properties* only being changed."[90] These categories were also the key to the Lutheran Scholastics' understanding of the status of the image of God after the fall of the first parents: the substance of humanity (the "image") was not lost, but the accidental qualities of holiness (the "likeness") were lost.[91]

The Reformed Scholastics also tended to argue that justification is an exterior judicial declaratory act and most assuredly not an interior change in the person who is justified. Peter van Mastricht even made this definitive: "Protestants never think that justification denotes an inward change in man, but always an outward one procured by declaration."[92] Reformed theologians during this period often referred to Christ's righteousness as being given to believers by attribution; this is the case, for example, in the 1625 Leiden Synopsis (33.11). On this model attributes do not have a substantial impact, but merely a relational one. Perhaps Johannes Wollebius exhibits the strongest reliance on Aristotelian categories; he notes that the righteousness of sanctification belongs to the "category of quality," while the righteousness of justification belongs to the "category of relation."[93] This bifurcation between substance and accident and the insistence that regeneration touches only the latter created difficulties in Scholastic teaching on Baptism, since they also wanted Baptism to affect the substance of the

89. D. Hollaz, *Examen Theologicum Acroamaticum* (1707); quoted in H. Schmid, *The Doctrinal Theology of the Evangelical Lutheran Church* (3d ed.; trans. C. Hay and H. Jacobs; repr. Minneapolis: Augsburg, 1961), 428, 464.

90. J. A. Quenstedt, *Theologia Didactico-Olemica* (1685); quoted in Schmid, *Doctrinal Theology of the Evangelical Lutheran Church*, 463 (emphasis added).

91. For analysis, see chapter 10 of my *Reforming Theological Anthropology*.

92. P. van Mastricht, *Theoretio-Practica Theologia* (1725); quoted in H. Heppe, *Reformed Dogmatics: Set out and Illustrated from the Sources* (London: Allen, 1950), 544.

93. J. Wollebius, *Christianae Theologiae Compendium* (Basel, 1626), 149; quoted in Heppe, *Reformed Dogmatics*, 566.

infant's soul, removing the stain of inherited sin (which the Scholastics called *peccatum substantiale*). Under the constraints of the presuppositions of this dichotomy, forgiveness either does too much (completely changing the real inner substance of a person) or accomplishes too little (merely touching the relational attributes, but not the real person).

The dialogue among philosophers and theologians over these issues did not stand still after the seventeenth century, although these early modern categories still stand at the center of some contemporary articulations of the doctrine of salvation. Unanswered philosophical questions in the debates over substance led John Locke to argue in *An Essay concerning Human Understanding* (1690) that the ideas of substance and accidents are not of much use, because we do not know what substance is, except that which supports accidents. In his *Enquiry concerning Human Understanding* (1748) David Hume followed the implications of this assertion to its logical conclusion: if substance is merely a "something we know not what," then we cannot predicate anything of it or know anything about what it is. By the time of Hume, many theologians had hitched their theological carts to the philosophical horse of substance metaphysics, and so this powerful skepticism threatened to derail the convoy of Protestant Scholastic doctrine. Immanuel Kant, who credited Hume for waking him from his "dogmatic slumbers," offered his own table of categories in his *Critique of Pure Reason* (1787) and explicitly reversed Aristotle, making "substance and accident" a sub-category of his category "Of Relation." Despite this significant revision, Kant still viewed substance as permanence and alteration as the changing of accidents.

G. W. F. Hegel more radically challenged the basic separation of the category of accident from the category of substance. In his *Science of Logic*, he insisted that the phenomena of relationality is essential not only to the reflective movement of knowing but also to *being* itself, which is self-related. The core of his argument is expressed in two closely related sections: "The Absolute Relation" (the final chapter of *Objective Logic*; 1812) and "The Notion" (the first chapter of *Subjective Logic*; 1819).[94] For Hegel, both substantiality and accidentality refer to determinations of the whole; this whole is neither being nor essence, however, but their dialectical unity in the reflective movement of the *absolute relation*, which is the highest category in the objective logic. "Substance, as this identity of the reflective movement, is the totality of the whole and embraces accidentality within it, and accidentality is the whole substance itself." Hegel speaks of an "immediate identity"

---

94. Published together in *Hegel's Science of Logic* (trans. A. V. Miller; ed. H. D. Lewis; Amherst, N.Y.: Humanity Books, 1999).

and a "unity" of substance and accidents; here again these are manifestations of the movement of the absolute relation. The extremes of accidentality and substantiality have no subsistence on their own. Accidentality is "in itself indeed substance," but as the "actuosity" of substance coming forth of itself, and substantiality is not substance "as substance," for it "has only accidentality for its shape or positedness."[95] For Hegel, form and content are inseparable in the dialectical process of logic, and method cannot be so easily separated from being: "The method is the pure Notion that relates itself only to itself; it is therefore the *simple self-relation* that is *being*."[96]

The emphasis on the ontological and epistemological importance of the category of relationality was taken up and refigured in the work of nineteenth-century philosophers like Søren Kierkegaard (for whom the self is "a relation that relates itself to itself") and Charles Saunders Peirce (who developed his own list of categories in which relation was central). Two of the most influential twentieth-century philosophers, Martin Heidegger and Jean-Paul Sartre, both struggled with the relations inherent in being, although they interpreted it differently insofar as they focused on the phenomenon of time and nothingness, respectively. Alfred North Whitehead explicitly rejected the Aristotelian substance-quality doctrine of actuality in *Process and Reality* (1929). He argued that to be an actual occasion is to be a *relatum* in the nexus of the organic physical world. Whitehead was in part responding to developments in science, which had moved beyond reliance on "substance" language. The early modern focus on the substances of discrete bodies in motion had been replaced by more relational thought-forms such as relativity and field theory.

Many theoretical models in contemporary psychological science, such as "object relations theory" and "family systems theory," are also embedded in this broader philosophical trajectory. Today most people do not think of their souls as immaterial substances with stains that need to be washed, but they do find themselves embedded in painful relations that hinder them from the wholeness and salvation they seek. If human existence really is substantially relational and if not only substances but also relations are real, then forgiveness must bear on the real transformation of these relations. This idea is not foreign to Scripture; biblical language about salvation and forgiveness is about the healing of relations in community. I argue elsewhere that the relational intuitions of Christian theology, as well as the relational praxis and piety of Christian life, are in part responsible for the (re)turn to relationality evident in wider culture and phi-

95. Quotations from *Hegel's Science of Logic*, 555–56.
96. Ibid., 842.

losophy.[97] This shift opens up conceptual space for an articulation of salvation and forgiveness that connects with the real ordering of human persons in community.

From Ordo Salutis to Salutary Ordering

This section introduces some (relatively) recent theological developments that illustrate the positive impact of the philosophical (re)turn to relationality on Christian soteriology. In the seventeenth century, the primary biblical warrant for putting so much energy into the debate over the "order of salvation" was Romans 8:29–30: "For those whom he foreknew he also predestined. . . . And those whom he predestined he also called; and those whom he called he also justified; and those whom he justified he also glorified." Paul's main focus in this context, however, was not on setting up an "order" but providing assurance that those who are suffering will also be glorified (8:17). Because God is the one who elects and justifies (8:33), nothing can separate us from God's love, not even death (8:38). Paul is describing the "large family" (8:29b) of God in which persons are set free from their selfish passion through life in the Spirit (8:2–8), the walls of hostility that divide cultures are broken down (8:9–11), and the "many" become "one body in Christ" (12:5). Paul is not so much interested in identifying the effective mechanical causes of an *ordo salutis* that moves an individual from one predetermined state to another, as he is in depicting the *salutary ordering* of persons in community, which is the manifestation of the in-breaking reality of the redemptive reign of the Spirit of Christ among the people of God.

A prominent feature of many recent theological proposals that attend to the community-transforming dynamics of Christian salvation is the insistence that soteriology must be embedded in the real praxis of social life. Redemption really liberates people from oppressing political structures, whether this oppressive policing is based on race, class, or gender. In his classical work on liberation theology, Gustavo Gutierrez argues that salvation is inherently related to liberation: "Salvation embraces all persons and the whole person; the liberating action of Christ . . . is at the heart of the historical current of humanity; the struggle for a just society is in its own right very much a part of salvation history."[98] Latin America was the context of Gutierrez's work, but theologians representing oppressed

97. F. L. Shults, "The Philosophical Turn to Relationality and the Responsibility of Practical Theology," in *Redemptive Transformation in Practical Theology* (ed. D. Wright; Grand Rapids: Eerdmans, forthcoming).

98. G. Gutierrez, *A Theology of Liberation* (rev. ed.; trans. C. Inda and J. Eagleson; Maryknoll, N.Y.: Orbis, 1988), 97.

peoples from many contexts emphasize the link between salvation and liberated community. The experience of Christians within Asian cultures led to a recognition of the need to complement the Western concern for dealing with guilt with an Eastern concern for the healing of shame in community. For example, in light of the Korean concept of *han* (frustrated hope, resentful bitterness, wounded heart), Andrew Sun Park focuses both on the "forgiven-ness" of wrongdoers and the "forgiving-ness" of victims. From this perspective, repentance is "an open-ended process which continues throughout our relational life."[99] For many African American theologians, salvation and forgiveness are unthinkable apart from real liberation of blacks from white domination: "Salvation is intended for the poor and the helpless, and it is identical with their liberation from oppression."[100]

The connection between forgiveness and politics is clear in the chilling title of a recent book by South African Archbishop Desmond Tutu: *No Future without Forgiveness*.[101] Apartheid, the Holocaust, and so many other atrocities of the twentieth century continue to overshadow dialogue about forgiveness. Today, human violence continues in old forms like ethnic cleansing and in new forms like suicide bombings—often with religious motivation. In this context, does a decision not to demand retribution make sense? Would such a transactional forgiveness be enough? Judicial declarations surely help but they do not always heal. Would even the healing of inner anger and shame be enough? Miroslav Volf describes forgiveness as "the boundary between exclusion and embrace." In this sense, forgiveness may remove the power of the rule to divide the parties, but "it leaves a distance between people, an empty space of neutrality, that allows them either to go their separate ways in what is sometimes called 'peace' or to fall into each other's arms and to restore broken communion."[102] Sometimes reconciliation may not be possible, but surely it should be the ultimate goal of Christian forgiveness even if its fulfillment is eschatological. Forgiveness works for justice now by pursuing the rule of love, which brings persons and communities into right relation. Discerning how Christian forgiveness should be worked out in particular cases is a difficult and perennial task. Nevertheless, that the task is being pursued with renewed vigor is a

99. A. S. Park, *The Wounded Heart of God* (Nashville: Abingdon, 1993), 91–92.

100. J. Cone, *God of the Oppressed* (rev. ed.; Maryknoll, N.Y.: Orbis, 1997), 210.

101. D. Tutu, *No Future without Forgiveness* (New York: Doubleday, 2000). For a summary of Tutu's view of forgiveness, see M. Battle, "A Theology of Community: The Ubuntu Theology of Desmond Tutu," *Interpretation* 54 (2000): 173–82.

102. M. Volf, *Exclusion and Embrace: A Theological Exploration of Identity, Otherness, and Reconciliation* (Nashville: Abingdon, 1996), 125–26.

promising development.[103] To share in the ministry of reconciliation, the church must extend its concern with forgiveness beyond the domain of theoretical jurisprudence and engage in the prudent and just praxis of healing and redemption.

Some of the most compelling voices in the call for a return to relational and transformational models of salvation and forgiveness are found among feminist theologians. Forgiveness must be about more than the individual's feelings of guilt; it must include a recognition of the pervasiveness of social ills, "intentionally meeting this evil with the will toward well-being."[104] If forgiveness is merely a legal transaction that does not actually transform power structures, then this is "good news" to the oppressor but not to the oppressed. Elsa Tamez observes that

> justification viewed from an abstract, individual and generic plane is good news more for the oppressors than for the poor. By beginning with the event of justification, the former can feel relieved of guilt—pardoned of their sins—by grace without confronting the "wrath of God" or judgment, or the justice of God, and without any need for any conversion or change of practice.[105]

Cynthia Crysdale argues that redemption in relation to the cross of Christ may begin in two ways: either with a recognition of one's own forgiveness or with a recognition of one's own woundedness. For those whose actions have been primarily oppressive, the approach to the cross should usually begin with a confession of sins; for those who have primarily experienced oppression, redemption begins by acknowledging one's wounds, finding one's voice, and seeking healing.[106] Every person, Crysdale argues, is to some extent both perpetrator and victim, so eventually both "sides" of the cross must be engaged in order for the cycle to be broken.[107] Among womanist theologians,

103. See, e.g., D. W. Shriver Jr., *An Ethic for Enemies: Forgiveness in Politics* (Oxford: Oxford University Press, 1995); H. Wells, "Theology for Reconciliation: Biblical Perspectives on Forgiveness and Grace," in *The Reconciliation of Peoples: Challenge to the Churches* (ed. G. Baum and H. Wells; Maryknoll, N.Y.: Orbis, 1997), 1–15; M. Volf, "The Social Meaning of Reconciliation," *Interpretation* 54 (2000): 158–72; R. G. Helmick and R. L. Petersen (eds.), *Forgiveness and Reconciliation: Religion, Public Policy, and Conflict Transformation* (Radnor, Pa.: Templeton Foundation, 2001).

104. M. H. Suchocki, *The Fall to Violence* (New York: Continuum, 1994), 155.

105. E. Tamez, *Amnesty of Grace: Justification by Faith from a Latin American Perspective* (trans. S. H. Ringe; Nashville: Abingdon, 1993), 21.

106. C. Crysdale, *Embracing Travail: Retrieving the Cross Today* (New York: Continuum, 2001).

107. For a psychological appropriation of Crysdale's theological proposal, see S. J. Sandage and T. W. Wiens, "Contextualizing Models of Humility and Forgiveness: A Reply to Gassin," *Journal of Psychology and Theology* 29 (2001): 201–11.

who integrate both feminist and liberation concerns, we find explicit critiques of white male–dominated soteriology in which Anselm's model of satisfaction has been privileged. It is not hard to understand why protecting the honor of the "landlord" does not really sound like salvation to African American female ears. Out of their own contexts and personal experiences, these theologians are exploring new ways to articulate the Christian doctrines of atonement and forgiveness.[108]

It is not only the voices of those who have been marginalized, however, that are increasingly calling for a soteriological focus on community, on salutary ordering rather than *ordo salutis*. In some mainline Protestant denominations,[109] this is evident in the fresh retrieval of insights from Luther and Calvin. Eberhard Jüngel argues that Luther's "rediscovery" of Paul's gospel of the justification of the ungodly was a recognition that God's righteousness is decisively *not* legal righteousness, but a sharing of divine righteousness that makes others righteous as the creative eschatological word of God is pronounced over them.[110] Luther is often misunderstood because interpreters fail to see that he views God's righteousness (or justification—the Greek word *dikaiosunē* covers both meanings) as an inherently *relational* concept.[111] The gospel is all about relations; Christ exposes himself to our relationlessness, creates new relations, sharing "the relational riches of his own life with us, so that new relationships, new ways of living, might emerge in us."[112]

On the Reformed side, the (re)turn to relationality is illustrated in the work of Colin Gunton, who draws our attention to those places in Calvin's corpus where his trinitarian intuitions are most evident. Gunton argues that despite his appropriation of juridical metaphors, Calvin's main purpose in book III of the *Institutes* is to show that justification is not a legal fiction. Justification has to do with a real participation with Christ by the Spirit in relation to the Father. Yes, justifica-

108. For a survey of several of these proposals, see J. D. Weaver, *The Nonviolent Atonement* (Grand Rapids: Eerdmans, 2001).

109. This shift is not limited to Protestant churches. Many Roman Catholic theologians are also moving in this direction; e.g., Fink ("History of the Sacrament of Reconciliation," 87) argues that "the time is ripe for this sacramental tradition to open itself beyond the realm of personal sin and individual absolution to new and broader experiences of sin in the interpersonal, communal and social realms."

110. E. Jüngel, *Justification: The Heart of the Christian Faith* (trans. J. F. Cayzer; Edinburgh: Clark, 2001), 73–77.

111. Ibid., 62–66. Jüngel's interpretation of Luther may be overly generous. For an examination of the essential relationality in biblical concepts of righteousness, which were at least insufficiently emphasized by Luther, see J. Ripley, "Covenantal Concepts of Justice and Righteousness, and Catholic-Protestant Reconciliation: Theological Implications and Explorations," *Journal of Ecumenical Studies* 38 (2001): 95–108.

112. Jüngel, *Justification*, 88.

tion by faith is central to theology and the Christian life for Calvin. However, "what he does not do with it, as generations after him did try to do, was to turn it into a theory, or into part of a theory, of an *ordo salutis*."[113] As I suggested above, salvation for Calvin is a salutary ordering of believers as they participate in an intimate relation with God. Even the title of book IV of the *Institutes*, "The External Means or Aids by Which God Invites Us into the Society of Christ and Holds Us Therein," is an expression of this insight.

The shift in soteriology also had a profound effect upon ecclesiology, as might be expected. Speaking from a free-church tradition, Miroslav Volf argues that redemption is mediated through real relations in community, not simply "immediately" to the individual. On the other hand, grace is not controlled by the Episcopal dispensation of the sacraments either; salvation occurs within and among the mutual fellowship of believers.[114] The *ordo salutis* model does not fit well with the biblical witness, as we have seen, and this is sufficient reason for suspicion among evangelical theologians. In the Protestant Scholastic exposition of doctrine and in many systematic presentations today, the order of salvation is treated in the context of justification and sanctification, well ahead of the treatment of ecclesiology. Telford Work suggests that theologians need to bring the church back to salvation and to bring salvation back to the church: "The salvation of discrete persons does not belong in categories of justification and sanctification abstracted from social relationships. . . . Ecclesiology should be the category within which the *ordo salutis* is treated."[115] Stanley Grenz proposes a revisioning of theology from an explicitly evangelical perspective in which community is the integrating motif for all of doctrine, including soteriology.[116]

This new focus on the communal aspects of salvation inevitably shapes the way that theologians think about forgiveness. One of the most influential attempts to link theological reflection on forgiveness with the redemptive practices of the Christian community is L. Gregory Jones's *Embodying Forgiveness*. Jones speaks of the "craft" of forgiveness and argues that learning this craft requires participation in

113. C. E. Gunton, "Aspects of Salvation," in Gunton's *Intellect and Action: Elucidation on Christian Theology and the Life of Faith* (Edinburgh: Clark, 2000), 136.

114. M. Volf, *After Our Likeness: The Church as the Image of the Trinity* (Grand Rapids: Eerdmans, 1998).

115. T. Work, "Reordering Salvation: Church as the Proper Context for an Evangelical *Ordo Salutis*," in *Ecumenical Theology in Worship, Doctrine, and Life* (ed. D. S. Cunningham et al.; Oxford: Oxford University Press, 1999), 182–95 at 187.

116. S. Grenz, *Theology for the Community of God* (Grand Rapids: Eerdmans, 2001). For an examination of other evangelical proposals, see F. L. Shults, "The Body of Christ in Evangelical Theology," *Word and World* 22 (2002): 178–85.

communities that embody particular practices.[117] In a more recent article, he offers this summary:

> Christian forgiveness includes words spoken and the transformation of inner emotions, but it is much more than that. Christian forgiveness recognizes the timeful process by which God's grace works in our lives and in our relations. It also involves us in activities where we learn to be forgiven and forgiving by engaging in activities other than those associated with forgiveness. Christian forgiveness aims at reconciliation and involves the task of responding to God's forgiving love by *crafting communities* of forgiven and forgiving people.[118]

In chapter 5 I will explore the dynamics of such communities and revisit these theological concerns with explicit reference to the Christian understanding and practice of faith, love, and hope in sacramental, baptized, and eucharistic community. Before turning to this reconstructive task, however, I need to describe the broader theological developments in which my proposal is embedded.

Salvation as Sharing in the Divine Nature

An important element in the therapeutic treatment of forgiveness, as Steve emphasized in chapter 3, is the extending of horizons. A theological treatment also requires an expansion of the field in which forgiveness is to be understood and practiced. The ultimate theological horizon is the relation to God. This means that forgiveness must be reframed within a general understanding of this relation. This subsection briefly describes the broader doctrine of the God world relation that will guide my exploration of forgiveness in chapter 5. Here I am explicitly appropriating developments in the doctrine of God in Western theology that have engaged the Eastern emphasis on salvation as "sharing in the divine nature."[119]

The reason so many of us in the West are resistant to the idea expressed in 2 Peter 1:4—that believers are called to become sharers in (or of) the divine nature—may lie deep in the presuppositions that shape our doctrine of God. Often we imagine "all that is" as divided

117. L. G. Jones, *Embodying Forgiveness: A Theological Analysis* (Grand Rapids: Eerdmans, 1995).

118. L. G. Jones, "Crafting Communities of Forgiveness," *Interpretation* 54 (2000): 121–34 at 122 (emphasis added).

119. I trace these developments in more detail in F. L. Shults, "Sharing in the Divine Nature: Transformation, *Koinōnia*, and the Doctrine of God," in *On Being Christian . . . and Human* (ed. T. Speidell; Eugene, Ore.: Wipf & Stock, 2002), part 1, and parts of that analysis are incorporated in what follows. For more on the exegetical issues surrounding this important phrase, see J. M. Starr, *Sharers in Divine Nature: 2 Peter 1:4 in Its Hellenistic Context* (Stockholm: Almqvist & Wiksell, 2000).

into two generic kinds: divine and nondivine. This way of construing the distinction between Creator and creation succeeds in protecting against pantheism, but it easily leads us into the opposite problem: conceptualizing the relation between Infinity and finitude (or between Eternity and time) in terms of a simple dualism in which God and the world are two parts of a broader whole. This in turn leads to the difficulty of understanding the distinction and unity of the immanent and economic Trinity. When pantheism and dualism are perceived as the only options, Western theology has most often leaned toward dualism in order to protect the transcendence of God. The early modern ways of speaking about God as a rational object, a single subject, and first cause buttressed this dualism, creating a worldview in which any talk of the participation of humanity in the Creator's *nature* (i.e., substance) seemed to entail that the nondivine creature *becomes* divine.

Space does not allow examination of the many theologians who reacted against these early modern conceptions of God, but we may get a sense of the scope of the reconstruction that has occurred by describing the role of Karl Barth in this process. Although Barth appropriates the judicial metaphors of the Reformed tradition, he is not bound by them. At the beginning of his massive treatment of the doctrine of reconciliation he insists that salvation "consists in participation in the being of God" (*Church Dogmatics* IV/1,8). Barth's broader work on the doctrine of God and its application to soteriology cleared the ground for many of the constructive theological proposals of the late twentieth century. Barth's material contribution can be summarized as initiating a fresh retrieval of the concepts of Infinity, Trinity, and Futurity. Despite his general appreciation of the Protestant Scholastics, at each of these three points Barth self-consciously departs from their models. He argues that their decentering of the doctrine of the Trinity is what led them to focus on proving the existence of God as an immaterial substance over against the world as its first cause. Overcoming these tendencies was the beginning of a new era of theological reflection in which the concepts of God, salvation, and relationality have been increasingly brought together.

Barth's emphasis on divine Infinity is already evident in his earlier *The Epistle to the Romans*. In the preface to the second edition, he announces: "If I have a system, it is limited to a recognition of what Kierkegaard called the 'infinite qualitative distinction' between time and eternity, and to my regarding this as possessing negative as well as positive significance: 'God is in heaven, and thou art on earth.'"[120] This

---

120. K. Barth, *The Epistle to the Romans* (1st German ed. 1919; trans. E. C. Hoskyns; London: Oxford University Press, 1933), 10.

emphasis is linked to Barth's well-known insistence that God is "wholly other." Later in his career, Barth admits that his early focus on the *diastasis* between God and humanity abstracted the wholly other and absolutized it over against humanity. He comes to realize that insofar as the word of God in Jesus Christ reveals that God is made known to creatures as for us and with us, and insofar as we experience life in the Spirit by whose power God is in and among us, we also need to speak of the "humanity of God."[121] If God is wholly other without qualification, this might imply that God is *defined* as that which is over against creation. Barth recognizes the need to avoid a naïve metaphysical dualism between God and the world that would imagine two universes (finite and infinite) that can be spanned by human language or thought.

In his *Church Dogmatics*, Barth provides a more detailed treatment of the idea of Infinity. He explicitly rejects the seventeenth-century Protestant Scholastic view of Infinity as a comprehensive attribute that describes the divine essence over against the world. Yes, God is infinite, but "*He is also finite—without destroying, but in his Infinity—*in the fact that as love He is His own basis, goal, standard, and law." Barth argues that properly predicating Infinity of God requires that we do so in a way that "does not involve any contradiction that it is *finitude as well.*"[122] Barth explains that God "is infinite in a manner in which the antithesis and mutual exclusiveness of the infinite and the finite . . . do not enclose and imprison Him. . . . The infinity which as a concept stands in antithesis to finitude . . . is quite insufficient to describe what God is in relation to space and time" (II/1,467). He tries to avoid the tendency, which was all too common in early modernity, to depict God as one of the objects of human reason, even as that object that is on the other side of the finite/infinite distinction. God is not simply the infinite as dialectically defined over against and so bound to the finite. God is "completely different,"[123] beyond and yet encompassing the distinction between infinite and finite. If one conceptualizes the God-world relation in terms of two kinds of being (infinite and finite) that together compose "All," then this All replaces God as the Absolute. Both God and world become parts of the "Whole." As

---

121. K. Barth, *The Humanity of God* (trans. J. N. Thomas and T. Wieser; Richmond: John Knox, 1960), 44–45.

122. K. Barth, *Church Dogmatics* (ed. G. W. Bromiley and T. F. Torrance; Edinburgh: Clark, 1936–77), II/1,467–68 (emphasis added).

123. S. Johnson, *The Mystery of God: Karl Barth and the Postmodern Foundations of Theology* (Louisville: Westminster John Knox, 1997), 20, suggests that this translation of *ganz anders* better captures Barth's intention. See also the comparison between Barth's theological method and Derrida's economy of *différance* in G. Ward, *Barth, Derrida, and the Language of Theology* (Cambridge: Cambridge University Press, 1995).

Barth recognizes, this way of speaking is not consistent with the idea of God as the unlimited and unconditioned, but marks "God" off as that part of the Whole that is limited (and so conditioned) by the finite. This debate continues today as philosophical theologians attempt to articulate a concept of true Infinity.[124]

The doctrine of the Trinity attracted fresh attention in late twentieth-century systematic theology, and this too was due in part to Barth's revival of traditional trinitarian emphases. In the first volume of his *Church Dogmatics* Barth self-consciously diverges from the custom of the Protestant Scholastics and their followers. Why, he asks, did they treat the "that" and "what" of God first, as though these could be separated from the "who"? (I/1,301). This separation in the doctrine of God was solidified when Thomas Aquinas tried to establish the unity of God (in his *Summa Theologica*) before turning to a treatment of the three persons of God revealed in Scripture. Although the trinitarian dynamics of the Christian experience of justification by faith were central for the early Reformers, their seventeenth-century followers returned to the medieval model of Thomas, privileging abstract unity and simplicity over the dynamic relationality of the persons of the Trinity. During the eighteenth century, which saw the rise of modern atheism, the majority of Protestant theologians in the West tried to ground their systems on broadly theistic concepts of the divine as a single subject with an all-powerful will and an all-knowing intellect, rather than on an explicitly Christian (trinitarian) idea of God.[125] Meanwhile, treatment of the Trinity was moved further and further from the center of the doctrine of God, so that by the nineteenth century Schleiermacher relegated it to a brief section at the end of *The Christian Faith* (1831).

Barth helped to reverse this trend by making "The Triune God" his first material topic after chapter 1, which was entitled "The Word

124. P. Clayton observes: "The infinite may without contradiction include within itself things that are by nature finite, but it may not stand *outside of* the finite. For if something finite exits, and if the infinite is 'excluded' by the finite, then it is not truly infinite or without limit. To put it differently, there is simply no place for finite things to 'be' outside of that which is *absolutely unlimited*"; *God and Contemporary Science* (Grand Rapids: Eerdmans, 1997), 99.

125. As M. J. Buckley notes (*At the Origins of Modern Atheism* [New Haven: Yale, 1987], 346–47), in early modernity Christianity "transmuted itself into theism" in order to protect its God from the challenges of mechanistic science; the Christian religion alienated itself from its own resources disclosed in the revelation of Christ long before "atheists" arose. Atheists simply drew out the logical implications of a "theism" that had become detached from the trinitarian God. Orthodox Protestant Scholastic theologians *affirmed* the doctrine of the Trinity, as they had the idea of Infinity, but these affirmations were not always integral to their systematic presentations.

of God as the Criterion of Dogmatics." It was precisely this criterion that led him to a reconsideration of the place of the doctrine in the structure of theological presentation. However, simply putting Trinity first in the order of treatment is not enough: its content must be "decisive and controlling for the whole of dogmatics" (*Church Dogmatics* I/1,303). Despite this formal revolution, materially Barth still imagines God as a single subject: "*God* reveals Himself. He reveals Himself *through Himself*. He reveals *Himself*" (I/2,296). The statement that "God reveals Himself as the Lord" is for Barth the root of the doctrine of the Trinity. When speaking about the Trinity, only to the one Lord does Barth believe the term *person* should be properly applied; here he defines a person as "an I existing in and for itself with its own thought and will" (I/1,358). Many theologians note that Barth's application of the self-reflection logic of German idealism to the one divine ego collapses into the same problems that Barth himself saw in Augustine's psychological analogies: the projection of our own experience as single subjects onto the divine nature. These problems led other theologians to articulate more robust presentations of the doctrine of the Trinity.

Barth provides a fresh impetus for the renewal of theological discourse on the concept of Futurity as well. In *The Epistle to the Romans*, he rejects the idea that human conduct could be traced to the will of God as its efficient cause; who would dare, he asks, speak of God and humanity as "links in a chain of causality?"[126] Barth insists that God confronts humanity not as first cause, but as primal origin: "If Christianity be not altogether thoroughgoing eschatology, there remains in it no relationship whatever with Christ."[127] This connection between eschatology and Christology is spelled out further in the *Church Dogmatics*. They are inherently linked because the incarnation of the divine word in Jesus Christ leads us to speak of divine Eternity as a true Eternity that "includes this possibility, the potentiality of time . . . [that] has the power to take time to itself" (II/1,617). For Barth, God's Eternity embraces time in three forms, which he calls pre-temporality, supra-temporality, and post-temporality. He argues that the Reformers (and many theologians before them) showed a dangerous one-sided interest in *pre*-temporality that led to the problems of determinism in the doctrines of election and provi-

126. Barth, *Epistle to the Romans*, 356.
127. Ibid., 314. B. McCormack shows how Barth exchanged one model of eschatology for another between the two editions of *Romans*. In the second edition of *The Epistle to the Romans* Barth "abandoned the process eschatology of *Romans I* in favor of a radically futurist 'consistent' eschatology"; *Karl Barth's Critically Realistic Dialectical Theology* (Oxford: Clarendon, 1995), 208.

dence.[128] Barth also criticizes much of the theology of the eighteenth and nineteenth centuries, which emphasized the present moment of human consciousness and its dependence on the divine, as too focused on God's *supra*temporality.

In the second volume of the *Church Dogmatics*, Barth recognizes that in his early writings his enthusiasm for thinking "with new seriousness about God's futurity" (II/1,636) led him into the danger of collapsing into an equally reductionistic obsession with *post*temporality. The idea that human history does not finally share in the wholly other Futurity of God, however, is not consonant with the biblical message that history moves toward a real end. To avoid posttemporal reductionism, Barth argues that the three forms of Eternity are equally God's Eternity and "therefore the living God Himself" (II/1,638).[129] In the last completed volume of the *Church Dogmatics*, he returns to the intimate connection between Christology and eschatology; the expectation of the Parousia of Jesus Christ as the "end, and therefore the dawn of eternal light" permeates the Christian life in hope (IV/3.2, 934). Barth's argument for a positive embracing relation between Eternity and time leads to a radical reconsideration of both the ideas of God as first cause and "eternal now." Many of those who followed in his wake realized that God and temporality must be thought together and that Futurity must somehow be included.

After the (re)turn to relationality, the metaphysics of substance that forced the choice between pantheism (one substance) and dualism (two substances) was severely challenged. If the divine nature is truly Infinite, so that God embraces while transcending the distinction between infinite and finite, then finite creaturely sharing in this nature does not have to mean that the finite becomes (substantially) infinite, nor that the finite is a constitutive "part" of the infinite, nor that God's nature is one (infinite) substance defined over against other (finite) substances. If God's nature is robust Trinity, then sharing in this nature will not be an impersonal absorption of the creature into a divine substance, but an intensification of personal being-in-relation through fellowship (*koinōnia*) in the Son's relation to the Father by the Spirit. If God's nature is primal Futurity, then human sharing in the divine nature is never comprehensive, because creaturely temporality cannot

128. C. E. Gunton suggests that the Reformers began the process of replacing abstract concepts of causality with concepts that connote more personal and loving agency. Cf. "The End of Causality? The Reformers and Their Predecessors," in *The Doctrine of Creation* (ed. C. E. Gunton; Edinburgh: Clark, 1997), 63–82.

129. For a discussion of Barth's view of Eternity and time, see G. Hunsinger, *Disruptive Grace: Studies in the Theology of Karl Barth* (Grand Rapids: Eerdmans, 2000), 186–209; and I. Dalferth, "Karl Barth's Eschatological Realism," in *Karl Barth: Centenary Essays* (ed. S. W. Sykes; Cambridge: Cambridge University Press, 1989), 14–45.

grasp or catch up with Eternity, although its very being is contingent on its orientation toward it.

For our purposes here, I suggest a terminological distinction between existing, participating, and sharing in the divine nature. Romans 11:36 tells us that *all things* are from, through, and to God. This means that to be creaturely is to *exist* in this dynamic movement in relation to God. Like the rest of creation, humans are created in and for the Logos, and human existence is upheld by the Spirit of life; God is the one *in* whom "we live and move and have our being" (Acts 17:28). What makes the human experience of creaturely existence "in God" unique, however, is the possibility of thematizing this relation as a searching and groping for the divine (17:27). Human persons *participate* in a way that is qualitatively different than the experience of other creatures; self-conscious creatures experience a personal knowing, acting, and being as a *becoming*. The Christian doctrine of creation implies that this participation (which is made possible by the ordering differentiation of the divine Logos and the dynamic unifying power of the divine Spirit) is real regardless of the extent to which persons explicitly reflect on their relation to the Creator. In what follows I normally reserve the term *sharing* for the intensification of the religious relation to God, which Christians experience as the indwelling and transforming presence of the Spirit of the one who raised Christ from the dead (Romans 8:11).

A renewed emphasis on the Infinite Trinitarian Futurity of God opens up conceptual space for making sense of human sharing in the divine nature and provides resources for speaking of this *koinōnia* in concrete relation to Jesus Christ.[130] However, Christology must be inherently correlated to Pneumatology, for this *koinōnia* is contingent upon the presence of the Spirit of the biblical God. Salvation and forgiveness are about grace. Human beings are not able on their own strength to manifest forgiving grace toward their friends, much less their enemies. Forgiveness must therefore be a sharing in divine grace. In the next chapter, I will explore ways in which the real presence of the gracious God of the Bible transforms epistemic, ethical, and ontological anxiety into faith, love, and hope—this is the existential space in which the praxis of Christian forgiveness takes concrete form.

---

130. Even in early Eastern patristic theology, the real meaning of "deification" was "Christification," as P. Nellas shows in *Deification in Christ* (trans. N. Russell; Crestwood, N.Y.: St. Vladimir's, 1997), esp. chap. 1.

5

FORGIVENESS AS SHARING
IN DIVINE GRACE

In our introduction, we delineated three general domains of meaning in which the word *forgiveness* operates: forensic, therapeutic, and redemptive. My purpose in this chapter is to elucidate the third semantic field by articulating a Christian understanding of redemptive forgiveness as "sharing in divine grace." Chapter 4 explored the significance of the concepts of facing and forgiveness in Scripture and the Christian tradition, revealing a need to extend the horizon of the doctrine of salvation in ways that move beyond merely legal and therapeutic metaphors. In the last subsection, I traced some of the developments in soteriology that have responded reconstructively to the philosophical (re)turn to relationality and suggested that moving from the conceptual (and existential) space of "observing" God to a model (and experience) of "participating in" God opens up new opportunities for expressing (and practicing) Christian forgiveness as sharing in divine grace.[1]

1. This participative model is gaining ground in Western theology. P. Fiddes suggests that "the path of Jesus, our own acts of giving and receiving forgiveness, and God's being as triune love interact in one event of participation"; *Participating in God: A Pastoral Doctrine of the Trinity* (Louisville: Westminster John Knox, 2000), 200. Cf. L. W. Countryman, *Forgiven and Forgiving* (Harrisburg, Pa.: Morehouse, 1998), who claims that "by forgiving, we actually share in the life and work of God—we share in God's creation of the future" (59). One of the most popular metaphors for this participation is "embrace," in which the forgiver embraces others as she is embraced by God. See, e.g., M. Volf, *Exclusion and Embrace: A Theological Exploration of Identity, Otherness, and Reconciliation* (Nashville: Abingdon, 1996).

Discourse on *redemptive* forgiveness attends to the reality of religious experience, the human relation to the divine. For Christian theology, salvation is by grace (e.g., Ephesians 2:8). So too, I argue, is Christian forgiveness. Trying to work up the energy to forgive another exhausts human resources. Divine forgiveness makes room for humans to share in the grace and joy of trinitarian love, which provides an infinite resource for human forgiveness. The Ephesians (4:32) were urged to forgive (*charizomai*) one another, as God in Christ had forgiven (*charizomai*) them. In other words, believers are called to face one another in a way that manifests grace as they are faced by the gracious face of God. Salvation is joyful participation in divine forgiveness, through which human life is drawn into the grace and peace of an eternal trinitarian facing that "blesses" and "keeps" the interfacing of communal fellowship. As we saw in chapter 4, the God of the Bible is essentially gracious, opening up space and time for human life and holding out the promise of new life. Divine forgiveness liberates the Christian community into a real sharing of real relations that manifest divine grace. Through forgiveness (*charizomai*) the Christian community shares in this divine grace (*charis*), as it receives the manifold gifts (*charismata*) of the Spirit that characterize its joyful (*chara*) and thanksgiving (*eucharistia*) worship and service and as it calls others into a life of wholeness and salvation in Christ.[2]

Because the idea of sharing (*koinōnia*) is so open to misunderstanding, it will be helpful to summarize what I said above regarding "sharing in the divine nature" with special attention to the dynamics of grace. Emphasizing Infinity, Trinity, and Futurity can protect us from the danger of thinking of this sharing either as a fusion of the divine and human or as a mere cooperation between them. If one imagines the divine being as an immense substance, sharing may imply that finite humans are ultimately absorbed into this substance. If one imagines the divine being as a single subject, sharing could indicate that humans either share some of God's thoughts or that humans (and all creatures) simply are these thoughts. If one imagines God merely as standing in a negative relation to time (i.e., timeless) or as before time, the sharing of temporal creatures in divine grace will sound either like no relation at all or like a totalitarian predetermination of temporality in which creatures are forced to share. If, however, one

---

2. Etymological observation is not yet theological argumentation, but even these philological connections have an intrinsic heuristic value. Full interpretation of the meaning of these terms and the concepts of faith, love, and hope requires examining not just the words but the semantic contexts in which they appear. Cf. J. Barr, *The Semantics of Biblical Language* (repr. Harrisburg, Pa.: Trinity, 1991). My discussion here privileges *charizomai* (to manifest grace) over *aphiēmi* (to put away), not in the sense that the latter is ignored or denied; rather, it aims at and is for the sake of the former.

imagines divine grace in relation to the infinite trinitarian God of promise, the prospects are not so bleak. If divine grace is perfectly Infinite, then human sharing in it does not leave less grace for God or make more grace than God had "before," because God is infinitely gracious. If divine grace is grounded in the eternal *koinōnia* of the persons of the Trinity, then it is not an impersonal causal force but a personal calling to share ever more intensely in this relational life. If divine grace is the faithful and loving presence of eternal Futurity, then human sharing in it is not a comprehensive grasping of grace but a redemptive orientation in relation to God, whose gracious coming makes humanity and all things new.

The Christian tradition has often treated the doctrine of salvation with special reference to faith, hope, and love (1 Corinthians 13:13)—the three that "remain" when all other objects of desire pass away. In other contexts, the same triad is emphasized, though more often in the order of faith, love, and hope (e.g., Colossians 1:4–5; 1 Thessalonians 1:2–3; 5:8), which is the order I follow in my presentation. My exploration of forgiveness in this chapter is structured by these abiding desiderata, which refer us to the ultimate meaning of life in relation to God. We must not think of these merely as substances[3] but as real substantive relations in which Christians are held through being-in-relation to God and one another. While these interrelated dynamics of the Christian life may not ultimately be separated, I make a conceptual distinction for the sake of analysis. Each of the three major sections has three subsections. I focus first on the various forms of anxiety that give rise to the human longing for forgiveness and render forgiving so difficult. Humans worry about what they *know*, how they should *act*, and who they will *be*, and so they struggle for control of rationality, morality, and reality. Although they are typically repressed, these anxieties wholly encompass human life. This means that the three basic arenas of philosophical reflection (epistemology, ethics, and ontology) must be brought to bear on our discussion of forgiveness.

Forgiveness must be understood within a horizon this expansive if we want more than a quick fix, a shallow functional solution to a deeper existential problem.[4] Forgiving has to do with everything, with life and with death. Cheap forgiveness, like cheap grace, does not truly save, although it may save face for a little while. Such facetious attempts at redemption only maintain the artificial façades that we have constructed to cover over our dread. Facing our anxiety involves rec-

---

3. As Augustine explicitly did with reference to love; *On the Trinity* 9.4.6.
4. Cf. F. L. Shults, "Pedagogy of the Repressed," *Theological Education* 36 (1999): 157–69.

ognizing the agony as well as the ecstasy of the dynamics of forgiveness. The infinite ecstasy of resurrection comes on the other side of the infinite agony of the cross. Redemptive forgiveness is infinitely painful, but it opens up human life to the infinite pleasure of sharing in grace. Superficial forms of therapy and theology that hide their faces from the void can only (at their best) heal or explain at the surface; at their worst, they efface the passion of the human longing for salvation. In what follows, I explore the conceptual, moral, and liturgical space opened up by the biblical tradition in search of illuminating and transforming interpretations of the agonistic and ecstatic experiences of forgiveness.

The task of the second subsection in each part of this chapter explores the specific way in which a Christian's understanding of and relation to Jesus Christ may shape her experience of forgiving vis-à-vis her neighbors (the biblical word for the postmodern "other"). Sharing in divine grace is life *in*, *with*, and *toward* Christ. From the fullness of the word manifested in Jesus, "we have all received, grace upon grace" (John 1:16). It is through him that "we have obtained access to this grace in which we stand" (Romans 5:2). Forgiveness is not a singular step in an individualistic *ordo salutis*, but a dynamic following of the *way* of salvation in Jesus Christ (John 14:6; Acts 9:2). Our entry into this way is trinitarian: it is through Christ that believers "have access in one Spirit to the Father" (Ephesians 2:18). In these subsections, I explore how the overlapping and interlacing of Christology and anthropology may shed light on the experience of redemptive forgiveness. In other writings, I have traced the historical development of the traditional themes of theological anthropology (personal identity, sin, and the image of God), explored directions for their reconstruction in late modern culture, and outlined Christian *koinōnia* in terms of sharing in the knowledge, suffering, and glory of Jesus Christ.[5] In what follows, these themes are intermingled within a specific treatment of the dynamics of forgiveness in soteriology.

The task of the third subsection within each part of this chapter is to interpret forgiveness in explicit dialogue with ecclesiological, pneumatological, and eschatological concerns. Treating these areas in detail is beyond the scope of the present book, but even the detection of recurrent constellations of ideas may itself be illuminative. Forgiveness, blessing, grace, peace, mercy—these all have to do with the way Christians actually live together day by day. It is to the generous Phil-

---

5. See F. L. Shults, *Reforming Theological Anthropology: After the Philosophical Turn to Relationality* (Grand Rapids: Eerdmans, 2003), chaps. 8–10; and idem, "Sharing in the Divine Nature," in *On Being Christian . . . and Human: Essays in Celebration of Ray S. Anderson* (ed. Todd Speidell; Eugene, Ore.: Wipf and Stock, 2002), part 2.

ippians that Paul writes: "You share in God's grace with me" (1:7). As we saw in chapter 4, salvation generally and forgiveness in particular have always been intimately linked to the sacramental life of the Christian church and especially to Baptism and the Eucharist. These too must be integrated into any Christian articulation of forgiveness. If forgiveness is only a celestial legal transaction that occurs over our heads, it does not really heal us. If forgiveness is only a therapeutic transformation of the systems of our lived world, it does not really save us. Forgiveness must also involve a real experience of the infinite reality of God's peaceful facing, so that we are able to face ourselves and others peacefully. Redemptive forgiveness opens us up to life in the Spirit so that we may live without anxiety, freely risking our being in the joy of belonging in relation to God and neighbor, because we already share in the coming reign of divine peace. Salvation occurs in real communal living—actually sharing God's forgiveness with the world, participating in the manifestation of divine grace, and becoming ministers of reconciliation. This chapter does not provide ordered steps to forgiveness; sharing in grace does not work that way. I believe, however, that a programmatic outline of discernible patterns of forgiveness in the context of a broader treatment of faith, love, and hope may provide a basis for clearer dialogue among theologians, psychologists, and anyone else who agonizes over the faces of forgiveness.

Forgiveness and Faith

The concept of faith is essential to the Christian understanding of salvation: "Therefore, since we are justified by faith, we have peace with God through our Lord Jesus Christ" (Romans 5:1). But what is the relation of faith to forgiveness? Let us examine this relation in three stages. First, the horizon for interpreting faith must be extended so that we can attend to its role in our broader experience of knowing and being known. The lack of faithfulness in our relations to others gives rise to epistemic anxiety—we worry about truth and trust. Second, the dynamics of faith in this general sense shape our identity as persons; for this reason, epistemic anxiety threatens our very selfhood. Christian faith has to do with finding personal identity in Jesus Christ through life in the Spirit. Third, faith is not only about our assenting to theoretical propositions or our noting the relevance of particular events—it also has to do with our fiduciary experiences,[6] with

6. Here I am playing with the common distinction in Christian soteriology between the three senses of faith as *notitia*, *assensus*, and *fiducia*.

the ties that bind us together as the church. Forgiveness occurs (or fails to occur) in the context of knowing (and being known) in sacramental community.

Facing Epistemic Anxiety

> Wisdom is better than jewels,
>> and all that you may desire cannot compare with her.
>>> —Proverbs 8:11

> Wisdom makes one's face shine.
>> —Ecclesiastes 8:1

Why do we seek forgiveness and struggle with forgiving others? Approaching this question epistemologically, we may say that part of the reason is that we do not know everything. Forgiving is so difficult because we are anxious about our knowledge of the other. Human self-conscious experience is driven by the need to believe, to trust, to belong in faithful communion. Forgiveness is needed when someone has broken faith. It is hard to forgive without knowing whether the other will break faith again.

Infidelity sparks a search for wisdom, a desire for confidence in our ability to negotiate relations with a perfidious offender. A convict must have enough credibility to convince a parole board if he wishes for his penalty to be diminished. An abusive or unfaithful husband needs to persuade his wife to trust him again. Both the board (for the sake of society) and the wife (for the sake of her children if not herself) are anxious about making true judgments about the perpetrator's past and future. In these cases, forgiveness waits for understanding. We would like to know and to be known in peaceful community, but we do not trust the other, and so we are afraid to forgive, to put away that which separates us from the other, that which protects us from being fooled again. The infidel is beyond belief; we refuse to be bound to him any longer. And do we even know or believe in ourselves enough to trust our own promises to forgive? If knowledge is power, we feel powerless. If our own ability to ascertain the future fidelity of the other is a precondition of forgiveness, we will never forgive. Manifesting grace to the other involves a dangerous renewal of the facial bonding necessary for interpersonal knowing. Negotiating these bonds requires knowledge, but human knowing is finite and fallible.

Redemptive forgiveness is supposed to remedy this anxiety, but how? Before the ecstasy of forgiveness comes the agony of facing our own limitations, acknowledging our inability to hold together the intelligibility of our lived world. As we become aware of the limits of our knowing, we become anxious about what we believe and worry about our relation to the truth. If we could grasp the truth with certainty and could render all things intelligible, then knowing would not be a problem and the painful struggle with forgiveness would diminish (although in such a scenario it might be meaningless to speak of forgiveness at all). In other words, humans need faith.[7] Although faith and knowledge have often been opposed, especially during the Enlightenment, late modern philosophy increasingly acknowledges the inherent trust involved in every knowing event. Even etymologically the word faith (*pistis*) is linked to knowledge (*epistēmē*). The root meaning of these Greek words has to do with "binding."[8]

The Christian conception of faith has its roots in the ancient Hebrew understanding of knowing, which expresses a concern for faithfulness in face-to-face covenantal relations. In the Hebrew Bible, truth (*emeth*) is that which is disclosed in history as dependable, reliable, and faithful. Knowing (*yada*) is not the contemplation of abstract eternal forms, but a faithful moving into relation. It involves a commitment that encompasses but transcends the Western focus on intellectual assent. Knowledge is oriented toward gaining wisdom, and wise persons orient themselves in upright and faithful relations in community. Human knowing implicates the whole person within the relational dynamics of life with God and neighbors.[9] The Hebrew Bible does not have an abstract noun that correlates precisely to the English term *faith*. The word *emunah* means "faithfulness" (or "faithful") and is typically applied to a person who is known and trusted. Here too we may trace an etymological connection between faithfulness (*emunah*) and truth (*emeth*). The thought world of the ancient Israelites was not bound by modernist theories about abstract and neutral knowledge— for them knowing was oriented toward faithful relations.

Epistemic anxiety is clearly connected to our theme of facing. The fear and desire that pervade the intersubjectivity of facing lead persons to deal with the threat to the self in a variety of ways, which oc-

7. See F. L. Shults, "Is It 'Natural' to Be Religious?" in *The Person: Perspectives from Science and Theology* (ed. N.-H. Gregersen; Studies in Theology and Science 6; Geneva: Labor et Fides, 2000), 103–13. B. Gerrish distinguishes between the generic or "elemental" faith held in common among human beings and the vision of the world that guides theistic and specifically Christian meaning-making and action in the world; *Saving and Secular Faith: An Introduction to Systematic Theology* (Minneapolis: Fortress, 1999).

8. Also in Latin one sees a connection between faith (*fides*) and being bound in relations of fidelity. Cf. F. L. Shults, "'Holding On' to the Theology-Psychology Relationship: The Underlying Fiduciary Structures of Interdisciplinary Method," *Journal of Psychology and Theology* 25 (1997): 329–40; and idem, *Reforming Theological Anthropology*, chap. 2.

9. The semantic range of the word *knowing* even covers sexual intercourse, a connection that is carried over into English in the King James Version: "Now Adam knew (*yada*) Eve his wife; and she conceived" (Genesis 4:1).

cur in the tension between two extremes: imploding into shameful self-facing to hide from the other or exploding through prideful facing down of the other. Both are attempts to secure the identity of the self over against the other. As we noted, a consistent loving face (usually the mother or primary caregiver) provides the developmental space (and time) for the healthy emergence of a child's ego functions, through which she then faces the world as a distinct personality. If our knowing is mediated through these dynamics of facing, so also will be our forgiving of one another. We are terrified by our inability to calm the cognitive dissonance in our relations to others, and yet we cannot escape our desire for an intimate knowing and being known. We worry about not being known at all, on the one hand, and about being known too intimately, on the other. The lack of trust clouds the vis-à-vis of human interaction and creates a haze that inhibits forgiveness.

The link between knowledge and forgiveness is also illustrated by the frequent pairing of forgiveness with forgetting. Forgive and forget, we are told. But can we simply forget what has happened—"ignore" (in the literal sense) the faithlessness of the past? Although Scripture uses the idiom of God's forgetting our sins, this is just as anthropomorphic as God's casting them into the sea. Christian forgiveness is not ignorant—it knows, but still offers grace. This knowing in faith cannot be deceived insofar as it truly shares in God's faithful embracing of the other. Redemptive forgiveness bears and overcomes sin not by forgetting or ignoring (i.e., not knowing) it, but by embracing the sinner in a way that heals the broken relations through infinite fidelity. This is possible only by sharing in divine grace. On the one hand, the need to forgive another means that one must get beyond ruminating on the offense, which easily leads to depression.[10] Yet, forgiveness is not necessarily a matter of altering one's judgment about the offense or of forcing oneself to suppress the memory. A forgiving person recognizes the offense as an offense, or the act would no longer be perceived as forgiveness. It is not the discernment of guilt but the emotional response and practical demand for retribution that may be altered. Further, forgiveness in the redemptive sense may be fully offered *along with* a prudent and just treatment of the other, which may include the provision of space and time for the other to fulfill the requirements of a legal transaction and/or to experience therapeutic transformation.

Commenting on the precept "know yourself," Augustine observes that "when it is said to the mind, Know yourself; then it knows itself

---

10. Cf. M. L. Bringle, "'I Just Can't Stop Thinking about It': Depression, Rumination, and Forgiveness," *Word and World* 16 (1996): 340–46.

by that very act by which it understands the word *yourself*" (*On the Trinity* 10.9.12). What is the origin of this self-relation in which *I* know *my self*? It cannot be the "I" (ego), for what I call my ego emerged only within self-conscious reflection on my "self." It cannot be the "self," for this is the object of "my" reflection through which I find myself. The relationality is irreducible. This self-reflective aspect of what I have been calling epistemic anxiety is a recurrent theme in philosophy.[11] For Christians, the origin of the relationality of the self's knowing of itself is the knowledge of God. Calvin explicitly linked knowledge of self to knowledge of God. The first two subsections of the *Institutes* are titled "Without Knowledge of Self There Is No Knowledge of God" and "Without Knowledge of God There Is No Knowledge of Self." The search for personal identity is intrinsically bound to the search for the absolute origin of our longing to know and be known. As Kierkegaard expresses it, the self as a relation that relates itself to itself is in despair until "in relating itself to itself and in willing to be itself, the self rests transparently in the power that established it,"[12] namely the power of the Eternal or the Infinite.

The limitations of human knowledge are ultimately revealed in confrontation with the idea of Infinity. We long for a secure relation to truth, to get a hold on reality. Yet, we cannot get our minds around the Infinite, and this inability evokes both fear and fascination. The inherent connection between infinity and divinity was recognized by the earliest human cultures; this can be traced from the end of the last ice age to the early Egyptian, Babylonian, and Chinese mathematicians. In ancient Greece, however, the main streams of philosophical thought developed a strong distaste for the idea of the limitless (*apeiron*). The power of reason to comprehend was privileged to such an extent that the idea of a reality beyond the grasp of the human mind was, well, hard to imagine. An infinite being (an unlimited substance beyond comprehension) either would not be good or simply could not exist.[13] Among early church theologians, it was tempting to follow these philosophical sentiments and concede that God is finite, an object that

11. The realization that the self cannot be the ground of its knowing of itself drove thinkers in the Enlightenment to reflection on the Infinite or the Absolute as the transcendental condition of human knowing. Cf. D. Klemm and G. Zöller (eds.), *Figuring the Self: Subject, Absolute, and Others in Classical German Philosophy* (Albany: State University of New York Press, 1997).

12. S. Kierkegaard, *The Sickness unto Death* (trans. H. V. Hong and E. H. Hong; Princeton: Princeton University Press, 1980), 14.

13. Plato's *Philebus* illustrates the position that because the unlimited is indefinite, it is imperfect; for this reason, it should not be attributed to the supreme divinity. For Aristotle "being" is categorized in terms of "matter" and "form"—the "formless" would not have being. In both cases, "infinite" did not seem an appropriate predicate for the absolutely good being.

may be grasped by natural human reason. The heretic Eunomious, for example, posited precisely this. Against this heresy, the Cappadocian fathers of the fourth century and especially Gregory of Nyssa insisted on the inscrutability of God. They articulated a positive view of Infinity as superabundant absolute perfection instead of the negative (more quantitatively oriented) view of Infinity as indefinite. Unlike his philosophical contemporaries who disliked the infinite because they could not grasp it mentally, Gregory delighted in knowing God as a being-grasped by the perfectly Infinite divine presence.

Paul rejoices that the Galatians "have come to know God," but immediately clarifies himself: "or rather to be *known* by God" (Galatians 4:9, emphasis added). For Christians, epistemic anxiety is eased not by grasping a concept of the divine but by an experience of knowing the love of Christ "that surpasses knowledge, so that you may be filled with all the fullness of God" (Ephesians 3:19). The inscrutable trinitarian God of the New Testament is the one by whom and through whom and in whom we know and are known (cf. Romans 11:33–36). "Knowledge puffs up," Paul observes, "but anyone who loves God is *known by* him" (1 Corinthians 8:2–3, emphasis added). Moreover, the believer's knowing of God is not static or "finished"—Paul recognizes that now he knows "in part" but he anticipates knowing fully "even as I have been fully *known*" (13:12, emphasis added). The good news of the gospel is that the mystery of the unknown God is made known by the Holy Spirit through the incarnation of the Logos in Jesus Christ. It is through the Spirit, who "is the truth" (1 John 5:6), and through the Son of God, who "has given us understanding," that we "know him who is true" (5:20).

The surprisingly intimate nature of this knowing, however, is that "we are in him who is true, in his Son Jesus Christ" (1 John 5:20), and the gift of the Spirit is what makes possible our abiding in God and God's abiding in us (3:24). Through the Spirit of Christ it is made known that divine Infinity is not simply beyond the finite but comprehends the finite—the Infinite knows the finite into existence, so to speak, and binds it together. The biblical God is not simply one of (and not even the greatest of all) the objects of human comprehension. When Paul corrects the Athenians' view of the unknown God, he does not provide them with a new object for them to idolize along with their other concepts of the divine. Instead he urges them to remember that God is the one "in whom we live and move and have our being" (Acts 17:28). The infinite God grants this life so that creatures might grope after God (17:27). Redemptive forgiveness is not ignorant or agnostic—it is an incursive and evocative "prognosis" that faces the other with perfect fidelity.

Human beings anxiously search for a faithful face that will never go away. They long to know and to be fully known while bound in faithful promising love. According to Jeremiah's prophecy, the manifestation of divine forgiveness in the new covenant of the LORD will resolve this anxiety: "No longer shall they . . . say to each other, 'Know the LORD,' for they shall all know me . . . ; for I will forgive their iniquity, and remember their sin no more" (31:34). Christians believe that this promise is fulfilled in the face of Jesus Christ through the presence of the Spirit. In faith they find themselves embraced by an all-encompassing divine countenance. Through faith in Christ they are bound together by the Spirit of truth. By faith they enter into a new way of knowing themselves and others *as* they are known by God. Believers still hold, still trust, but this is a peaceful knowing because it emerges out of a being-known by the one whose faithfulness upholds all things. Growing in Christian faith means learning not to depend on one's own finite epistemic power to secure one's identity, learning not to withhold forgiveness as a way of protecting the self. It means finding one's identity in relation to the Father of Jesus Christ through life in the Spirit, which opens up the self to share in the joy of redemptive forgiveness.

Finding Personal Identity in Jesus Christ

Paul describes his new identity in Christ by explaining to the Galatians that "it is no longer I who live, but it is Christ who lives in me. And the life I now live in the flesh I live by faith in the Son of God, who loved me and gave himself for me" (Galatians 2:20). This union with Christ is so intimate that Paul is elsewhere compelled to speak of the person who is connected to the Lord as "one spirit" with him (1 Corinthians 6:17). On the assumptions of classical metaphysics with its anthropology of substances,[14] this idea of finding personal identity "in Christ" is vexing. A radical union with or in another person would mean being identical to him or her. In this case the particularity of one identity is absorbed into or crushed by the substance of the other. The turn to relationality, however, may help us articulate an understanding of union with Christ by the Spirit in a way that both coheres with the intuitions of the biblical tradition and illuminates religious experience.

14. Moving beyond the ancient and early modern idea of the *soul* as an immaterial individual substance, R. Williams suggests instead that we use *soul* to refer to "a whole way of speaking, of presenting and 'uttering' the self, that presupposes *relation* as the ground that gives the self room to exist, a relation developing in time, a relation with an agency which addresses or summons the self, but is in itself no part of the system of interacting and negotiating speakers in the world"; *Lost Icons: Reflections on Cultural Bereavement* (Edinburgh: Clark, 2000), 160.

Experiencing forgiveness as sharing in divine grace involves the formation of a special kind of identity. In light of Paul's dialectic between "I" and "not-I," we will speak of this as the Christian's "dialectical identity."[15] First, it is essential to realize that every person's identity is *already* dialectical. As persons, we find ourselves in an ongoing process of receiving our identity in relation to others. The self emerges in the field of consciousness already confronted by and confronting others. The self knows itself in an ongoing self-identification as it is known and identified by others. This self-identifying is not grounded in the self; the self *finds* itself *already known* by others, already being identified by those who are beyond the self. The personal identity of an individual, then, is conditioned by the relation of the self to others.[16] The ego is the agency by which a person attempts to "found" the self in relation to that which is beyond the self (the "not-I"). A person struggles to hold together the meaning of the world through this agency. The fact that the ego is both centripetally figured (self-centered) and centrifugally oriented (other-facing) explains the epistemic dizziness that drives the self to find and secure its identity. Ultimately, however, the self cannot secure its own identity, for it is given by others. However, it is "given" not as a completed substance, but as a "call" from the other(s) to come into relation. Personal identity is found in the relating of the self to others, in the knowing of others who are relating to the self. If the gift and call to find one's identity is mediated to the self in ways that threaten abuse or desertion, the ego is terrified. If self-identification depends wholly on relations with finite others, then the particularity of the self will always be in danger of being crushed or abandoned.

Persons long for relations to other persons in which they can know and be known without epistemic anxiety. Only by finding one's identity in relation to an infinite Other, however, is it possible to become oneself peacefully. If personal identity is found as one is known by a *truly infinite* Other, the self has space and time to become itself without losing its finite historical particularity. This is what Christian faith is all about: finding oneself in "the peace of God, which surpasses all understanding," which guards one's heart and mind "in Christ Jesus" (Philippians 4:7). Christian faith is knowing oneself as dependent on being known by God. The believer finds personal identity outside of

15. J. E. Loder and W. J. Neidhardt use this phrase in *The Knight's Move: The Relational Logic of the Spirit in Theology and Science* (Colorado Springs: Helmers & Howard, 1992), 188–89, 236. I treat these dynamics in more detail in F. L. Shults, "Becoming 'One Spirit' with the Lord," *Princeton Theological Review* 7 (2000): 17–26.

16. P. Ricoeur argues "that the selfhood of oneself implies otherness to such an intimate degree that one cannot be thought of without the other"; *Oneself as Another* (trans. K. Blamey; Chicago: University of Chicago Press, 1992), 3.

herself in Christ, that is, in an epistemic relation upheld through life "in the Spirit." Eternal life is connected to knowing God: "And this is eternal life, that they may know you, the only true God, and Jesus Christ whom you have sent" (John 17:3). The believer *as believer* knows God as she is known by God; she is *already* identified and bound in spiritual union with the Lord, although she longs for an ever increasing intensification of that union. She is filled with Christ, who is all and in all (Colossians 3:11). This filling does not crush her particularity but faithfully holds it together, granting her space and time to grow in wisdom. Finding herself "in Christ," she is freed to manifest grace to the other, even to forgive her enemies, because her desire for knowing and being known—her very identity—is hid with Christ in God (3:3). Free from epistemic anxiety in this infinitely safe relationality, she is able to face her neighbor in faithfulness—not by trying to "found" the identity of the other but by inviting him into relation to the only one who can: the biblical God who delights in manifesting grace.

Why is the relation to Jesus Christ so important in this dialectical identity? Because it is through the history of this man's relation to the one he called Father that the ideal human relation to God is revealed. The very concept of "person" itself was shaped by reflection on the history of Jesus and his reliance on the Spirit in relation to the Father. The knowledge of God, the mystery of the human relation to the divine, was revealed in the *prosōpon* of Jesus Christ. The Greek word *prosōpon*, which as we saw in chapter 4 can mean face or presence, can also be rendered "person." As K. P. Wesche explains, early Christian theology departed from the universal psychology model of ancient Greece and started with the particular individual Jesus Christ. What it meant to be a person was radically impacted by the resulting christological debates.[17] Wolfhart Pannenberg argues that early theologians came to view individuals as persons by virtue of their special relation to God, "either (like Jesus) in openness to fellowship with [God], or in being closed to this destiny."[18] In Pannenberg's own constructive proposal, he defines person as "the presence of the self in the moment of the ego," a presence mediated by the Spirit. If this presence is based on the relation to God, then "persons can be free in the face of their social situation."[19] This is how Jesus found his own identity, and Christians are called to become persons in the same way.

17. K. P. Wesche, "The Soul and Personality: Tracing the Roots of the Christological Problem," *Pro Ecclesia* 5 (1996): 23–42 at 38–39.

18. W. Pannenberg, *Systematic Theology* (trans. G. W. Bromiley; Grand Rapids: Eerdmans, 1994), 2.199.

19. W. Pannenberg, *Anthropology in Theological Perspective* (trans. M. J. O'Connell; Philadelphia: Westminster, 1985), 240–41.

Practicing redemptive forgiveness requires participation "in Christ," a theme that is crucial in Pauline theology.[20] Not only are we in Christ but Christ is being formed "in us" (Galatians 4:19). The mutuality of this prepositional use of *in* suggests that Paul is not thinking of spatial relations but of personal *koinōnia*. Sharing in divine grace is spelled out in Paul's writings in terms of the material plenitude of life in Christ. This fellowship of believers in Christ includes the experiences of sanctification (1 Corinthians 1:2); grace (Ephesians 2:7; 1 Corinthians 1:4); connection to the source of life (Romans 6:23; 1 Corinthians 1:30); new creation (2 Corinthians 5:17); righteousness (5:21; Ephesians 2:10); every spiritual blessing, including calling, adoption, and forgiveness (1:3–10); release from condemnation (Romans 8:1–2); being built up spiritually in faith (Colossians 2:7) into a dwelling place for God (Ephesians 2:22); fullness (Colossians 2:10); the peace of God (Philippians 4:7); satisfaction of every need (4:19); racial, class, and gender reconciliation (Galatians 3:28); and the presence and promise of abiding with God (John 15:1–7; 1 John 2:24–25). Being in Christ means finding oneself identified through one's relation to the Spirit in whom the Son is faithfully bound to the Father. It is through the Spirit that we know Christ and have the "mind" of Christ (1 Corinthians 2:10–16). Only those who have the Spirit belong to Christ (Romans 8:9). As observed in chapter 4, the early Reformers retrieved Paul's emphasis on spiritual union with God in Christ as the main point of salvation.

It is important to realize that Jesus found his own identity as a human person not only in relation to the Father and the Spirit, but in relation to the community that formed around him. In the presence of his disciples, Jesus prays: "As you, Father, are in me and I am in you, may they also be in us. . . . The glory that you have given me I have given them, so that they may be one, as we are one, I in them and you in me, that they may become completely one" (John 17:21–23). Jesus is one with the Father, but this identity is a dialectical unity in the Spirit, not an undifferentiated unity. Throughout his gospel, John portrays Jesus as making God known by inviting others to be born anew of the Spirit and into the mutual fellowship of the Son and the Father. Jesus welcomes those who believe into the relational union of this shared knowledge. Through the power of the Spirit, Jesus lived a life of radical faithfulness to God the Father as he ministered to his neighbors. In his facing of others, Jesus responded to the call to entrust

20. J. D. G. Dunn argues that participation in Christ "leads more directly into the rest of Paul's theology than justification"; *The Theology of Paul the Apostle* (Grand Rapids: Eerdmans, 1998), 395. E. P. Sanders suggests that the heart of Paul's theology is expressed in "participationist terms of being found in Christ"; *Paul and Palestinian Judaism: A Comparison of Patterns of Religion* (London: SCM, 1977), 505.

himself to God (1 Peter 2:23) even when suffering at the hands of his enemies; believers are encouraged to follow his example and "entrust themselves to a faithful Creator" (4:19). Like Christ, the identity of the Christian is not primarily determined by her relations to the angry and shameful interfacing of others but by her relation in the Spirit to the gracious Face of the Father; by her confident trust in God she is identified by her neighbors as a fiduciary of divine grace.

Christians long to "be found" in Christ (Philippians 3:9), to "grow in the knowledge of God" (Colossians 1:10). The use of the gerund *finding* in the title of this subsection is not accidental. Finding oneself in Christ is a process. The new self of the believer "is being renewed in knowledge" (3:10). In the experience of knowing and being known by God, wherein the Other that mediates the self to itself is the presence of the Spirit of Christ, the identity of the self is always newly composed by this infinite Other. The faithful arrival of this new creation (and composition) cancels the need for the ego to hold together the world. A person can enter into rest (Hebrews 4:11). Being distinct from God is accepted as the gift of finitude, and one no longer anxiously tries to hold God to the self or to secure God as one rational object among others.

This does *not* mean going against reason or accepting a logical contradiction. It means humbly recognizing the limits of human rationality and its inherent dependence upon and orientation toward that which is beyond it. Skeptics will perceive this reference to mystery as a way of hiding behind a religious illusion (Freud) or as a sign of weakness (Nietzsche). I want to make a clear distinction between *appealing to mystery* at the end of one's argument when it leads to a contradiction, and the *appeal of mystery* when one begins to face the infinite God made known in Christ, whose Spirit fulfills our longings for knowing and being known.[21] The mystery of God's wisdom is not a puzzling secret for individual reflection. Yes, *my* salvation, *my* identity, is secured by God's grace, but as I am being saved, my journey toward wholeness, health, and faithfulness is socially located, mediated by the meaning-making of a particular community.

Knowing in Sacramental Community

The Christian community experiences salvation as the transformation of knowing and being known in embodied[22] or sacramental fellowship. Sacramentality is essential to the corporate identity of those

21. Cf. F. L. Shults, *The Postfoundationalist Task of Theology* (Grand Rapids: Eerdmans, 1999), chap. 5.

22. The early church had to fight against Gnosticism, the view that redemption comes through an abstract gnosis (knowledge) that escapes from concrete embodied existence and mutual interdependence on others.

who are called into this life of faithful forgiving. My sacramental emphasis in a discussion of forgiveness may initially seem puzzling, but the use of the term is more than an effort to transverse ecumenical boundaries. The Latin word *sacramentum*[23] translates the Greek *mystērion*, which is explicitly linked in the New Testament to knowledge of God in Christ. The revelation of Jesus Christ is the primal sacrament, the mystery of divine redemption that has been *made known* (Ephesians 1:9; 3:3–10). This mystery is itself the knowing and being known that comes from sharing in the divine knowledge: the riches of the glory of the mystery of God is "Christ in you" (Colossians 1:27). The mystery (*sacramentum*) of God's wisdom was manifested in the history of Jesus Christ, through whom believers now share in eternal life through the Spirit (cf. 2 Corinthians 5:11; 1 John 1:3; 2:17, 25; 3:24; 5:11, 20; Philemon 6). Paul is given grace "to make everyone see" the mystery that was hidden in God "so that through the church the wisdom of God in its rich variety might now be made known" (Ephesians 3:9–10).

Forgiveness and the sacraments have always been linked in church history, as we saw in chapter 4. Under the reign of the *ordo salutis*, sacramentality was imprisoned by substance metaphysics. In response to Roman excesses, the mediating role of the church in redemption was downplayed in much of Protestant theology; however, the adverse effects of this neglect on the dynamism of fellowship in the church eventually sparked a renewal of ecclesiological reflection. After the (re)turn to relationality, the *real* presence of divine grace may more easily be articulated and found consonant with the ecclesial experience of knowing and being known in *real relations*.[24] The sacramental life of the church is a response to the revelation of the mystery of God made known in Christ. This life together takes shape in a communal sharing in the Spirit (*koinōnia pneumatos*; Philippians 2:1). The church is the communion of those who believe in and are bound to the relational mystery revealed in Christ. This is not merely an aggregate of separate individuals who all have the same object of knowledge. Rather, the sacramental community is a dynamic nexus of concrete relations; the church is constituted by the relational presence of the Spirit of Christ in which it coheres and to which it adheres. As we will see in the next two sections, this shift has radical implications for

23. In ancient Rome, the term originally indicated something set aside for a religious purpose. The decision to translate the Greek term *mystērion* in the Latin Vulgate with *sacramentum* registered its effect on the later sacramental debates.

24. For Calvin, the sacraments were all about relations, as his Catholic interlocutors realized. Presupposing the Aristotelian categories of substance versus relations, however, they saw his view as non-substantial. Cf. G. C. Berkouwer's review of this debate in *The Sacraments* (Grand Rapids: Eerdmans, 1969), 56–89.

understanding Baptism and the Eucharist. However, it also affects other activities traditionally considered sacramental, such as the confession of sins and the confirmation of faith in the promising word of grace.

Sacraments have often been defined in the tradition as visible signs of invisible grace. To avoid the Platonic dualism lurking behind this definition, we might capture the same intuition by saying that sacraments are the manifestation of infinite grace in and through finite signs. Humans are sign-making and symbol-constructing creatures; every social group and culture tries in its own way to respond to that which is beyond its finite control. Christians too make *signs* that express their intentionality in relation to God and their neighbors. The sacraments signify the community's dependence on God's tending and the awareness of its members that they are called to attend to one another. The signs we make as the church, as we work out our salvation together in fear and trembling (Philippians 2:12), signal our identity. Sacramental practice is linked to the word (*logos*) of God in which Christians discover the intention of creaturely existence. Through the sacraments, the community signals its freedom from the painful signification of guilt and shame and interprets itself as a fellowship subtended by the *koinōnia*-creating presence of the Spirit of Christ (cf. Matthew 18:20; 1 Corinthians 12:13; Acts 1–2; Ephesians 2:22; 2 Corinthians 13:13; Romans 8:9–27; 5:5; Colossians 1:8). As Rowan Williams notes, the significance of Jesus' life and death is unprecedentedly effective:

> By offering and effecting forgiveness, and forming a community around this reality, human relationships and potentialities are set free from the paralysing and self-intensifying consequences of hostility and aggression to each other and to ourselves, from the lethal symbiosis of violence and guilt. There is a "new creation"; so that this sign, the identity of Jesus, is of fundamental significance. . . . In these [sacramental] acts the Church "makes sense" of itself . . . but its "sense" is seen as dependent on the creative act of God in Christ. . . . The Church's sacramental action is the Father's art. . . . They are the drawing of believers into the life of the kingdom of God.[25]

In the light of divine forgiveness, the sacraments of the church signify the comprehensive effect of the revelation of the mystery of God's redeeming presence in Christ by the power of the Spirit.

Forgiveness as sharing in divine grace is constitutive for the Christian community. It is the gift and call of the corporate identity of the church. Jesus gave this commission to his disciples: "'As the Father

25. R. Williams, *On Christian Theology* (Oxford: Blackwell, 2000), 205–6.

has sent me, so I send you.' When he had said this, he breathed on them and said to them 'Receive the Holy Spirit. If you forgive the sins of any, they are forgiven them; if you retain the sins of any, they are retained'" (John 20:21b–23). The outpouring of the Spirit of the resurrected Christ creates a particular community in history. As the "body" of Christ, those in this fellowship share together a knowing and being known by God, who holds them together in the Spirit as they experience the delightful terror of the sacraments. As the community receives the Spirit of grace, it becomes a gracious fellowship, finding its identity as it shares in redemptive forgiveness. The forgiveness of sins, as part of the mystery of God's wisdom, is not merely something Christians announce; it *is* the dynamic reality of communal knowing and being known in the *koinōnia* of the Spirit. Forgiveness is an act of faith, that is, a faithful knowing that identifies itself in sharing with the other. Knowing in sacramental community takes shape in worship and service, whereby the church receives the gift of its corporate identity and calling anew. The church finds its identity in the reception and sharing of this gracious presence of the Spirit of Christ. The church does not have or control its identity through its own power, but receives it in response to divine grace. The members of the church are bound together in grace as they face one another faithfully and rely together on the saving Face of God. The sacramental community that worships and serves the biblical God is becoming itself as it responds to and shares in the mystery of God: the intimacy of the Son's knowledge of the Father in the Spirit.

Knowing in sacramental community is an *intensification* of life in the Spirit of Christ. This idea may help us resolve the tension between the general creative versus the particular redemptive presence of the divine Spirit, which we noted in chapter 4. The same Spirit who gives life to all creatures calls self-conscious creatures toward an intensification of new life. As the third person of the Trinity, the Holy Spirit is the origin, condition, and goal of the intensification of creaturely existence. The presence of the divine Spirit is the origin of all life and holds all life in a unifying tension. Self-conscious human life exists in this same tensive field of finitude upheld by the Spirit, but it experiences this field as a self-intensification in relation to other creatures. As the condition for this intensifying of the self in communion with others, the evocative presence of the Spirit calls human life toward ever more intense participation in the fellowship of the Son with the Father. For this reason, we may say that the Spirit is also the eternal goal of the intense human search for *koinōnia*. The Holy Spirit is personal in all of these ways, but only and always as the Spirit of the Father and the Son. In the painful but redemptive process of seeking salvation, humans exist on the basis of the Spirit as the general source of life in which they live and move and have their being. Redemption involves an intensification of this relational existence as a sharing in divine grace.

Redemptive forgiveness is political. Forgiving is not the isolated act of an individual will, but an intensification of salutary ordering in the Spirit in which persons are drawn more deeply into fellowship through divine grace: "There is no longer Jew or Greek, there is no longer slave or free, there is no longer male and female; for all of you are one in Christ Jesus" (Galatians 3:28). This means that all of our political relations, whether rooted in differences of race, class, or gender, will no longer wholly define our identity. As the sacramental community that is "one in Christ Jesus" we seek to become the *polis* of the God of peace; for this reason, our policing of one another should not be characterized primarily by institutional policies that keep "us" in and "them" out of power—by conflicts of interest. Sacramental politics should transform persons in community so that they come to have the "same mind" that was in Christ Jesus, who looked not to his own interests but considered the interests of others (Philippians 2:4–7). In Christ, God was reconciling the world to himself, and now the church (as the body of Christ) finds its identity as it shares in God's ministry of reconciliation in the world (2 Corinthians 5:19–20). The political life of the church should be a sign of divine faithfulness.

Knowing in the Spirit means finding oneself in the embrace of God and other believers.[26] The goal of Christ's prayer to the Father in John is that the disciples may be "one" and "in us"—"so that the world may *believe* . . . so that the world may *know*" (17:21–23). The whole world is called to share in this fellowship as it is confronted by a community of persons whose knowing of one another manifests the faithfulness of God, signaling the presence of the Spirit of Christ. Trying to face one's own sin or to have faith without seeing the "face" of the other is *spiritual* prosopagnosia.[27] Confession of sin and confession of faith occur before others, facing other persons (cf. James

26. Volf illustrates the explanatory power of focusing on relations in his analysis of the apparent impasses between Episcopal models, which stress the mediation of grace through the bishop, and free-church models, which speak of the unmediated presence of the grace of Christ. Volf observes that "both models underestimate the enormous ecclesiological significance of concrete relations with other Christians, relations through which every Christian becomes a Christian and in which that person lives as a Christian"; *After Our Likeness: The Church as the Image of the Trinity* (Grand Rapids: Eerdmans, 1998), 134.

27. Prosopagnosia is a psychological condition in which a person is unable to recognize or sometimes even see the faces of others. Cf. O. Sacks, *The Man Who Mistook His Wife for a Hat* (New York: Touchstone, 1998).

5:16; Matthew 10:32–33). Understanding and practicing Christian forgiveness, then, requires sharing in the life of the community. This is why Jones speaks of the need for crafting communities of forgiveness, engaging persons in practices that are crucial for sustaining forgiven and forgiving identities: "Learning to be forgiven and to forgive requires us also to learn to speak (and listen) truthfully, pray, heal, confess, and engage in mutual admonition. Further, activities such as hospitality . . . are also crucial to forming and sustaining Christian community and enabling us to discover what it means to be forgiven."[28]

Becoming a forgiven and forgiving self involves finding one's identity in relation to other selves in community. Just as not having enough faithful faces in one's life leads to anxiety, so too does having too many faces. In other words, it is possible to be overwhelmed by the call to face every "other." As will become clear in the remainder of this chapter, I am not suggesting that the Christian should become self-effacing or pusillanimous, but that through life in Christ she can develop a disposition of fidelity and openness to others that maintains appropriate and permeable boundaries—as she finds herself overwhelmed by God's grace.[29]

Placing forgiveness and the sacraments within an ecclesiological context does not mean limiting them to events inside a church building. The church is the called *out* (*ekklēsia*) community but it finds its identity in being called *to* faithful ministry in the real systems of the lived world. The sacramental community is *elected*[30] to move faithfully into the world, sharing the knowledge of Jesus Christ. The unique sacramentality of Christianity expresses its particularity, but it must do more than this if the church wants to avoid cultic solipsism. Sacramental activities like confession of sin and confirmation of faith should also be signs in and to the world of the in-breaking reign of divine peace. The mystery of God revealed in Christ is not a contradiction, and sacramental life is not secretive. The manifestation of the reality of the infinite trini-

---

28. L. G. Jones, "Crafting Communities of Forgiveness," *Interpretation* 54 (2000): 121–34 at 131.

29. For a practical Christian treatment of the challenge of being overwhelmed, see D. F. Ford, *The Shape of Living: Spiritual Directions for Everyday Life* (Grand Rapids: Baker, 1997).

30. In both the Hebrew Bible and the New Testament, election is not primarily about the status of individuals based on a decision in the past, but about the call of the community (or the person who leads the community) that orients it toward the future (cf. Genesis 12:1–3; Deuteronomy 7:6; Isaiah 42:1; Romans 8:28–30; Ephesians 1:4–9; Luke 9:35). The New Testament word usually translated "election" is *eklegomai*, which was used in Greek antiquity to denote the calling of a person or a group to perform a particular task (e.g., Plato's *Republic*).

tarian God makes us known to ourselves and to each other, so that we truly know *as* we are known. In and through the Spirit of Christ the sacramental community signals the liberation of the world from guilt and shame through the real experience of redemptive forgiveness.[31]

Forgiveness and Love

Like faith, love is essential to the Christian understanding of salvation: "Everyone who loves is born of God and knows God. Whoever does not love does not know God, for God is love" (1 John 4:7b–8). "The only thing that counts is faith working through love" (Galatians 5:6b). In what way is love related to forgiveness? I explore this relation in three steps. First, our horizon for understanding love must be expanded, and so I observe the generic sense in which human *eros* desires ostensible goods. Broadly conceived, love strives for the good life; and ethical anxiety emerges in the context of this struggle. Second, I outline the theological claim that human agents may become righteous by sharing in Jesus Christ's "dying to sin"; cruciformity and redemptive forgiveness come together. Third, I argue that the forgiveness of sins really does have to do with Baptism, but suggest that we may gain new insight into these dynamics if we think not simply of the washing of individual souls, but more broadly of baptized living in pneumatological, ecclesiological, and eschatological perspective.

My exploration of the relation between forgiveness and love will be guided by John's straightforward definition: "We know *love* by this, that he laid down his life for us—and we ought to *lay down our lives* for one another. How does God's love abide in anyone who has the world's *goods* and sees a brother or sister in need and yet refuses help?" (1 John 3:16–17). Knowing in faith is not enough for redemptive forgiveness. Perhaps intellectually I can work up an abstract mental forgiveness. But to *act* lovingly toward my enemy who has acted wickedly toward me—this is something else entirely. How should we approach this overwhelming task of sharing in God's loving grace by laying down our lives for one another?

31. M. Welker argues that "it is the forgiveness of sins that creates the unity of human beings with God. The forgiveness of sins awakens the world-overcoming power of sacrifice and free self-withdrawal—a power that proceeds from the communion of the sanctified in a self-endangering world. By the act of liberation from the power of sin, the presence of the Holy Spirit as a saving public person comes to be felt in worldwide influence and effectiveness"; *God the Spirit* (trans. J. F. Hoffmeyer; Minneapolis: Fortress, 1994), 315.

Facing Ethical Anxiety

I can will what is right, but I cannot do it. For I do not do the good I want, but the evil I do not want is what I do. . . . Wretched man that I am! Who will rescue me from this body of death?

—Romans 7:18b–19, 24

Do not sin to save face.

—Sirach 42:1

Why do we agonize over God's forgiveness of us, and why is it such hard work for us to forgive others? Examining these questions from an ethical perspective, we may say that this agony is partially due to our not having the power to secure all of our desires. What's love got to do with it? Human persons are essentially lovers, seeking to relate themselves to objects of desire. We *act* intentionally because we *love* objects that we judge to be *good*. Desire for a particular (putative) good leads us to act. This is the structural pattern of personal agency.

If humans are sometimes called moral animals, this is not because they are all good and just, but because their identity as agents is characterized by an ambiguous orientation toward doing what seems right or desiring what seems good to them. Ethical anxiety emerges not only in relation to choices about particular goods, but also more deeply in the existential worry that our very capacity to choose, our finite power to relate to goodness, will ultimately fail. Specific questions about which objects a particular moral agent should desire are dependent on a prior and more basic question: what is the ultimate origin, condition, and goal of human agency? With this question, we enter the arena of philosophical and religious discourse. In Plato's *Symposium*, Socrates tells his interlocutors the story of his encounter with Diotima. She taught him that the god Eros helps the soul move toward the Good. In Aristotle's *Nichomachean Ethics*, human agency moves toward the goal of personal happiness; this teleological movement is ultimately ("finally") caused by the Unmoved Mover. These are only two examples of the philosophical intuition that action, love, and goodness are inherently connected to a religious reality.[32]

Even nontheological anthropological theories must explain why humans act in ways that are self-alienating and other-abusing rather than in ways that promote love and goodness. For example, psychological explanations of human misery may find its roots in the sup-

---

32. "The word 'religion' is derived from the Latin 'religare' which means 'to bind together': a religion binds together the believer and that which is most real, through practices the very performance of which is to assume the relation that is taken to be the chief human good"; J. Stone, "A Theory of Religion," *Religious Studies* 27 (1991): 337–51 at 339.

pression of the intellect (Spinoza) or the repression of sexuality (Freud). Sociological explanations of the agony of social life may identify its origin in prehistoric times when happy naked savages piled up more wheat than necessary (Rousseau) or in the primal accumulation of capital (Marx). More recently biologists like Richard Dawkins and E. O. Wilson argue that moral failure may be explained as nothing more than the functioning of selfish genes trying to survive. Each nontheological hamartiology brings with it a nontheological soteriology, proposing various salvations: better intellectual training, therapy, a social contract, the revolution of the proletariat, or perhaps genetic engineering. Whether self-consciously "religious" or not, most persons are concerned with *acting* in ways that provide them with what they perceive to be the good life. Philosophical anthropological reflection is a search for the ultimate source of this life, whether or not this source is explicitly called the "divine."

This ethical tension so dominates human existence that some philosophers grant ethics primacy over epistemology or metaphysics. For the purposes of our exploration of forgiveness, Emmanuel Levinas provides a particularly good example because his work in ethics explicitly deals with the importance of the face. Levinas writes of the "epiphany" of the face, the intersubjective space of the "face to face" that is the irreducible and ultimate relation.[33] This mutual facing occurs within (or as) a dynamic intersubjective field; the call of the face of the other obliges the self as it emerges within this primordial relation. Suffering confrontation in the face of the other is "otherwise than being," for the face confronts us not as a static object but as the "*way* of the neighbor."[34] All of our anxiety about loving and being loved—about community, responsibility, domination, and liberation—appears in this interpersonal field of facing and being faced. Levinas recognizes that we are dealing with something that cannot be reduced to the social interaction of human individuals. While "the face opens the primordial discourse whose first word is obligation which no 'interiority' permits avoiding," it also raises essential religious questions: "The welcoming of the face is peaceable from the first, for it answers to the unquenchable Desire for Infinity."[35]

When we think of ourselves as "lovers," we usually are not referring to objects but to our desire for other persons. Individual intentional agency is characterized by a struggle to resolve the obligatory tension

33. E. Levinas, *Totality and Infinity* (trans. A. Lingis; Pittsburgh: Duquesne University Press, 1969), 295.

34. E. Levinas, *Otherwise than Being; or, Beyond Essence* (trans. A. Lingis; Pittsburgh: Duquesne University Press, 1998), 88. Cf. idem, "Is Ontology Fundamental?," in his *Basic Philosophical Writings* (Bloomington: Indiana University Press, 1996), 1–10.

35. Levinas, *Totality and Infinity*, 201, 150.

between the self and other personal agents. The problem is that moral subjectivity as a structured self-relation is not and cannot be established by the self.[36] Persons lack power not only over the objects of their desire, but over desire itself. A personal agent discovers her "self" already emplotted in a historical trajectory, with intentions and obligations that operate within a community that mediates criteria for discerning good actions. Agents are embedded in an unfolding story in which they find themselves already loving and longing to be loved. This agency is characterized by an intense longing for intimacy.[37] At about age two, a child begins to realize that she cannot control her relations to others; intimacy is threatened and becomes threatening. To protect herself, she says "no" to everything, sharply differentiating the self from any and all "not-I" whatsoever. Here on the field of interpersonal anxiety, the ego has landed.

Ego functions develop as increasingly complex ways of acting aimed at composing and controlling the relation between self and other. This is normally characterized by an attempt to maintain equilibrium between independence on the one side and inclusion (or assimilation) on the other.[38] The child longs to be intimate with the other (to love and be loved), but she is also afraid of being absorbed by the other. Although most of us learn to repress these fears after they are embarrassingly displayed in adolescence, we continue trying to negotiate our relations with others in ways that protect our own agency. Yet, simultaneously we long to be embraced wholly and nakedly by the loving agency of the other. The power of the ego is insufficient: we cannot keep the self in and the other out and concomitantly become united with the other in love. Why do we suffer this separation from the ultimate good that we desire? Because we depend on the erotic power of our own egos to secure the finite goods of our lived worlds, rather than facing God as the infinite Good. Our desire for objects or other persons becomes the ground of our hope for the good life, and we fail to see that the only ultimate resolution to our moral tension is immersion in divine love. The solution to ethical anxiety is

36. Over against the early modern concept of a person as a neutral or "punctual" self, C. Taylor argues that the self exists in the space of constitutive concerns that "touch on the nature of the good that I orient myself by and on the way I am placed in relation to it"; *Sources of the Self: The Making of Modern Identity* (Cambridge: Harvard University Press, 1989), 50.

37. Cf. E. Storkey, *The Search for Intimacy* (Grand Rapids: Eerdmans, 1995).

38. Object-relations psychologist R. Kegan points to five life stages in which we reach a place of equilibrium during these negotiations: impulsive, imperial, interpersonal, institutional, and interindividual; *The Evolving Self: Problem and Process in Human Development* (Cambridge: Harvard University Press, 1982), 226. Resolving the dynamic tension between self and other is the task of each new stage, which involves anxiety and struggle throughout life.

facing and being faced by God so that we can ask with Thomas Merton: "Why should I fear anything that cannot rob me of God, and why should I desire anything that cannot give me possession of Him?"[39]

The Christian gospel claims that the human longing for love may be fulfilled in relation to the infinite love of the trinitarian God. When the early Christian believers (or should I say "lovers"?) experienced the confirmation of Jesus' claim that the Spirit of the Lord was upon him (Luke 4:18) and that he and the Father were one (John 10:30) through his resurrection (Romans 1:4), they concluded that their very understanding of God must incorporate the agency of the Father, the Son, and the Spirit. Reflection on these revelatory events eventually gave rise to what became known as the doctrine of the Trinity. As pastors concerned to lead their flocks to a saving relation with God, patristic theologians exhausted themselves in the development, articulation, and defense of the Christian doctrine that the one essence of God *is* the communion of these three persons: God *is* love. Christian belief in atonement and regeneration (freedom from sin) presupposes robust relations among the persons of the Trinity, for it is through Christ that we "have access in one Spirit to the Father" (Ephesians 2:18). The whole experience of salvation is captured by this trinitarian structure: "If the Spirit of him who raised Jesus from the dead dwells in you, he who raised Christ from the dead will give life to your mortal bodies also through his Spirit that dwells in you" (Romans 8:11). Christian lovers are reconciled with the trinitarian God, who *is love* (1 John 4:8); this frees them from depending on their own ego agencies, liberating them for the intimacy of true love.

If our desire is for God alone, if we first seek God's righteousness, we will not strive for finite things like "the Gentiles" do; "all these things will be given" to us but we will not desperately grasp them—we will not "worry about tomorrow" (Matthew 6:31–34)—because our agency is upheld in the infinite goodness of the God of love. The ethics of Jesus is summarized in the two commandments on which all the law and the prophets hang: "You shall love the Lord your God with all your heart, and with all your soul, and with all your mind. . . . You shall love your neighbor as yourself" (22:37–40). The face of the other and the face of the self are morally held together vis-à-vis the loving face of God. Rather than struggling with our neighbors over finite goods, we are able to manifest the generosity of forgiving grace out of the superabundance of joy.

Jesus claimed that God alone is good (e.g., Matthew 19:17). God's goodness, however, makes others righteous by granting a share in divine holiness. This is ultimately disclosed in the life of Jesus Christ,

39. T. Merton, *New Seeds of Contemplation* (New York: New Directions, 1961), 159.

who refused to exploit or grasp equality with God and was obedient even to death on a cross (Philippians 2:6–8). Through Christ "the righteousness of God has been disclosed" (Romans 3:21–22). "No one has greater love than this, to lay down one's life for one's friends" (John 15:13). God's goodness is manifested in the sending of the Son, and God's love is "poured into our hearts through the Holy Spirit" (Romans 5:5). The righteousness of God has been revealed so that in Christ "we might become the righteousness of God" (2 Corinthians 5:21). Human agency is transformed as we share in a righteousness that is not our own, but that comes from life in the Spirit of Christ.

Jesus Christ shows us the proper relation of human agency to God by his refusal to secure goodness by doing his own will, up to and including the temptations at Gethsemane and on the cross. Before breathing his last, Jesus commends his spirit into the hands of the Father (Luke 23:46), showing his dependence on the grace of God to the very end. From the beginning and throughout his ministry, Jesus resisted the temptation to control his life through his own agency. Jesus does not do anything on his own, but only what he "sees the Father doing" (John 5:19). This was possible because he was filled with the Holy Spirit (Luke 4:1–13). His whole ministry was an agency immersed in the Spirit of life, intending the glory of the one he called Father. Through his dependence on the eternal Spirit (Hebrews 9:14), he offered his life for the sake of manifesting the Father's love in community (John 17:26). Jesus himself was "justified (*edikaiōthē*) by the Spirit" (1 Timothy 3:16). He was made perfect through sufferings (Hebrews 2:10), and "he learned obedience through what he suffered" (5:8). How do Christian lovers share in Christ's victory over sin and death so that they too may be united to the goodness and righteousness and justice of God? How may our ethical anxiety be overcome so that we receive the power to love truly and so to forgive?

Dying to Sin with Jesus Christ

In other words, how does Christ's death bring us salvation from sin? The forgiveness manifested on the cross is related to the real dynamics of grace in community, wherein we are called to forgive others. If forgiveness is infinitely good for us, then we must expand our horizons for understanding it even beyond death. As we saw in chapter 4, theologians are increasingly challenging the sufficiency of legal understandings of the atonement for explaining the relation of Christ's death to the forgiveness of sins. Forensic applications of forgiveness explain the remittance of a penalty for one's guilty actions, but they do not address the need for the real transformation of anger and shame in relation to self, other, and God. Placing all the emphasis on a judicial payment on the cross leaves out the role of the *resurrection* of Jesus in making new life possible. Further, such theories tend to focus on the relation of the Father and Son, leaving out the work of the *Holy Spirit*, whose redemptive activity then seems to be tacked on after the real objective transaction is completed. Space does not allow a full treatment of the theory of atonement, but we may at least point to some promising opportunities in soteriology after the (re)turn to relationality. In this subsection, I explore a more robustly trinitarian way of thinking about forgiveness as sharing in divine grace through dying to sin with Jesus Christ by the power of the Spirit.

How can we think of sin and death in a way that makes sense of the overcoming of one through the other? First, the term *sin* (and related terms like *iniquity* and *transgression*) in Scripture does not refer to an abstract substance; it indicates ways of relating to ourselves, others, and God that prevent us from facing one another in love. In the Hebrew Bible sin is what hinders persons from being in proper relation to divine goodness.[40] In the New Testament sin describes agencies that resist the grace and love of God. For Paul sin is that which is opposed to and overcome by grace (Romans 5:15–21; 6:1, 14–15, 23). Sin is slavery, a binding from which we are unable to free ourselves (6:16–17; 7:14, 25). For John, a lack of love is at the root of all forms of sinning; these actions keep us from the good life we desire and so are essentially opposed to righteousness (John 16:8; 1 John 2:1). Human agency is agonizing because we are aware of our inability to secure goodness over against the threat of evil. No matter how hard we try, we are bound by our sinning: this impotence terrifies us because our personal activity cannot hold off the various faces of the void—loneliness, depression, anger, shame—much less death itself.

Second, the term *death* in the New Testament and especially in Paul does not mean simply the cessation of bodily functioning; it may also refer to the relational dynamics that keep humans from the full flourishing of life in righteousness:

> How can we who died to sin go on living in it? Do you not know that all of us who have been baptized into Christ Jesus were baptized into his

40. In Poetry and Wisdom literature, we find an emphasis on corruption of the heart and the inability of anyone to do good (Proverbs 20:9). Sinful actions produce guilt (Psalm 38:4), and punishment is inevitable, either on earth (7:16) or before "the heavens" (Job 20:27). In the Law, the focus is on the breaking of rules and transgressing against the divine commands, which are oriented toward goodness (Numbers 22:18; Leviticus 5:5; 26:40). Similarly, in the Historical Books, sin is generally related to rebelling against God: everyone "did what was right in their own eyes" (Judges 21:25). A common theme in the Prophetic Books is the chastisement of the rich for oppressing the poor (Amos 4:1; 5:12) or for abusing orphans and widows (Ezekiel 22:7). Isaiah 53:4–12 also connects death and sin, both of which separate us from God.

death? Therefore we have been buried with him by baptism into death, so that, just as Christ was raised from the dead by the glory of the Father, so we too might walk in newness of life.

For if we have been united with him in a death like his, we will certainly be united with him in a resurrection like his. We know that our old self was crucified with him so that the body of sin might be destroyed, and we might no longer be enslaved to sin. For whoever has died is freed from sin. But if we have died with Christ, we believe that we will also live with him. We know that Christ, being raised from the dead, will never die again; death no longer has dominion over him. The death he died, he died to sin, once for all; but the life he lives, he lives to God. So you also must consider yourselves dead to sin and alive to God in Christ Jesus.

—Romans 6:2–11

Notice that Paul says the Christian "has died" and should consider herself "dead" to sin. This is obviously not physical death, but it is the annihilation of something—namely, the destruction of the bonds by which sin enslaves us. In the previous chapter Paul said that "death exercised dominion from Adam to Moses" (Romans 5:14). Yet, we know that *physical* death did not stop with Moses. In 5:12–21 Paul makes a threefold comparison between Adam, Moses, and Jesus. Life and righteousness cannot be achieved by those who depend on the passions of the flesh (represented by Adam) or on the keeping of the law (represented by Moses). It is through Jesus Christ that we now have both righteousness and life (5:21). In the later Pauline literature as well, readers are told that they "were dead" (Ephesians 2:1, 5; Colossians 2:13) because of their sins. Here we are dealing with a theological view of death that is broader than the final dissolution of our current embodiment. Moribundity already crushes human life as agents face themselves and others in sin. Yet, sharing in the life of God is also already possible now as human agents are freed from this morbid interfacing through the manifestation of God's gracious forgiveness in the Spirit of Christ.

Dying to sin is not possible apart from divine grace. We cannot absolutely secure the objects of our desire on our own ego strength, because we cannot control the future. Moreover, we cannot rescue ourselves from this bondage (as Paul confesses in Romans 7). Human agents are aware that they are not what they *ought* to be, and this makes them miserable. Conviction of this failure is part of the gospel, because it points us toward our need for the infinite grace and goodness of God. The convicting power of the Spirit intensifies remorse over the past and anxiety over the future until one finally cries out for deliverance. This mortification of our ego agency makes room for the vivification of a new agency that relies on God, from whom we receive "every good and perfect gift" (James 1:17 New International Version). The ego cannot kill itself and still live, nor can it grant itself new life. Yes, the Spirit gives new life—but first the Spirit kills. Even this dying that comes before redemptive living is gracious, because here the Spirit negates the agency bound by sin, thereby freeing it for the freedom of life in Christ. As we die to our attempts to control death, sin no longer stings us (1 Corinthians 15:56) because we receive a new life of love from which not even death can separate us (Romans 8:37–39). Divine grace is primal, and our sharing in this grace involves receptivity, but it is a real reception of the infinite power of divine love through which real human agency is transformed.

The life of forgiveness that shares in divine grace takes shape in Christ as a life of cruciformity.[41] All three Synoptic Gospels (Matthew 10:38–39; Mark 8:34–35; Luke 9:23–24; cf. John 12:25) report Jesus' saying that those who would follow him must deny themselves and "take up the cross"—only the one who loses her life for Jesus' sake will find (or save) it. Having been made perfect through suffering, Jesus "became the source of eternal salvation" (Hebrews 5:9) for us. How? When we are "crucified with Christ," it is no longer we who live but Christ who lives in us (Galatians 2:19–20); yet, we live as we are united to him in faith that is "made effective through love" (5:6 New Revised Standard Version margin). "Those who belong to Christ Jesus have crucified the flesh with its passions and desires" (5:24).[42] Paul urges the Romans to present their bodies as a "living sacrifice" (12:1). Loving and being loved by God is not merely an abstract inner feeling, but a concrete experience of fellowship that intensifies as we actively share in the self-giving love of Jesus Christ. This is how we become ministers of reconciliation (2 Corinthians 5:18), drawing others into fellowship with God's infinite goodness. Jesus shows us that love is laying down one's life (1 John 3:16). This means that Christian agency is *cruciform*, shaped by concrete acts of love to and with and for the neighbor. By dying to sin with Jesus Christ by the power of the Spirit, the Christian is freed to fulfill the call to love and forgive not only her neighbors but even her enemies.

The agony of this dying brings the ecstasy of new life, and not only once but throughout our lives. The readers of 1 Peter are urged to "rejoice insofar as you are sharing (*koinōneite*) Christ's sufferings" because whoever has suffered in the flesh (in the way Christ did) "has

41. Cf. M. J. Gorman, *Cruciformity: Paul's Narrative Spirituality of the Cross* (Grand Rapids: Eerdmans, 2001).

42. "The world," Paul insists "has been crucified to me, and I to the world" (Galatians 6:14). "I die every day!" he tells the Corinthians (1 Corinthians 15:31). "If we have died with him, we will also live with him" (2 Timothy 2:11).

finished with sin" (4:1, 13). This initially does not appear to be good news—until we realize that it opens us up to an intimate fellowship with and in the infinite goodness and love of the trinitarian God. Paul announces to the Philippians that the righteousness of God is available to them as they are bound to Christ; he prays that he may "know Christ and the power of his resurrection" and may share "his sufferings by becoming like him in his death," that if possible he "may attain the resurrection from the dead" (Philippians 3:10–11; cf. Romans 6:3–11). Timothy is encouraged to join "in suffering for the gospel, relying on the power of God" (2 Timothy 1:8), and he is expected to "share in suffering" as a soldier of Christ (2:3, 9), for "all who want to live a godly life in Christ Jesus will be persecuted" (3:12).[43]

As Christian lovers, we can be vulnerable in our relations to our neighbors because our life is infinitely secure in divine love. Our lives are held together as we intimately share in God's reconciling activity. This does not mean seeking affliction to get sympathy or telling others to stop complaining about their affliction. It is rather an *active* movement toward the afflicted other in the power of love that cannot be crushed in affliction (2 Corinthians 4:8). The goodness of divine life is revealed to others as we "walk just as he walked" (1 John 2:6), laying down our lives for one another (3:16). Redeemed life is eternal life and so beyond the reach of death. The Christian is freed to a life of "always carrying in the body the death of Jesus" and "always being given up to death for Jesus' sake, so that the life of Jesus may also be made visible in our mortal flesh" (2 Corinthians 4:10–11). Having lost our lives (Matthew 16:25), we receive a new life that shares in God's goodness and manifests divine righteousness in concrete acts of vulnerable love. As Dietrich Bonhoeffer puts it, "forgiveness is the Christlike suffering which it is the Christian's duty to bear."[44]

This concept of "bearing" reminds us of 1 Peter 2:24, which says that Jesus "bore our sins in his body on the cross, so that, free from sins, we might live for righteousness." This bearing has sometimes been taken to mean that Jesus was punished in the place of us. As we saw in our analysis of the biblical concept of forgiveness in chapter 4, this is probably not the intended meaning of this term as typically

43. Suffering for Christ is graciously granted by God to believers as a privilege (Philippians 1:29). The Thessalonians are commended for suffering for the kingdom of God (2 Thessalonians 1:5), for they suffer the "same things" that Jesus suffered (1 Thessalonians 2:14). *Koinōnia* in Christ's suffering is also *koinōnia* in one another's suffering (2 Corinthians 1:4–7), because Christ suffered (and was raised) for the sake of others: "And he died for all, so that those who live might live no longer for themselves, but for him who died and was raised for them" (5:15).

44. D. Bonhoeffer, *The Cost of Discipleship* (trans. R. H. Fuller; New York: Macmillan, 1949), 100 = 2d ed. (1959), 80.

used in the Hebrew Bible. Bearing sin is not primarily a penal concept; it has to do with providing a way for stricken people to be released from their painful relations, opening up the possibility of reconciliation. In the New Testament, too, discourse about the ministry
and cross of Christ is not focused on its forensic application. In 1 Peter 2 Jesus' bearing of sin is explicitly introduced with a reference to
Isaiah's Suffering Servant and is surrounded by this commentary:
"Christ also suffered for you, leaving you an example, so that you
should follow in his steps. . . . When he was abused, he did not return
abuse; when he suffered, he did not threaten; but he entrusted himself
to the one who judges justly" (2:21b–23). Through his personal agency
that led to the cross, Jesus "bore" the weight of sin, the misery that
humans experience in separation from God; he manifested a life of total dependence on the love and goodness of the Father, made possible
by his reliance on the Holy Spirit. Jesus' message of God's forgiving
grace was attested by his resurrection from the dead, marking his life
as the way of salvation—an example that we should follow. Penal substitutionary theories focus on Jesus' taking of our place or dying "for
us" in a way that *excludes* us. On the hypothesis of substance metaphysics, it seems that Jesus' place-taking would have to push the substance of humanity away from the place of atonement (or mercy seat).
However, Jesus' place-taking is also *inclusive;* his agency opened up to
us the possibility of incorporation into the intimate relationality of the
divine life.

Christ's dying to sin was substitutionary atonement. "Substitution"
does not, however, have to be understood only in terms of a legal
transaction. Being released from a financial or criminal debt is wonderful news, but it does not necessarily free the agent from shame or
alter the binding structures of agency that led to the original transgression. As Christof Gestrich notes, we find substitutionary action in
a general sense throughout nature. Parents give up their own pleasure
and sometimes their lives to care for their children: "In this sense they
are acting as substitutes for their young."[45] Such substitutionary action makes room for another to grow by taking up tasks that they otherwise would have to fulfill themselves. For example, a mother substitutes for an infant, providing nourishment, caring for wounds, and
creating space and time for him to mature. Christ's substitution for us
has as its goal our atonement or reconciliation with God. His place-
taking for and among human agents created space and time for this to

45. C. Gestrich, *The Return of Splendor* (trans. D. W. Bloesch; Grand Rapids: Eerdmans, 1997), 297. For a more detailed philosophical argument, see idem, "God Takes
Our Place: A Religious-Philosophical Approach to the Concept of *Stellvertretung*," *Modern Theology* 17 (2001): 313–34.

occur, for us to take our place within the infinite "seat" of divine mercy.

This is what Jesus did during his whole life; *already* in his ministry and healing the disciples saw the fulfillment of Isaiah's reference to the Suffering Servant who would "take" and "bear" the agony of the people (Matt. 8:17). However, the cross grasps our attention in a particularly powerful way. Like the bronze serpent that Moses lifted up on a pole (Numbers 21:9), "so must the Son of Man be lifted up, that whoever believes on him may have eternal life" (John 3:14–15). The cross of Jesus showed us the results of human sin and violence, and his resurrection and sending of the Spirit made a way for us to be released from the misery of our sinning. When we look on the cross, we face one who is stricken and yet wholly trusts in God (1 Peter 2:23). We are reminded of our own suffering and the shadow of death that hangs over our longing to secure the good life. The place-taking that occurred in the manifestation of the Son of God in the history of Jesus provides a redemptive place for us—as we take the "way" of Christ we share in the infinite love of the triune God. We are called to bind ourselves to this *way* of living—to forgive others in the radical sense of acting as substitutes for them, providing space and time for them through our own actions so that they might become whole. Bonhoeffer again: whoever forgives the other's sins takes his sin "upon himself, because he knows that Christ bears his sin. Therefore, he can take the sin of the other."[46]

Forgiveness is linked not only to Good Friday, but also to Easter and the day of Pentecost; it is because the same Spirit that raised Christ from the dead dwells in us (Romans 8:11) that we are empowered to forgive. Our response to the affliction of others will be to share in their sufferings, even to the point of dying for the sake of righteousness. This is possible only if we "rely not on ourselves but on God who raises the dead" (2 Corinthians 1:9). Having died to death, we are freed to manifest the power of forgiveness that initiates a new life in community through grace. In the context of his "going up to Jerusalem," Jesus tells his disciples that the Son of Man will be handed over, killed, and then raised again (Mark 10:32–35). James and John express their desire to be right next to Jesus in glory. Jesus asked them if they are able "to be baptized with the baptism that I am baptized with." They claim that they are, and Jesus acknowledges that indeed they will be (10:35–40). Jesus is referring here not to water Baptism, but to his experience of death and resurrection. What does it mean for the disciples to share in *this* Baptism?

46. D. Bonhoeffer, "Das Wesen der Kirche," 269; quoted and translated in Gestrich, *Return of Splendor*, 295.

Acting in Baptized Community

Scripture clearly links Baptism to salvation and forgiveness (e.g., Acts 2:38; 1 Peter 3:21; Colossians 2:11–12; Mark 16:16; Romans 6:3–5; Matthew 28:19). However, an interpretation of Baptism that focuses primarily on the washing of the vitiated substances of individual souls (as with Augustine) may occlude the broader relational context in which salvation takes shape in real community. Baptism is indeed a key part of the Christian answer to the problem of evil, suffering, and sin. My goal here is to press toward a more robust understanding of the lived existence of the baptized community, the body of Christ, which works[47] to manifest God's love and forgiveness to and in the world. Might we think of Baptism not merely as one step in the *ordo salutis*, but as a *salutary ordering* of persons in community? Redemptive forgiveness is not just about guilty individuals—it is about healing the wounds of our communities.[48] In order to expand the theological horizon within which our life as Christian lovers is to be conceptualized and carried out, I will examine Baptism more broadly in pneumatological, ecclesiological, and eschatological perspective.

To grasp the significance of acting in baptized community, we must recognize that Baptism has to do with more than water in the New Testament. We might even say that, after Jesus, Baptism is primarily about being immersed in the Holy Spirit. All four of the gospels go out of their way to emphasize that while John baptizes with water, the greater one who comes after him will baptize with the Holy Spirit (Matthew 3:11; Mark 1:8; Luke 3:16; John 1:33). The outpouring of the Spirit constitutes the church, and the postresurrection promise to the disciples explicitly distinguishes again between John's Baptism and "the promise of the Father . . . for John baptized with water, but you will be baptized with the Holy Spirit" (Acts 1:4–5). After Pentecost, Peter calls his listeners to be baptized "in the name of Jesus Christ so that your sins may be forgiven; and you will receive the gift of the Holy Spirit" (2:38). In the context of defending his interaction with Cornelius and his household (during which the Holy Spirit was poured out even on Gentiles), Peter remembers again this distinction between Baptism only by water and the Baptism with the Holy Spirit promised by Jesus to his followers (10:45; 11:16).

My purpose here is not to argue about whether water Baptism and Spirit Baptism are identical, or whether they occur in a particular dia-

47. As the title of E. Hong's book suggests—and as everyone who struggles with it knows from experience—*Forgiveness Is a Work as Well as a Grace* (Minneapolis: Augsburg, 1984).

48. As J. Sobrino notes, the purpose of forgiveness "is not simply to heal the guilt of the sinner but the purpose of all *love*: to come into *communion*"; "Latin America: Place of Sin and Place of Forgiveness," *Concilium* 184 (1986): 51 (emphasis added).

chronic order, or about the distinctions between being filled with, indwelled, and baptized by the Spirit. Rather, I want to point to the ever intensifying pattern of life-death-new life, which characterizes the agency of lovers who are drawn into spiritual union with God in Christ. Being-baptized in the Spirit is the ongoing salutary ordering of human life as it shares in the gracious being-in-relation of the trinitarian God. The washing of water signifies a union with Christ in death and resurrection. This union is an immersion (*baptizō*)[49] in the Spirit that intensifies throughout life and takes shape in community. This is life "in the Spirit." It is "the Spirit of him who raised Jesus from the dead" that dwells "in you (plural)" (Romans 8:11). As we also dwell in the Spirit, our lives are conformed to Christ.[50] Those who are gathered together (*ekklēsia*) as the "temple of the Spirit" are immersed in the gifts (12:3–8), the fruit (Galatians 5:22), and the manifestations (1 Corinthians 12:7–11) of the Spirit, which display the good life of fellowship with God: "For in the one Spirit we were all baptized into one body—Jews or Greeks, slaves or free—and we were all made to drink of one Spirit" (12:13). This shared life of love, this ever intensifying immersion ties us to one another in love so that we are free to love fully. We become righteous together as we love one another, which is possible only as we abide in God and God abides in us, as John never tires of reminding his readers in his first epistle. The Johannine "abiding" is another way of describing our fellowship or sharing in the divine love.

This salutary ordering is not a legal abstraction. It takes concrete shape in real life activities. To join the ecclesial community of those being-immersed in the Spirit of God is to take specific actions that reorder the way one faces one's neighbors. The inability to give up one's self-reliance hinders the full experience of salvation. To share in eternal life is to rely on the goodness of God, who loves the other with infinite generosity. Baptism is an essential religious practice for the Christian—not only the singular act related to the river, font, or baptistery—but the whole set of practices through which lovers are immersed in the real source of goodness. In this sense, redemptive forgiveness depicts the whole of Christian activity. Agential relations are real, and being-baptized by and into the relational *koinōnia* of the Spirit, being-immersed in the fellowship of the body of Christ, really saves by reordering human agency in salubrious community.

49. The spatial picture of immersion is ultimately limited here, because life in the Spirit is also the life of the Spirit in us. For a discussion of this mutual indwelling, see Shults, *Reforming Theological Anthropology*, chap. 5.

50. The Ephesians are urged to "be imitators of God . . . and live in love, as Christ loved us and gave himself up for us" (Ephesians 5:1–2).

Relating Baptism in this broader sense to the life of the whole community immersed in the Spirit requires moving beyond the early modern obsession with the *ordo salutis* of an individual's experience of salvation. The New Testament describes the dynamics of redemption in several ways. It involves a call to conversion, a turning to faith in which the believer is bound to the Father through the Son and the Spirit (Mark 1:14–15; John 17:20–23; Acts 2:38–39; 16:31; Romans 10:9; 1 John 3:23–24). Redemption is described as a declaring and making holy (Romans 3:20–26; 1 Corinthians 1:8–9; 2 Corinthians 5:17–21; Galatians 2:16–21; 2 Thessalonians 2:13–14) as well as the giving of regeneration (John 3:5–7, 16; 6:40; 20:31; Romans 8:11; Titus 3:4–7; 1 Peter 1:3, 23). Some early modern theologians separated these dynamics into steps and tried to determine the order in which an individual experiences them. On this model, Baptism is one of the steps in the order of salvation, and the question arises regarding its function at a particular point in the order (e.g., before, after, or with regeneration).

If we attend to the broader sense of Baptism—acting together immersed "in the Spirit"—we can see that all of these biblical dynamics of redemption occur as concrete events in community, transforming our agency through saving faces. The turning, making, and giving depicted in the Scriptures listed above are oriented toward an ordering of human life in community in relation to the only source of true goodness: the love of the trinitarian God. Conversion is not simply a decision at a singular point in time.[51] Christian life is a dynamic converting, a turning-with others into the fellowship of divine love. We may also speak of this same salutary ordering as being called, being made righteous, being given new life, etc. Instead of an anxious self-examination of one's status in the order of salvation, a new kind of question comes to the fore: how may *we* experience an ordering of life together that is really good for us? The answer of the gospel is that this occurs by the gracious presence of the Spirit who dwells in the community and in whom the community dwells.

As we noted above, human love aims for ordering ourselves salutarily in relation to others. We desire to organize ourselves in ways that will bring goodness (*salus*) to our lives. The salutary ordering of a just community requires righteous agents. Sharing in God's righteousness is made possible through Baptism into the community of Christ. This is not a magical transubstantiation, but a dynamic, historical reordering of our real relations to one another and to God. Being saved means being brought into the good life of divine love. Jesus said that people

51. Cf. R. V. Peace, *Conversion in the New Testament: Paul and the Twelve* (Grand Rapids: Eerdmans, 1999).

would know his disciples by their love for one another (John 13:35). Redemption from sin is primarily about entering into *koinōnia* with the trinitarian God, a dynamic fellowship that is mediated through and transforms our loving activity in community. This means that the church ought to be a place where people discover the good life, where they are confronted by righteous people in communities of justice.

Forgiveness and unforgiveness are about power. Who has the power to secure objects of desire? Who gets to decide the boundaries of and rules for community? Ordering based on finite power may occur on the basis of geography, socioeconomic status, ethnicity, gender, or any "otherness" that threatens the power establishment of a community. When the disciples began to struggle over who would have the seat of power in the kingdom, Jesus said, "It will not be so among you; but whoever wishes to be great among you must be your servant" (Matthew 20:26). Human *economies* (in the broadest sense of the word) order communal life. The "root of all evils" is the love for finite goods (1 Timothy 6:9–10), which is why those who want to be rich (regardless of the desired commodity) have so much difficulty sharing in the righteousness of the kingdom. Communities are threatened (from within or without) when agents begin to fight over the finite goods available and struggle for the finite power to establish the distribution of goods, material or otherwise.

The divine economy, however, is the *oikonōmia* of salvation in which infinite goodness overflows boundaries and infinite love conquers fear. Christians anticipate a new heaven and a new earth, in which "righteousness dwells" (2 Peter 3:13 Revised Standard Version), but they are called together now as a sign of the in-breaking promise of divine peace. The baptized community signals the arrival of divine forgiveness by actively manifesting divine grace. The *koinōnia* created by the Spirit binds us together in love. Because we are "baptized into Christ" and are "one in Christ" (Galatians 3:27–28), the distinctions between Jew and Greek (race), slave and free (class), male and female (gender) are no longer determinative for the way we act toward each other. We do not need to control the "others" by marking them off and acting over against them to secure our own good, because we have been secured together by the infinite goodness of divine love.

How does redemptive forgiveness operate in this community? Frederick Keene points out that we never have a case in the Hebrew Bible or in the New Testament in which a weak person is told to forgive a stronger person.[52] Especially in the culture of the first century, forgive-

---

52. F. W. Keene, "Structures of Forgiveness in the New Testament," in *Violence against Women and Children* (ed. C. J. Adams and M. M. Fortune; New York: Continuum, 1995), 122–23.

ness was something offered by a person with more power (or money, i.e., a creditor) to a person with less power (or money, i.e., a debtor). Sometimes persons on equal footing would offer forgiveness, but the idea of a person with less power offering forgiveness to a person with power over them was foreign to the cultures in which the biblical texts were written. Keene's analysis suggests that only by giving up power and placing themselves before their victims as equals (at most) or as servants (at best) would it even be *possible* for an oppressor to receive forgiveness. It is common today, however, to hear that forgiveness should be offered by Christian victims to all perpetrators, Christian or otherwise.[53] Such forgiveness is considered virtuous. Does Keene's observation mean that we should stop asking abused Christians to forgive their powerful abusers or to withhold forgiveness until the abuser is brought low?

Here our delineation of the three semantic domains of forgiveness may help clarify such questions. If we are applying forgiveness forensically, the answer to the question may very well be "no." For the victim to forgive may be completely out of place or even meaningless here.[54] In the field of therapeutic transformation, however, we may hope that a victim could come to a place where she at least desires to move toward the healing of wounded relations. Therapeutic forgiveness in this sense could emerge from the side of the victim and move toward the transformation of communal relations with the more powerful perpetrator. In some contexts, quick reconciliation may not be practical or wise, and it is important to determine appropriate boundaries to check evil and stimulate repentance.[55] In reference to redemptive forgiveness, however, we should answer "yes"—Christian lovers should always strive to manifest forgiveness. "Sharing in divine grace" works precisely by the weak showing love to the strong by refusing to participate in the power struggle that defines human economies. This means loving even one's enemies (Luke 6:27–36). For some victims, however, the road to sharing in redemptive forgiveness may be *through* the process of therapeutic transformation and may occur *as* the perpetrator is being held accountable to judicial regulations.

Jesus prayed for his disciples that the same love with which the Father had loved him would also be "in them" (John 17:26). Sharing in the gracious love of the trinitarian God is not an impotent acceptance of victimization, but an active *koinōnia* in the omnipotent vulnerabil-

---

53. For example, M. Hurley, "Reconciliation and Forgiveness," *Jurist* 56 (1996): 456–86 at 467.

54. Cf. A. S. Park and S. L. Nelson (eds.), *The Other Side of Sin: Woundedness from the Perspective of the Sinned-Against* (Albany: State University of New York Press, 2001).

55. See S. Tracy, "Sexual Abuse and Forgiveness," *Journal of Psychology and Theology* 27 (1999): 219–29 at 225–26.

ity of divine grace. This infinite power of love absorbs all wounds, transforming the wounded as it works for justice in the face of unholy powers. This vulnerable love may also convict the wounders by challenging their violent control over others. The Christian community does not simply accept the suffering of the poor and the abused as a necessary part of the world. We respond to suffering with love because evil is finite and cannot ultimately separate us from God's goodness. Christian agency is not seduced by finite goods, because these do not provide that for which we are truly longing: righteous relations within loving community. Sin and death no longer bind and terrify, and wealth no longer deceives us. Redemptive forgiveness works against generic suffering by sharing in the reconciling praxis of divine love, which gives itself up for the other. As we die to our obsession with acting in ways that secure our own finite goods, we may have fellowship in divine goodness, which moves into the world with the infinite power of love.

The community that is being-baptized in the Spirit of Christ is immersed in the reconciling activity of God. The gospel is appealing not only as a relevant message, but because it is "the power of God for salvation" (Romans 1:16–17), which is manifested in the righteousness of God among those who believe. The shared life of Christian lovers is an alluring reality that draws people into the good life. Persons in baptized community are able to show love in a way that is radically vulnerable, because the source of their life is infinite love: their intimate fellowship is borne up in the infinite buoyancy of eternal life. As we suffer with, in, and for the world, we "consider it nothing but joy" (James 1:2) because our communal good is not secured by the power of our institutional structures, but by our sharing in the arrival of divine grace and peace that creates and holds us in *koinōnia*. Unforgiveness and death do not have the final word: "For if we have been united with him in a death like his, we shall certainly be united with him in a resurrection like his" (Romans 6:5). God's faithful love orients us in hope to the eschatological promise of sharing in divine grace, which breaks into the ontological structures of our being in the world and recreates us through divine forgiveness, granting us a share in that hopeful forgiving.

Forgiveness and Hope

Of the three that "remain" (1 Corinthians 13:13), hope has not received as much attention in the theological tradition as have faith and love. Nevertheless, hope is essential to the New Testament understanding and experience of salvation. Like faith, hope is that in which and by which we are saved: "For in [or by] hope we were saved" (Romans 8:24). Like love, hope is that into which and for which we are saved: "He has given us a new birth into a living hope" (1 Peter 1:3). The Book of Hebrews urges its readers "to seize the hope set before us," a hope we already have as the "anchor of the soul," a hope that enters into the depths of divine communion (6:18–19). Paul prays for the Romans: "May the God of hope fill you with all joy and peace in believing, so that you may abound in hope by the power of the Holy Spirit" (15:13).

How should we speak of the relation of hope to forgiveness? So far I have discussed forgiveness in epistemic and ethical perspective. While these are essential, we must not leave out the way in which (un)forgiveness shapes our very being as well as our knowing and acting. Corresponding to the treatments of faith and love, I will divide my analysis into three sections. First, our horizon for understanding hope must also be expanded. If hope is merely a docile wishing or vapid optimism, then it will not help us in dealing with reality here and now. I suggest that we think of hope as real human being, as a real personal relation to God through which ontological anxiety is overcome. Second, I examine the meaning of the "image of God" revealed in Jesus Christ and the dynamics by which persons may be conformed into his image through the Spirit (Galatians 5:5) and so liberated from existential dread. Third, I describe forgiveness as a sharing of hope through being in eucharistic community. Redemptive forgiveness releases our present from the totalizing painful determination of the past so that we may face the future full of hope and extend that hope to others.

Facing Ontological Anxiety

> I will sing praise to my God while I have being.
> —Psalm 104:33b

> Do not, O Lord, turn your face away from me.
> For it is better for me to die
>   than to see so much distress in my life.
> —Tobit 3:6b

Why does despair often overshadow our longing for divine forgiveness? Why does the prospect of forgiving another person sometimes seem worse than death? Reflecting on these questions from the perspective of ontology we may say that part of the reason is that we do not have enough metaphysical weight to establish our being among others in the systems of the lived world. Underlying guilt and shame is an existential dread that most of us are afraid to face. We repress this ontological anxiety with all kinds of neurotic busyness. At the same time, we find it difficult to suppress our hope for a future in which the particularity of our being will not be annihilated. We hope to belong in a peaceful and joyful pattern of harmonious relations with others. Redemptive forgiveness as sharing in divine grace opens up that future.

First we must face the real threat to our continued existence and admit that we do not have the power to determine the reality of our own future. To be a human person is to wonder what the future holds. Facing the uncertainty of the future, we realize that our very being is at stake. Personal being is a becoming in openness to a future outside the self. Healthy persons hope for being in relation to that future. When hope begins to fade, the well-being of the person dissipates.[56] Giving up hope provides an anaesthetic for ontological anxiety that may temporarily numb the pain but does not heal. The hope for a continuation of our reality drives us to survive. Hope "comes close to being the very heart and center of a human being."[57] We want to belong in the future, to find our place in an ultimate reality in which the dissolution of our reality no longer hangs over us. This ambiguous longing for the future is part of our nature as human persons. With the rise of self-consciousness comes an intense awareness of some reality beyond human life that determines the future of personal being, even after death. We see evidence of this awareness not only in the great cultures of the iron and bronze ages but also in the art and burial practices of the earliest *homo sapiens*. Religions strive to mediate the human relation to that reality. Under the threat of perishing, humans strive for a secure existence in the future that includes their personal particularity. Human hope takes shape in the anticipation of a future reality in which our belonging is no longer at risk.

Hope and being may also be linked to the concept of beauty. Humans are drawn to aesthetically pleasing patterns, whether in the form of music, art, literature, or peaceful community. Moving beyond questions about which particular things are beautiful or about how to secure this or that particular thing in a pattern of peaceful existence, we enter the religious domain by asking: what are the conditions that make possible the longing itself? Human hope is called into existence through the gracious gift of the Aesthetic. Beauty draws us toward itself. Here I do not mean merely the pleasure or feelings we get in rela-

56. For a summary of research demonstrating the importance of hope for human health, see C. R. Snyder, "The Past and Possible Futures of Hope," *Journal of Social and Clinical Psychology* 19 (2000): 11–28; idem, "Conceptualizing, Measuring, and Nurturing Hope," *Journal of Counseling and Development* 73 (1995): 355–60.

57. W. Lynch, *Images of Hope: Imagination as Healer of the Hopeless* (Notre Dame: University of Notre Dame Press, 1965), 31.

tion to pretty things, but the transcendental condition of our aesthetic longings. As social beings, humans desire harmony; they are attracted to patterns of belonging that promise to hold personal life together without crushing it. The passion for a transcendent reality sets humans apart from other creatures. Dare we hope for a metaphysical matrix in which joy and peace flourish eternally? The human struggle to "be" exists as a searching for transcendence, as a desire to belong with others beyond the threat of the violent absorption or destruction of the particularity of our lives. Our being is in peril, however, and so we often resort to violence—exerting our will to *be* by crushing or manipulating the beauty of the other, utilizing physical or social structures to secure our own pleasure.

Late modern culture palpably exhibits not only an obsession with pleasure and beauty but also the terrible violence that arises from ontological anxiety. The work of René Girard is especially insightful on this issue. Although his theories of mimetic desire and the foundation of religion in sacred violence[58] are important in general for the doctrine of Christian salvation, his analysis of the scapegoat phenomenon is perhaps most relevant to our discussion of forgiveness. Girard examines both the ancient practice of sending out an actual goat into the wilderness to rid the community of its sins as well as the modern use of the term *scapegoat*: violent urges are directed by an individual or group toward the "other" to keep the violence from destroying the self or the community. For example, he refers to an employee who doesn't dare kick his boss, but kicks the dog when he gets home or generally mistreats his family.[59] This mechanism is an attempt to secure the being of the person or society by destroying or abusing an other who putatively deserves it. Underlying this behavior is a longing for the "plenitude of being," or what Girard calls "metaphysical desire." His work has been appropriated by Christian scholars for theological and pastoral purposes,[60] and Girard himself explicitly points to the cross of Christ as unveiling the reality and inadequacy of the scapegoat mechanism inherent in all victimization. Throughout the world, in politics, families, and every sphere, "the murderers remain convinced of the worthiness of their sacrifices. They, too, know not

---

58. See R. Girard, *Violence and the Sacred* (trans. P. Gregory; Baltimore: Johns Hopkins University Press, 1977); and idem, *Things Hidden since the Foundation of the World* (trans. S. Bann and M. Metteer; Stanford: Stanford University Press, 1987).

59. R. Girard, *I See Satan Falling Like Lightning* (trans. J. G. Williams; Maryknoll, N.Y.: Orbis, 2001), 156.

60. For example, R. G. Hamerton-Kelly, *Sacred Violence: Paul's Hermeneutic of the Cross* (Minneapolis: Fortress, 1992); D. W. Augsburger, *Helping People Forgive* (Louisville: Westminster John Knox, 1996); P. J. Watson, "Girard and Integration," *Journal of Psychology and Theology* 26 (1998): 311–21.

what they do and we must forgive them. The time has come for us to forgive one another. If we wait any longer there will not be time enough."[61]

In the New Testament, salvation is commonly described as sharing in divine *glory*. This emphasis is especially prevalent in the Pauline literature.[62] Being saved has to do with "being transformed into" the image of Christ "from one degree of glory to another" (2 Corinthians 3:18), while sinning has to do with falling "short of the glory of God" (Romans 3:23). The author of 1 Peter describes himself as "one who shares in the glory (*doxēs koinōnos*) to be revealed" (5:1). This is why he can encourage his readers to "rejoice insofar as you are sharing Christ's sufferings, so that you may also be glad and shout for joy when his glory is revealed" (4:13). They have been called to God's "eternal glory in Christ" (5:10), and their sharing in God's gracious movement toward others is "so that God may be glorified in all things through Jesus Christ" (4:11). In 2 Peter, the phrase *sharers of the divine nature* is preceded by the announcement that God has "called us to his own glory and excellence" (1:3 Revised Standard Version). The author of Hebrews describes the Son as "the reflection of God's glory" (1:3) who is "now crowned with glory" (2:9) and through whom God brings "many children to glory" (2:10). Here too we see that the glory of God is shared with human creatures. The Christian does not simply have or become God's glory; rather, her whole being as being in relation is oriented toward the arriving kingdom of glory: "We wait for the blessed hope and the manifestation of the glory of our great God" (Titus 2:13). Believers are urged to trust God, who is able "to make you stand without blemish in the presence of his glory with rejoicing" (Jude 24).

How is glory related to ontological anxiety, and what does this mean for forgiveness? The root meaning of the Hebrew word for glory (*kabod*) is "heaviness." Our own being is not heavy enough to hold down reality and to secure our place within it. This ontic weightlessness terrifies us. We long for a share in the being of God, to be secured in the weighty presence of divine glory. This longing is what is most

---

61. R. Girard, *The Scapegoat* (trans. Y. Freccero; Baltimore: Johns Hopkins University Press, 1986), 212.

62. God calls us "into his own kingdom and glory" (1 Thessalonians 2:12). Believers are sanctified by the Spirit so that we "may obtain the glory of our Lord Jesus Christ" (2 Thessalonians 2:14). It is by God's grace that we are made worthy of the call, "so that the name of our Lord Jesus may be glorified in you, and you in him" (1:12). Already here and now the believer shares in the divine glory through life in the Spirit of Christ. This sharing does not occur all at once; rather, it is a dynamic process of becoming: "Momentary affliction is preparing us for an eternal weight of glory beyond all measure" (2 Corinthians 4:17).

real about us as personal creatures. To be a human person is to be subjected in hope by the God of hope and so to long for a reality that grants peace and the beauty of belonging.[63] The hope to which God calls us (Ephesians 1:18) is a glorious inheritance, which is sealed by the promised Holy Spirit (1:13). Our being free in Christ is linked to the promise of the Spirit of God through whom we hope (Galatians 5:5). The gospel is the good news about life in the Spirit of Christ, a new life that provides ultimate ontological peace because nothing, not even death, can separate us from the freedom of divine love (Romans 8:38–39). Paul tells the Galatians that he has "freedom . . . in Christ Jesus" (2:4) and that they were "called to freedom" (5:13). It is "for freedom that Christ has set us free" (5:1). This freedom is tied both to glory and to the future: "Creation itself will be set free from its bondage to decay and will obtain the freedom of the glory of the children of God" (Romans 8:21).

Real freedom is an anticipatory sharing of the promising presence of divine glory. This *hopeful* being emerges in relation to the divine presence, for "where the Spirit of the Lord is, there is freedom" (2 Corinthians 3:17). Christians must neither forget the past nor live oblivious to the present, but they are called to an active hope that shares in the Futurity of the peaceful presence of God, which transforms all temporality. The eternal future of God's glory has been manifested in the face of Jesus Christ, and makes possible Christian life as a gracious fellowship in the Holy Spirit. The divine determination that orients us toward the beauty of holiness does not compete with human freedom, but calls it into being. This gift and call of freedom is the real *being* of human persons. This being is a becoming that finds its origin, condition, and goal in the call of the triune Creator to an ever intensifying share in the relation of the Son to the Father in the Spirit. In other words, our ontological anxiety dissolves in the presence of the infinite beauty of the divine countenance. With the arrival of every new future, which is God's gift, comes the gift of the freedom to hope. God's presence makes all things new and human freedom reaches out for a share in this donated *novum*. The Futurity of the biblical God of hope is revealed in the face of Christ by the power of the Spirit: this discloses the essential relationality of the divine Trinity, whose perfect Infinity embraces and calls human persons into the fullness of being.

How is this related to forgiveness? Playing off of Paul Jensen's suggestion that "to forgive means to exhaust in one's own *being* the consequences one has suffered so that those consequences will not cause

---

63. Not only human being, but indeed every creaturely being is "subjected . . . in hope" (Romans 8:20).

further damage . . . to the victimizer," I would like to explore what kind of being one must have in order to forgive. Jensen notes that "when God forgives, God determines to absorb into his own being the consequences of human sin and thus exhaust its virulence."[64] However, humans do not have enough being for this kind of forgiveness. Our being is limited. But as Karl Barth poignantly observes: "salvation is more than being" (*Church Dogmatics* IV/1,8). We need more than sufficient weight to hold the other away from us so we will not be wounded. Redemptive forgiveness requires a hopeful relation to the transcendent source of being.[65] Hope and forgiveness can exhaust the consequences of violence and suffering only as they share in divine grace, which is infinitely glorious, and so able to absorb all wounds, making space and time for the movement of the other toward wholeness and salvation. Overcoming the violence of unforgiveness will require a new ontology that transcends the zero-sum game of finite conflict and competition.[66] Being forgiven means receiving new being. It means finding one's very nature wholly renewed and open to a whole and healing future. Forgiving others donates the possibility of new being.

The ontological anxiety of the early Christian believers (or dare I say "hopers"?) was dissolved in relation to the God of hope. All of their attention was on the future that is breaking into the present, on the presence of the promising one who is coming so that they may be glorified with him along with all of creation (Romans 8:10–25). They cast all of their metaphysical hope on the risen Lord, whose Parousia is at the same time both anticipated as a final fulfillment in which God will be "all in all" (1 Corinthians 15:28) and also already experienced proleptically through the indwelling Holy Spirit who is its "pledge" (Ephesians 1:14). Jesus' message focused on the arrival of the coming kingdom of God: "The hour is coming, and is now here" (John 4:23). After his resurrection and the outpouring of the Holy Spirit at Pentecost, those who hope in God now anticipate the consummation of the

64. P. Jensen, "Forgiveness and Atonement," *Scottish Journal of Theology* 46 (1993): 141–59 at 154 (emphasis added).

65. As G. Tinder notes, "Forgiveness in the midst of suffering is the means by which we situate our lives in God's time and undertake to carry on our destinies. . . . Thus forgiveness, in the company of suffering, is the decisive act of hope. . . . Every human being is stubbornly inclined to seek things . . . that bring forgetfulness of our finitude and mortality. Unless life has a transcendental dimension, in which that inclination is uprooted and its consequences forgiven, true hope is doomed"; *The Fabric of Hope: An Essay* (Emory University Studies in Law and Religion 6; Atlanta: Scholars Press, 1999), 70–71.

66. Cf. J. Hughes, "The Politics of Forgiveness," *Modern Theology* 17 (2001): 261–87 at 276: "A different ontology is required to sustain reciprocity without commodification."

new creation that has already begun in them. They are consumed by a passion for participating in the reconciling activity of the one who is "making all things new" (Revelation 21:5). They "are receiving" salvation as life in hope, anticipating *koinōnia* in divine glory (1 Peter 1:9; 5:1).

In chapter 4 we observed the importance of Paul's language about "the glory of God in the face of Jesus Christ" (2 Corinthians 4:6). Only of Jesus is it said that he *is* the image of God (Colossians 1:15; 2 Corinthians 4:4; cf. Hebrews 1:3). Genesis 1:26–27 describes human beings as created "in" or "according to" God's image, but the New Testament makes it clear that human imaging of God is essentially linked to Christ. How may we speak of Jesus Christ as the "the image of God" in a way that makes sense of our being called to share in divine glory so that we too may redemptively forgive one another?

Conforming to the Image of Jesus Christ

For those who hope in Christ, the image of God is still future: "we will also bear the image of the man of heaven" (1 Corinthians 15:49). Christ "will transform" our humble body so "that it may be conformed to the body of his glory" (Philippians 3:21). "We will be like him, for we will see him as he is" (1 John 3:2). Yet, the life of hope in Christ is already an experience *now* of this arriving future. The person whose hope is in the Spirit "is being renewed in knowledge according to the image of its creator," and this renewal is through Christ who "is all and in all" (Colossians 3:10–11). The new self is being "created according to the likeness of God in true righteousness and holiness" (Ephesians 4:24); it is called "to be conformed to the image of his Son" (Romans 8:29). The hopeful Christian finds her being in this spiritual becoming, which is a being-transformed by the Spirit into the image of Christ, through whom she enters into the *koinōnia* of divine glory. In order to clarify these dynamics, let us explore more carefully the interrelation between the biblical ideas of glory and image as manifested in the reality of Jesus Christ.

The divine glory is the shared relational being of the triune God, not an attribute of the heaviest single person in the universe. The *trinitarian* structure of divine glory is especially evident in John's Gospel: "We have beheld his glory, glory as of the only Son from the Father" (John 1:14 Revised Standard Version). This glory is both the Father's and the Son's. The glory of Jesus is manifested in his signs (2:11), and the disciples believe in him. But Jesus does not seek his own glory (8:50); he recognizes that it is his "Father who glorifies" him (8:54). Jesus tells the disciples: "Now is the Son of man glorified, and in him God is glorified; if God is glorified in him, God will also glorify him in himself, and glorify him at once" (13:31–32 Revised Standard Version). Further, it is the coming "Spirit of truth" who "will glorify" Christ "because he will take what is mine and declare it to you" (16:13–14). What does the Spirit take and declare in this act of glorifying? "All that the Father has" (16:15), which he has given to the Son.

We are not dealing here with a single subject obsessed with *self*-glorification, but with a *mutual* glorification among the trinitarian persons. Immediately before his betrayal, Jesus speaks to the Father: "Glorify your Son so that the Son may glorify you. . . . I glorified you on earth by finishing the work that you gave me to do" (John 17:1, 4). The disciples are being drawn by the Spirit into this mutual glorifying of the Father and the Son; they too are called to do the same works "so that the Father may be glorified in the Son" (14:12–13). The fellowship (or abiding; 15:4–10) of the disciples in the Son's relation to the Father also redounds to the glory of Jesus, who prays: "I am glorified in them" (17:10 Revised Standard Version). The glorious relation between the Father and the Son is mediated by the Holy Spirit, who is sent to dwell with and in believers and to call them into relational unity. Creaturely sharing in the trinitarian glory of God is made possible by the unifying work of the Spirit (as Paraclete; 14:16), who mediates the promise of Jesus: "The glory that you have given me I have given them, so that they may be one, as we are one" (17:22).

The worry that affirming biblical language about "sharing" glory will inevitably lead to an apotheosizing of humanity may be allayed by the observation that persons are called to image God by sharing in the way of Jesus Christ: glorifying the Father in total reliance on the Spirit so that we, like him, might be made "perfect through sufferings" (Hebrews 2:10). Sharing in the divine glory does not mean striving to be "just like" God, but *imaging* God the way Jesus did. Jesus reveals the proper human relation to God—taking the form of a servant, becoming obedient even to death on a cross (Philippians 2:8): "Therefore God also highly exalted him . . . to the glory of God the Father. . . . Therefore . . . work out your own salvation" as God works in you (2:9–12). In case we miss the point, Paul comes back to it later in the same letter, proclaiming that he wants to know Christ, to share in his sufferings "by becoming like him in his death, if somehow I may attain the resurrection from the dead" (3:10–11). He makes the same point in Romans about our following in the way of Jesus: "If in fact, we suffer with him so that we may also be glorified with him" (8:17). Sharing in divine glory, and so human salvation, is not about static substances being transmogrified but about *becoming free* as one enters into the dynamic relational being of the living God. Although this glory is future for us, we already share in it by grace as we are being drawn into union with God through spiritual life in Christ.

The gift of the call to image God cannot be controlled by and integrated into the individual's ego functions, but must be received as gift (grace) day by day, moment by moment. It is a *being*-conformed. Imaging God (manifesting God's glory) means becoming like Christ, receiving the gift of being from the Father upheld by the Spirit. The redeemed life of imaging God is not simply a restoration of initial paradisaic conditions that have been lost, but a granting of the fullness of life "abundantly far more than all we can ask or imagine" (Ephesians 3:20). Only in the granting of hope by the word of promise are persons enabled to turn away from their self-composing anxiety and lean wholly on the ontological source of personal being. Christian hope is a throwing of oneself into the being of the one true God who addresses and calls creatures into an eternal future, which is the peace of trinitarian life. The presence of eternal Futurity evokes a freedom that takes shape as hope. In the Spirit of Christ this hope rests in loving trust in the ontological ground of beauty as it is drawn toward infinite pleasure and joy; this is an active hope that responds to the call of God into ever more intense and glorious fellowship.

The term *image* connotes the idea of a manifestation or disclosure, a re-presentation of the presence of something or someone to someone else. In his ministry, Jesus manifested the presence of God. He confronted others with the "face" of the Father's forgiveness and the promise of life in the Spirit. This was not an abstract facing, but the real presence of God's grace to and for the neighbor. Facing Jesus Christ, we are confronted with the presence of God's gracious promise; as the image of God, he re-presents God. This presence of God's glory is the manifest promise of grace, and the presence of God's grace is the manifest glory of the promise. Jesus presents us with a life of hope in the promise of the Father to grant life through the Spirit. In his facing of God in this way and in his sharing of that hope with others, Jesus is the image of God. Those who follow him find grace through the presence of the attentive life-giving Spirit of God and re-present that grace to others in community. Although in hope the Christian already experiences this grace through the Spirit, it is still future. As Paul observes, "Now we see in a mirror, dimly [enigmatically], but then we shall see face to face" (1 Corinthians 13:12). This promised face-to-face existence is "not yet," but also "already" as we share now in the creative reality of the divine promise and represent the promise to others.[67]

67. This life of promising is not alien to our personhood: we find our being as persons in promising and being promised by others into the future. For a treatment of the importance of the Christian concepts of hope and promise for responding to the "modern" problem of the self, see A. Thiselton, *Interpreting God and the Postmodern Self* (Grand Rapids: Eerdmans, 1995), 145–52.

Image also implies similarity or likeness. By manifesting the Son's relation to the Father in the Spirit, Jesus shows us what God is "like." The trinitarian countenance is essentially *koinōnia* and so an infinitely welcoming Face that invites peaceful participation. In his facing of others, the reign of God's peace appeared. Jesus did not image God by sitting around by himself, but by manifesting God's glory in concrete acts that confronted his neighbors with the divine promise—by facing others in his community in a way that called them toward a life of shared grace and peace. We too are called to *face* God and our neighbors in a way that is "like Christ." We might even speak of a "family resemblance" among those who are adopted into God's family. This similarity is not based on physical appearance but on a "way of appearing" as we face others with the peace of God. Facing God (like Jesus), our faces shine with the glory of the divine countenance as we attend to the other. The Book of James urges its readers not to be like someone who observes her own face in a mirror and walks away forgetting her own likeness (1:22–25). This facing of the self is self-deceiving; instead we should look into the perfect "law of liberty," which opens us up in freedom to works of love that provide hope for those in distress, such as orphans and widows (1:27). This faithful love that faces the neighbor is willing to give itself fully because it is full of hope in the glory of the divine promise of eternal peace. As we confront others in faithfulness and love, opening them up to the divine promise, we are fulfilling our call to be conformed to the image of Jesus Christ.

The forgiveness manifested in the history of Jesus Christ means more than simply the satisfaction on the cross of a legal penalty for the transgressive activity of the guilty. Forensic applications of the forgiving work of Christ focus primarily on the past, and indeed the cross and all of Jesus' historical activity are central for Christian hope. What makes them good news, however, is that they manifested the in-breaking of God's promise to forgive and heal, an in-breaking that continues to constitute the reality of Christian hope *now*. The legal "salvation" of a judicial verdict releases me from a punishment, but it does not cure my ontological anxiety. Paying a debt to justice may take care of guilt, but it does not heal shame.[68] A punitive concept of forgiveness may help a person who feels guilt about an activity, but for the deeper existential dread that accompanies repeated shaming, we need a complementary concept of forgiveness that is oriented toward wholeness

---

68. The tendency to pay attention to shame is more prevalent in pastoral theology, where practitioners and theorists recognize the role of shame in blocking wholeness and salvation. See, for example, R. H. Albers, "The Shame Factor: Theological and Pastoral Reflections Relating to Forgiveness," *Word and World* 16 (1996): 347–53.

and reconciliation.[69] We need our sins to be remitted not only in a judicial sense, but also in a medical sense: we want to be healed and made whole.

For Matthew, it was not only at the cross but already in the healing ministry of Jesus that he saw the fulfillment of Isaiah 53:4—in his ministry to hurting people "he took our infirmities and bore our diseases" (Matthew 8:17). Jesus' whole ministry bore (took away) the pain of sin and death. However, the ultimate cost of this bearing became most clear at Golgotha. The cross was "the final and total expression of his bearing our sins. . . . [It] becomes both the supreme act of his self-giving and the symbol of his complete solidarity with us in our behalf."[70] As we articulate the power of the cross and resurrection, we should be sensitive to how people feel the brokenness of sin in different ways: sometimes as guilt for attempts to oppress and sometimes as shame under oppression.

Conforming to the image of Jesus Christ means facing our neighbors and enemies with the promise of hope as we find ultimate belonging in the presence of the God of hope. This occurs in community. Several theological treatments of the idea of the image of God explore its application beyond the focus on the individual's rationality or holiness that characterized large streams of the Christian tradition.[71] Christians hope in fellowship with God, a *koinōnia* in and through the Spirit of Christ whose Parousia brings the reign of divine peace so near that it is in and among us now. All of our lives are spent longing for a face that will grant us peaceful loving attention, a face that will secure us and call us into a hopeful future. In Christ, we find that face; by the Spirit, we become that face for one another.

Being in Eucharistic Community

Why *eucharistic* community? In what sense *being*? What does any of this have to do with *forgiveness*? These questions are all interrelated and must be answered together. As in our previous analyses of the dynamics of forgiveness in the Christian community, the (re)turn to rela-

69. For discussion of the psychological and therapeutic issues around these two ways of conceiving forgiveness, see E. M. Pattison, "Punitive and Reconciliation Models of Forgiveness," in *Counseling and the Human Predicament: A Study of Sin, Guilt, and Forgiveness* (ed. L. Aden and D. G. Benner; Grand Rapids: Baker, 1989), 162–76.

70. Cf. C. N. Kraus, *Jesus Christ Our Lord* (Scottsdale, Pa.: Herald, 1987), 226.

71. Cf. Shults, *Reforming Theological Anthropology*, chap. 10. D. J. Hall's *Imaging God* (Grand Rapids: Eerdmans, 1986) explores the way in which a communal emphasis alters the way we think of the command to have "dominion," which is linked to the creation of humanity in God's image in Genesis. He develops an "ontology of communion" that allows him to articulate a view of dominion as "stewardship," not only of nonhuman creation, but also of our being with others. See also S. Grenz, *The Social God and the Relational Self* (Louisville: Westminster John Knox, 2001).

tionality opens up new possibilities for understanding and experiencing the "real presence" of Christ. If what is most real about the presence of Christ is the gracious relationality of divine peace, then we may be able to move beyond debates over the presence of the Lord in or with the elements. Perhaps the Lord's Supper is not about *substance*-iation at all, but about the substantive transformation of broken relations into new beautiful patterns of living that share in the community-healing reality of divine grace. We might then say that the church is ontologically made new as it gathers around the table, responding in joy and gratitude to the real presence of the forgiving Spirit of Christ, through whom it receives its calling to manifest divine grace and peace to and in the systems of the lived world. In other words, the eucharistic community exists[72] through the blessing and keeping of the gracious and peaceful Face of God.

First, let us reflect on the meaning of the Eucharist in the context of the community that formed around Jesus of Nazareth and his ministry and message of forgiveness. Jesus gave thanks during that last supper with his disciples, as they had fellowship for the final time before his death. Not only his "last supper," however, but all of Jesus' suppers should teach us about how to manifest God's forgiveness to others. Jesus' own ministry of forgiveness was a welcoming of others, especially "sinners," into eucharistic (thankful) and joyful community. It is important to recognize the cultural significance of table fellowship for the Jewish people during Jesus' time. The ancient Israelites structured their experience of time around feasting (Feast of Weeks, Feast of Tabernacles, etc.), as they anticipated the promised peace (*shalom*) of God's reign. Even the regular sharing of meals together represented a "communion" that should be extended only to certain people at certain times. The Pharisees had developed explicit rules for excluding particular persons from *koinōnia*. As Jesus traveled through ancient Palestine, he upset many of the cultural standards and religious regulations that guided Jewish community life. Jesus' being in openness to his neighbors was not constrained by the culinary policies of his culture. His intimate communion with social outcasts enacted the peaceful *koinōnia* of the reign of God. The Christian church is called to the same kind of communal living, which is possible only if by the Spirit, we can say with Jesus: "My food is to do the will of him who sent me"

72. Eastern Orthodox theologian J. Zizioulas notes that in the patristic era "the eucharist was not the act of a pre-existing Church; it was an event *constitutive* of the being of the Church, enabling the church to *be*"; *Being as Communion* (Crestwood, N.Y.: St. Vladimir's, 1997), 21. D. Farrow points to Irenaeus's claim that "it is only eucharistically that creation can hope to enjoy the liberty for which it is made"; *Ascension and Ecclesia: On the Significance of the Doctrine of the Ascension for Ecclesiology and Christian Cosmology* (Grand Rapids: Eerdmans, 1999), 70.

(John 4:34). The sustenance of the hopeful follower of Christ is the eschatological activity of the divine Spirit who draws all things toward renewal in God.

Jesus' table fellowship was primarily with those who had little hope, whose ontological anxiety had been intensified by a variety of psychological and social factors. The woman who is "forgiven much" in Luke 7:36–50 approaches Jesus during a meal, and although defaced by the Pharisees, she receives grace as Jesus calls her into a new life: "Go in peace." The first miracle recorded in John's Gospel is the turning of water into wine at Cana, and while this manifested Jesus' glory to the disciples (John 2:11), its practical purpose seems to have been to keep the table fellowship going. When Matthew the tax collector is called by Jesus, he does what comes naturally—he throws a party (Matthew 9:9–13). This table fellowship with sinners is upsetting to the Pharisees, but Jesus counters: "Go and learn what this means, 'I desire mercy, not sacrifice.'" When Jesus invites himself to Zacchaeus's house (Luke 19:1–10), the latter "was happy to welcome him." Although officially the guest, Jesus' gracious presence at the table of this sinner allowed him to host a transforming fellowship so powerful that it led Zacchaeus to act in radically hospitable ways in his community. Even after the resurrection, Jesus' presence during meals is revelatory. The eyes of the disciples on the road to Emmaus were opened only after Jesus took, blessed, and broke bread and gave it to them (24:30–31). His way of being at table was so unique that it had to be him! Later in Acts, we hear that the table fellowship of the early church was characterized by "glad and generous hearts" (2:42–47), which led to their sharing all things in common. Peter had to learn that this call to communion ultimately extends even to the unclean Gentiles, such as Cornelius (10:9–20).

In the face of Jesus Christ, the early disciples were confronted by a grace so radical that they could interpret his presence only as the arrival of the kingdom of God: "From his fullness we have all received, grace upon grace" (John 1:16). The eucharistic community gives thanks (*eucharistia*) to God in response to this *charis* (grace). The church as the body of Christ calls others to share in the salutary ordering of divine grace. Forgiveness is what this community is all about. Its calling is fulfilled by concrete acts of self-giving service to those who, like us, cannot secure their own existence in the world. The joy (*chara*) of the thanksgiving community naturally flows toward God as a response to grace and overflows in the gifts (*charismata*) of the Spirit that shape the community. The gifts of each member are oriented toward serving the others; together, we are "stewards of the manifold grace of God" (1 Peter 4:10). The church shares grace by welcoming others into a new way of being, a new space and time that is opened up by the divine promise. Christian *koinōnia* is a being-filled with the Spirit in graceful, joyful, and thankful community (Ephesians 5:4, 20), an inviting fellowship that calls others to become "sharers in the promise" (3:6), so that they too may be liberated from ontological anxiety.

This has everything in the world to do with forgiving. The eucharistic community can expend itself, exhaust the violence of the other in its own being, because its being is not its own, but the reception of the inexhaustible being of divine life. The gratitude and joy that emerge from sharing in divine grace provide an ontological stability that enables redemptive forgiveness. This is how we participate as ambassadors of God's grace, as ministers of reconciliation: "In Christ God was reconciling the world to himself. . . . [Now] God is making his appeal through us" (2 Corinthians 5:19–20). Eucharistic life is grace-giving thanks and joy. Paul calls his readers to rejoice in the Lord always (Philippians 4:4; 1 Thessalonians 5:16). James urges the believers to "consider it nothing but joy" when they suffer various trials (1:2). This is possible only if our being is no longer threatened by those whom we need to forgive. Offering forgiveness provides space and time for the other to be nourished, to be welcomed into face-to-face fellowship. The *telos* of forgiveness is described in Jesus' parables in terms of feasting (e.g., the prodigal son; Luke 15:11–32) and banqueting (e.g., 14:12–24; Matthew 22:1–10). The Eucharist signifies the nourishing presence of God's promising grace to the community; this grace aims at increasing thanksgiving (*eucharistia*) "as it extends to more and more people . . . to the glory of God" (2 Corinthians 4:15).

The particular act of having "communion" together signifies our recognition that our whole lives are dependent on God's gracious opening up of the future through the resurrection of Christ. The Eastern Orthodox liturgical practice of *epiclesis* (invoking the Spirit) during the Eucharist complements the practice of *anamnesis* (remembering the death of Jesus). Forgiveness not only remembers but also anticipates. We gratefully welcome the *koinōnia*-creating presence of the Spirit, whose being-there for and with us is not limited to the "sacred" space/time of the table. The Eucharist may be an intensification of our communion, but it signals our dependence on the Spirit in all the places and moments of our communal lives. Some churches report that the sacraments are no longer experienced as significant in their communities. The problem may not be the emptiness of the sacraments as "signs" but the unfortunate reality that those who are engaging in this signification are themselves empty—ontologically bereft of the hopeful relation to others and to God. If being in communion is the metaphysical origin of forgiveness, it is no wonder that so many ruggedly individualistic Christians struggle to forgive.

The members of the eucharistic community make room for one another around the table. What about the stranger—should the "other" also be welcomed into table fellowship? In the testimony of the early church, the exclusion of others did not seem to be the major concern at the Lord's Supper as it is so often today. In fact, exclusion was precisely the problem Paul addressed in his First Letter to the Corinthians.[73] Paul notes that the cup of blessing and the broken bread are a sharing (*koinōnia*) in the blood and body of Christ (1 Corinthians 10:14–16). Partaking of one meal represents their being "one body" (10:17). They are called to orient themselves wholly to the Lord in all aspects of their lives (10:21). Partaking of the Lord's Supper should affect the way one has table fellowship with those outside the church as well. Paul encourages them: "If an unbeliever invites you to a meal and you are disposed to go, eat whatever is set before you" (10:27). If one partakes with thanksgiving, Paul does not see a problem—as long as it is done "for the glory of God" (10:31). After a discussion of prayer during the assembly, he provides instructions in 1 Corinthians 11 to guide them when they come together for a meal. Because they are not waiting for one another, but some are going hungry while others are gorged, Paul tells them that it is not really the Lord's Supper that they eat (11:20)! It becomes the Lord's Supper as the table fellowship of Christ's ministry takes form in the whole life of the community. Surely the main question in the practice of the Lord's Supper is not whom we should exclude from it. Instead, we might attend instead to the exclusive practices that characterize our whole lives as we eat our fill in a hungry world.

In his being with others, Jesus also manifested the reign of God's *peace*. Forgiveness opens up the possibility for a peaceable future in relation to the other. It promises being to the other, wholly new being. Therefore, only God can forgive. But we (like Christ) can manifest redemptive forgiveness by sharing in divine grace and peace. Those who gather around tables for communion can rejoice that "he is our peace" because the peace of God breaks down the walls of hostility between them (Ephesians 2:14). Redemptive forgiveness is possible in the presence of the God of peace who gives to believers "peace at all times in all ways" (2 Thessalonians 3:16). How will this peace be manifest? Through the promised advocate, the Holy Spirit (John 14:26). The gracious presence of God is the promise of divine fellowship, which is the only kind of peace that is a fruit of the Holy Spirit. This promise is already received as it is anticipated in hope (Galatians 3:14–19). We are drawn into the peace of God as our lives are "hidden

---

73. Cf. James's concern about similar practices of exclusion in the assembly (2:1–17).

with Christ in God" (Colossians 3:3). The eucharistic meal celebrates the eschatological one (*ho eschatos adam*; 1 Corinthians 15:45), the coming prince of peace. Those who exist in this hope are attentive to the Parousia of the life-giving Spirit who is present at the table fellowship of those gathered in the name of Christ. The regular practice of gathering at the table signals our recognition that our whole lives are caught up in the festivity of the Spirit.

Salvation is the reception of a peace that passes understanding, that keeps our hearts and minds in Christ Jesus (Philippians 4:7). This is peace not as the world gives (John 14:27), but the infinite peace of communion with the trinitarian God. The body of Christ shares in Jesus' glory precisely by sharing in his intending[74] of God's forgiving presence to others. The Ephesians are urged to "maintain the unity of the Spirit in the bond of peace" (4:3). The apostles preached the gospel of peace (Acts 10:36). The author of Hebrews exhorts: "Pursue peace with everyone, and the holiness without which no one will see the Lord" (12:14). Paul encourages the Romans to "pursue what makes for peace and mutual upbuilding" (14:19). By the power of the Spirit, we face our neighbors with the presence of the divine promise of peace. We glorify God by turning away from our own attempts to grasp ontological security at the expense of the being of the other, resting instead in the peace of the divine presence.

We must understand and practice forgiveness in light of the most radical extension of horizons possible—the ontological arrival of divine grace and peace. Our struggle to forgive others will fail if we depend on our own ontic weight. In communion with God, however, we (like Christ) may manifest divine grace by facing others in a way that both calls them to fellowship and also provides them time and space to face their own anxiety. Sharing in the divine glory with Christ radically frees the one who hopes, empowering her to face the other with promising grace—to forgive. The practice of gathering together at the Eucharist should emerge out of and lead toward a deep festiveness in the everyday life of the community, overflowing the boundaries of the sanctuary. The real presence of Jesus Christ was and is a promising presence, a call to share in the joy of divine forgiveness through life together in the Spirit. And so I end by returning to the point at which I began in chapter 4: with the grace and peace that come only from the shining divine countenance, the blessing and keeping face of God (Numbers 6:23–27), whose presence is the hope of salvation.

74. A. McFadyen describes the image of God in terms of the call to become persons, a call that is mediated not only through Christ and the Spirit, but also through social relations. He argues that "Jesus *intended* others as forgiven . . . pulling future freedom into the present"; *The Call to Personhood* (Cambridge: Cambridge University Press, 1990), 118.

Modeling Forgiveness: Interdisciplinary Explorations

Steven J. Sandage and F. LeRon Shults

6

FACIAL HERMENEUTICS

Scholarly treatments of forgiveness should engage the front lines of the relational battlefield of life. In part 3, our goal is to test the psychological and theological models of forgiveness developed in parts 1–2 by applying them to particular case studies. The clinical cases are based on the real stories of individuals who worked with Steve in therapy, although we have changed names and other information in order to protect their identities. The biblical cases we selected are stories, parables, and instruction about facing and forgiveness. These texts and contexts illustrate the dramatic struggle of people entangled in the pain of denial, hatred, pride, and shame—people searching for wholeness and salvation.

In this chapter, we focus on facial hermeneutics. After setting out the clinical case study, we then provide a brief psychological interpretation. Finally, we set out the biblical cases and explore ways in which our disciplinary perspectives overlap, mutually enhance one another, and open up new implications for therapeutic practice and theological articulation. As you read these case stories, we encourage you to pay attention to your own internal reactions to the people and issues involved. What do you feel? By whom are you most angered? With whom do you most empathize? What concerns you most about the dilemmas they face? What kinds of psychological and theological questions arise as you read?

Case Study: "Faces of Contempt"

Sandra (Native American, age 37) and David (Swedish American, age 41) were an interracial couple who came to marital therapy shortly after separating for the second time in their three-year marriage. David, who arranged the first session, struck me as articulate, polite, and detail oriented on the phone. Seeing him now in person as he entered the office first, his posture was stiff and his complexion pale. Nevertheless, he smiled as he shook my hand and said, "It's nice to meet you," before sitting down. Sandra came in second and threw herself into one of the chairs, mumbling "hi" with minimal eye contact. She stared out the window as if she were alone in the room.

I must have given some standard therapist-like opening (e.g., "What brings you in?") when David reached into his briefcase and pulled out a small notebook. Sandra's head did not turn from facing the window but she did sneak a peak to catch David's move. He started, "Well, I made note of a few issues I'm concerned about." Looking down at his notebook, he explained, "First, Sandra goes into rages at the drop of a hat, no matter where we are or who is around. Even at our church. It is embarrassing and I can't deal with it anymore." At that, Sandra whirled around in her chair, now facing him, and said, "I am so sick of hearing you whine! What you 'can't deal with' is anything that distracts you from your precious career." David looked toward me nervously and said, "Do you see what I mean? She's out of control and she's like this all the time. She has no concept of forgiveness." "Oh! I can't even stand to look at you!" Sandra countered as she turned back toward the window.

David and Sandra were struggling against many stressors. David was a computer software consultant who was making a career transition into professional ministry. He had started both seminary and a part-time church staff position that year while trying to keep his business afloat. Sandra was working half-time as a shift manager at a department store in a job she detested, as well as carrying the lead role in taking care of their eighteen-month-old daughter, Anna. David had been married for a short period in his mid-twenties to Angela and had a fourteen-year-old daughter, Brittany, from that marriage. Brittany stayed with David and Sandra every other weekend and for longer periods in the summer.

Sandra was also dealing with some other very painful issues. Within the past year a coworker had made a series of blatantly racist remarks to Sandra, and that person had received only a mild reprimand when Sandra reported it to her superiors. The racism and lack of support she felt at work brought to a head a growing frustration that had been brewing for a long time. She found herself deeply embedded in a white community (family and in-laws, friends, and church) that was oblivious, at best, to issues of racism. This would have been hard enough but it also reactivated anxious feelings of victimization from her adolescent experience of being physically abused by a volatile stepfather. She had never discussed this abuse with anyone but David.

Sandra and David had deeply loved each other earlier in their journey together, but at this point they were caught in a powerful vortex of unforgiveness. They both felt hopeless about their marriage. David could not understand Sandra's anger nor could he make sense out of the changes that were just emerging in her sense of self-identity. He hated conflict and wanted to find a logical way to fix his marriage so "things could run smoothly again." Sandra had idealized David when they were first married. He seemed calm and confident of his faith and life goals. She also liked his large, close family, which she never had. She was an only child, and her mother had died of cancer seven years earlier. She had not spoken to her stepfather for nearly that long. But now David seemed self-absorbed and insensitive to her, and his family felt intrusive. After a fight David would stay with one of his siblings, while Sandra sat home alone. She felt determined that somehow her life had to change, and every time David used the word *forgiveness* she felt an intense rush of fear and rage. For her, forgiveness meant "accept getting abused again."

David said he felt closest to God when he was teaching or leading a Bible study at church. He believed his marital problems were getting in the way of "what God wants to do with" his life. He often felt distant from God when at home, which usually involved tension between him and Sandra. He said he was concerned "God might give up" on him, and he frequently worried about whether he might be "losing his salvation."

Sandra did not readily talk about her faith at this point in her journey, as the topic generated a mix of confusion, frustration, and shame. She said, "I don't have any idea where God is right now, and I don't feel like searching for him." She admitted she felt torn between wishing punishment would fall upon her racist coworkers and feeling guilty for "being in spiritual exile."

Case Interpretation

Sandra and David are a couple facing one another with contempt rather than forgiveness and repair. They were lacking a sense of inter-subjective attunement and empathy for one another and caught in a volatile shame-anger spiral that led both to feel emotionally over-whelmed. When face to face in conflict, their faces flashed expressions of painful shame and angry contempt back and forth until they were simply too defensive to face each other at all. They both lapsed into defensive maneuvers in an attempt to save face at the expense of the face needs of the other. As John Gottman finds in his research with couples in conflict, the physiological stress alone of this process of contemptuous facing is enough to lead couples like Sandra and David to search for ways of avoiding each other.[1] Both Sandra and David failed to understand their own subjective experience very well, much less that of the other. And this lack of mutual intersubjective attune-ment and empathy left them gripped by estranging forces of unfor-giveness and sliding toward hopelessness about the future horizon of their marriage.

Despite the serious problems in their relationship, Sandra and David each had important strengths as individuals. Both were in-telligent, responsible people who valued and worked hard at their commitments. They were both caring and responsive parents to Anna and were eager to make sacrifices for her well-being, al-though their marital conflict was probably impacting her emerg-ing development. David valued his role as a father to Brittany, and Sandra mostly enjoyed her own connection with Brittany. Both David and Sandra were flexible about nontraditional domestic roles, at least in theory, and had some success with flexible role assign-ments to facilitate their family functioning. Sandra was extremely loyal, though she was at a point where she was wrestling with how to balance that virtue with other virtues like justice. She was also quite compassionate toward those who are suffering, a compas-sion she rarely extended to herself. David was effective at rational problem solving, a strength he relied upon too much in his mar-riage. Both David and Sandra were committed to their religious faith, even if neither their internalized forms of that faith nor their religious community were particularly helpful in dealing with their marital conflicts at the start of therapy. They were eager to join ed-ucational small groups at church, but those social groups tended

---

1. J. M. Gottman, "A Theory of Marital Dissolution and Stability," *Journal of Family Psychology* 7 (1993): 57–75.

to fail in facilitating the integration of cognitive and emotional understanding.[2]

In the estranging context of facing each other in conflict, Sandra and David experienced each other very differently. Sandra experienced David as controlling, self-absorbed, and nonempathic. His note taking felt like surveillance to gain incriminating evidence against her. She experienced his ministry and work focus as bordering on an addiction that gave him a self-aggrandizing stage for gaining strokes from others. She felt that he didn't understand her feelings or what was going on in her life, and she became cynical about his willingness to consider alternatives to their current church and life situation. At a deeper level, his lack of empathy for her subjectivity, particularly the injustice she was experiencing, activated feelings of being abandoned and alone in her suffering. This was an experience she previously encountered with her mother, whom she loved but who was also complicit by failing to protect her from an abusive stepfather. David's general lack of emotional support and advocacy for Sandra moved him into a complicit role of his own. She had usually apologized after getting angry at David and dropped her complaints but she had become unwilling to do so anymore.

David tended to experience Sandra as volatile, aggressive, and arrogant. His subjective experience that she did not value his feelings provoked a sense that he was being attacked and publicly shamed, which was hauntingly reminiscent of ways in which David's father and mother would spontaneously erupt in verbal attacks on each other. He felt that he was calm and rational and that her attacks came out of nowhere. Her face of contempt scared him, leaving him defensively clamoring to stipulate rules and eventually turning to shaming attacks himself. He was also experiencing Sandra as something of a stranger, different than she used to be in the way she related to him. He was overwhelmed by what he felt was her constant negativity and complaining and frustrated that she was frequently "letting the sun go down on her anger" (Ephesians 4:26) rather than apologizing and making up.

Several systemic dynamics of intersubjective estrangement were at work in this case. First, Sandra recently awakened to the racist context in which she lived. Not only was she experiencing explicit racism and injustice in her workplace but she was becoming aware of more insidious implicit racism in her church and David's family. Their inter-

---

2. K. I. Pargament and M. S. Rye, "Forgiveness as a Method of Religious Coping," in *Dimensions of Forgiveness: Psychological Research and Theological Perspectives* (ed. E. L. Worthington Jr.; Philadelphia: Templeton Foundation, 1998), 62–64; R. Wuthnow, "How Religious Groups Promote Forgiving: A National Study," *Journal for the Scientific Study of Religion* 39 (2000): 125–39.

racial relationship was accepted by David's family and friends on the surface, but Sandra started to realize what Miroslav Volf calls the as-similating form of exclusion.[3] Sandra would not be openly excluded as long as she fit in by adapting herself to the dominant white culture. In various systemic contexts, she was being faced in contempt and non-recognition, both powerful forms of shaming. She served as a scape-goat, an easy target of blame not only in her current contexts but in the abusive relationship with her stepfather, who had wanted a wife but not a daughter. Her burgeoning awareness of racism was impor-tant but also came as another loss for a woman who had experienced a number of painful losses and abandonments. She was giving up what we call self-surveillance, but that had left her wandering in a psy-chological and spiritual desert that offered few empowering sources for constructing a healthy self-identity. As is the case with many vic-tims of abuse, God seemed mostly absent and at times accusatory to Sandra.[4]

David and Sandra were also part of a systemic context that chal-lenged their abilities to make healthy space for their relationship. Most couples experience a decline in marital satisfaction after the birth of their first child, so they were facing a normal life-cycle chal-lenge. And forming a blended family added another degree of diffi-culty to their marriage. But these challenges were further complicated by workplaces that did not support work/family boundaries. David, in particular, had not developed the ability to set boundaries with work and the church, feeling that work and ministry demands should al-ways come first. He also felt entitled to having Sandra adapt her needs to his calling. This paralleled his narcissistic family-of-origin experi-ence, where his parents' needs took precedence, and he gained ap-proval by denying his emotional needs and working hard to achieve the kind of success that would make his family look good. This was an intergenerational pattern in the families of both of his parents—lots of exterior success and periodic interior ruptures in relationships that were covered over rather than repaired. David and Sandra each lacked an "internal museum" of faces from their family and relational histo-ries with whom they had experienced forgiveness and repair.[5]

David was also using his skills at record keeping as a form of sur-veillance to triangulate others into supporting his position against

3. M. Volf, *Exclusion and Embrace: A Theological Exploration of Identity, Otherness, and Reconciliation* (Nashville: Abingdon, 1996).

4. C. Doehring, *Internal Desecration* (Lanham, Md.: University Press of America, 1993); idem, "The Absent God: When Neglect Follows Sexual Violence," *Journal of Pas-toral Care* 47 (1993): 3–12.

5. The "internal museum" concept and metaphor comes from D. W. Augsburger, *Helping People Forgive* (Louisville: Westminster John Knox, 1996).

Sandra's resistance. This was a symptom of his anxiety and lack of self-differentiation. Like many men raised in his cultural context, David had not been socialized to take the perspective of others or admit when he was wrong. His lack of humility reflected an insecure grasping for power and, at a deeper level, an existential fear of any diminishment that symbolized the underlying void of negation. His spirituality was rooted in an image of a God whose affirming face (or presence) was selectively responsive to successful performance. His early development involved a frustrated need for mirroring and the experience of parents who selectively affirmed effective performance, resulting in the internal representation of a God who mirrors back competence to David. This was not an image of a God who is accepting and forgiving, and David's relationship with Sandra was testing the limits of his representation of God. Sandra no longer looked at David with a face of idealization. This stress contributed to David's anxiety and anger being manifested as unforgiveness and as attempts to control Sandra.

Based on the anxiety and pain of their conflicts, David and Sandra also succumbed to totalizing one another. Each used global attributions about the character and motives of the other person to interpret the chaos in their relationship. David viewed Sandra as "nothing-more-than" an angry woman who was trying to get in the way of his work and ministry, and Sandra viewed David as "nothing-more-than" a self-absorbed man who was unwilling to share power. From those perspectives, conflicts became a zero-sum game where one person wins and one person loses and both try to establish who is most to blame. At best, forgiveness could take only the form of forensic transaction where one or both apologize after a conflict out of shame or fatigue, but this did not result in a deeper transformation of their relationship.

Forgiveness was not appropriate as an initial goal for therapy with this couple, especially for Sandra who was experiencing the reactivation of trauma and was taking initial steps toward asserting herself against injustice. David and Sandra each entered individual therapy with separate therapists and worked with me in couples therapy. Several systemic dynamics had to change before anything approximating transformative forgiveness would happen. First, safe space had to be created for Sandra and David to pursue healing and wholeness as individuals and as a couple. This meant setting firmer boundaries against outside intrusions, primarily David's extended family and the unrealistic demands of his workload. David began to enter into Sandra's perspective with regard to his family and the church, and this led to some decisions about boundaries that helped save space for David and Sandra to face each other. This disembedding from the familiarity of community enmeshment also meant tolerating feeling somewhat like strangers for a time, particularly for David.

These moves also reflected a greater sharing of power between David and Sandra. David began to realize he had allowed his performance-based sense of self to be determined by outside validation, a position that was inherently insecure and left him chronically anxious and empty. As he faced his own internal emptiness and shame, he eventually moved toward a healthier sense of self-acceptance that did not require so much mirroring from others. This allowed him to be less defensive about Sandra's complaints and to admit he even shared many of her concerns about his family and church. He began to differentiate by developing his own voice in his family and church to maintain boundaries and to try to repair estranged relationships.

Individual therapy helped Sandra grieve and lament the series of losses in her life and to work on the traumatic impact of racism and abuse. She was also empowered to develop and affirm her sense of self as she explored her racial and gender identity. She was surprised to find this latter endeavor to be spiritually rejuvenating as she explored Native American spirituality. She began to feel less defensive about asserting her own agency and voice.

As a couple, Sandra and David worked on developing the communicative competence to face each other in intersubjective dialogue.[6] They found that they were each misinterpreting the other person and casting projections based on their worst fears. It became safer to lose face and admit being wrong, angry, or simply feeling vulnerable. When this began to happen they found they could apologize and repair most conflicts rather than maneuvering to save face. This was not without periodic relapses of defensiveness and hurt, but there was gradual movement toward the healing transformation of living with each other in more just and forgiving ways.

Intertextual Explorations

The Christian Scriptures also contain a variety of cases in which persons struggle with forgiveness in the context of faces of contempt. Our goal in the following is to explore some of the facial hermeneutics in some key texts from the Gospel of Matthew and to ask how these may be woven into the context of Sandra and David's story. Two of the most enigmatic New Testament passages that deal with both divine

6. D. S. Browning, B. J. Miller-McLemore, P. D. Couture, K. B. Lyon, and R. M. Franklin, *From Culture Wars to Common Ground: Religion and the American Family Debate* (2d ed.; Louisville: Westminster John Knox, 2000).

and interhuman forgiveness appear in Matthew: the Lord's Prayer and the parable of the unforgiving slave. Our entry into the first passage begins with attention to its broader context, in which Jesus is teaching his disciples about facial hermeneutics (6:1–18):

> Beware of practicing your piety before others in order to be seen by them; for then you have no reward from your Father in heaven.
>
> So whenever you give alms, do not sound a trumpet before you, as the hypocrites do in the synagogues and in the streets, so that they may be praised by others. Truly I tell you, they have received their reward. But when you give alms, do not let your left hand know what your right hand is doing, so that your alms may be done in secret; and your Father who sees in secret will reward you.
>
> And whenever you pray, do not be like the hypocrites; for they love to stand and pray in the synagogues and at the street corners, so that they may be seen by others. Truly I tell you, they have received their reward. But whenever you pray, go into your room and shut the door and pray to your Father who is in secret; and your Father who sees in secret will reward you.
>
> When you are praying, do not heap up empty phrases as the Gentiles do; for they think that they will be heard because of their many words. Do not be like them, for your Father knows what you need before you ask him.
>
> Pray then in this way:
>> Our Father in heaven,
>>> hallowed be your name.
>>> Your kingdom come.
>>> Your will be done,
>>>> on earth as it is in heaven.
>>> Give us this day our daily bread.
>>> And forgive us our debts,
>>>> as we also have forgiven our debtors.
>>> And do not bring us to the time of trial,
>>>> but rescue us from the evil one.
>
> For if you forgive others their trespasses, your heavenly Father will also forgive you; but if you do not forgive others, neither will your Father forgive your trespasses.
>
> And whenever you fast, do not look dismal, like the hypocrites, for they disfigure their faces so as to show others that they are fasting. Truly I tell you, they have received their reward. But when you fast, put oil on your head and wash your face, so that your fasting may be seen not by others but by your Father who is in secret; and your Father who sees in secret will reward you.

First, Jesus tells his disciples not to practice piety "before others in order to be seen by them" (6:1). The hypocrites pray and give alms where everyone can face them: in the synagogues and streets, announced with trumpets in case someone might not notice. Jesus teaches his disciples to pray in secret, facing only the Father. In the presence of this Face, it is not necessary to "heap up empty phrases" and "many words," because this Face knows the one who prays more deeply than she knows herself. After describing the way in which the disciples should pray, Jesus continues to teach them about practicing piety: Do not "look dismal, like the hypocrites" who "disfigure their faces" to ensure that those facing them are aware they are fasting. No, "wash your face," Jesus says, so as not to "be seen" by others but by the Father.

Examination of the broader context sheds light on the way devotion to God frees us from anxiety. Epistemic anxiety arises because we do not know where our next meal will come from or what will happen tomorrow. The prayer places our trust in the faithfulness of God. Ethical anxiety is a result of our trying to determine how to act in ways that secure the good life. But we are not strong enough to keep evil away, to overcome trials, and so the prayer focuses our desire on the one whose infinite power elevates us into the presence of a Face that releases us from the determining power of finite goods and evils. The overcoming of ontological anxiety is also evident in the prayer. The idea of the Father "in heaven" borrows from the Israelite understanding of the presence of the glory of God, the "place" of the divine, to which we do not have immediate access but which nevertheless "dwells" in the earth. Invoking the kingdom of the heavenly Father, the reign of divine peace, is a way of expressing hope in the faithful promising presence of divine love that already secures our existence as we share in the grace that binds us together as the church.

If we widen our scope further we note that the Lord's Prayer is placed by Matthew in the Sermon on the Mount. This broader context provides insight into the three phases of forgiveness. Jesus' teaching in these chapters is all about the relation to God and others in community. Here we can find resources for understanding the three general phases in the process of forgiveness. Engaging in lament, in the sense defined in chapter 3, is evident in several places. For example, the sermon begins with the blessing on the "poor in spirit" and those who are reviled and "persecuted for righteousness' sake" (5:3–11). Readers are challenged to hold their own behavior up to the law, a higher law that requires loving their enemies (5:44), and to judge themselves according to it. This leads to a practice of piety that includes honest expression and acknowledging one's faults in the presence of God, who already knows one's needs (6:6, 8). In the prayer itself, we find a cry for protection against evil and times of trial (6:13). The practice of fasting also traditionally involves time for reflecting on one's life situation and reminding oneself of the total dependence on

God for life. Empathy and appropriate humility are encouraged by the use of the plural "we" as the prayer calls the reader to an awareness that she too is a debtor from the perspective of others whom she has offended. Facing one's own faults is inherent in the prayer. Finally, the extension of narrative horizons is also evident in the prayer. The follower of Christ is not to interpret her story only in light of earthly horizons, but in light of the arrival of the kingdom of heaven, which stands for the in-breaking presence of the God of peace in the lived systems of daily life. Treasures are not to be stored up on earth; such a horizon is too narrow or shallow for the full experience of forgiveness. Extending one's horizons so that one values the presence of God (the kingdom of heaven) above all radically sets one free to discover new meaning in the ongoing narrative of divine grace.

Does God forgive us *as* we forgive our neighbors? Yes. But if we understand forgiving only in terms of a legal or financial transaction, this text easily becomes a tool for manipulating victims through fear. Limited to the forensic domain, the fifth petition of the Lord's Prayer sounds like a threat: "God will take away your ticket to heaven if you do not grant absolution to those who have hurt you." Understood within the semantic field of redemptive forgiveness outlined in chapter 5, however, the petition suggests that one will experience the "putting away" of one's own sins only as one "puts away" the sins of others. In other words, the painful shame and guilt that bind our relations to others keep us from receiving the wholeness of divine salvation. Redemptive forgiveness heals us and transforms us, and our reception of this forgiveness over time takes concrete shape in new healthier relations to ourselves and with our neighbors. If divine forgiveness is the manifestation of infinite grace that embraces us within the trinitarian life of love and peace, then our new life will also manifest this grace as we embrace others. The phrase *as we forgive our neighbors* might even be taken as a performative utterance[7] in the context of a liturgical activity that expresses our move toward the healing of relations with the other. As we are being forgiven, as we share in divine grace, we are opened up to a peaceful future and empowered to embrace others as we call them into that kingdom of peace. *As* we manifest grace toward our neighbors, we receive the fullness of life in relation to God. We are saved.

The Lord's Prayer also raises the contrast between an authentic, internalized spirituality and an attention-seeking, external spirituality. Jesus affirms the former and warns against the latter. The psychological research reviewed in chapter 3 suggests a contemporary parallel to

7. This is the suggestion of A. J. Hultgren, "Forgive Us, As We Forgive (Matthew 6:12)," *Word and World* 16 (1996): 284–90.

the spiritual wisdom of Jesus' teaching in this passage. People who are high in intrinsic religiosity, that is, those who hold an authentic commitment to their faith as an end in itself, tend to be higher in forgivingness than those who are lower in intrinsic religiosity.[8] In contrast, extrinsic religiosity, that is, the orientation of those whom Jesus describes as simply wanting to be seen as spiritual by others, is not conducive to forgivingness. This hypocritical desire to be seen as pious by others (Matthew 6:2) connotes the excessive need for mirroring and external validation that is described by contemporary psychologists as symptomatic of pathology. Jesus is suggesting that authentic disciples should focus on seeking God's Face rather than on seeking the face of others. This seems to invite what Murray Bowen and contemporary family therapists call "differentiation of self,"[9] a trait that we suggested in chapter 2 as also being related to the capacity to forgive others.

The reciprocity of forgiving and being forgiven alluded to in Matthew 6:12–15 also finds a contemporary parallel in numerous psychological models of forgiveness.[10] Anyone can experience offenders who are hard or seemingly impossible to forgive, but the general capacity to forgive others reflects an integration of humility and healthy selfhood. Nevertheless, the moral and spiritual gravity of the reciprocity of forgiveness described by Jesus (i.e., one is forgiven *if* and *as* one forgives others) probably seems more culturally congruent in the collectivistic context of the ancient world than in the contemporary individualistic context of Western societies. A focus on the rights and merits of individual selves renders this text challenging for psychological and spiritual contextualization.[11]

The parable of the unforgiving slave occurs in Matthew 18:23–35, immediately following Peter's question about how many times to forgive another member of the church. Peter's inquiry appears to have been prompted by Jesus' instructions to members of the church: those who have been sinned against should face the offender alone first, then with two or three other faces, then ask the person to face the whole church (18:15–20). The use of the term *church* suggests that

8. M. E. McCullough and E. L. Worthington Jr., "Religion and the Forgiving Personality," *Journal of Personality* 67 (1999): 1141–64.

9. M. Bowen, *Family Therapy in Clinical Practice* (New York: Aronson, 1978).

10. D. B. Allender and T. Longman III, *Bold Love* (Colorado Springs: Navpress, 1992); R. D. Enright and the Human Development Study Group, "Counseling within the Forgiveness Triad: On Forgiving, Receiving Forgiveness, and Self-forgiveness," *Counseling and Values* 40 (1996): 107–26; J. P. Pingleton, "Why We Don't Forgive: A Biblical and Object Relations Theoretical Model for Understanding Failures in the Forgiveness Process," *Journal of Psychology and Theology* 25 (1997): 403–13.

11. S. J. Sandage and T. W. Wiens, "Contextualizing Models of Humility and Forgiveness: A Reply to Gassin," *Journal of Psychology and Theology* 29 (2001): 201–11.

Matthew placed together a set of specific teachings by Jesus intended to guide the early Christian community. The facial hermeneutics of intersubjectivity also illuminate the story of the unforgiving slave. Twice the slave falls down before the king, but only once does it have the desired effect. Between these facings of the king, the slave grabbed a fellow slave "by the throat"—we may assume the anger in the first slave's face was quickly interpreted since the latter slave cries out for mercy. Their fellow slaves "saw" what had happened and were "distressed." The process of forgiveness had gone horribly awry.

The apparent lamentation of the slave in the presence of the king is shown to be false by his later actions. For this reason, the king does not have pity on him again. The anxiety that he expressed at first was revealed to be a shallow anxiety, focused only on the immediate occasion and not based on a deeper existential evaluation of his life situation. He fails to show any empathy whatsoever when he faces his fellow slave almost immediately ("as he went out" from the king). This illustrates that he does not have the "constructive sorrow" (2 Corinthians 7:8 13)[12] that characterizes mature humility when he approaches the king. He also lacks formation in the virtue of gratitude for forgiveness received, which contemporary psychologists find to be positively correlated with a disposition to forgive.[13] He is concerned only for himself and does not show love-oriented concern for the well-being of the other. He tried to save face with the king, but was unwilling to lose face and show mercy to his neighbor. Finally, we can see the limitations of the slave's horizons. His attention span is limited to each particular act in his narrative. Positive movement toward forgiveness in the sense of therapeutic transformation would require extending his horizon both temporally and spatially so that he could imaginatively envision his own place in the broader human community.

The parable of the unforgiving slave illustrates the dynamics of anxiety that make forgiveness so agonizing. Unfortunately, in this story none of the characters achieve the ecstasy of forgiveness. Yet this is what Matthew is holding out to his reading community as the ideal. The parable occurs within a broader didactic context. The overall concern of the author seems to be not simply with the individual getting to heaven, but with corporate forgiveness.[14] The context sug-

12. For an integrative treatment of guilt and constructive sorrow, see S. B. Narramore, *No Condemnation: Rethinking Guilt Motivation Counseling, Preaching, and Parenting* (Grand Rapids: Zondervan, 1987).

13. M. E. McCullough, R. A. Emmons, and J. Tsang, "The Grateful Disposition: A Conceptual and Empirical Topography," *Journal of Personality and Social Psychology* 82 (2002): 112–27.

14. For a discussion of this, see S. E. Hylen, "Forgiveness and Life in Community," *Interpretation* 54 (2000): 146–57.

gests that the community for which Matthew was writing was struggling with problems of power in their way of ordering their life together and needed instruction and exhortation on manifesting grace toward each other. It is important to recognize that this is a parable and meant to be metaphorical. Think, for example, of the unjust judge of Luke 18:1–8 who does not want to show justice to the widow who keeps bothering him, but finally her persistence wears him down. Obviously, the parable does not expect us to attribute a lack of justice or patience to God. Earlier Luke had reported the story of the rich man in Hades and Lazarus in the bosom of Abraham (16:19–31). This parable seems less interested in describing the actual facial interaction of persons after death than it does in motivating persons to face those who are oppressed *now* in mercy rather than in contempt. Unfortunately, the disanalogies between God and the king in Matthew 18 are too often overlooked, and a tit-for-tat view of forgiveness is used to compel victims to stop complaining about their abusers.

David and Sandra's struggle demonstrates the relation between divine and interhuman forgiveness. One of the most interesting aspects of this psychological case from a theological perspective is David's worry about losing his own salvation. This illustrates that his conception of divine forgiveness is affecting and being affected by his struggle with human forgiveness. His attitude also illustrates a common conception of salvation among many conservative Protestants in North America. Salvation is imagined primarily as a "ticket to heaven." Either you have one or you don't. This is a great example of how theology affects life. His view of divine forgiveness seems to be primarily limited to a transaction. So why is it so hard for Sandra to forgive? It is just a transaction, thinks David, a mere decision of the will. But in fact, his anxiety about his being forgiven by God reveals that he is not really satisfied with this abstract legal model of salvation. His belief that God has forgiven him, understood as a single past decision that means he does not have to pay a debt, has not helped him experience *salus* (or health) in his life, and so he begins to question his salvation. The spirituality and religiosity of both Sandra and David began to change as they were healed individually and as a couple. David's initial forensic view of forgiveness lacked the power to heal their estrangement and lacked a politic that would transform their relational system. Therapeutic forgiveness paved the way for formation in redemptive forgiveness. David came to value both grace and social justice more strongly. Sandra came to feel less spiritually incompetent and abandoned and more grounded in a secure sense of God's presence. Both became less anxiety driven in their approach to the sacred, and this allowed them both to differentiate from one another and, eventually, to reconnect spiritually. They began to image God for one another by allowing space for the other instead of fighting against each other for intersubjective space.

The theological idea that God creates "space" for the human experience of grace resonates with the theme of space in several schools of psychoanalytic thought.[15] Healthy parents are described as being accessible and present for their children but also allowing space for creativity and play. Securely attached infants use their caregivers as a base for exploratory play interspersed with the pleasure of mutual recognition, shared discovery, and warm reunion. These are forms of relationality that Sandra and David had not experienced with their own parents, and it was challenging for them to internalize these kinds of relational images of God. The idea that God's saving and forgiving presence opens health-generating and creative space for humanity connects the doctrines of creation and redemption in a way that may seem foreign to those accustomed to forensic models of forgiveness. It suggests, however, an artistic motif or an aesthetic dimension to human forgiveness that echoes or shares in the creativity of God.

David and Sandra were headed toward the social fate of many Christian ministers who get trapped in a systemic double bind that can promote the hypocrisy Jesus warned about. Spiritual leaders are too often held to perfectionistic standards by those they are serving. Unfair use of biblical texts about leaders "having their houses in order" can create a pressure to hide personal and relational struggles behind a surface veneer of external piety. At times a leader's career and family income is at stake. The pernicious cycle of this bind is that as the exterior façade of spiritual and relational perfection is constructed and maintained, the interior life of the leader and family becomes more and more barren. Early in the process David could not appreciate the value of having the façade torn down before entering into the throes of full-time ministry, but later he and Sandra both felt grateful they had established a different approach to community. They cultivated a healthy and authentic Christian community of friends who were able to face and accept them in their brokenness, and they made a commitment to maintaining relationships with formative stakeholders in their marriage.

The psychological and spiritual process of healing and forgiveness experienced by Sandra and David also resonates with Cynthia Crysdale's integrative theology of salvation reviewed in chapters 3 and 4.[16] Crysdale's two sides of the cross suggest that the way we come to the

15. J. Benjamin, *Like Subjects, Love Objects: Essays on Recognition and Sexual Difference* (New Haven: Yale University Press, 1995).

16. C. Crysdale, *Embracing Travail: Retrieving the Cross Today* (New York: Continuum, 2001).

Christ event is conditioned by our social location. If we come from a place of social privilege, as many white males like David do, the initial invitation of the cross may be to the humility of repentance and the forgiveness of sins. David moved toward a more authentic and less anxiety-driven form of psychological and spiritual repentance and forgiveness. If we come to the cross from a place of social oppression, Crysdale suggests that the initial invitation of the cross may be one of God's identification with innocent victims and the healing of wounds of shame.[17] Sandra moved toward the cross from this direction and began to face herself with greater affirmation and empowerment as she felt faced by a God of love rather than exclusion. Crysdale argues that both sides of the cross—the healing of wounds of shame and the forgiveness of sins—are relevant to the overall process of realizing the healing and wholeness of salvation and breaking the victim-perpetrator cycle that perpetuates estrangement. Facing both sides of the cross invites a more holistic and just model of forgiveness and salvation.[18]

The robust experience of having been saved, being saved, and anticipating salvation involves an ongoing process of living like Christ with others in real space and time. This is related to the discussion of substitutionary atonement in chapter 5. Human intimacy with God (atonement) is made possible by Christ's place-taking among humanity, making room in the Spirit for us to be reconciled to God. The church is called to share in this gracious place-taking, making room for others in the *koinōnia* of the Spirit. These dynamics are analogous to the way a mother provides her children with hospitable space and time to live, grow, heal, and flourish. The child could not survive unless another substitutes for the life-sustaining activities that he is not yet able to perform on his own. The love of the mother bears the burden of the child's stress by maintaining spatiotemporal boundaries within which the child can grow into the capacity for intimate self-giving relations with others; this is the atoning power of love. In cases like Sandra and David's, the sacramental community is called to provide space and time for their healing; this substitutionary work of the church signals the manifestation of divine grace. Drawing them into a life immersed in the Spirit of grace, the church may participate in God's reconciliation through a charismatic nourishing of their lives that opens them up to face one another graciously. As this couple is faithfully upheld within the baptized and eucharistic community, they may receive grace for the real experience of "dying to sin" with and "conforming to the image" of Jesus Christ. Redemptive forgiveness takes time and space . . . and transforms them.

17. Also, see Volf, *Exclusion and Embrace*.
18. Cf. Sandage and Wiens, "Contextualizing Models of Humility and Forgiveness."

7

SALVATION BY FACE

In Christian theology, we are accustomed to hearing about salvation by grace and salvation by faith, but salvation by face? As we showed throughout parts 1–2, the human search for wholeness and salvation is a longing to belong in a peaceful fellowship of facing and being faced. For the ancient Israelites, this was expressed as a desire to be in the presence of the shining divine countenance. The early Christians found salvation in the face of Jesus Christ through the presence of the Holy Spirit. Salvation comes in relation to the face of God. This redemptive vis-à-vis is an experience of being faithfully restored and bound to the gracious divine presence: "For by grace you have been saved through faith, and this is not your own doing; it is the gift of God" (Ephesians 2:8). Our discussion of forgiveness has been guided by this basic intuition of Christian experience and doctrine.

Another key intuition of lived Christian experience is that salvation is a process, a becoming in relation to God, that involves an actual change in one's way of living: "You see that a person is justified by works and not by faith alone. . . . Faith without works is . . . dead" (James 2:24, 26). That is to say, our being saved by the divine face involves the transformation of our facing of others. We "are receiving . . . salvation" as the outcome of our faith (1 Peter 1:9) as we share in the manifestation of divine grace. Both are true: salvation is God's gift, which we do not earn, and salvation is worked out by us in daily life: "Work out your own salvation with fear and trembling; for it is God who is at work in you, enabling you both to will and to work for his good pleasure" (Philippians 2:12b–13). Salvation involves not only the Face of God but the redemptive transformation of the way we face ourselves and our neighbors.

Case Study: "Demanding to Be Faced"

Kevin (Irish American, age 33) was referred to therapy by a singles' pastor of a large, nondenominational church. Mike (the pastor) had approached Kevin, who had recently started attending the singles group, after several women complained that he had been "hitting on them." Mike recounted to me the sharp contrast he first noticed as Kevin stood alone by the refreshment table at the singles group. Kevin's form-fitting shirt and tight jeans outlined the muscular physique of a bodybuilder, but his nervous fidgeting and vigilant eyes revealed profound insecurity. Mike expressed his concern to Kevin that the goal of the singles group was to encourage spiritual growth and not to provide a dating service. Kevin said he was just trying to meet people, but when Mike pressed it by suggesting he put off asking out any more women from the group for awhile, Kevin exploded, "I'm just so sick of being alone!" and stormed out of the room. Later that week he met with Mike over breakfast and began to tell his painful story, which had reached a point of crisis.

Kevin was enraged by a recent experience of unrequited love with Tammy (age 21), who lived in a neighboring state about eight hours away. He had met Tammy through a mutual acquaintance and had visited several times for long weekends. Tammy was on the heels of a series of difficult relationships with men, one of which had resulted in a pregnancy. She was unemployed and had little family support but decided to keep the child. She and her family belonged to a conservative Protestant church, and when the elders learned she was pregnant they met with her and said she would need to publicly repent during a church service and seek forgiveness from the congregation for becoming pregnant outside of marriage. When Tammy refused, they informed her she would undergo church discipline and was barred from church activities until she was willing to repent.

Kevin had been eager to help her out by doing odd jobs and errands, and they eventually had sex on several occasions. Kevin decided he wanted to marry Tammy and, despite being unemployed himself, bought an engagement ring by cashing in some family money he borrowed to return to college. When he proposed, he was shocked to hear Tammy say she really considered him nothing more than a friend and did not want a romantic relationship. She then laughed and said, "Basically, you get on my nerves because you're too nice."

Kevin was numb as he returned home. He was living with his parents while returning to college part-time after several frustrating years in a series of retail sales jobs. His shock soon turned to anger, and he began calling Tammy several times a day demanding a better explanation. Kevin felt betrayed and led on. Soon, Tammy simply quit answering the phone. There had been another guy at her place the last couple of times she had answered, and Kevin had tape-recorded those conversations. He was planning another trip to demand an explanation in person, even if it meant waiting on her doorstep until she faced him. All he lacked was the money to make the trip. He could not stop thinking about Tammy and his need to see her again.

Most of us could probably understand Kevin's feeling deeply hurt and rejected, but the rest of his life also provided little buffer against the anxious desperation that was spinning out of control. He felt so keyed up that he had been getting drunk every couple of nights. He was spending his days working out, surfing the Internet, or attending class. With no close friends, his evenings involved either going to a bar by himself or simply driving around town.

Kevin's parents were retired and home most of the time, which made him eager to be elsewhere. He experienced his mom as opinionated and critical and said she was bugging him to get a job. He described his dad as off in his own world and a TV addict. Kevin's older sister, Lisa (age 34), was a CPA and married with two young daughters. She and Kevin were not close. Kevin's family was Irish and Catholic on both sides, though his family had minimal involvement with religion or the church while he was growing up. He had recently started attending the worship service and singles group at the nondenominational church near his gym after he noticed a lot of people his age in the parking lot one Sunday morning. He said he had hoped "to meet some people and maybe find a purpose or something." Kevin said he also worried that, if he didn't find a way to forgive Tammy, God would never forgive him for his sins.

Case Interpretation

Kevin's pain over Tammy's rejection was propelling him toward dangerous self-destructive behavior. He felt his only salvation or relief would come from demanding that Tammy face him. In reality, sitting on her step with such a demand would risk arrest for stalking. So why was Kevin so obsessed with seeing Tammy?

Numerous psychological dynamics shaped the context of Kevin's estrangement. He had a growing sense of shame and worthlessness due to a lengthy period of unemployment that put him living back at home with his parents. He had stumbled between a series of jobs he didn't enjoy and had never landed on a career path. Interestingly, he had shown talent in acting and dance in high school but his family had never embraced his enthusiasm for those pursuits, often not even showing up for his performances. Yet he had learned that he had the power to entertain people, and he was famished for the attention that generated. He enjoyed being seen.

As he entered his thirties, Kevin also felt hungry for connection and intimacy. He knew how to use his body to get close to women but he did not know how to pursue emotional and spiritual intimacy. His attachment style could be described as anxious-ambivalent (see chap. 2), meaning that he never felt quite close enough to other people and battled a constant anxiety that he would be rejected again. Women he dated quickly experienced him as clingy, and as soon as they started to pull back Kevin would become agitated or even angry. This, of course, made the women nervous, and they would distance themselves further.

Kevin would also engage in sacrificial efforts to ensure the closeness of others by doing favors, as he did for Tammy. Generosity and helping others were among Kevin's strengths. He failed, however, to see how these sacrifices were not always invited and appreciated, and he lacked awareness of how this consistently set him up to feel resentful. These problems represented deficits in intersubjectivity and empathy, resulting in episodes of unforgiveness.

At a deeper existential level, Tammy's rejection and absence (i.e., not even answering his calls) symbolized the negation and loneliness of the void.[1] Kevin started to construct a story line in his own mind where he sacrificially rescued a woman he really cared for, thereby breathing purpose back into his life, which felt hopelessly empty. Tammy ruptured his fantasy with a narcissistic wound that left him groping for an affirming face to save him from despair.

Several psychological dynamics help explain Kevin's difficulty in forgiving Tammy. First, he was shamed by her rejection of his proposal, which took him by surprise in an awful reversal of fortunes. The shocking estrangement of a dashed hope can generate a potent source of rage. Tammy's casual response to Kevin's proposal also demonstrated a lack of intersubjective attunement and empathy, which compounded the loss of face. Second, this psychological sequence over-

---

1. J. E. Loder, *The Logic of the Spirit: Human Development in Theological Perspective* (San Francisco: Jossey-Bass, 1998).

whelmed Kevin's fragile ego and sent him into a narcissistic rage that impeded his own empathy for Tammy. Third, Kevin became stuck in a cycle of ruminating on the unfairness of Tammy's rejection, then trying to solve the mystery of her motives, and finally feeling so horrible that he would search out a quick source of self-medication (e.g., alcohol). Then he would start the cycle over again.

This conflict between Tammy and Kevin also unfolded within several systemic contexts. The first context is that of Kevin's family system. His parents seemed to detour their marital conflict toward Kevin and modeled the poor interpersonal boundaries that he adopted. Kevin felt that his older sister was the family star, and he both envied and resented her success.

Tammy's systemic context included recent exclusion by a Christian community that had shamed and stigmatized her for becoming pregnant. Her own family had seemingly capitulated to the moral police at their church, leaving her cynical about God and the reality of forgiveness. And the father of her child was absent from involvement. It seems that the shame and pain of both Tammy and Kevin prevented them from empathic intersubjectivity as they faced the perspective of the other.

The nondenominational church Kevin was visiting provided yet another systemic context for this conflict. Kevin's lack of formative involvement in the church or other sources of community while he was growing up meant he did not really know how to approach Christian community. So he approached people in the church as we all do, at least initially, by trying to use what had worked for him in the past. In Kevin's case what had worked was his body. He feared people would not accept him unless he did something for them (e.g., entertained them, helped them, seduced them). This is reflected in his anxiety that, despite his hurt and anger, unless he forgave Tammy (i.e., did something) God would not forgive him. Stating this psychologically, Kevin seemed to fear that unless he bridled his rage against people who had rejected him, he would not only drive away those people but also lose the face of God.

Therapy with Kevin started by helping him form the boundaries to create safe space, in this case primarily to protect him from contact with Tammy that could escalate. His primary motivation for not going to face Tammy was initially to simply avoid getting in trouble. He also started antidepressant medication, worked on boundaries with his parents, stopped drinking, and responded to other interventions aimed at alleviating his depressive symptoms. This provided a measure of restored face and emotional stabilization necessary to make engaging in lament a constructive process.

Kevin began to extend his narrative horizons by examining the reasons for his pain and frustration about his life and relationships. His unforgiveness of Tammy had roots of shaming estrangement in other family relationships. His increasing capacity to sustain eye contact during therapy sessions was a good index of his progress in overcoming this shame. Gradually, he grew in his ability to face and sit with his anxieties and pain without demanding immediate relief, and he even sent Tammy a card wishing her well with her pregnancy. This gesture of goodwill was unlike his previous efforts to secure acceptance from others through sacrificial acts. It was a step of forgiving closure as evidenced by his not continuing to ruminate on her feelings about him. Like many clinical cases involving forgiveness, there was no ultimate reconciliation between Kevin and Tammy. Kevin had to move forward tolerating a less-than-perfect ending and without fully knowing the systemic impact of his commitment to forgiveness.

Intertextual Explorations

In this section we examine some New Testament texts on forgiveness and the search for salvation, exploring how they may illuminate the contexts of Kevin and Tammy. What are the dynamics of "salvation by facing" that overlap and connect these "texts"? Our primary biblical cases are the story of the forgiven woman, who appears only in Luke's Gospel, and a composite of the stories of the rich young ruler, who appears in each of the Synoptic Gospels. We begin with the forgiven woman in Luke 7:36–50:

> One of the Pharisees asked Jesus to eat with him, and he went into the Pharisee's house and took his place at the table. And a woman in the city, who was a sinner, having learned that he was eating in the Pharisee's house, brought an alabaster jar of ointment. She stood behind him at his feet, weeping, and began to bathe his feet with her tears and to dry them with her hair. Then she continued kissing his feet and anointing them with the ointment. Now when the Pharisee who had invited him saw it, he said to himself, "If this man were a prophet, he would have known who and what kind of woman this is who is touching him— that she is a sinner." Jesus spoke up and said to him, "Simon, I have something to say to you." "Teacher," he replied, "Speak." "A certain creditor had two debtors; one owed five hundred denarii, and the other fifty. When they could not pay, he canceled the debts for both of them. Now which of them will love him more?" Simon answered, "I suppose the one for whom he canceled the greater debt." And Jesus said to him, "You have judged rightly." Then turning toward the woman, he said to Simon, "Do you see this woman? I entered your house; you gave me no

water for my feet, but she has bathed my feet with her tears and dried them with her hair. You gave me no kiss, but from the time I came in she has not stopped kissing my feet. You did not anoint my head with oil, but she has anointed my feet with ointment. Therefore, I tell you, her sins, which were many, have been forgiven; hence she has shown great love. But the one to whom little is forgiven, loves little." Then he said to her, "Your sins are forgiven." But those who were at the table with him began to say among themselves, "Who is this who even forgives sins?" And he said to the woman, "Your faith has saved you; go in peace."

Much of the scholarly debate[2] over this story revolves around the issues of whether the woman was already forgiven *before* she came to the table and precisely *why* she was crying. These two issues are related: was she weeping out of lament for her past life (which led to Jesus' forgiving her) or out of joy for having already received forgiveness from Jesus at some earlier time? These questions presuppose that forgiveness is a one-time transaction. Jesus' parable about forgiving financial debts obviously lends initial support to this interpretation. We must, however, allow the parable to be iconic: to point beyond itself to the reality of redemption. Clearly, the woman's mind was not filled with images of financial ledgers. She was a "sinner in the city," and, whether or not this means she was a prostitute,[3] her experience of being shamed in the community led her to face her anxiety about her desiring goodness, and it intensified her search for salvation.

The parable points to the contrast between two of those facing Jesus during table fellowship—Simon the Pharisee and this unnamed forgiven woman. The woman demonstrates the virtue of *gratitude* in response to the benevolent grace of Jesus. Moreover, by crashing the party and anointing Jesus' feet, she shows the intensity of gratitude that contemporary psychologists link to psychological and spiritual health and to virtues like hope, empathy, and forgivingness.[4] In con-

---

2. For a review of the exegetical literature on this story, see R. Holst, "The One Anointing of Jesus: Another Application of the Form-Critical Method," *Journal of Biblical Literature* 95 (1976): 435–46; D. A. S. Ravens, "The Setting of Luke's Account of the Anointing: Luke 7.2–8.3," *New Testament Studies* 34 (1988): 282–92; J. Kilgallen, "Forgiveness of Sins (Luke 7:36–50)," *Novum Testamentum* 40 (1998): 105–16.

3. For a fascinating discussion of the tendencies of male interpreters to project gender bias into the text, see J. K. Applegate, "'And She Wet His Feet with Her Tears': A Feminist Interpretation of Luke 7.36–50," in *Escaping Eden: New Feminist Perspectives on the Bible* (ed. H. C. Washington et al.; New York: New York University Press, 1999), 69–90. For an argument against the idea that she was a prostitute, see T. J. Hornsby, "Why Is She Crying?" in the same volume, 91–103.

4. Cf. M. E. McCullough, R. A. Emmons, and J. Tsang, "The Grateful Disposition: A Conceptual and Empirical Topography," *Journal of Personality and Social Psychology* 82 (2002): 112–27.

trast, Simon displays the kind of superiority and lack of empathy that psychologists describe as narcissism. Her gratitude and humility provoke something in Simon. He believes religious figures like he and Jesus should exclude people like this woman, seemingly out of an anxiety of some kind of contagion. British psychoanalyst Melanie Klein[5] describes envy as the opposite of gratitude, and characters who fit Simon's profile might be read as envious of those who somehow found the freedom to surrender their defenses against authentic saving love. Jesus' parable also serves to diagnose Simon's barrier to forgiveness. He lacks the humility to face the depth of his own need to be forgiven, no doubt as a result of protecting his social face; he has not been formed by forgiveness-catalyzing gratitude.

At the end of the pericope, Jesus makes it clear that the woman's *faith* had saved her. Although salvation is tied to forgiveness here, they are not simply conflated. Salvation is the broader reality in which forgiveness is experienced as the healing of ethical anxiety. Her faith indicates that she also had faced her epistemic anxiety. In Christ she found one who bound himself faithfully to God and others. His final words to her, "go in peace," open up to her a new promise for a life in relation to the God of peace who establishes her agency in a new way. Her ontological anxiety is diminished as she sets aside her own attempts to secure her existence in the face of condemning others. In the face of Christ, she found no condemnation, only *hope* for new being. We should not let the language of debts overwhelm us and lose sight that *love* is the main point in her response. The woman showed "great love" (Luke 7:47). We should not be put off by the sensuality of her expression of love to Jesus (touching, wiping, kissing). Jesus certainly was not. This does not mean that her love was only sensual, but that she expressed herself in these intimate ways out of an overflow of joyous gratitude in response to Jesus' own love. This was her way of showing that she had fallen in love. She was saved.

The forgiven woman offers a wonderful example of the three phases of the forgiveness process. She is clearly engaging in lament. Although some commentators argue that her tears are tears of joy, joy and lament are not mutually exclusive, especially in the experience of one who was led to this kind of radical behavior. We can say that her ego defenses were undone, she died to her attempts to hold her world together. Now, all that matters is love—expressing love to this one who opened her life up to grace. Jesus encourages ego-humility. He does not deny her past or suggest that it was not that bad. Yet, he also affirms her strengths, her courage in confronting him in a place where

5. M. Klein, *Envy and Gratitude* (New York: Basic Books, 1957).

she was sure to be scorned. Finally, Jesus expands her horizons: "Your faith has saved you; go in peace."

This story also illustrates the dynamics of facial hermeneutics. The woman is apparently behind Jesus, so that he does not face her. Simon the Pharisee looks at her with contempt. We think of a parable that Jesus told "to some who trusted in themselves . . . and regarded others with contempt"—the story of the Pharisee and tax collector (Luke 18:9–14). The patterns of their intersubjective facing are blatant and radically different, one prays while standing and boasting, the other not even looking up to heaven but crying out for mercy. Similarly, the forgiven woman does not seem embarrassed at all, but is wholly intent on her expression of love, as she attends fully to providing bodily hospitality. Jesus *looks* at Simon and tells the parable of the two debtors, implicating him. But then Jesus turns to the woman and announces that her sins are forgiven. The other guests face each other in astonishment: "Who is this who even forgives sins?" Jesus maintains his gaze on the woman as he intends her into a life of peace. We are not told how this took shape in community, but we can imagine that her new life of peace was an ongoing experience of being saved and falling more deeply in love. Perhaps she even left everything to follow Jesus (as the rich young ruler refused to do), joining the women who began traveling with Jesus "soon afterwards" in Luke 8:1–3.

In sharp contrast to the ecstasy of the forgiven woman, the stories of the rich young ruler (Matthew 19:16–26; Mark 10:17–27; Luke 18:18–27) provide an example of the failure to receive therapeutic and redemptive forgiveness. The intersubjective dynamics of facial hermeneutics are also explicit here. The language of *looking* captures this. The ruler comes to Jesus for guidance in his quest for eternal life. After he got an answer he didn't like, Jesus looked at him and said: "How hard it is for those who have wealth to enter the kingdom of God!" (Luke 18:24). The ruler was looking to his own resources to secure the salutary ordering of his life. As one who rules, he had reached a level of comfort in the way he was faced by others, and he was able to rule through his facing of them. In Mark's version of the story, the looking is even more pronounced. The story is preceded by Jesus' seeing the way the disciples were treating the little children and calling the latter to face him for a blessing (Mark 10:14–15). Mark portrays the man running up to Jesus and kneeling before him. After the man's claim to have kept the commandments "since my youth," Mark tells us that Jesus "looking at him, loved him" (10:21). When the man hears Jesus' description of the one thing he lacked, "at that saying his *countenance* fell" (Revised Standard Version). When the disciples are astonished that the rich will find it hard to enter the kingdom, Mark emphasizes that Jesus looked at them before answering. Peter's response to the dialogue is to say to Jesus: "Look, we have left our homes and followed you" (Luke 18:28).

The stories indicate that the man respected Jesus' authority, but there is no sense of deep lament, no expression of passionate remorse for his failure to face others properly. In fact, he claims to have kept the commandments from his youth. Jesus challenges him to face himself honestly, to recognize that he depends on his wealth for his salvation. The man is unable to do so; his face falls, he walks away grieving. Yet, he does not allow this grief to drive him toward the depth of self-facing that would open him up to new ways of facing others and facing God as the only source of salvation. Jesus radically expands his horizon, but it is overwhelming. The rich young ruler becomes dizzy at this prospect and collapses back into a horizon that he has learned to control. He is unable to reframe his struggle for forgiveness and salvation. This is not unlike the experience of therapy for many clients who want to forgive but must first enter into the unsettling process of lament and explore their underlying resistance to forgiveness.

Matthew has the young man put the question most blatantly: "What good *deed* must I do to have eternal life?" (19:16). Clearly the emphasis is on doing. He is trying to act in ways that will secure his salvation. Not only ethical, but also epistemic anxiety is evident here. He wants to know the answer to a question that plagues him, that has driven him to seek out this "Good Teacher" (as Jesus is called in Mark's and Luke's accounts). He has been trying his whole life to keep the commandments. We can assume that he, like every other human being, failed at some point, but that he engaged in the proper remedy according to the religious law of his day. He even uses the language of inheriting salvation, an obvious financial metaphor. What must he do, what transaction must occur for him to procure what he desires? Jesus challenges him directly at the point of his ethical anxiety: "Why do you ask me about what is good? There is only one who is good" (19:17; cf. Mark 10:18, "Why do you call me good? No one is good but God alone."). The source of goodness, the true resolution for one's desires, is God alone. Jesus is the way to this infinite source of goodness precisely by pointing away from himself toward the Father. If God alone is good, then becoming good must involve sharing in the divine goodness, which is love. Elsewhere Jesus summarizes the commandments as loving God and neighbor (Matthew 22:37–39). In this context, however, he lists several other commandments. Mark includes "you shall not defraud" in the list (10:19), which may have hit home to the rich man. To this the man responds: "I have kept all these since my youth."

What does he lack? If he wants to be perfect, says Jesus, he should sell his possessions, give to the poor, and follow him. Because he had many possessions he "went away grieving." This young man, whom Mark portrays as rich and a ruler, is unwilling and unable to restructure his activities. He has done well in securing the goods that he desires. The one thing that matters infinitely, however, he was unable to receive—precisely because of his reliance on his own moral power to order his own life. Unfortunately, the man's response to Jesus' explanation of the one thing he lacked shows that he had not faced his anxiety deeply enough: "Sell all that you own and distribute the money to the poor, and you will have treasure in heaven; then come, follow me" (Luke 18:22). Most contemporary lay readers of the Bible, especially those who are not poor, tend to take Jesus' statement to the man as spiritual or allegorical. Even if Jesus meant it literally when he spoke to the man, it should not be taken literally as applying to us today.[6] Among biblical scholars, however, this spiritual reading is increasingly seen as implausible. In light of (a) first-century political conditions in Israel, (b) the Jewish expectation of the Messiah for the fulfillment of the Jubilee in which the land would be redistributed, and (c) general considerations in form criticism and redaction criticism of the Gospel writer's intentions, it seems that Jesus really did mean what he said.[7] After all, Peter and the other disciples took him literally. It is fascinating that here (if nowhere else) the *metaphorical* nature of financial-transaction models of salvation is taken with great seriousness by conservative North American Christians!

As a wealthy person and a ruler, the young man had learned to establish and secure his own being in the world. He had learned to suppress his ontological anxiety. Jesus was calling him to give up all of this and to depend wholly on God as the only hope of salvation. Christ was the revelation of such a life. He entrusted himself completely to God's care, relying on the life-preserving power of the Spirit. Jesus found his identity in his being faced by God, in his giving glory to the Father and thereby sharing in the Spirit of life. Being young, perhaps the rich ruler had not yet experienced enough failure in life to know that no finite power is able to secure creaturely being in the world. Rich people build and store up treasure in barns, but they may miss what really matters metaphysically: joyful delight in God that over-

6. See the study and comments of J. A. Draper, "Exegesis and Proclamation: 'Go Sell All That You Have . . .' (Mark 10:17–30)," *Journal of Theology for South Africa* 79 (1992): 63–69.

7. Cf. G. D. Kisner, "Jesus' Encounter with the Rich Young Ruler and Its Implications for Theology and Development," *Journal of Religious Thought* 49 (1992–93): 81–86; D. M. May, "Leaving and Receiving: A Social-Scientific Exegesis of Mark 10:29–31," *Perspectives in Religious Studies* 17 (1990): 141–54.

flows into sharing with others. In each of the Synoptics, the rich young ruler story is immediately preceded by Jesus' call to attend to and provide for the infants, little ones, and children whom he gathered around him for a blessing. Jesus was calling the young man to "die to sin" (as Paul would put it later), to put to death his desire to secure the world on his own strength. In Jesus, the ruler was confronted by the image of God and was called to be "conformed to that image" by manifesting divine grace to his neighbors through self-giving acts of love. What must I do to inherit eternal life? Give up my political power over others through which I attempt to secure my existence and depend wholly on the presence of the face of God for blessing and keeping.

When we look at Jesus' ministry of forgiveness, the problem was not simply the evils of physical suffering and social oppression, but also the "goods" of this life that seduced the healthy into thinking they do not need a doctor and the rich into believing that they do not need a deliverer. In response to the finite evils of sickness and oppression, Jesus heals and sets free, but salvation is more difficult for those who are defining their lives by their own attempts to maintain control over finite goods. Their psychological attachments keep them from facing their deeper existential longing to be attached to the ultimate source of good—divine grace. The forgiven woman who had suffered under the oppression of others was able to receive forgiveness, while the arrogant religious leaders who thought their deeds made them exemplars of goodness were not. The rich young ruler was unable to respond to the gospel because of the "problem of good"—the goods of this world had seduced him into relying on his own moral agency. We cannot fulfill our thirst for goodness no matter how much we drink up the goods of the finite world. As we struggle between the repulsion of finite evils and the seduction of finite goods, we are torn apart. God's love transcends this pushing and pulling, yet it is precisely in this tension that God is immanently present to us, calling us to share in the infinite goodness of the trinitarian life. Knowing ourselves as forgiven and forgiving others require that even our healthy and good attachments in this life be subsumed within a deeper attachment to God.[8]

How is our understanding of the contemporary and biblical cases enhanced when we explore them intertextually? In our clinical case, Tammy's story was like that of the Luke 7 woman: both faced judgment of their sexuality by religious leaders who scapegoated and excluded them. In the case of the rich younger ruler, Jesus made a well-

---

8. Cf. R. C. Roberts, "Attachment: Bowlby and the Bible," in *Limning the Psyche: Explorations in a Christian Psychology* (ed. R. C. Roberts and M. R. Talbot; Grand Rapids: Eerdmans, 1997), 206–28.

diagnosed invitation to the repentance and forgiveness that saves. Tammy was not so fortunate. The religious leaders who surrounded her attempted to shame her in a way that seemed oriented toward saving their own face needs. The religious leaders in Tammy's case seemed to have missed the relational implications of their exclusion for the child growing inside of her and, consequently, denied the child space and time during the most formative period of all. It is easy to critique such legalistic persons, but larger social and religious systems are also responsible for perpetuating theologies and psychologies that do not actually lead to wholeness and salvation. Unfortunately, we do not know whether Tammy ever encountered a forgiving face that helped restore her to spiritual community.

Kevin was helped through being faced by Mike, the singles' pastor, who met with him for one-on-one discipleship. This was a unique relationship of acceptance for Kevin and one not based on his body or persona. Like the forgiven woman in Luke, Kevin had been searching for someone whose face would see and accept him beneath his sexuality and beyond his utility. This enabled him gradually to surrender his pursuit of other faces for validation, faces that had only been confirming his shame. This may be the kind of freedom Jesus was speaking of when he told the forgiven woman to "go in peace." Unlike the rich young ruler, Kevin found the courage to surrender his idols of control in the realization that, like all idols, they did not actually bring health and peace. Kevin had always been good at physical disciplines, and he began to transfer this discipline to Christian spiritual practices. Kevin was able to experience a therapeutic form of forgiveness in his episode of estrangement from Tammy, which helped save him from disaster. He also started to develop boundaries that created space for the formation of his own identity and relationship with God. And he moved toward a relational context of community where he could potentially realize deeper redemptive encounters with the holy face of Jesus, the one whose coming saves. During the course of therapy Kevin responded to a forensically oriented gospel presentation at the church he was attending, and he reported being deeply moved that even his worst sins could be forgiven and "remembered no more." This highlights that forensic transactional images of forgiveness can be meaningful for many people, particularly those early in a process of faith development or those who experience their own souls as caged in a "prison-house."[9]

---

9. William James employs this image of a "prison-house" to describe the inner experience of individuals with the "sick soul" religious temperament in *The Varieties of Religious Experience: A Study in Human Nature* (1902; repr. New York: New American Library, 1958), 118. James suggests that such individuals need a religion of deliverance that starts by adequately resolving the evil they sense within.

Salvation and forgiveness should be understood in relation to the dynamics of healing and redemption that operate in the real experience of those who respond to divine grace by worshiping and serving the God of Jesus Christ in the power of the Spirit. Redemptive forgiveness reinterprets and reforms the world, creating new bindings that liberate us into the grace of eternity. "What must I do to be saved?" This is like asking: "What must I do to fall in love?" The answer in both cases involves facing the other. Knowing that another has received forgiveness is like gazing into the shining face of a child who is free of anxiety—whose lack of façade evokes a smile. Knowing you are forgiven by another can be like knowing you are in love. No one has to tell you—you just know. Christians experience salvation in and through the struggle to forgive. Salvation is believing, loving, and hoping in the Face of God, as we call one another into a fellowship of gracious and peaceful facing, searching together for the wholeness of thanksgiving joy that comes from the blessing and keeping of the divine countenance. We forgive each other as we live together in ways that manifest and share in divine grace, so that we may face each other free of anxiety and say:

> The LORD bless you and keep you;
> the LORD make his face to shine upon you, and be gracious to you;
> the LORD life up his countenance upon you, and give you peace.

BIBLIOGRAPHY

Albers, R. H. "The Shame Factor: Theological and Pastoral Reflections Relating to Forgiveness." *Word and World* 16 (1996): 347–53.

Allender, D. "Emotions and the Pathway to God." *Christian Counseling Today* 4 (1996): 32–35.

Allender, D., and T. Longman III. *Bold Love*. Colorado Springs: Navpress, 1992.

Alter, M. G. *Resurrection Psychology: An Understanding of Human Personality Based on the Life and Teachings of Jesus.* Chicago: Loyola University Press, 1994.

Anderson, P. N. *The Christology of the Fourth Gospel.* Valley Forge, Pa.: Trinity, 1996.

Applegate, J. K. "'And She Wet His Feet with Her Tears': A Feminist Interpretation of Luke 7.36–50." Pp. 69–90 in *Escaping Eden: New Feminist Perspectives on the Bible.* Edited by H. C. Washington et al. New York: New York University Press, 1999.

Arendt, H. *The Human Condition.* Garden City: Doubleday, 1959.

Aron, L. *A Meeting of the Minds: Mutuality in Psychoanalysis.* Hillsdale, N.J.: Analytic Press, 1996.

Atwood, G. E., and R. D. Stolorow. *Structures of Subjectivity: Explorations in Psychoanalytic Phenomenology.* Hillsdale, N.J.: Analytic Press, 1984.

Auerbach, J. S., and S. J. Blatt. "Self-Reflexivity, Intersubjectivity, and Therapeutic Change." *Psychoanalytic Psychology* 18 (2001): 427–50.

Augsburger, D. W. *Conflict Mediation across Cultures: Pathways and Patterns.* Louisville: Westminster John Knox, 1992.

———. *Helping People Forgive.* Louisville: Westminster John Knox, 1996.

Aulén, G. *Christus Victor.* New York: Macmillan, 1954.

Bailey, D. P. "Concepts of *Stellvertretung* in the Interpretation of Isaiah 53 and the Suffering Servant: Recent Tübingen Scholarship on Isaiah 53." Pp. 223–59 in *Jesus and the Suffering Servant: Isaiah 53 and Christian Origins.* Edited by W. H. Bellinger Jr. and W. R. Farmer. Harrisburg, Pa.: Trinity, 1998.

Balentine, S. E. *The Hidden God: The Hiding of the Face of God in the Old Testament.* Oxford: Oxford University Press, 1993.

Barr, J. *The Semantics of Biblical Language.* Originally 1961. Reprinted Harrisburg, Pa.: Trinity, 1991.

Barth, K. *Church Dogmatics.* 4 vols. Translated and edited by G. W. Bromiley and T. F. Torrance. Edinburgh: Clark, 1936–77.

———. *The Epistle to the Romans.* Translated by E. C. Hoskyns. London: Oxford University Press, 1933.

———. *The Humanity of God.* Translated by J. N. Thomas and T. Wieser. Richmond: John Knox, 1960.

Bass, E., and L. Davis. *Courage to Heal: A Guide for Women Survivors of Sexual Abuse.* 3d edition. San Francisco: Harper, 1994.

Battle, M. "A Theology of Community: The Ubuntu Theology of Desmond Tutu." *Interpretation* 54 (2000): 173–82.

Baumeister, R. F., L. Smart, and J. M. Boden. "Relation of Threatened Egotism to Violence and Aggression: The Dark Side of High Self-Esteem." *Psychological Review* 103 (1996): 5–33.

Baumeister, R. F., A. M. Stillwell, and T. F. Heatherton. "Guilt: An Interpersonal Approach." *Psychological Bulletin* 115 (1994): 243–67.

Baumeister, R. F., S. R. Wotman, and A. M. Stillwell. "Unrequited Love: On Heartbreak, Anger, Guilt, Scriptlessness, and Humiliation." *Journal of Personality and Social Psychology* 64 (1993): 377–94.

Belenky, M. F., B. M. Clinchy, N. R. Goldberger, and J. M. Tarule. *Women's Ways of Knowing: The Development of Self, Voice, and Mind.* Revised edition. New York: Basic Books, 1997.

Benjamin, J. Afterword to *Relational Psychoanalysis: The Emergence of a Tradition.* Edited by S. A. Mitchell and L. Aron. Pp. 201–10. Hillsdale, N.J.: Analytic Press, 1999.

———. *Like Subjects, Love Objects: Essays on Recognition and Sexual Difference.* New Haven: Yale University Press, 1995.

———. *Shadow of the Other: Intersubjectivity and Gender in Psychoanalysis.* New York: Routledge, 1998.

Berkouwer, G. C. *The Sacraments.* Grand Rapids: Eerdmans, 1969.

Berry, J. W., and E. L. Worthington Jr. "Forgiveness, Relationship Quality, Stress While Imagining Relationship Events, and Physical and Mental Health." *Journal of Counseling Psychology* 48 (2001): 447–55.

Berry, J. W., E. L. Worthington Jr., L. Parrott III, L. E. O'Connor, and N. G. Wade. "Dispositional Forgivingness: Development and Construct Validity of the Transgression Narrative Test." Forthcoming.

Best, S., and D. Kellner. *The Postmodern Turn.* New York: Guilford, 1997.

Bolt, P. G. "Jesus and Forgiveness in Mark's Gospel." *Reformed Theological Review* 57 (1998): 53–69.

Bonhoeffer, D. *The Cost of Discipleship.* Translated by R. H. Fuller. New York: Macmillan, 1949. 2d edition in 1959.

Bowen, M. *Family Therapy in Clinical Practice.* New York: Aronson, 1978.

Braaten, C. E., and R. W. Jenson (eds.). *Union with Christ: The New Finnish Interpretation of Luther.* Grand Rapids: Eerdmans, 1998.

Braithwaite, J. *Crime, Shame, and Reintegration.* Cambridge: Cambridge University Press, 1989.

———. *Restorative Justice and Responsive Regulation.* Oxford: Oxford University Press, 2001.

Brandsma, J. M. "Forgiveness: A Dynamic, Theological, and Therapeutic Analysis." *Pastoral Psychology* 31 (1982): 40–50.

Breck, J. "The Face of the Spirit." *Pro Ecclesia* 3 (1994): 165–78.

———. *Spirit of Truth.* Crestwood, N.Y.: St. Vladimir's, 1991.

Bringle, M. L. "'I Just Can't Stop Thinking about It': Depression, Rumination, and Forgiveness." *Word and World* 16 (1996): 340–46.

Browning, D. S., B. J. Miller-McLemore, P. D. Couture, K. B. Lyon, and R. M. Franklin. *From Culture Wars to Common Ground: Religion and the American Family Debate.* 2d edition. Louisville: Westminster John Knox, 2000.

Brueggemann, W. *Theology of the Old Testament: Testimony, Dispute, Advocacy.* Minneapolis: Fortress, 1997.

Buckley, M. J. *At the Origins of Modern Atheism.* New Haven: Yale University Press, 1987.

Calvin, J. *Institutes of the Christian Religion.* 2 vols. Edited by J. T. McNeill. Translated by F. L. Battles. Library of Christian Classics 20–21. Philadelphia: Westminster, 1960.

Cole, J. *About Face.* Cambridge, Mass.: MIT Press, 1998.

Coles, R. *The Spiritual Life of Children.* Boston: Houghton Mifflin, 1990.

Collins, K. "A Hermeneutical Model for the Wesleyan *Ordo Salutis.*" *Wesleyan Theological Journal* 19/2 (1984): 23–37.

Cone, J. *God of the Oppressed.* Revised edition. Maryknoll, N.Y.: Orbis, 1997.

Countryman, L. W. *Forgiven and Forgiving.* Harrisburg, Pa.: Morehouse, 1998.

Crossan, J. D. "Our Own Faces in Deep Wells: A Future for Historical Jesus Research." Pp. 282–310 in *God the Gift and Postmodernism.* Edited by J. D. Caputo and M. J. Scanlon. Bloomington: Indiana University Press, 1999.

Crysdale, C. *Embracing Travail: Retrieving the Cross Today.* New York: Continuum, 2001.

Dalferth, I. "Karl Barth's Eschatological Realism." Pp. 147–70 in *Karl Barth: Centenary Essays.* Edited by S. W. Sykes. Cambridge: Cambridge University Press, 1989.

Darwin, C. *The Expression of Emotions in Man and Animals.* Chicago: University of Chicago Press, 1872.

Davidson, D. L., and G. J. Jurkovic. "Forgiveness and Narcissism: Consistency in Experience across Real and Hypothetical Hurt Situation." Paper presented at the First National Convention on Forgiveness, Kansas City, 1993.

Davis, A. Y. "Race, Gender, and Prison History: From the Convict Lease System to the Supermax Prison." Pp. 35–45 in *Prison Masculinities.* Edited by D. Sabo, T. A. Kupers, and

W. London. Philadelphia: Temple University Press, 2001.

Dimburg, U., M. Thunberg, and K. Elmehed. "Unconscious Facial Reactions to Emotional Facial Expressions." *Psychological Science* 11 (2000): 86–89.

Doehring, C. "The Absent God: When Neglect Follows Sexual Violence." *Journal of Pastoral Care* 47 (1993). 3–12.

———. *Internal Desecration.* Lanham, Md.: University Press of America, 1993.

Doherty, W. J. *Soul Searching: Why Psychotherapy Must Promote Moral Responsibility.* New York: Basic Books, 1995.

Dollinger, S. J. "Religious Identity: An Autophotographic Study." *International Journal for the Psychology of Religion* 11 (2001): 71–92.

Donaldson-Pressman, S., and R. M. Pressman. *The Narcissistic Family: Diagnosis and Treatment.* New York: Lexington, 1994.

Draper, J. A. "Exegesis and Proclamation: 'Go Sell All That You Have . . .' (Mark 10·17–30)." *Journal of Theology for South Africa* 79 (1992): 63–69.

Dunn, J. D. G. *The Theology of Paul the Apostle.* Grand Rapids: Eerdmans, 1998.

Eichrodt, W. *Theology of the Old Testament.* 2 vols. Translated by J. A. Baker. Philadelphia, Westminster, 1967.

Ekman, P., and E. Rosenberg (eds.). *What the Face Reveals: Basic and Applied Studies of Spontaneous Expression Using the Facial Action Coding System.* New York: Oxford University Press, 1998.

Emmons, R. A. "Personality and Forgiveness." Pp. 156–75 in *Forgiveness: Theory, Research, and Practice.* Edited by M. E. McCullough, K. I. Pargament, and C. E. Thoresen. New York: Guilford, 2000.

Enright, R. D. *Forgiveness Is a Choice: A Step-by-Step Process for Resolving Anger and Restoring Hope.* Washington, D.C.: American Psychological Association, 2001.

Enright, R. D., and R. P. Fitzgibbons. *Helping Clients Forgive: An Empirical Guide for Resolving Anger and Restoring Hope.* Washington, D.C.: American Psychological Association, 2000.

Enright, R. D., and the Human Development Study Group. "Counseling within the Forgiveness Triad: On Forgiving, Receiving Forgiveness, and Self-Forgiveness." *Counseling and Values* 40 (1996): 107–26.

Enright, R. D., and the Human Development Study Group. "Piaget on the Moral Development of Forgiveness: Identity or Reciprocity?" *Human Development* 37 (1994): 63–80.

Enright, R. D., and J. North (eds.). *Exploring Forgiveness.* Madison: University of Wisconsin Press, 1998.

Exline, J. J., W. K. Campbell, R. F. Baumeister, T. Joiner, and J. Krueger. "Humility and Modesty." In *The Values in Action (VIA) Classification of Strengths.* Edited by C. Peterson and M. Seligman. Cincinnati: Values in Action Institute, forthcoming.

Exline, J. J., and N. Molnar. "Letters, Logic, and a Lack of Self-Righteousness: Facilitators of Forgiveness?" Paper presented in "Forgiveness as Positive Science: Theory, Research, and Clinical Applications." A symposium cochaired by P. C. Hill and S. J. Sandage and conducted at the annual meeting of the American Psychological Association, San Francisco, 2001.

Fairweather, A., and L. Zagzebski (eds.). *Virtue Epistemology: Essays on Epistemic Virtue and Responsibility.* New York: Oxford University Press, 2001.

Farley, E. *Good and Evil: Interpreting a Human Condition.* Minneapolis: Fortress, 1990.

Farrow, D. *Ascension and Ecclesia: On the Significance of the Doctrine of the Ascension for Ecclesiology and Christian Cosmology.* Grand Rapids: Eerdmans, 1999.

Fiddes, P. *Participating in God: A Pastoral Doctrine of the Trinity.* Louisville: Westminster John Knox, 2000.

Fincham, F. D. "The Kiss of the Porcupines: From Attributing Responsibility to Forgiving." *Personal Relationships* 7 (2000): 1–23.

Fink, P. E. "History of the Sacrament of Reconciliation." Pp. 73–89 in *Alternative Futures for Worship,* vol. 4: *Reconciliation.* Edited by P. E. Fink. Collegeville, Minn.: Liturgical Press, 1987.

Finkel, E. J., C. E. Rusbult, M. Kumashiro, and P. A. Hannon. "Dealing with Betrayal in Close Relationships: Does Commitment Promote Forgiveness?" *Journal of Personality and Social Psychology* 82 (2002): 956–74.

Fonagy, P., and M. Target. "Mentalization and the Changing Aims of Child Psychoanalysis." *Psychoanalytic Dialogues* 8 (1998): 87–114.

Ford, D. *Self and Salvation: Being Transformed.* Cambridge: Cambridge University Press, 1999.

———. *The Shape of Living: Spiritual Directions for Everyday Life.* Grand Rapids: Baker, 1997.

Forde, G. O. *Christian Life in Christian Dogmatics.* Edited by C. E. Braaten and R. W. Jenson. Philadelphia: Fortress, 1984.

Forest, J. *Confession: Doorway to Forgiveness*. Maryknoll, N.Y.: Orbis, 2002.

Foucault, M. "About the Beginnings of the Hermeneutics of the Self: Two Lectures at Dartmouth." *Political Theory* 21 (1993): 198–227.

———. *Discipline and Punish: The Birth of the Modern Prison*. New York: Pantheon, 1977.

Freedman, S. R. "Forgiveness and Reconciliation: The Importance of Understanding How They Differ." *Counseling and Values* 42 (1998): 200–216.

Freedman, S. R., and R. D. Enright. "Forgiveness as an Intervention Goal with Incest Survivors." *Journal of Consulting and Clinical Psychology* 64 (1996): 983–92.

Friedman, R. E. *The Hidden Face of God*. San Francisco: HarperCollins, 1995.

Gartner, J. "The Capacity to Forgive: An Object Relations Perspective." *Journal of Religion and Health* 27 (1988): 313–20.

Gassin, E. A., and R. D. Enright. "The Will to Meaning in the Process of Forgiveness." *Journal of Psychology and Christianity* 14 (1995): 38–49.

Gerrish, B. *Saving and Secular Faith: An Introduction to Systematic Theology*. Minneapolis: Fortress, 1999.

Gestrich, C. *The Return of Splendor*. Translated by D. W. Bloesch. Grand Rapids: Eerdmans, 1997.

Gilligan, C. *In a Different Voice: Psychological Theory and Women's Development*. Cambridge: Harvard University Press, 1982.

Girard, R. *I See Satan Falling Like Lightning*. Translated by J. G. Williams. Maryknoll, N.Y.: Orbis, 2001.

———. *The Scapegoat*. Translated by Y. Freccero. Baltimore: Johns Hopkins University Press, 1986.

———. *Things Hidden since the Foundation of the World*. Translated by S. Bann and M. Metteer. Stanford: Stanford University Press, 1987.

———. *Violence and the Sacred*. Translated by P. Gregory. Baltimore: Johns Hopkins University Press, 1977.

Goffman, E. *Interaction Ritual: Essays on Face-to-Face Behavior*. New York: Aldine, 1967.

———. *The Presentation of Self in Everyday Life*. New York: Doubleday, 1959.

Gonzales, M. H., J. A. Haugen, and D. J. Manning. "Victims as Narrative Critics: Factors Influencing Rejoinders and Evaluative Responses to Offenders' Accounts." *Personality and Social Psychology Bulletin* 20 (1994): 691–704.

Gonzales, M. H., D. J. Manning, and J. A. Haugen. "Explaining Our Sins: Factors Influencing Offender Accounts and Anticipated Victim Responses." *Journal of Personality and Social Psychology* 62 (1992): 958–71.

Gordon, K. C., and D. H. Baucom. "Understanding Betrayals in Marriage: A Synthesized Model of Forgiveness." *Family Process* 37 (1998): 425–49.

Gorman, M. J. *Cruciformity: Paul's Narrative Spirituality of the Cross*. Grand Rapids: Eerdmans, 2001.

Gottman, J. M. "A Theory of Marital Dissolution and Stability." *Journal of Family Psychology* 7 (1993): 57–75.

Gottman, J. M., and N. Silver. *The Seven Principles for Making Marriage Work*. New York: Three Rivers Press, 1999.

Gottman, J. M., R. Levenson, and E. Woodin. "Facial Expressions during Marital Conflict." *Journal of Family Communication* 1 (2001): 37–57.

Grassie, W. "Postmodernism: What One Needs to Know." *Zygon: Journal of Religion and Science* 32 (1997): 83–94.

Grenz, S. *The Social God and the Relational Self*. Louisville: Westminster John Knox, 2001.

———. *Theology for the Community of God*. Grand Rapids: Eerdmans, 2001.

Gruber, M. I. "The Many Faces of Hebrew נשא פנים 'Lift up the Face.'" *Zeitschrift für die alttestamentliche Wissenschaft* 95 (1983): 252–60.

Gunton, C. E. "The End of Causality? The Reformers and Their Predecessors." Pp. 63–82 in *The Doctrine of Creation*. Edited by C. E. Gunton. Edinburgh: Clark, 1997.

———. *Intellect and Action: Elucidation on Christian Theology and the Life of Faith*. Edinburgh: Clark, 2000.

Gutierrez, G. *A Theology of Liberation*. Revised edition. Translated by C. Inda and J. Eagleson. Maryknoll, N.Y.: Orbis, 1988.

Habermas, J. *Justification and Application*. Cambridge: MIT Press, 1993.

———. *Moral Consciousness and Communicative Action*. Cambridge: MIT Press, 1990.

Hall, D. J. *Imaging God*. Grand Rapids: Eerdmans, 1986.

Halling, S. "Shame and Forgiveness." *Humanistic Psychologist* 22 (1994): 74–87.

Hamerton-Kelly, R. G. *Sacred Violence: Paul's Hermeneutic of the Cross*. Minneapolis: Fortress, 1992.

Hargraves, T. D. *Families and Forgiveness: Healing Intergenerational Wounds*. New York: Bruner/Mazel, 1994.

Hauser, M. D. *Wild Minds: What Animals Really Think*. New York: Holt, 2000.

Heinze, L. S., and C. R. Snyder. "Forgiveness Components: Mediators of PTSD and Hostility in Child Abuse." Paper presented at the annual meeting of the American Psychological Association, San Francisco, 2001.

Helmick, R. G., and R. L. Petersen (eds.). *Forgiveness and Reconciliation: Religion, Public Policy, and Conflict Transformation.* Radnor, Pa.: Templeton Foundation, 2001.

Heppe, H. *Reformed Dogmatics: Set Out and Illustrated from the Sources.* Revised and edited by Ernst Bizer. Translated by G. T. Thomson. London: Allen & Unwin, 1950.

Heron, A. I. C. *The Holy Spirit.* Philadelphia: Westminster, 1983.

Hess, U., S. Blairy, and R. E. Kleck. "The Influence of Facial Emotional Displays, Gender, and Ethnicity on Judgements of Dominance and Affiliation." *Journal of Nonverbal Behavior* 24 (2000): 265–83.

Hinlicky, P. R. "Theological Anthropology: Toward Integrating Theosis and Justification by Faith." *Journal of Ecumenical Studies* 34 (1997): 38–73.

Hodgins, H. S., E. Liebeskind, and W. Schwartz. "Getting out of Hot Water: Facework in Social Predicaments." *Journal of Personality and Social Psychology* 71 (1996): 300–314.

Hoffmann, N. *Sühne: Zur Theologie der Stellvertretung.* Einsiedeln: Johannes Verlag, 1981.

Holeman, V. "Mutual Forgiveness: A Catalyst for Relationship Transformation in the Moral Crucible of Marriage." *Marriage and Family: A Christian Journal* 2 (1999): 147–58.

Holst, R. "The One Anointing of Jesus: Another Application of the Form-Critical Method." *Journal of Biblical Literature* 95 (1976): 435–46.

Hong, E. *Forgiveness Is a Work as Well as a Grace.* Minneapolis: Augsburg, 1984.

Hornsby, T. J. "Why Is She Crying?" Pp. 91–103 in *Escaping Eden: New Feminist Perspectives on the Bible.* Edited by H. C. Washington et al. New York: New York University Press, 1999.

Huang, S. T., and R. D. Enright. "Forgiveness and Anger-Related Emotions in Taiwan: Implications for Therapy." *Psychotherapy* 37 (2000): 71–79.

Hughes, J. "The Politics of Forgiveness." *Modern Theology* 17 (2001): 261–87.

Hultgren, A. J. "Forgive Us, As We Forgive (Matthew 6:12)." *Word and World* 16 (1996): 284–90.

Hunsinger, G. *Disruptive Grace: Studies in the Theology of Karl Barth.* Grand Rapids: Eerdmans, 2000.

Hurley, M. "Reconciliation and Forgiveness." *Jurist* 56 (1996): 456–86.

Hylen, S. E. "Forgiveness and Life in Community." *Interpretation* 54 (2000): 146–57.

Ickert, S. "Defending and Defining the *Ordo Salutis*: Jacob van Hoogstraten vs. Martin Luther." *Archive for Reformation History* 78 (1987): 81–97.

Jensen, P. "Forgiveness and Atonement." *Scottish Journal of Theology* 46 (1993): 141–59.

Jenson, R. W. *Systematic Theology,* vol. 1. Oxford: Oxford University Press, 1997.

Johnson, S. *The Mystery of God: Karl Barth and the Postmodern Foundations of Theology.* Louisville: Westminster John Knox, 1997.

Jones, L. G. "Crafting Communities of Forgiveness." *Interpretation* 54 (2000): 121–34.

———. *Embodying Forgiveness: A Theological Analysis.* Grand Rapids: Eerdmans, 1995.

———. "For All the Saints: Autobiography in Christian Theology." *Asbury Theological Journal* 47 (1992): 27–42.

Jordan, J. V. "The Meaning of Mutuality." Pp. 81–96 in *Women's Growth in Connection: Writings from the Stone Center.* Edited by J. V. Jordan, A. G. Kaplan, J. B. Miller, I. P. Stiver, and J. L. Surrey. New York: Guilford, 1991.

Jüngel, E. *Justification: The Heart of the Christian Faith.* Translated by J. F. Cayzer. Edinburgh: Clark, 2001.

Kant, I. *Religion within the Limits of Reason Alone.* Originally 1793. Translated by T. M. Greene and H. H. Hudson. New York: Harper, 1960.

Karen, R. *Becoming Attached: First Relationships and How They Shape Our Capacity to Love.* New York: Oxford University Press, 1994.

———. *The Forgiving Self: The Road from Resentment to Connection.* New York: Doubleday, 2001.

Kaufman, G. *Shame: The Power of Caring.* Rochester, Vt.: Schenkman, 1985.

Keene, F. W. "Structures of Forgiveness in the New Testament." Pp. 121–34 in *Violence against Women and Children.* Edited by C. J. Adams and M. M. Fortune. New York: Continuum, 1995.

Kegan, R. *The Evolving Self: Problem and Process in Human Development.* Cambridge: Harvard University Press, 1982.

———. *In over Our Heads: The Mental Demands of Modern Life.* Cambridge: Harvard University Press, 1994.

Keltner, D., A. M. Kring, and G. A. Bonanno. "Fleeting Signs of the Course of Life: Facial Expression and Personal Adjustment." *Cur-*

rent Directions in Psychological Science 8 (1999): 18–22.

Kernis, M. H., and C. R. Sun. "Narcissism and Reactions to Interpersonal Feedback." *Journal of Research in Personality* 28 (1994): 4–13.

Kierkegaard, S. *The Sickness unto Death.* Translated by H. Hong and E. Hong. Princeton: Princeton University Press, 1980.

Kilgallen, J. "Forgiveness of Sins (Luke 7:36–50)." *Novum Testamentum* 40 (1998): 105–16.

Kisner, G. D. "Jesus' Encounter with the Rich Young Ruler and Its Implications for Theology and Development." *Journal of Religious Thought* 49 (1992–93): 81–86.

Klein, M. *Envy and Gratitude.* New York: Basic Books, 1957.

Klemm, D., and G. Zöller (eds.). *Figuring the Self: Subject, Absolute, and Others in Classical German Philosophy.* Albany: State University of New York Press, 1997.

Kohut, H. "Narcissism and Narcissistic Rage." *Psychoanalytic Study of the Child* 27 (1972): 379–92.

Kraus, C. N. *Jesus Christ Our Lord.* Scottsdale, Pa.: Herald, 1987.

Kristeva, J. *Desire in Language: A Semiotic Approach to Literature and Art.* Edited by L. S. Roudiez. Translated by A. Jardine, T. A. Gora, and L. S. Roudiez. New York: Columbia University Press, 1980.

———. *Strangers to Ourselves.* Translated by L. Roudiez. New York: Columbia University Press, 1991.

Kunz, G. *The Paradox of Power and Weakness: Levinas and an Alternative Paradigm for Psychology.* Albany: State University of New York Press, 1998.

Lakeland, P. *Postmodernity: Christian Identity in a Fragmented Age.* Minneapolis: Fortress, 1997.

Lamb, S., and J. G. Murphy. *Before Forgiving: Cautionary Views of Forgiveness in Psychotherapy.* Oxford: Oxford University Press, 2002.

Lehmann, P. *Ethics in a Christian Context.* New York: Harper & Row, 1963.

Levinas, E. *Ethics and Infinity.* Originally 1982. Translated by R. Cohen. Pittsburgh: Duquesne University Press, 1985.

———. "Is Ontology Fundamental?" Pp. 1–10 in Levinas's *Basic Philosophical Writings.* Bloomington: Indiana University Press, 1996.

———. *Otherwise Than Being; or, Beyond Essence.* Translated by A. Lingis. Pittsburgh: Duquesne University Press, 1998.

———. *Totality and Infinity.* Translated by A. Lingis. Pittsburgh: Duquesne University Press, 1969.

Lewis, H. B. *Shame and Guilt in Neurosis.* New York: International Universities Press, 1971.

Loder, J. E. *The Logic of the Spirit: Human Development in Theological Perspective.* San Francisco: Jossey-Bass, 1998.

———. *The Transforming Moment.* 2d edition. Colorado Springs: Helmers & Howard, 1989.

Loder, J. E., and W. J. Neidhardt. *The Knight's Move: The Relational Logic of the Spirit in Theology and Science.* Colorado Springs: Helmers & Howard, 1992.

Lossky, V. *The Mystical Theology of the Eastern Church.* Crestwood, N.Y.: St. Vladimir's, 1998.

Luskin, F. *Forgive for Good: A Proven Prescription for Health and Happiness.* San Francisco: Harper San Francisco, 2001.

Lynch, W. *Images of Hope: Imagination as Healer of the Hopeless.* Notre Dame: University of Notre Dame Press, 1965.

MacIntyre, A. *After Virtue: A Study in Moral Theory.* 2d edition. Notre Dame: University of Notre Dame Press, 1984.

Madanes, C. *Sex, Love, and Violence: Strategies for Transformation.* New York: Norton, 1991.

Marion, J.-L. "The Face: An Endless Hermeneutics." *Harvard Divinity Bulletin* 28/2 (1999): 9–10.

Marty, M. "The Ethos of Christian Forgiveness." Pp. 9–28 in *Dimensions of Forgiveness: Psychological Research and Theological Perspectives.* Edited by E. L. Worthington Jr. Philadelphia: Templeton Foundation, 1998.

Mason, M. *The Mystery of Marriage.* Portland: Multnomah, 1985.

May, D. M. "Leaving and Receiving: A Social-Scientific Exegesis of Mark 10:29–31." *Perspectives in Religious Studies* 17 (1990): 141–54.

McAdams, D. P. *The Stories We Live By: Personal Myths and the Making of the Self.* New York: Guilford, 1993.

McCormack, B. *Karl Barth's Critically Realistic Dialectical Theology.* Oxford: Clarendon, 1995.

McCullough, M. E. "Forgiveness: Who Does It and How Do They Do It?" *Current Directions in Psychological Science* 10 (2001): 194–97.

———. "Marital Forgiveness: Theoretical Foundations and an Approach to Prevention." *Marriage and Family: A Christian Journal* 1 (1997): 81–96.

McCullough, M. E., C. G. Bellah, S. D. Kilpatrick, and J. L. Johnson. "Vengefulness:

Relationships with Forgiveness, Rumination, Well-Being, and the Big Five." *Personality and Social Psychology Bulletin* 27 (2001): 601–10.

McCullough, M. E., R. A. Emmons, and J. Tsang. "The Grateful Disposition: A Conceptual and Empirical Topography." *Journal of Personality and Social Psychology* 82 (2002): 112–27.

McCullough, M. E., J. J. Exline, and R. F. Baumeister. "An Annotated Bibliography of Research on Forgiveness and Related Concepts." Pp. 193–317 in *Dimensions of Forgiveness: Psychological Research and Theological Perspectives*. Edited by E. L. Worthington Jr. Philadelphia: Templeton Foundation, 1998.

McCullough, M. E., K. I. Pargament, and C. E. Thoresen (eds.). *Forgiveness: Theory, Research, and Practice*. New York: Guilford, 2000.

———. "The Psychology of Forgiveness: History, Conceptual Issues, and Overview." Pp. 1–14 in *Forgiveness: Theory, Research, and Practice*. Edited by M. E. McCullough, K. I. Pargament, and C. E. Thoresen. New York: Guilford, 2000.

McCullough, M. E., K. C. Rachal, S. J. Sandage, E. L. Worthington Jr., S. W. Brown, and T. L. Hight. "Interpersonal Forgiving in Close Relationships, II: Theoretical Elaboration and Measurement." *Journal of Personality and Social Psychology* 75 (1998): 1586–1603.

McCullough, M. E., S. J. Sandage, and E. L. Worthington Jr. *To Forgive Is Human*. Downers Grove, Ill.: InterVarsity, 1997.

McCullough, M. E., and E. L. Worthington Jr. "Religion and the Forgiving Personality." *Journal of Personality* 67 (1999): 1141–64.

McCullough, M. E., E. L. Worthington Jr., and K. C. Rachal. "Interpersonal Forgiving in Close Relationships." *Journal of Personality and Social Psychology* 73 (1997): 321–36.

McFadyen, A. *The Call to Personhood*. Cambridge: Cambridge University Press, 1990.

McMinn, M. R. *Psychology, Theology, and Spirituality in Christian Counseling*. Wheaton, Ill.: Tyndale, 1996.

Merton, T. *New Seeds of Contemplation*. New York: New Directions, 1961.

Mettinger, T. N. D. *In Search of God: The Meaning and Message of the Everlasting Names*. Translated by F. H. Cryer. Philadelphia: Fortress, 1988.

Miller, A. *Banished Knowledge*. New York: Doubleday, 1990.

Mitchell, S. A. *Relationality: From Attachment to Intersubjectivity*. Hillsdale, N.J.: Analytic Press, 2000.

Moltmann, J. *The Source of Life: The Holy Spirit and the Theology of Life*. Translated by M. Kohl. Minneapolis: Fortress, 1997.

———. *The Spirit of Life: A Universal Affirmation*. Translated by M. Kohl. Minneapolis: Fortress, 2001.

Moule, C. F. D. "The Theology of Forgiveness." Pp. 250–60 in Moule's *Essays in New Testament Interpretation*. Cambridge: Cambridge University Press, 1982.

Muller, R. *Christ and the Decree: Christology and Predestination in Reformed Theology from Calvin to Perkin*. Durham, N.C.: Labyrinth, 1986.

———. "Perkin's *A Golden Chaine*." *Sixteenth Century Journal* 9 (1978): 69–81.

Müller-Fahrenholz, G. "Turn to the God of Mercy: New Perspectives on Reconciliation and Forgiveness." *Ecumenical Review* 50 (1998): 196–204.

Murray, J. C. *The Problem of God*. New Haven: Yale University Press, 1964.

Narramore, S. B. *No Condemnation: Rethinking Guilt Motivation Counseling, Preaching, and Parenting*. Grand Rapids: Zondervan, 1987.

Nathanson, D. L. *Shame and Pride: Affect, Sex, and the Birth of the Self*. New York: Norton, 1992.

Nellas, P. *Deification in Christ*. Translated by N. Russell. Crestwood, N.Y.: St. Vladimir's, 1997.

Niebuhr, R. *The Nature and Destiny of Man*. 2 vols. New York: Scribner, 1941–43.

Norcross, J. C. *Psychotherapy Relationships That Work*. New York: Oxford University Press, 2002.

O'Kennedy, D. F. "'It Shall Not Be': Divine Forgiveness in the Intercessory Prayers of Amos." *Old Testament Essays* 10 (1997): 92–108.

Orange, D. M., G. E. Atwood, and R. D. Stolorow. *Working Intersubjectively: Contextualism in Psychoanalytic Practice*. Hillsdale, N.J.: Analytic Press, 2001.

Ouspensky, L., and V. Lossky. *The Meaning of Icons*. 2d edition. Crestwood, N.Y.: St. Vladimir's, 1999.

Pannenberg, W. *Anthropology in Theological Perspective*. Translated by M. J. O'Connell. Philadelphia: Westminster, 1985.

———. *Systematic Theology*, vol. 1. Translated by G. W. Bromiley. Grand Rapids: Eerdmans, 1994.

Pargament, K. I., and M. S. Rye. "Forgiveness as a Method of Religious Coping." Pp. 59–78 in *Dimensions of Forgiveness: Psychological Research and Theological Perspectives*. Edited by E. L. Worthington Jr. Philadelphia: Templeton Foundation, 1998.

Park, A. S. *The Wounded Heart of God*. Nashville: Abingdon, 1993.

Park, A. S., and S. L. Nelson (eds.). *The Other Side of Sin: Woundedness from the Perspective of the Sinned-Against*. Albany: State University of New York Press, 2001.

Pattison, E. M. "Punitive and Reconciliation Models of Forgiveness." Pp. 162–76 in *Counseling and the Human Predicament: A Study of Sin, Guilt, and Forgiveness*. Edited by L. Aden and D. G. Benner. Grand Rapids: Baker, 1989.

Patton, J. *Is Human Forgiveness Possible? A Pastoral Care Perspective*. Nashville: Abingdon, 1985.

Peace, R. V. *Conversion in the New Testament: Paul and the Twelve*. Grand Rapids: Eerdmans, 1999.

Peck, M. S. *The Different Drum: Community Making and Peace*. New York: Simon & Schuster, 1987.

Peddle, N. A. "Forgiveness in Recovery/Resiliency from the Trauma of War among a Selected Group of Adolescents and Adult Refugees." Doctoral diss., Fielding Institute, 2001.

Pennebaker, J. W. *Emotion, Disclosure, and Health*. Washington, D.C.: American Psychological Association, 1995.

Peters, T. *Sin: Radical Evil in Soul and Society*. Grand Rapids: Eerdmans, 1994.

Phan, P. C. *Grace and the Human Condition*. Wilmington: Glazier, 1988.

Piehl, R. O. "Marbles, Clocks, and the Postmodern Self." *Journal of Psychology and Theology* 26 (1998): 83–100.

Pillari, V. *Scapegoating in Families: Intergenerational Patterns of Physical and Emotional Abuse*. Philadelphia: Brunner-Routledge, 1991.

Pingleton, J. P. "Why We Don't Forgive: A Biblical and Object Relations Theoretical Model for Understanding Failures in the Forgiveness Process." *Journal of Psychology and Theology* 25 (1997): 403–13.

Polinska, W. "Bodies under Siege: Eating Disorders and Self-Mutilation among Women." *Journal of the American Academy of Religion* 68 (2000): 569–89.

Pollack, S. D., D. Cichetti, K. Hornung, and A. Reed. "Recognizing Emotion in Faces: Developmental Effects of Child Abuse and Neglect." *Developmental Psychology* 36 (2000): 679–88.

Prilleltensky, I. "Values, Assumptions, and Practices: Assessing the Moral Implications of Psychological Discourse and Action." *American Psychologist* 52 (1997): 517–35.

Quinn, P. L. "Christian Atonement and Kantian Justification." *Faith and Philosophy* 3 (1986): 440–62.

Raitt, T. M. "Why Does God Forgive?" *Horizons in Biblical Theology* 13 (1991): 38–58.

Rakestraw, R. "Becoming Like God: An Evangelical Doctrine of Theosis." *Journal of the Evangelical Theological Society* 40 (1997): 257–69.

Ravens, D. A. S. "The Setting of Luke's Account of the Anointing: Luke 7.2–8.3." *New Testament Studies* 34 (1988): 282–92.

Reid, D. *Energies of the Spirit: Trinitarian Models in Eastern Orthodox and Western Theology*. Atlanta: Scholars Press, 1997.

Retzinger, S. M. "The Role of Shame in Marital Conflict." *Perspectives on Social Problems* 3 (1992): 135–54.

Rhodewalt, F., and C. C. Morf. "Self and Interpersonal Correlates of the Narcissistic Personality Inventory: A Review and New Findings." *Journal of Research in Personality* 29 (1995): 1–23.

Ricoeur, P. *Oneself as Another*. Translated by K. Blamey. Chicago: University of Chicago Press, 1992.

Ripley, J. "Covenantal Concepts of Justice and Righteousness, and Catholic-Protestant Reconciliation: Theological Implications and Explorations." *Journal of Ecumenical Studies* 38 (2001): 95–108.

Rizzuto, A.-M. *The Birth of the Living God: A Psychoanalytic Study*. Chicago: University of Chicago Press, 1979.

Roberts, R. C. "Attachment: Bowlby and the Bible." Pp. 206–28 in *Limning the Psyche: Explorations in Christian Psychology*. Edited by R. C. Roberts and M. R. Talbot. Grand Rapids: Eerdmans, 1997.

———. "Forgivingness." *American Philosophical Quarterly* 32 (1995): 289–306.

Rosenau, P. M. *Postmodernism and the Social Sciences*. Princeton: Princeton University Press, 1992.

Russell, J. A., and J. M. Fernandez-Dols. "What Does a Facial Expression Mean?" Pp. 3–30 in *The Psychology of Facial Expressions*. Edited by J. A. Russell and J. M. Fernandez-Dols. Cambridge: Cambridge University Press, 1997.

Sacks, O. *The Man Who Mistook His Wife for a Hat*. New York: Touchstone, 1998.

Safer, J. *Forgiving and Not Forgiving: A New Approach to Resolving Intimate Betrayal*. New York: Avon, 1999.

Sandage, S. J. "An Ego-Humility Model of For-giveness: Implications for Couple and Fam-ily Dynamics and Therapy." *Marriage and the Family: A Christian Journal* 2 (1999): 277–92.

———. "An Ego-Humility Model of Forgiveness: Theoretical Foundations." *Marriage and the Family: A Christian Journal* 2 (1999): 259–76.

———. "Power, Knowledge, and the Hermeneu-tics of Selfhood: Postmodern Wisdom for Christian Therapists." *Mars Hill Review* 12 (1999): 65–73.

Sandage, S. J., and P. C. Hill. "The Virtues of Positive Psychology: The Rapprochement and Challenges of an Affirmative Postmod-ern Perspective." *Journal for the Theory of Social Behaviour* 31 (2001): 241–60.

Sandage, S. J., P. C. Hill, and C. Vang. "Forgive-ness as a Culturally Embedded Virtue: Ex-amples in Hmong Communities." Paper pre-sented in "Forgiveness as Positive Science: Theory, Research, and Clinical Applica-tions." A symposium cochaired by P. C. Hill and S. J. Sandage and conducted at the an-nual meeting of the American Psychological Association, San Francisco, 2001.

Sandage, S. J., and T. W. Wiens. "Contextualiz-ing Models of Humility and Forgiveness: A Reply to Gassin." *Journal of Psychology and Theology* 29 (2001): 201–11.

Sandage, S. J., and E. L. Worthington Jr. "An Ego Humility Model of Forgiveness: An Em-pirical Test of Group Interventions." Poster presented at the annual meeting of the American Psychological Association, Bos-ton, 1999.

Sandage, S. J., E. L. Worthington Jr., T. L. Hight, and J. W. Berry. "Seeking Forgiveness: Theo-retical Context and an Initial Empirical Study." *Journal of Psychology and Theology* 28 (2000): 21–35.

Sanders, E. P. *Paul and Palestinian Judaism: A Comparison of Patterns of Religion*. London: SCM, 1977.

Scheff, T. J. "Emotion and Illness: Anger, By-passed Shame, and Heart Disease." *Perspec-tives on Social Problems* 3 (1992): 117–34.

———. "Shame and Related Emotions: An Over-view." *American Behavioral Scientist* 38 (1995): 1053–59.

Scheff, T. J., and S. M. Retzinger. *Emotions and Violence: Shame and Rage in Destructive Con-flicts*. Lexington, Mass.: Lexington, 2001.

Schiano, D. J., S. Ehrlich, K. Rahardja, and K. Sheridan. "Measuring and Modeling Facial Affect." *Behavior Research Methods, Instru-ments, and Computers* 32 (2000): 505–14.

Schmid, H. *The Doctrinal Theology of the Evan-gelical Lutheran Church*. 3d edition. Trans-lated by C. Hay and H. Jacobs. Reprinted Minneapolis: Augsburg, 1961.

Schnarch, D. M. *Constructing the Sexual Cruci-ble: An Integration of Sexual and Marital Therapy*. New York: Norton, 1991.

———. *Passionate Marriage: Keeping Love and Intimacy Alive in Committed Relationships*. New York: Norton, 1997.

Schonbach, P. *Account Episodes: The Manage-ment and Escalation of Conflict*. Cambridge: Cambridge University Press, 1990.

Schore, A. N. "Early Shame Experiences and In-fant Brain Development." Pp. 57–77 in *Shame: Interpersonal Behavior, Psychopa-thology, and Culture*. Edited by P. Gilbert and B. Andrews. New York: Oxford University Press, 1998.

Searles, H. F. "The Role of the Analyst's Facial Expressions in Psychoanalysis and Psycho-analytic Therapy." *International Journal of Psychoanalytic Psychotherapy* 10 (1984–85): 47–73.

Seibold, M. "When the Wounds Run Deep: En-couragement for Those on the Road to For-giveness." Pp. 294–308 in *Care for the Soul: Exploring the Intersection of Psychology and Theology*. Edited by M. R. McMinn and T. R. Phillips. Downers Grove, Ill.: InterVarsity, 2001.

Shaull, R., and W. Cesar. *Pentecostalism and the Future of the Christian Churches*. Grand Rapids: Eerdmans, 2000.

Shriver, D. W., Jr. *An Ethic for Enemies: Forgive-ness in Politics*. Oxford: Oxford University Press, 1995.

Shults, F. L. "Becoming 'One Spirit' with the Lord." *Princeton Theological Review* 7 (2000): 17–26.

———. "The Body of Christ in Evangelical Theol-ogy." *Word and World* 22 (2002): 178–85.

———. "Holding on to the Psychology-Theol-ogy Relationship." *Journal of Psychology and Theology* 25 (1997): 329–40.

———. "Is It 'Natural' to Be Religious?" Pp. 103–13 in *The Person: Perspectives from Sci-ence and Theology*. Edited by N.-H. Gregersen. Studies in Theology and Science 6. Geneva: Labor et Fides, 2000.

———. "Pedagogy of the Repressed." *Theologi-cal Education* 36 (1999): 157–70.

———. "The Philosophical Turn to Relational-ity and the Responsibility of Practical Theol-ogy." In *Redemptive Transformation in Prac-tical Theology*. Edited by D. Wright. Grand Rapids: Eerdmans, forthcoming.

———. *The Postfoundationalist Task of Theology.* Grand Rapids: Eerdmans, 1999.

———. *Reforming Theological Anthropology: After the Philosophical Turn to Relationality.* Grand Rapids: Eerdmans, 2003.

———. "Sharing in the Divine Nature: Transformation, *Koinōnia,* and the Doctrine of God." Pp. 87–127 in *On Being Christian . . . and Human.* Edited by T. Speidell. Eugene, Ore.: Wipf & Stock, 2002.

Smedes, L. *The Art of Forgiving.* Nashville: Moorings, 1996.

———. *Forgive and Forget.* Dallas: Word, 1984.

Snyder, C. R. "Conceptualizing, Measuring, and Nurturing Hope." *Journal of Counseling and Development* 73 (1995): 355–60.

———. "The Past and Possible Futures of Hope." *Journal of Social and Clinical Psychology* 19 (2000): 11–28.

Snyder, C. R., L. Y. Thompson, S. T. Michael, L. Hoffman, H. N. Rasmussen, L. S. Billings, L. Heinze, J. E. Neufeld, C. M. Robinson, J. R. Roberts, and D. E. Roberts. "The Heartland Forgiveness Scale: Development and Validation of a New Measure of Dispositional Forgiveness." Unpublished paper, 2001.

Sobrino, J. "Latin America: Place of Sin and Place of Forgiveness." *Concilium* 184 (1986): 45–56.

Starr, J. M. *Sharers in Divine Nature: 2 Peter 1:4 in Its Hellenistic Context.* Stockholm: Almqvist & Wiksell, 2000.

Staub, E., and A. Gubin. "Healing through Connection and Understanding Project Research Findings: Results from Community Members." Unpublished paper, 2001.

Staub, E., and L. A. Pearlman. "Healing, Forgiveness, and Reconciliation in Rwanda: Project Summary and Outcome." Unpublished paper, 2000.

Staub, E., and L. A. Pearlman. "Healing, Reconciliation, and Forgiving after Genocide and Other Collective Violence." Pp. 195–218 in *Forgiveness and Reconciliation: Religion, Public Policy, and Conflict Transformation.* Edited by R. G. Helmick and R. L. Petersen. Philadelphia: Templeton Foundation, 2001.

Stern, D. N. *The Interpersonal World of the Infant: A Viewpoint from Psychoanalysis and Developmental Psychology.* London: Karnac, 1985.

Stolorow, R. D., D. M. Orange, and G. E. Atwood. "Cartesian and Post-Cartesian Trends in Relational Psychoanalysis." *Psychoanalytic Psychology* 18 (2001): 468–84.

Stone, J. "A Theory of Religion." *Religious Studies* 27 (1991): 337–51.

Storkey, E. *The Search for Intimacy.* Grand Rapids: Eerdmans, 1995.

Stump, E. "Atonement according to Aquinas." Pp. 61–91 in *Philosophy and the Christian Faith.* Edited by T. V. Morris. Notre Dame: University of Notre Dame Press, 1988.

Suchocki, M. H. *The Fall to Violence: Original Sin in Relational Theology.* New York: Continuum, 1994.

Surakka, V., M. Sams, and J. K. Hietanen. "Modulation of Neutral Face Evaluation by Laterally Presented Emotional Expressions." *Perceptual and Motor Skills* 88 (1991): 595–606.

Tamburello, D. E. *Union with Christ: John Calvin and the Mysticism of St. Bernard.* Louisville: Westminster John Knox, 1994.

Tamez, E. *Amnesty of Grace: Justification by Faith from a Latin American Perspective.* Translated by S. H. Ringe. Nashville: Abingdon, 1993.

Tangney, J. P. "Humility: Theoretical Perspectives, Empirical Findings, and Directions for Future Research." *Journal of Social and Clinical Psychology* 19 (2000): 70–82.

———. "Shame and Guilt in Interpersonal Relationships." Pp. 114–39 in *Self-Conscious Emotions: Shame, Guilt, Embarrassment, and Pride.* Edited by J. P. Tangney and K. W. Fischer. New York: Guilford, 1995.

Tangney, J. P., S. A. Burggraf, H. Hamme, and P. E. Wagner. "Shame-Proneness, Guilt-Proneness, and Psychological Symptoms." Pp. 343–67 in *Self-Conscious Emotions: Shame, Guilt, Embarrassment, and Pride.* Edited by J. P. Tangney and K. W. Fischer. New York: Guilford, 1995.

Tangney, J. P., R. Fee, C. Reinsmith, A. L. Boone, and N. Lee. "Assessing Individual Differences in the Propensity to Forgive." Paper presented at the annual meeting of the American Psychological Association, Boston, 1999.

Tangney, J. P., P. E. Wagner, D. H. Barlow, D. E. Marschall, and R. Gramzow. "The Relation of Shame and Guilt to Constructive vs. Destructive Responses to Anger across the Lifespan." *Journal of Personality and Social Psychology* 62 (1996): 669–75.

Taylor, C. *Sources of the Self: The Making of Modern Identity.* Cambridge: Harvard University Press, 1989.

Taylor, V. *Forgiveness and Reconciliation: A Study in New Testament Theology.* London: Macmillan, 1952.

Thiselton, A. *Interpreting God and the Postmodern Self.* Grand Rapids: Eerdmans, 1995.

Tillich, P. *Systematic Theology.* 3 vols. Chicago: University of Chicago Press, 1951–63.

Tinder, G. *The Fabric of Hope: An Essay.* Emory University Studies in Law and Religion 6. Atlanta: Scholars Press, 1999.

Tomkins, S. S. *Affect, Imagery, and Consciousness,* vol. 1: *The Positive Affects.* New York: Springer, 1962.

Tracy, S. "Sexual Abuse and Forgiveness." *Journal of Psychology and Theology* 27 (1999): 219–29.

Triandis, H. C. *Individualism and Collectivism.* Boulder, Colo.: Westview, 1995.

Tsang, J., M. E. McCullough, and W. T. Hoyt. "Psychometric and Rationalization Accounts for the Religion-Forgiveness Discrepancy." Forthcoming.

Tutu, D. *No Future without Forgiveness.* New York: Doubleday, 2000.

Ulanov, A. B. *Finding Space: Winnicott, God, and Psychic Reality.* Louisville: Westminster John Knox, 2001.

van Asselt, W. J. "*Amicitia Dei* as Ultimate Reality: An Outline of the Covenant Theology of Johannes Cocceius." *Ultimate Reality and Meaning* 21 (1998): 35–47.

Vandenberg, B. "Levinas and the Ethical Context of Human Development." *Human Development* 42 (1999): 31–44.

Vitz, P. C., and P. Mango. "Kernbergian Psychodynamics and Religious Aspects of the Forgiveness Process." *Journal of Psychology and Theology* 25 (1997): 72–80.

———. "Kleinian Psychodynamics and Religious Aspects of Hatred as a Defense Mechanism." *Journal of Psychology and Theology* 25 (1997): 64–71.

Volf, M. *After Our Likeness: The Church as the Image of the Trinity.* Grand Rapids: Eerdmans, 1998.

———. *Exclusion and Embrace: A Theological Exploration of Identity, Otherness, and Reconciliation.* Nashville: Abingdon, 1996.

———. "The Social Meaning of Reconciliation." *Interpretation* 54 (2000): 158–72.

Vygotsky, L. S. *Thought and Language.* Edited and translated by E. Haufmann and G. Vakar. Cambridge: MIT Press, 1962.

Walker, D. and R. Gorsuch. "Dimensions Underlying Seventeen Models of Forgiveness and Reconciliation." Forthcoming.

Ward, G. *Barth, Derrida, and the Language of Theology.* Cambridge: Cambridge University Press, 1995.

Ware, K. *The Inner Kingdom.* Crestwood, N.Y.: St. Vladimir's, 2000.

Washington, H. C. "The Lord's Mercy Endures Forever: Toward a Post-Shoah Reading of Grace in the Hebrew Scriptures." *Interpretation* 54 (2000): 135–45.

Watson, P. J. "Girard and Integration." *Journal of Psychology and Theology* 26 (1998): 311–21.

Watson, R. A. "Toward Union in Love: The Contemplative Spiritual Tradition and Contemporary Psychoanalytic Theory in the Formation of Persons." *Journal of Psychology and Theology* 28 (2000): 282–92.

Watzlawick, P., J. Weakland, and R. Fisch. *Change: Principles of Problem Formation and Problem Resolution.* New York: Norton, 1974.

Weaver, J. D. *The Nonviolent Atonement.* Grand Rapids: Eerdmans, 2001.

Weil, S. *Waiting for God.* Originally 1951. Translated by E. Craufurd. New York: Harper & Row, 1973.

Weiner, B. "On Sin versus Sickness: A Theory of Perceived Responsibility and Social Motivation." *American Psychologist* 48 (1993): 957–65.

Welker, M. *God the Spirit.* Translated by J. F. Hoffmeyer. Minneapolis: Fortress, 1994.

Wells, H. "Theology for Reconciliation: Biblical Perspectives on Forgiveness and Grace." Pp. 1–15 in *The Reconciliation of Peoples: Challenge to the Churches.* Edited by G. Baum and H. Wells. Maryknoll, N.Y.: Orbis, 1997.

Wesche, K. P. "'Mind' and 'Self' in the Christology of Saint Gregory the Theologian: Saint Gregory's Contribution to Christology and Christian Anthropology." *Greek Orthodox Theological Review* 39 (1994): 33–61.

———. "The Soul and Personality: Tracing the Roots of the Christological Problem." *Pro Ecclesia* 5 (1996): 23–42.

Wharton, H. "The Hidden Face of Shame: The Shadow, Shame, and Separation." *Journal of Analytical Psychology* 35 (1990): 279–99.

White, M., and D. Epston. *Narrative Means to Therapeutic Ends.* New York: Norton, 1990.

Williams, R. *Lost Icons: Reflections on Cultural Bereavement.* Edinburgh: Clark, 2000.

———. *On Christian Theology.* Oxford: Blackwell, 2000.

Winnicott, D. W. *Playing and Reality.* Originally 1971. Reprinted New York: Tavistock, 1982.

Witvliet, C. V., T. E. Ludwig, and K. L. Vander Laan. "Granting Forgiveness or Harboring Grudges: Implications for Emotion, Physiology, and Health." *Psychological Science* 12 (2001): 117–23.

Work, T. "Reordering Salvation: Church as the Proper Context for an Evangelical *Ordo Salutis.*" Pp. 182–95 in *Ecumenical Theology in Worship, Doctrine, and Life.* Edited by D. S.

Cunningham et al. Oxford: Oxford University Press, 1999.

Worthington, E. L., Jr. "An Empathy-Humility-Commitment Model of Forgiveness Applied within Family Dyads." *Journal of Family Therapy* 20 (1998): 59–76.

———. *Five Steps to Forgiving: The Art and Science of Forgiving*. New York: Crown, 2001.

———. "The Pyramid Model of Forgiveness: Some Interdisciplinary Speculations about Unforgiveness and Forgiveness." Pp. 107–38 in *Dimensions of Forgiveness: Psychological Research and Theological Perspectives*. Edited by E. L. Worthington Jr. Philadelphia: Templeton Foundation, 1998.

Worthington, E. L., Jr., and D. T. Drinkard. "Promoting Reconciliation through Psychoeducation and Therapeutic Interventions." *Journal of Marriage and Family Therapy* 26 (2000): 93–101.

Worthington, E. L., Jr., S. J. Sandage, and J. W. Berry. "Group Interventions to Promote Forgiveness: What Researchers and Clinicians Ought to Know." Pp. 228–53 in *Forgiveness: Theory, Research, and Practice*. Edited by M. E. McCullough, K. Pargament, and C. Thoresen. New York: Guilford, 2000.

Worthington, E. L., Jr., and N. G. Wade. "The Psychology of Unforgiveness and Forgiveness and Implications for Clinical Practice." *Journal of Social and Clinical Psychology* 18 (1999): 385–418.

Wuthnow, R. "How Religious Groups Promote Forgiving: A National Study." *Journal for the Scientific Study of Religion* 39 (2000): 125–39.

Zizioulas, J. *Being as Communion*. Crestwood, N.Y.: St. Vladimir's, 1997.

INDEX